When Dempsey Fought Tunney

When Dempsey Fought Tunney

Heroes, Hokum, and Storytelling in the Jazz Age

Bruce J. Evensen

THE UNIVERSITY OF TENNESSEE PRESS / KNOXVILLE

Library of Congress Cataloging in Publication Data

Evensen, Bruce J.
  When Dempsey fought Tunney : heroes, hokum, and storytelling in
the Jazz Age / Bruce J. Evensen. — 1st ed.
    p.   cm.
  Includes bibliographical references and index.
  ISBN 0-87049-919-X (cloth: alk. paper)
  ISBN 0-87049-918-1 (pbk.: alk. paper)
  1. Dempsey, Jack, 1895– . 2. Tunney, Gene, 1898– . 3. Boxers
(Sports)—United States—Biography. 4. Sports journalism—United
States—History—20th century. 5. Sportswriters—United States—
History—20th century. 6. Hero worship—United States—
History—20th century. I. Title.
GV1132.D4E84 1996
796.8'3'092'2—dc20
[B]   95-32483
                                             CIP

This one is for our two terrific kids—Stephen and Katherine. It was begun with Steve on the way and ends at Katie's arrival.

Contents

Illustrations

Introduction

When Jack Dempsey fought Gene Tunney for the heavyweight championship of the world on the evening of September 23, 1926, the event was witnessed by more people than any other civic spectacle in the history of the Americas. Beyond the record-setting 130,000 spectators gathered at Philadelphia's Sesquicentennial Stadium lay an estimated thirty-nine-million listeners across a thirty-one–station nationwide radio network. They collected communally in city centers, storefronts, parks, athletic clubs, in drug stores, radio shops, hotels, theaters, on street corners and porches, and before open windows and newspaper offices, wherever speakers could be heard broadcasting one of the great stories of the American jazz age. Minutes later they would snap up special edition newspapers in greater numbers than ever before to read about what they had just witnessed. There was no getting enough of the biggest news since the Armistice. Dempsey, their beautiful Dempsey, poets would soon write, had been done in by a former shipping clerk. Everywhere cultural credulity was taxed.

It meant something to be publicly present at the great fight, and everywhere the pattern was repeated. In city after city, pictures show men in coats and ties and hats and slickers as the early autumn rains fell. Several thousand stood "barely a foot apart" in St. Paul before the *Pioneer Press and Dispatch* office at Fourth and Minnesota streets to hear the magnetic megaphone voice of Auctioneer Baer. Among them were a freckle-faced boy who ditched his sister at a Tom Mix movie because he simply "had to come" and popcorn venders who strained out of the windows of their carts, eagerly listening to the fight's returns.[1] In Kansas City, the *Star* and *Times* hosted a "fight party" at Star Plaza and sold thousands of extra editions which were anxiously read by dash and dome light as the crowd dispersed in cars crammed along Twelfth Street.[2]

In Denver, the *Post* congratulated itself on "pace-setting civic service" in generating "the largest crowd in the history of Denver" to hear Tod Sloan's megaphone call of the fight from its office on Champa Street. The competing *Rocky Mountain News* and *Times* at Welton Street claimed in seven-column certainty that more women had come to hear sports editor Ed Lyons's call of the contest than had ever gathered at any event in city history.[3]

And in Salt Lake City, Dempsey's mother sat in the home that Jack bought and listened to J. Andrew White and Graham McNamee's account of the fight on the infant National Broadcasting Company, while twenty thousand of her neighbors clogged Main Street between first and Second South to hear the battle over loudspeakers provided by the *Salt Lake Tribune*. Even the Mormon Church's *Deseret News* could not resist the excitement, quadrupling its telephone service to answer calls from fight fans who couldn't find a radio nor wait for the paper's special editions on the fight.[4]

At the *New York Times* office on Times Square, three stenographers from the State Law Reporting Company worked in relays to provide a verbatim record of NBC's nationwide broadcast of the event. Theirs would be among the two million words filed by eight hundred correspondents on the fight under headlines that had not been seen since the signing of the armistice.[5] Our generation might consider Babe Ruth the most extraordinary sports celebrity of the 1920s, but jazz-age circulation managers knew better. Jack Dempsey meant a 50 percent leap in readership in the weeks before and in the days following his title defenses. He was good copy whether divorcing, marrying, acting in films, appearing in vaudeville, or standing trial for evading the draft. That was why these managers named him the century's "greatest stimulus to circulation."[6]

This book analyzes two parallel struggles during America's jazz age. The first is the story of two fighters of very different temperament and background whose personal drama was staged in a squared ring through the promotional genius of the era's greatest showman. The other contest was fought between star sports writers and senior editors of different dispositions and values, whose struggle over tall-tale telling in the nation's sports pages, and eventually its radio, reflected journalism's uncertain complicity in the manufacture of celebrity in an era of personal publicity. Each battle sheds light on the role of sport, celebrity, and mass-mediated civic spectacle in defining and stylizing competing values of urban America during the nation's interwar era.

The best-known, most widely read, and highest-paid sports writers of the jazz age tended to see their own careers linked to that of the sports heroes their stories carefully cultivated. The tall tales they told seized upon boxing's traditional ability to signify what it meant to be a man at a time in which the requirements of corporate America seemed to favor bureaucrats who quietly and cooperatively went about their work, rather than the few of passionate intensity whose paths were chronicled in the pages of Fitzgerald's Gatsby or West's Miss Lonelyhearts. The stories star sports writers spun about Dempsey and Tunney and their two heavyweight championship fights—the first fought in Philadelphia in 1926, the second in Chicago one year later—self-consciously played to this uncertainty.

Worthy of endless embellishment was the fundamental fact that Jack Dempsey was from the West and Gene Tunney the East. That permitted wordsmiths like Ring Lardner, Damon Runyon, Grantland Rice, Heywood Broun, Paul Gallico, and others rich opportunities in representing what was at stake when Dempsey fought Tunney, that a diverse urban readership easily understood. Dempsey's upbringing in small mining towns and hobo camps could be shaped by the nationally syndicated sports establishment as the story of the country's rugged individualist who subdues the wilderness and defeats implacable enemies at a time that saw the closing of the frontier. Dempsey's self-actualization seemed to reaffirm the efficacy of individual initiative at a time in which individual autonomy appeared threatened by increasing bureaucratization and industrialization.

Gene Tunney's association with New York's Greenwich Village and his steady, if unspectacular, rise to doughboy and dockside shipping clerk could be made to mean something quite different from Dempsey's image in the nation's press. Here was a man of careful estimates and cool calculation, lacking in Dempsey's raw aggression, but more than a match for his guile. Tunney's defense earnestly embraced a seamless strategy that was guided by the fine art of self-preservation. His technique, honed within an urban landscape requiring accommodation among competing constituencies, could be portrayed in the nation's press as the antithesis of the values that pushed early Americans beyond the Appalachians and saw them rushing down the Ohio in pursuit of personal gain and national destiny. That had been a life course taken by Dempsey's ancestors in an era that seemed more recent than distant in the nostalgia of interwar readership. The contrast mass media drew between Dempsey and Tunney could be made to personify a certain anxiety of living in the 1920s, a generation rushing to the future while remaining passionate about its past. This ambivalence created a moving target for the period's great sports storytellers and their canny circulation managers. And as much as senior editors might deplore the hokum and civic spectacle attached to heavyweight championship fights, it was hard to quarrel with the record circulations stimulated by such storytelling.

The cultivation of sports celebrity and mass-mediated hero worship during the 1920s is a commentary on a generation's search for significance during a period in American history when for many the world seemed increasingly insensible. For some writers the world appeared suddenly broken in two; others saw one "civilization" disintegrating with another taking its place. America's secularization had been commented on for years, but now the acceleration of this tendency seemed for many dangerously heightened.[7] Central to this tendency was the modern infatuation with the profane imagery of the marketplace, and fundamental to this trend was the engine of a rapidly growing media and promotional industry. The confluence of interests between sports promoters and circulation–seeking sports writers provided a new and socially sanctioned forum for rehearsing the many meanings of postwar industrial living for America's expanding leisure culture. That made the Dempsey-Tunney title fights an important text in how one might interpret the predicament of living in what Lewis Mumford describes as "the hyper-active commercial town, governed by standards of factory and market" that leaves vast urban masses with little sense of a shared vision to frame the community's self-identity.[8] The shaping of the many meanings of these civic spectacles fell to artists in the age of ballyhoo— the sports writers and promoters—who became nearly as celebrated as the heroes of their texts.

For months following Tunney's ten-round decision over Dempsey in Philadelphia, the nation's newspaper editors and cultural critics still wrangled over what the fascination with Dempsey and the furor over the Dempsey-Tunney title fight said about a country with an insatiable appetite for mass-mediated spectacle.[9] Veteran observers who noted that "since the war the national nerves have not returned to normal" thought the media circus surrounding the title fight signified a certain bewilderment in jazz-age journalism and the reading publics it served. Self-conscious defenders of journalistic professionalism and leisure class probity charged that creating public spectacles and "playing them to the hilt" fed mob sentiment and contributed to the withering of communal virtue, while undermining the integrity of journalism. But opponents of the bureaucratized cheerlessness of industrial living and establishment journalism's "emotional commitment to conventionality" argued that telling tales about Dempsey and the fight game reassured jazz-age readers that the individual could still make a difference.[10]

While Lindbergh's solo crossing of the Atlantic is the period's best-remembered act of individual courage, it was, even as Lindbergh pointed out, ultimately a triumph of technology. What made Dempsey so eminently exploitable and the greatest boon to circulation in twenty years was that he stood alone as the hard, primitive man of the ring. The media's portrayal of Lindbergh's flight and Dempsey's fights reflected a search for simplicity in an era peculiarly desperate for heroic figures.[11] A nation of 110 million that had known something approaching "unity of purpose" and "spiritual resolve" during the Great War, jazz-age editors observed, now appeared to suffer from "moral anesthesia." A country "young and bursting with energy" seemed paradoxically enervated, torn between cynicism and sentiment, or as later cultural commentators would describe it, a tension between the promise of progress and the comfort of nostalgia.[12]

In recent years, skeptics have openly challenged assertions about American "mentality" in the 1920s or any other period. They note that almost every conceivable value or trait has been imputed to American character or personality, and they charge that historical thinking in the twenty-first century must move beyond simple categories of what national groups are "like."[13] One way of attempting to do this has been to analyze the communication patterns of the leisure world, a place where twentieth-century Americans tend to define themselves through public play. This space is a world of personal transparency in the otherwise "opaque surface of everyday living," a collective forum for thinking out loud and ascribing meaning to personal and relational existence.[14] The game becomes a measure of character because it demands what ordinary life inhibits—individual initiative beyond what is merely required. For Emile Durkheim, sports participation and spectatorship are the "moral equivalent of religious activity" because they encourage the "moral remaking of individual as well as collective life." For Johan Huizinga, twentieth-century sport is a secular ceremony, where mass-mediated heroes and villains describe tensions and ambiguities within the social order. The struggle on the field of play serves as a metaphor for man's reluctant encounter with modernity.[15]

Journalists of the 1920s were not unmindful of the public's passion for sports and the stories that could be crafted in exploiting that fascination. Sports had gained respectability with the middle class during the first two decades of the twentieth century as it became associated with personal regeneration, social renewal, and "a desire to live forever." The image of Teddy Roosevelt as the national embodiment of vigor further legitimized preoccupation with sports as a test of individual capacity and character.

By the twenties, an estimated twelve million Americans watched boxing matches or fought themselves. Military training for doughboys during World War I included lessons in the manly art. Another fifteen million Americans during the jazz age watched football or played the sport, made famous on the professional level by Red Grange. Ten million Americans attended baseball games. Four million golfed. One million played tennis. Two hundred thousand ran track. One hundred thousand played soccer. Sports, and media attention to it, had significantly rationalized the leisure time of a growing fraction of the middle class and was celebrated in the popular literature of the youth culture as a proving ground for the thoroughly modern man and woman.[16]

Four billion dollars was spent on seats to sporting events during the decade of the twenties, an enthusiasm not lost on circulation managers of the twelve billion newspapers annually produced in the United States. Dempsey fights got million dollar gates and strongly stimulated short-term circulation, a testimony to the punching power of fistiana's Tiger Man as much as the power of publicity. Dempsey was a skinny-legged Colorado hobo with a high-pitched voice and a mediocre record over unknowns when his wily manager Jack Kearns brought him to New York just after the outbreak of the first World War. Kearns hawked the unassuming youth to newspaper offices throughout the city and used personal publicity to force fights with local challengers. "Like a strip teaser," Kearns observed, "I always figured you couldn't get anywhere without exposure." Kearns built Dempsey up as a "killer" and made sure he scowled, went unshaved, and soaked his face in brine to "look the part." New York sports writers began to embrace and embellish the image, making Dempsey as well known "as a member of your own family." Paul Gallico of the *New York Daily News* observed that creating and cultivating sports "legends" was a "meal ticket" few papers could pass up.[17]

Journalistic preoccupation with sports extravaganzas crested with the Dempsey-Tunney title fights of 1926 and 1927. For the first, Dempsey was ending a self-imposed three-year retirement during which he had made millions in Hollywood, on Broadway, in appearance fees, and in fighting occasional exhibitions. Public anticipation of his return to the ring was so great that Associated Press was forced to establish a sports department of first eight, then twelve men to cover the event. United Press followed this example by trebling sports coverage to participating papers and International News did the same, raising from five thousand to forty-five thousand the word hole daily filled by sports reporters.[18]

Dempseymania provoked a crisis in journalistic professionalism and deepened divisions within the American Society of Newspaper Editors, the organization established in 1923 to "protect the integrity of the profession." ASNE conservatives, angered by the growing independence of sports writers and editors, found that 40 percent of all local news coverage was now devoted to sports with the number rising to 60 percent in many of the nation's largest dailies. Veteran editors told ASNE investigators that they were "worn out" trying to prevent their sports departments from "going hog wild." City editors and managing editors were uncertain how this "young giant" should be handled and complained that publishers did not care how big the sports page was "so long as it had advertising." They were opposed in curtailing the excesses of sports departments by circulation managers who calculated that one in every four readers bought a paper primarily because of its sports coverage. ASNE investigators bemoaned a 50 percent increase in sports news over twenty years, since there was now "no end in sight."[19]

The controversy over the Dempsey fights and the trend in sports reporting reflects deepening tensions within jazz-age journalism and the fast-fading Victorian culture it chronicled. The emergence of the tabloid press with its emphasis on crime news, pictures, and self-promotion led to charges by H. L. Mencken and others that newspapers were being overrun by "ham-minded men who are forcing newspapers to be ham hooks with which to get their ham." Critics maintained newspapers were now "gigantic commercial operations" that compelled publishers "to appeal to larger and larger masses of undifferentiated readers." Senior editors argued that the growing independence and lucrative salaries of certain sports writers symbolized the profession's loss of moral direction.

The issue was not simply the controversial cultivation of sports promoters and personalities but the editorial authority that appeared threatened by this development. Three out of every four sports departments edited their own copy and sent it directly to the composing room, permitting puffing "that would not be tolerated on any other page." This is what made the excitement over Dempsey a measure of journalistic anxiety as well as cultural credulity during America's jazz age.[20]

Probing the civic spectacle of the Dempsey-Tunney fights is a way of analyzing not only the link between mass media and the rise of sport, but also the controversy over national "character" and tensions between modernity and tradition in the interwar period. The representation of Dempsey as "a hard and primitive man" who "fought our battles" and Tunney as "a no account clerk," "a man in an arrow collar" essentially pitted type against type. Dempsey was a modern day Neanderthal with "the backward sloping brow of a man born to be a fighter." Tunney had "a full and well-developed forehead—the head of a student." Even the *Nation*, which resisted taking such storytelling seriously, observed that in an era where "the taste of presidents runs to vaudeville and detective stories, the cause of culture" might be materially advanced if "mind were to triumph over matter."[21]

At a distance of thirty-five years, Paul Gallico, one of the most self-reflective of the jazz-age sports writers and editors, could not remember whether the representation of sports celebrities in the press followed or helped form public sentiment toward boxers, baseball players, and other popular heroes.[22] The depiction of the heavyweight champion as his generation's symbol of manliness, physical courage, and virility had long been a good story. One hundred years before Dempsey stepped into the ring, Pierce Egan was popularizing the fight game to the English fancy by promoting it as "a science that adds generosity to the national disposition, humanity to our conduct, and courage to our character." In sixteen volumes published during Britain's boxing craze between

1813 and 1824, Egan's *Boxiana* promised "to convey amusement if not information for those who prefer rough sincerity to affected politeness."[23] The thirty-seven-round draw between Benicia Boy John C. Heenan and English champion Tom Sayers outside London on April 17, 1860, drew praise from Thackeray and sent *New York Herald* editor James Gordon Bennett scurrying to beat his competition with fight results in an extra edition.[24] And a generation later, Richard K. Fox, publisher of the *National Police Gazette*, manufactured a diamond-studded silver belt and offered it as a prize to the challenger who would "restore dignity" to American manhood by beating Boston strongboy John L. Sullivan.[25]

If Dempsey's portrait in the press as the quintessential American man of action was nothing new, both the magnitude of the promotion and the popular response were new. Gallico's view was that Dempsey became his generation's "beloved alter ego" because his personification of rugged individualism mitigated the civilizing demands of a rapidly industrializing and bureaucratizing America. That's what allowed him to "overshadow his era," transforming him, as Grantland Rice put it, into "the greatest drawing card in the history of sports."[26]

The press made sure the public knew Dempsey better than a member of their own family so that when Dempsey fought there was more than a title at stake. Someone long known intimately for his virtues, failings, strengths, and weaknesses was about to enter a kind of public ordeal. So it meant something to be present. Tickets were printed large and dusted in gold leaf to prove the point. And larger still was media attention which "let you in on everything." The event and the chronicling of the event became inseparable not only to readers and listeners but the chroniclers themselves. "We were all part of the Dempsey cult," Gallico recalls, "and were blinded by our own ballyhoo."[27]

The million dollar gates that witnessed the Dempsey drama during the 1920s, and the millions more who gathered at communal listening outposts across America to be a personal part of fight night, testify to the success of mass media in making images that captured the public imagination in a new era of personal publicity. The unparalleled success of the promotion appears to have been the portrayal of Dempsey as "unspoiled, natural, himself" in his "truculence, pugnacity and aggressiveness," an "everyman, fighting our battles," through the careful "cultivation of his brutality" and the liberal exercise of his "bottomless well of cold fury."[28] This depiction of Dempsey within conventional wisdom made him a compensatory figure to men who needed to be reminded of the continuing utility of individual action in an era in which personal autonomy appeared increasingly threatened.[29]

The stories that surrounded Dempsey's capturing of the heavyweight title and each of his title defenses helped elevate the son of a frontier family into the first rank of urban folk heroes. For Americans inarticulate in the face of industrial change, celebrating Dempsey's violence was a pre-modern reassurance that you were as good as the next man.[30] That was why poets lamented his passing, speaking in behalf of "the million men and a million boys" who loved their "big boy," their "beautiful Dempsey." These were the ones who prayed that God might raise Dempsey from boxing's dead "to hit him again Dempsey," to "kill him for me Dempsey" with that "God in heaven smile."[31]

The year before Dempsey's birth in Manassa, Colorado, George Santayana, writing in *The Harvard Monthly,* commented on the "sudden eruption of the sporting spirit" in America by observing that modernity had left "nothing to conquer or defend except the honor of success." This meant that men sought standards to lift them from the "vulgarity" of everyday living, finding in sports "feasts of strength, skill and courage," a place to celebrate human freedom where "the soul might assert its own independence."[32] The arena of mass-mediated sports spectatorship with its promotion of expressive involvement became a ritual of social life during the jazz age through which audiences either bonded as intimates or separated themselves from those who saw the fight and fighters differently. Depicting this text and assisting in its interpretation was a job that fell to the nation's star sports writers, who were writing social history while serving their own interests. Their determination to write the story of Dempsey's career as if he were "always 12 feet tall" reflected readership's appetite for moral epistles drawn from tall-tale telling.[33]

The civic spectacles carefully managed by sports promoters and sports writers during America's jazz age were not an unbroken string of successes. Dempsey's July 1923 title defense against Tommy Gibbons in Shelby, Montana, and Gene Tunney's 1928 knockout of Tom Heeney in New York cost their promoters plenty. These failures demonstrate that although mass media had strategies in storytelling, audiences had the ability to resist the seduction of those messages.[34]

That makes the chronicling of the 1926 heavyweight title fight between Jack Dempsey and Gene Tunney and their 1927 title rematch more than a case study in hyperbole and successful storytelling during America's jazz age. Read a different way, the stories that journalists told about the great fighters and their battles were parts of a single story, the story of living in America during the 1920s and what Americans wanted to believe about that America and their place in it. Read this way, the Philadelphia and Chicago fights depict a cultural collision between two warring tendencies in early modern living—the struggle of the individual versus the communal. Behind this typology rested a certain nostalgia for what many Americans understood to be their common frontier past, a reminiscence in the 1920s that contended uneasily with the requirements of urban, industrial living. Mass media was one of the sites where this dialogue took place. The media's depiction of Dempsey, Tunney, their careers, and their fights offered jazz-age readers the seduction of recreating one's own life in so far as you embraced the attributes ascribed to a favorite fighter.

Jack Dempsey was born at that moment in American history in which the receding frontier and the rise of cities raised anew the relationship between self-reliance and community. The closing of the frontier in 1890 was followed three years later by Frederick Jackson Turner's assertion that the ever-expanding frontier with its limitless opportunity to acquire free land had fundamentally contributed to the shaping of American national character. Onto that imaginative landscape was projected a specific conception of America and the American hero. The West became a place of primitive, uncomplicated contact with nature. The men who made trails into the West to test their limits explored the limits of their own potential, or so the story went. The moral of the myth offered psychic solace to readers momentarily rescued from the monotonous work of industrial living.[35]

The myth of frontier individualism and the transformation of Jack Dempsey into the embodiment of the frontier ethos was largely the construction of the eastern, urban press. Trans-Mississippi newspapers that followed his career were less tempted to imbue their native son with qualities of the existential hero. If anything, newspapers in his native Colorado castigated Dempsey for failing to fight for his country during the first World War. The determination of a San Francisco draft board to classify Dempsey 4-A because his parents depended on his fight income struck the *Creede* (Colorado) *Candle* as difficult to justify when only "yellow-streaked pacifists" failed to fight for their country.[36] The *Leadville Carbonate Weekly Chronicle* viewed Dempsey's knockout of Jess Willard for the heavyweight title with little more than contempt. Even "a continuous flow of clever advertising," the paper declared, could not obscure the fact that "only a few months ago our sons and brothers were called to the colors, where they risked life and limb for their country." The paper thought Dempsey had proven himself to be "an ordinary fighter" bent on money-making.[37]

Dempsey never believed the ballyhoo that went with the heavyweight title. In his own mind he was no more a national symbol of frontier virtue than the crowds that gathered earnestly in the East to see their man in action.[38] He was born to a man, however, who believed in advertising and went west in search of a small fortune. The pretty promises of the frontier's booster press took Hyrum and, reluctantly, Mary Smoot Dempsey from settlement to settlement. Eleven-pound William Harrison Dempsey, the ninth of thirteen children, was born on June 24, 1895, at a stopover in Manassa, Colorado, folklore had it, as his mother read John L. Sullivan's *Life of a 19th Century Gladiator.* Whether the story was true or not, it later made good copy. And the eighteen years that followed formed the basis of the Dempsey legend that fired his generation in a blaze expertly stoked by the jazz-age press.[39]

Dempsey and the Doctor

The early career of Jack Dempsey demonstrates the importance of self-promotion and mass media in the rise of a fighter from also-ran to championship material. By early 1917, Dempsey was ready to throw in the sponge after five years of ring beatings which had earned him the reputation by the age of twenty-one of being punched out. It was a serendipitous meeting with a wily promoter, equally down on his luck, that resuscitated Dempsey's sagging career and showed what careful cultivation in the nation's sports pages could do in making and breaking champions. The prize fighting culture of Dempsey's youth rewarded fast talk as much as it did fast fists. A good promoter could manufacture headlines that got his fighter fights. In Doc Kearns, Dempsey found a manager who well understood that rhetorical warfare was every bit as important in building a fighter's following as what went on in the ring.

From the earliest days of a rootless childhood in the Colorado outback, Jack Dempsey wanted to be "somebody." It was the promise of reputation and recognition that first lured him into fighting and sustained his hard and often bitter advance to the title. As an adolescent, Dempsey turned to the pulp press in his search for heroic identity. He was "devoted" to the *National Police Gazette,* the four-page nickel shocker that became the Bible of the American barber shop by staging sports spectacles that built the personality of sports celebrities. Dempsey would cut and tack pictures of his favorite sports heroes to his bedroom wall and carefully remove them one by one during the family's many moves across the Colorado and Utah frontiers.

The *Gazette's* pink-paged sports section and loudmouthed headlines were the brainchild of Irishman Richard K. Fox, who had acquired the paper in 1877 to settle a $5,000 debt. His canny promotion of the Paddy Ryan–Joe Goss title fight in 1880 meant a record circulation run of four hundred thousand and persuaded him that profits were to be made in backing boxing. Fox's editorial policy was to "write the stuff the dailies don't dare use" to make the *Police Gazette* "the national arbiter of the masses in sports and the gay life." This determination had made the *Police Gazette* a million dollar enterprise and led it into a noisy and highly personal print campaign to wrest the heavyweight championship from John L. Sullivan.[1]

None of Dempsey's heroes stood taller than the Great John L.[2] The Boston Strongboy had earned Fox's everlasting enmity by a personal slight. One evening in the spring of 1881, the two men shared adjoining tables at Harry Hill's Dance Hall and Boxing Emporium in New York. When Sullivan refused Fox's invitation to come to the publisher's table for a business talk, the feud was on. The fact that Sullivan won the heavyweight title the following year from Paddy Ryan in a widely publicized title fight, witnessed by Jesse and Frank James in Mississippi City, Mississippi, along with a crowd of bank robbers, confidence men, and cutthroats as if out "on a Sunday school picnic," only deepened Fox's dislike.[3] He was certain that only the *Police Gazette* should be in the business of staging title fights. When Sullivan refused to fight Fox's hand-picked contender, Jake Kilrain, the publisher declared Sullivan had forfeited the title. The *Police Gazette* commissioned a diamond-studded silver belt for its champion, and Sullivan's backers in the Boston press retaliated with a belt of their own, spelling out the name of the "people's champion" in 397 diamonds against a background of American eagles and Irish harps.[4] Sullivan's 1889 pasting of Big Jake in their title fight annoyed Fox further, but record circulations fixed that. More than a decade passed before young Dempsey first became aware of the fight, but by that time it had passed into legend. Sullivan's seventy-five-round win "upon an emerald plain" in one hundred degree heat before bare knuckle fans outside New Orleans assured him his place as one of America's first mass-mediated cultural heroes.[5]

The championship had passed from the Great John L. to James J. Corbett by the time of Dempsey's birth and "Gentleman Jim" was making most of his money out of the ring, just as Dempsey would a generation later. Sullivan's press wars with Fox had helped win him a faithful following, a lesson quickly learned by San Francisco's fighting bank clerk. Corbett's choice of theatrical manager William A. Brady as press agent, manager, and producer showed the intimate link between a fast-track boxing career and cultivating an entertaining image in the big city press. Brady seized upon the press's portrait of Corbett as a different kind of champion in creating the play, *Gentleman Jack,* in which

This is an early publicity photo of Dempsey in training. Dempsey's manager Doc Kearns arranged many photo opportunities with the press in an effort to keep his fighter's face before the public. The publicity campaign paid off and led to a title fight with champion Jess Willard on July 4, 1919, in Toledo, Ohio. Photograph courtesy of Lyle Whiteman.

Corbett played a Princeton student of impeccable moral character. The hero's formal wear was an effort to sanitize the public persona of the pugilist, and although Corbett proved "an agreeable disappointment as an actor," his nightly performances played to packed houses on both sides of the Atlantic.[6]

The Ivy League hero stood beside local terrors as front-page news in Rocky Mountain country on June 25, 1895, the day William Harrison Dempsey was born. Columbia oarsmen used their broad reach and "beef at the start of the stroke" to beat back a challenge from Cornell and Pennsylvania to win the four-mile rowing race on the Hudson at Poughkeepsie in a record twenty-one minutes and twenty seconds. At that hour, William Middleton, a Denver vegetable peddler, lay unconscious on the banks of the Platte River, his skull caved in by two men, posing as police officers, who were certain he had $1,000 sewed in the lining of his shirt.[7] Played less prominently on the same day was the passing of the middleweight heavyweight championship to an Australian. Dan Creedon and Boston's Billy Hennessy were to have fought twenty rounds in that city, but only six were necessary when Hennessy "dropped over on his head" and had to be "carried unconscious out of the arena apparently unharmed."[8]

The press that daily and weekly chronicled the boom and bust cycles of life in Colorado's mining districts nurtured Dempsey on the news of how little separated personal fortune from misfortune. Typical was the investigation by Routt County authorities into the apparent suicide of a mining engineer named Wills outside a prospecting camp near Craig. The local paper observed that Wills attended medical college in Louisville before making $75,000 in mining near Helena. Before opening his mouth to a 44-40 Marlin safety gun, he had pinned a note to his coat saying, "I cease the struggle for existence. I do myself the mercy to escape the horrors which poverty heaps upon us. Do what you please with what I leave and stick my carcass in a hole anywhere."[9]

Shortly after Jack's birth, attended by a midwife who received two bits for her trouble, Hyrum lost his farm, the family was fed by the Mormon Church, and life on and off the dole began. The family moved to Creede, along the Great Divide. A succession of flights followed, from Antonito to Alamosa, Uncompahgre to Steamboat Springs, and Leadville to Meeker and Rio Blanco, followed by Delta and Rifle, all in a dispiriting pattern. "You learned to work hard or starve," Dempsey remembers.[10] Hyrum had a faculty for finding boom towns after the boom at a time of depressed economic conditions across the centennial state and much of the West. Meeker's booster press gave a new spin to falling farm prices and played out mines. "The deadest of dead things was a boom town after the boom," the paper commented. That was why Meeker and Rio Blanco counties "have never had a boom, don't want any at the present time, or any future time."[11]

The family's many moves were in part stimulated by press accounts promising riches for those who were patient. A stopover in Antonito in the San Luis Valley noted that "the wheel of fortune rolls swiftly around. The rich are likely to become poor and the poor rich."[12] The propaganda of presses in other stops along the way was more overt. They transformed Steamboat Springs, in the northwest corner of Colorado, into "an American Eden" and Alamosa on the banks of the Rio Grande into "a vast empire" with "the best wheat, oats and barley in the nation."[13] Leadville leaders admitted "a temporary dullness" but predicted it would be of some good, "ridding the district of the flotsam that was of no use to the business of the city."[14] The Dempsey family was presumably part of that flotsam, arriving in Alamosa to find mineral prices in sharp decline and the town newspaper admonishing "if any more people come here what on earth are they going to do for a living?"[15]

Dempsey's mother, a no-nonsense Scotch Irishwoman who claimed Utah Senator Reed Smoot as a distant relative, attempted to retrieve the expanding family's failing resources by opening an eating house for railroad work crews in Montrose, Colorado, as Dempsey's father found and then lost a ranching job. The eastern press would later celebrate Dempsey as America's prototypical individualist, but Dempsey's recollection of westerners was their emphasis on community. While serving as bootblack and dishwasher in his mother's eatery, he noted that "companionship was very important to men in the West." The small town press of Dempsey's childhood affirms this view. "Individuals live and die in obscurity," the *Creede Candle* noted. That was why it was imperative for townspeople to face their challenges "in the proper spirit and work together for a common end."[16]

Dempsey devised strategies of survival during his Colorado years which served him well in the ring. One pressed hard against adversity even if it pressed back. His later ability to take a beating and keep on coming was a skill acquired in the requirements of daily living. The press liked a fighter who liked to fight, but Dempsey had never known another way. Pioneering culture in prospecting, farming, and ranching mirrored the impermanence of Dempsey's fragile family life. The youngster found that sometimes the threat one faced was inadvertent—like the Sterling County man who discovered his wife, mother, and two children were drowned when an eight-foot wall of water overturned their car after it stalled in the sands of Pawnee Creek.[17] Sometimes the cruelty was purposeful, if inexplicable, like the time a Routt County rancher hired a boy for a single cent and sent him to bed without supper. During the night authorities later learned he stole the penny and beat the boy for losing it.[18]

Jack's losses were less dramatic if equally consequential. In Lakeview, Utah, he shined shoes in a barber shop and was fired for accidentally breaking a comb. The indignity fueled his "impatience to grow up." He shoveled dung, fed pigs, worked sugar beet fields, and helped pitch circus tents. By sixteen, he joined his older brother Bernie as a copper mine mucker, loading ore three thousand feet down in Bingham Canyon, Utah, and Cripple Creek, Colorado.

Still small and skinny, Jack sparred with Bernie, sparing his older brother's glass chin, while the latter launched a brief boxing career as Jack Dempsey, the name of the famous Irish middleweight, the "Nonpareil" who had died the year of Jack's birth. The boy who would become the jazz age's Jack Dempsey sprinted against horses to test his speed and endurance. He followed Bernie's example by chewing pine gum to strengthen his jaw and bathed his face in beef brine to give it the roughhewn look of a well-worn saddle. The careful cultivation of the Dempsey look had already begun.[19]

Dempsey developed a name for his persona, Kid Blackie, and spent the next five years riding the rods, living out of hobo camps, and looking for a fight. A typical tactic was to swagger into a saloon and mimic the boast of John L. Sullivan that he could "lick anyone in the house." After the town bully was laid out and the hat was passed, the beetle-browed stranger sometimes had meal money. He would travel to the next town tied to the undercarriage of a Pullman car. He closed his eyes to avoid cinders, and when he wasn't numbed by cold, he found a way to sleep. He submitted himself to the deprivations of railway watchmen and hobo jungles by disciplining himself to think of "future rewards."[20]

Kid Blackie took fights wherever he could get them with "just about anyone willing" for purses not worth splitting. He experienced "a strong bond of brotherhood" within the hobo culture while living under its rules, disciplines, and caste system. He became a porter in the Hotel Utah for free room and board and got $2.50 instead of $5.00 when he knocked out "One Punch" Hancock, because the fight only lasted twelve seconds. To get the other $2.50 he knocked out Hancock's brother in twenty seconds. The night he substituted for Bernie in a bout in Cripple Creek, he fought for the first time under the name Jack Dempsey and badly beat George Copelin. But the promoter failed to part with a $10.00 purse. "Young Dempsey," as he sometimes billed himself, beat Slick Merrill in Tonopah and lost to Johnny Sudenberg in Goldfield, Nevada, a town made famous by fight promoter Tex Rickard. When Dempsey's manager skipped town with Jack's end of the purse, he began looking for another manager.[21]

Even as an unknown, Dempsey appreciated that a good press agent was as crucial as a solid left hook for a young fighter. He took on Andy Molloy as manager and publicist but "business was bad." A trip to the *Denver Post* introduced Dempsey to Otto Floto, the self-proclaimed "dean of American sports writers," who seemed known, Dempsey observed, "by crook and banker alike." The Cincinnati-born sports writer went west to escape his father's insistence that he submit himself to a Jesuit education. Arriving in Cripple Creek as its mines opened, he posted bills and did "what came naturally for a man in search of a meal." In Denver, he promoted fights at the old Coliseum at Eighteenth and Champa streets, organized a dog and pony show, and married a bareback rider. He launched a lithograph business, specializing in theatrical, race track, and fight news. Floto arranged some mining camp bouts for Dempsey until they were robbed at gun point in Grand Junction. This led Floto to return to his typewriter and to claim, several years later, that he had "discovered" Jack Dempsey.[22]

A series of "crumby" fights followed, some won, others lost, a few ending in draws. Dempsey was disillusioned and considered quitting. Then something happened that seemed to affirm Dempsey's faith in himself. He fought Johnny Sudenberg again, this time to a draw in Reno, and when he awoke the following morning found a single paragraph on the fight in a local paper. He scrounged as many copies of the edition as he could, clipped one and sent it home to his mother. Finally seeing his name in print "went a long way with me." Recognition in the press became Dempsey's ticket to "being somebody." So he began keeping track of his fight record. He intensified his training regimen, running six miles every morning. He built a four-foot-high cage and began sparring in it, perfecting the stalking crouch that was to become his signature in the ring. He felt his "enthusiasm" for fighting return. He then knocked out the Boston Bearcat in a single round in Ogden, Utah, and Sudenberg in two rounds in Ely, Nevada. Three quick knockouts over highly regarded western fighters followed.[23]

By mid-June 1916, Dempsey felt he was ready for the big time. He arrived in New York City with Jack Price, his new fight manager, and began making the rounds of the city's sports departments. He brought with him clippings of recent wins over the best in the West. The city's sports writers, while sympathetic, were unmoved. They had never heard of the Boston Bearcat or Johnny Sudenberg. When Dempsey ran out of money, stopped eating, and slept out in Central Park, he looked little more than "a dirty bum." Damon Runyon of the *New York American* and Nat Fleischer and Jim Price of the *New York Press* took pity on the fighter and used their columns to promote him into an exhibition bout at the Fairmont Athletic Club.[24]

The emaciated newcomer celebrated his twenty-first birthday by stepping into the ring giving up forty-two pounds to Andre Anderson, a promising heavyweight presumably on his way up. Dempsey was "badly battered" in the first round and returned to his corner "with gore smeared over his face." But as the fight progressed, Dempsey gave as good as he got. Each fighter was pounded to the canvas several times, but by the end of ten rounds Dempsey remained the aggressor and Anderson could barely stand. The newspaper decision went to Dempsey.[25]

Dempsey was both unassuming and hungry, two qualities admired by sports writers. They could color a fighter who liked to fight. The fight crowd came to see only one man standing at the final bell, and Dempsey's aggressive style gave them their money's worth. Under New York law, if there was no knockout in an exhibition bout, it was officially declared a draw. But the newspapermen present would unofficially declare a winner in the next edition, thereby launching or ending many a career. That is what made their careful cultivation by the boxer and his manager all the more crucial.

In three weeks Dempsey fought twice more, a certain sign he was becoming a fan favorite. His battles against Wild Bert Kenny at Fairmount and John Lester Johnson in Harlem were "classics in violence." Each were draws in which Dempsey took terrific punishment. Against Johnson, Dempsey fought eight rounds with a broken rib. Reporters admired his courage and liked the fact he could punch and take a punch. They noted that Dempsey lacked the ring experience to finish a fighter. In three fights he had made $150 which he split with Price. It wasn't enough. Price returned to Salt Lake City, and Dempsey painfully followed a few days later.[26]

More than Dempsey's body had been bruised in his first brush with New York. He had been promised $500 for fighting Johnson and received only $100. His broken rib pressed against his stomach "making things unbearable." Every breath "was like being stabbed with a sharp knife." On his way west, his only suitcase was stolen with his only pair of shoes inside. When he arrived in Pueblo, Colorado, the local blood bank refused his blood. "I looked like I could use it myself," he remembered.

He returned to the only support system he knew, the saloon culture of Commercial Street in Salt Lake City. On an impulse, he married a piano player from a local tavern. Maxine Cates, from Walla Walla, Washington, was fifteen years Dempsey's senior and did not lack in "experience." Dempsey reluctantly returned to the ring on February 13, 1917, and was knocked down four times in the first round by Jim Flynn in Murray, Utah. Bernie threw in the towel at the end of the round to avoid further humiliation.[27]

There would be, however, other humiliations. On an ill-conceived trip to San Francisco to restart his sagging career, Dempsey's wife left him. Unable to find a ring opponent, Dempsey hired out as a Seattle lumberjack. He could no longer beat even ordinary opponents when they could be found. His no-decision bouts with Al Norton and Willie Meehan in Oakland, fought "in the grip of grippe," were so uninspired that many of the few fans who gathered left before the fights were finished. Dempsey repeated his New York pattern of promoting himself to San Francisco sports departments, even posing to have his picture taken at the *San Francisco Bulletin*. But the Flynn fiasco had poisoned the press against him. At twenty-one, Dempsey appeared punched out and washed up.[28]

While working in a Tacoma shipyard, Dempsey thought seriously of quitting the ring and settling into a "normal" life. But he was laid off at the shipyard and simultaneously received word his youngest brother Bruce had been stabbed to death in a Salt Lake City street fight. While riding the rods back to Utah, he stopped in Oakland and went down along foundry row to White's Saloon where he thought he could beg a meal. There he came to the aid of a small man with a raspy voice and vested suit who had been cornered by four "barbed wire characters." They soon discovered that Dempsey's punching power was still enough to quickly settle matters.[29]

When Jack Dempsey arrived in Salt Lake City, he was too late for Bruce's funeral but just in time to bury any notion there was money or fame to be made in boxing. After six hard and lonely years on the road, "Harry," as his family knew him, was nearly twenty-two, separated, broke, tired, and had few prospects. Giving up the idea of having your name in the newspaper to signify you were good for "something," didn't seem like such a sacrifice now. From the days when he had read of the great fighters in the *National Police Gazette* and his mother had filled his head with stories of the Great John L. Sullivan, Harry Dempsey, who became "Kid Blackie," who briefly was "Young Dempsey" before begetting "Jack Dempsey," had hardly deflected from a single course. He had wanted to be "somebody."

As the nation plunged into a great war, a private battle waged by a largely anonymous western fighter appeared over. When someone suggested a Dempsey fight to an Oakland promoter, with the proceeds going to the war effort, he was given the horse laugh. "Dempsey's a bum," the promoter answered. "I've seen him fight and I've seen him licked."[30] Even as a hobo, Dempsey had angrily resented the suggestion he was a bum. A bum was someone who refused work and Dempsey had gladly washed dishes, mined coal, picked fruit and dug ditches to get to where he thought he was going.[31] Now the attraction of family and community seemed greater than the seduction of "being a success," even if it meant casting off the identity he had assiduously cultivated since late adolescence.

When Jack Dempsey, the great "Nonpareil," died in 1895 after a storied career as light heavyweight champion, there might never have been a second Dempsey to take his place had it not been for the most extraordinary of accidents.[32] For what the second Dempsey could not achieve through force of will and rigorous self-promotion, came to him almost through inadvertence. The "wheel of fortune" finally came around for Dempsey, just as the pioneering press had long before predicted it might. What's more, the press itself would become a willing and major player in the wheel's turn. First, however, it took a good doctor to diagnose what was ailing Dempsey, a specialist in the art of career management and promotion who realized the patient's self-esteem was inextricably bound to making a name for himself in the squared ring. That man was the fellow Dempsey had fought for at White's Saloon in Oakland. His name was John Leo McKernan.

In the spring of 1917, "Doc" Kearns was a thirty-four-year-old fight manager as much in need of a fighter as Dempsey was someone to fight for. Born in Michigan and raised in Oakland, McKernan left on the Alaska gold rush at fourteen, working saloons in Nome, White Horse, and Dawson as gold dust weigher and keeper of accounts. While still a youth he punched cows near Billings, Montana, and worked as a Barbary Coast bouncer. On the side, he manufactured fire extinguishers and drove a taxi in Seattle. While trying out with the Seattle baseball team of the Pacific Coast League, he started fighting as a lightweight under the name Jack Kearns. Kearns fought sixty-seven times, most of them as a mediocre welterweight. Although a master of the verbal ballyhoo, Kearns admitted, "I was always a poor judge of distance in a fight. I never knew how long or how fast I was going to fall."[33]

Even Kearns's detractors considered him "as cunning in his sphere as Talleyrand" who knew "every dark winding lane in the most crooked business in the world."[34] Kearns was an unabashed con artist, who raised the "divine right of the chisel" to new heights. Saturday afternoons found him on a ferryboat running between Oakland and San Francisco wearing his deceased father's preacher clothes. One of Kearns's wrestlers, posing as a city detective, interrogated young couples who had brought a suitcase on board. If they confessed they weren't married, the confidence man would threaten to arrest them when the ship docked. When they begged for mercy, Kearns interceded, offering to marry them "for nothing more than they had on them." His bogus wedding license was given gratis. When called a crook, he replied, "I prefer to be called a manipulator."[35]

Jack Dempsey's first brush with Jack Kearns came a year before the Oakland barroom brawl, when he bested Joe Bond, a promising heavyweight then managed by Kearns. The year since the fight had taken its toll on the youthful fighter. On the ferryboat over to San Francisco, Dempsey appeared to Kearns to be "really down in the dumps," his weary, deep-set eyes suggesting a "ready-for-anything look."[36] What Dempsey was not ready for was a return to the ring. When Kearns offered to manage him, Dempsey indicated he was through with fighting. He only wanted "a decent job" now. That's where things stood until Dempsey received a wire from Kearns in Salt Lake City. It included a train ticket to San Francisco with an offer to fight fireman Jim Flynn, the man who had given Dempsey his one-round defeat. Equally impressive was the five dollars in meal money Kearns enclosed for the trip. Dempsey accepted. It was the first time he had ridden "in a compartment instead of under one."[37]

The Dempsey that presented himself at Kearns's doorstep in May 1917 was "thin, haggard, and run-down," a six-footer, weighing 160 pounds, whose "ribs could be played like a xylophone."[38] Kearns's key contribution to Dempsey's career was restoring his confidence. Working on Dempsey's ring skills and persuading the press, as well as fellow promoters and the public, that Dempsey was a legitimate contender for the Jess Willard title would come soon enough. The Dempsey he inherited had failed to make the big time in both the East and West, and while ring watchers after the fact would write that "Dempsey

Doc Kearns, *right,* shakes hands obligingly with referee Tommy Milligan as newsreel and still photographers record the staged event. Kearns thought promotion a form of public "strip tease." One didn't "get anywhere," he often argued, "without exposure." Photograph courtesy of Lyle Whiteman.

didn't know quit from flit," the reality was he had already quit—twice—after six years of unaccomplished barroom and tank town brawling.

Kearns took to his boxer like a good doctor, peppering him with optimism delivered in the "cool persuasive ease of an evangelist." Dempsey began to believe in himself again, finding Kearns "a crafty alligator, who connived for success, a man who would stop at nothing and would not be stopped." Kearns's exuberance and sales pitch on Dempsey worked, because Kearns told Dempsey what he wanted to believe about himself, that he still had a chance to be "somebody." Dempsey found that that approach made it "hard to refuse the man." Kearns's "limitless faith that there would be another big payday" soon helped transform the dispirited Dempsey from a washed-up pug to a confident slugger on his way up.[39]

The restoration of Dempsey's fragile self-esteem was greatly aided by Kearns's creation of a support system for the fighter. Dempsey moved into the McKernan household in Oakland, enjoying Mrs. McKernan's home cooking as much as she welcomed the discovery of a "long-lost son." She called Dempsey

"Jack" and her own son "Kearns." Dempsey walked her to church, picked fruit she put up in preserves, built her a fruit cellar in the basement, and liked drying after-dinner dishes. Kearns observed that Dempsey "obviously enjoyed making himself useful." Mrs. McKernan became his biggest fan, urging Kearns "to pay more attention to Jack."[40] Although Dempsey's pride would later make him chafe at his dependence on Kearns, in the spring and summer of 1917 it was just what the doctor ordered and the patient needed.

The promised fight with Flynn had only been a pretext to get Dempsey to come to the coast. Instead, Kearns worked Dempsey out slowly in a makeshift gym behind the McKernan home. Dempsey sparred with Red Watson, a punishing puncher, and worked on developing his left by throwing a baseball left-handed for hours. Kearns taught Dempsey how to finish a fighter and saw to his "delight" that Dempsey had "an inborn killer instinct" that could be cultivated. Roadwork and ring conditioning developed Dempsey's quickness and left "a smoldering look about him" Kearns decided to test in a bout.[41]

What is more remarkable than Dempsey's four-round decision over "Fat" Willie Meehan on July 25, 1917, in Emeryville, outside Oakland, is that it attracted attention in the press the following day.[42] A flurry of Bay area fights followed at biweekly intervals, including a loss and two draws to Meehan, twin wins over Kearns crony "Handsome" Al Norton, a first-round knockout of Charley Miller and a four-round decision over well-regarded Bob McAllister. These contests culminated in Dempsey's October 2, 1917, game comeback over "Gunboat" Smith in San Francisco's Mission Park. The fight was Dempsey's first to generate banner headlines.[43]

Edward J. Smyth, who fought under the name "Gunboat" Smith, was the white heavyweight champion of the world when he defeated Arthur Pelkey in a January 1, 1914, fight in Daly City, California. Smith lost the title six months later to Georges Carpentier and at thirty was clearly past his prime when he fought Dempsey. Smith defeated Jess Willard before the "Pottawatomie Giant" floored Jack Johnson in 1915 for the heavyweight championship, but Smith had grown old and rusty waiting for the end of the war and a rematch with Willard.

Smith's fight with Dempsey nearly ended in the second round when a right to the head had Dempsey out on his feet. Returning to Oakland on the ferry afterwards, Dempsey apologized to Kearns, thinking he had lost the fight and unaware of the savage beating he had given his opponent in the two rounds that followed. After five years of ring failure, it was hard for Dempsey to believe he was anything other than an ordinary fighter. But for the first time since he had taken him on as a short-term meal ticket, Kearns began to believe his own publicity on Dempsey. The Smith fight convinced Kearns that Dempsey was championship material with "a gameness that went deeper than his consciousness."[44]

Kearns's "lust for publicity" and intimate ties with West Coast sports writers were now brought into play. "I'm gonna build you up as a killer," Kearns promised Dempsey, teaching him how to scowl and to walk the strut of a champion. While the *San Francisco Chronicle's* Harry B. Smith, with ties to "Gunboat" Smith's backer Harry Sullivan, saw the veteran's defeat as a loss in "stamina," the competing Hearst paper, the *San Francisco Examiner,* and its sports writer Warren Brown, were promoting Dempsey as a potential challenger to Willard in pieces planted by Kearns.[45] Kearns bought out the editions in which the article appeared and personally put it on the desk of every sports writer in San Francisco. Then he sent the article to a network of sports writers he knew across the nation.

The hype worked. Dempsey's defeat of Carl Morris, a six-foot, four-inch, 235-pound Oklahoma mastiff, at San Francisco's Dreamland Pavilion was the best attended and most widely covered of Dempsey's West Coast bouts. Morris had enjoyed pounding and demeaning Dempsey when Jack was his struggling, poorly paid sparring partner. Now Dempsey did the dishing, and although he rarely took fighting personally, he particularly delighted in pounding out a four-round decision over the "Sapulpa Giant." Al Jolson, Wyatt Earp, and Rube Goldberg were among celebrities who witnessed Kearns's "tiger man" in action that night, a sure sign that the doctor's tall-tale telling was just the right prescription.[46]

The decision by Jack Kearns to take his fighter east in late December 1917 was largely predicated on the need to generate greater publicity for more ambitious bouts and an eventual shot at Willard. Kearns's strategy was to force fights through the power of publicity. The campaign began in the editorial office of the *Denver Post*. Kearns was acquainted with the paper's owner, Harry H. Tammen, a man who was to the publishing world what Kearns would become to boxing promotion. Tammen was a former bartender who had bought the *Post* with partner Fred G. Bonfils in the year of Dempsey's birth. They practiced yellow journalism from red-painted offices while advertising themselves as "Your Big Brother" and "The People's Champion." Typical of the *Post's* front-page moralizing was the account of Agnes Marion, who came to Denver from Allegheny, Pennsylvania in search of her estranged husband William. Now a man of "great fortune," the husband was charged with desertion and forced to pay $15,000 alimony. "The story told in the complaint," the *Post* observed, "is the tale of a little family attempting to keep the wolf from the door after the husband and father left. They are a most pitiful spectacle."[47]

The paper's perpetual crusades and self-promoting exposés, printed in red-ink banner headlines, played well to Kearns's "creative" uses of the truth. He told sympathetic sports editor Otto Floto that Willard had agreed to meet Dempsey for the title. The contest, he imagined, would be put on in Chicago, with the proceeds going to the Salvation Army to aid American forces overseas. Floto, who knew a bit about the fine art of self-promotion in forcing fights through the press, gave the story two-column play. He had a personal stake in promoting Kearns's plans, since Floto had already picked Dempsey as the man most likely to topple Willard.[48]

Kearns's choice of Chicago as the site for his fictional fight was part of his cold calculation. He knew Willard would be working out at the Arcade gym in the Windy City and that Willard was using his appearance there to deflect criticism that he was refusing to face Fred Fulton, his number-one challenger, in the ring. Willard was engaged in his own propaganda offensive and made eight-column headlines by suggesting Chicago be the site of a ten-round, no-decision exhibition with Fulton, the proceeds from the million dollar gate going to the American Red Cross. Fulton's reported reply was, Why fight if the title was not on the line? A Red Cross representative, contacted by the *Chicago Tribune,* then nixed the ballyhoo by stating Willard had never approached the organization with the idea. The effect of the week-long wrangling was to make Willard look like he was ducking a fight and making a "serious mistake" by serving as his own publicity man.[49]

Willard's determination to manage his own career and to directly tell his story to the press bucked the pattern William A. Brady had set with "Gentleman Jim" Corbett and Kearns enjoyed with Dempsey. The development of the modern sports department with its hungry writers in hot pursuit of tall tales that would stimulate circulation while promoting their own careers meant that the days of John L. Sullivan were gone. A fighter needed a promoter who knew how to cultivate his image in the press. That meant that when Doc Kearns and Jack Dempsey arrived in Chicago on the evening of January 2, 1918, they may have been penniless but had an idea. Part of the plan was already in motion. Chicago sports writers had received copies of the story Kearns planted in Denver. Initial reaction to the report, however, was as cold as the weather settling over the city.[50] Just two days before, the *Chicago Tribune's* boxing writer Ray Pearson had listed the names of the country's fifty-five leading fighters in all weight categories. Dempsey's name was not among them. While he had fought some fair-to-middling Pacific Coast fighters, Dempsey remained a relative unknown east of the Rockies.[51]

Kearns and Dempsey finessed Chicago sports writers by playing the roles of "Big Time fight Manager and His Contender." It was a technique Kearns had learned from Bill Brady, who had finagled Jim Corbett into a title shot and his first million by keeping up appearances while living on the cuff. Brady's advice was that the manager should be the showman, offering reporters the "window dressing," and the fighter "should be kept in the background."

Kearns admitted he "dressed a lot of windows" for the usually taciturn

Dempsey.[52] Kearns and Dempsey, carrying leather valises and wearing patent leather shoes, three-piece suits, and linen handkerchiefs, bought on credit for the act. They checked into one of the best suites of the Morrison Hotel and invited the press up for a buffet, booze, and the opportunity to meet "the next heavyweight championship of the world." The gambit worked. On January 6, Kearns grabbed two columns in the Sunday *Chicago Tribune,* which introduced Dempsey as "a Pacific Coast heavyweight here seeking a battle with champion Willard." The taunting cut line below the face of the sartorially splendid Dempsey reads, "Here He Is, Jess!"[53]

By Dempsey's own admission, nearly a dozen well-qualified heavyweights stood between him and a crack at Willard. But it was Kearns's snake oil charm in giving the press a good story and Dempsey's making good in the ring which moved his stock up ahead of the others. Willard was already feeling the heat. Stories that Kearns and Dempsey were "looping the Loop" in search of Willard and that Willard had "betrayed" the war effort in refusing to fight Dempsey with the proceeds going to charity brought Willard to the boiling point. Kearns further infuriated Willard by sending a letter to his neighbors in Pottawatomie Country, Kansas, branding Willard a "slacker" for ducking Dempsey. When Kearns met Willard in "Kid" Howard's gym on the city's North Side, the Gentle Giant threatened him, "You can't pressure me. Get your boy a reputation."[54]

What Jess Willard failed to realize was that by angrily avoiding Dempsey, he was helping to build his challenger's reputation. Kearns exploited Willard's understandable reluctance to risk his title against a lightly regarded opponent into the moral equivalence of cowardice in the face of danger. The ruse was ably aided by western and midwestern sports writers who knew Kearns and were spoiling for a fight. They made their money telling tales of fighters who fought, not those who resisted getting into the ring. Their co-mingling of interests helped project Dempsey's image of up-and-coming contender to a wider segment of fight fans. It would be their vote as much as Dempsey's fists which would determine the fighter's future. That was why Kearns exercised a two-tier strategy in the year and a half before finally landing the title fight with Willard. On the one hand, he staged an elaborate elimination tournament in which Dempsey faced the fighters standing between him and the title. At the same time, Kearns created a vaudeville act that kept Dempsey's name in the newspapers in between bouts. The one-two punch worked because it gave sports writers and their readers what they wanted most—stories that invited vicarious pleasure in standing with Dempsey above the fallen foe.

Dempsey fought a remarkable twenty times in 1918, beginning the year with a one-round knockout of Homer Smith in Racine, Wisconsin, and ending it with a fourteen-second score-settling wipe out of Carl Morris in New Orleans. In between, Dempsey fought several well-known fighters, like Bill

Brennan and Billy Miske, and quite a few one-round wonders, such as Tom Riley and Kid McCarthy, whose clobberings were designed to pad Dempsey's knockout count while playing up his new moniker as the "Manassa Mauler." There appears to be some evidence that Kearns, at the last minute, may have twice substituted common sparring partners for better-known foes with the intention of adding to Dempsey's 60 percent knockout record.[55] There is also the claim by a sports writer who followed Dempsey's career closely that Kearns had his old pal "Handsome" Al Norton fight under several names to make Dempsey's numbers look even better.[56]

When the run to the championship got dull, Kearns resorted to hyperbole. He told reporters that Dempsey had hit Bill Brennan so hard in their six-round Milwaukee match that the challenger had broken a leg while twisting to the canvas. Reporters who checked the story would have found Brennan only suffered a sprained ankle. In Chicago, Kearns offered $10,000 he didn't have to any two fighters the press would pick for his "Man Eater" to fight on a single night. When Dempsey demurred, Kearns reminded him that "publicity is the name of the game" for those interested in the big time.[57]

Kearns's promotional ploys finally paid off when Fred Fulton agreed to meet Dempsey on the evening of July 27 in Harrison, New Jersey, just outside New York City. Fulton had little to gain and much to lose in fighting Dempsey. Dempsey had to beat him to get to Willard but the reverse was not true. By defeating Willard in a four-round exhibition shortly before Willard won the title from Jack Johnson in April 1915, the Minnesota plasterer had earned the reputation as the man Willard most wanted to avoid. But Kearns's deft use of "newspaper pressure" to force fights was nearly contagious, and Fulton reluctantly succumbed to it.[58] Fulton's sense that Kearns's bark was worse than Dempsey's bite proved a fatal mistake when Dempsey laid him out at eighteen seconds into the first round.[59]

The nine thousand dollars that Dempsey and Kearns split for the Fulton fight was more than Dempsey had made in six years of fighting. More importantly, press coverage of the contest finally won Dempsey a following. He remembers being "mobbed by enthusiastic fans" on the way to his dressing room after the fight. "They tore at everything," Dempsey said in some bewilderment. "They just wanted to take a little piece of me home." Fans later trailed Dempsey and Kearns to the Treat Hotel and seemed content just to be in the same room as their new hero.[60]

Kearns would give them every opportunity to watch their hero and make them pay for their pleasure. He created the Jack Dempsey Revue for Barney Gerard's American Burlesques and took it on the vaudeville circuit to keep Dempsey's name before the public. The program patterned itself after the theatrical appearances of boxing champions from Sullivan to Willard. The difference was Dempsey was not yet champion. The crowds that came to watch Dempsey shadowbox and jump rope did not seem to mind. Their payoff came when the Manassa Mauler leveled a volunteer Kearns picked at random from the audience at the end of each act. The man submitting himself to such pseudo-furious punishment all the way from Scranton to Bakersfield was Dempsey's trainer, Max "the Goose" Kaplan. The night in Trenton that a real challenger beat the Goose to the stage, Kearns made sure Dempsey's gloves were loaded.[61]

In the space of less than two years, the promotional genius of Doc Kearns had helped transform Jack Dempsey from a washed-up has-been to a Man Killer. He achieved this not simply by making Dempsey a better boxer, but by carefully creating an image for his fighter well suited to the appetites of friendly sports writers and fight fans hungry for heroes. Even Dempsey's defeat in a four-round exhibition to "Fat" Willie Meehan in between burlesque house engagements did little to tarnish the Manassa Mauler's title hopes. That was testimony to Kearns's success in cultivating the image of an invincible Dempsey by embellishing his ring successes and keeping out of the press his occasional failures.

Sports writers would later justify their complicity in creating the image of Dempsey as an impregnable warrior by noting that they were only "giving the public the Dempsey it wanted." But they were taking their cue from Kearns. His genius drew from an intuitive recognition of the public mood and an endless creativity in manufacturing stories which served that mood. Emerson has written that "times of heroism are times of terror," and this has rarely been more true than during the jazz age where a search for "great men" filled the pages of the daily press.[62] Contemporary critics saw hero worship in the jazz age arising out of "an increasing sense of insecurity" which fixed on civic spectacles as a central means of authenticating masculinity and individual potency.[63]

Kearns realized that the six-year journey Dempsey had taken from boxing jungle anonymity to budding sports celebrity was a fight fought for and within the public imagination. Armistice Day now created new conditions testing the Great Doctor's versatility. Willard had hidden out while the war was on, collecting his money from film, stage, and circus work while maintaining it was "unpatriotic" to stage fighting spectacles for profit while American boys were fighting and dying overseas. Now those soldiers were coming home, and the nation prepared for a release of nervous energy one contemporary commentator compared to "the experience of children let out of school."[64] Kearns prepared to profit from that release by stylizing a personality the public could get excited about. That led to an historic meeting with an old nemesis every bit as astute as he in giving the public what it wanted. In the newly emerging era of personal publicity and civic spectacle, they laid the foundation for what would become the Dempsey legend.

Tex and Toledo

John McGraw, the veteran manager of the New York Giants, who liked a good fight, need not have introduced Doc Kearns to Tex Rickard at the bar of the Biltmore Hotel in mid-July 1918. The two men knew each other, even if it took Rickard a while to remember it. Kearns had been a fourteen-year-old gold weigher at Rickard's Great Northern Saloon in Nome during the days of the Klondike gold rush. It was one of several fortunes that the tight-lipped, pokerfaced Texan had won and lost on his way to becoming general manager of New York's Madison Square Garden. Kearns would later claim that he had upbraided Rickard at the Biltmore bar for "stealing" one of his most promising heavyweights, Australian Les Darcy, years before. But since Kearns needed Rickard, who had Willard under contract, to arrange a title fight, it is more likely past differences were soothed by a bit of bourbon.[1]

Kearns and Rickard needed one another. The heavyweight division under the indolent and inactive Jess Willard was at a low ebb and costing the canny Rickard money. Willard's single title defense since knocking out Jack Johnson in a Rickard-backed bout in Havana, Cuba, three years before, had been a listless, no-decision, ten-round exhibition against Frank Moran in March 1916. That, too, had been a Rickard brainchild. His $42,000 guarantee had persuaded the dollar-wise Willard to forgo another tour with Buffalo Bill's Wild West Show and make some money in the ring. But since that bout, which had been panned in the press, Willard stayed away from the gym, added 50 pounds

Dempsey strikes a fighting pose. In the days leading up to and the years immediately following Dempsey's ascent to the championship, the Manassa Mauler made more money out of the ring than in it. The rich rewards of acting in vaudeville and Hollywood, and five-figure appearance fees testified to the lucrative business of cultivating celebrity and civic spectacle during the American jazz age. Photograph courtesy of Lyle Whiteman.

to his 250-pound frame, played a circus act, and casually reiterated his determination to remain retired from the ring until war's end.[2]

For Rickard, taking a chance on a possible Willard-Dempsey bout, seemed like a better bet than some high stakes promotions he had bet his bankroll on.[3] Rickard was a gambler who loved action. What sports writers saw as his "Midas touch at promotion" appeared guided by a "gorgeous imagination" honed by years of being "a great listener."[4] They were years that articulated a life course not unlike that of Dempsey and Kearns. All were men of the West who had come east to make their mint. Each were born to strong and resolute mothers who gave them their "fight" and fathers united in their unique inability to make money. Rickard's peculiar passion for promotion endeared him to the press, not only because they personally profited from the stories he conceived and they successfully spun, but because there was something quite singular in the man, a resolute steadfastness acquired in the face of many emergencies that reporters found particularly ingratiating. Rickard appeared to genuinely enjoy courting the press, and they seemed satisfied to play the cards he dealt. The reason, according to Will Rogers, was that most found Rickard "one of the few outstanding personalities of our time."[5]

Rickard's facility for tall-tale telling extended to details of his childhood. He was variously born in Missouri and Kansas, in either 1870 or 1871, but always within shooting range of the Jesse James family, whom he claimed as neighbors. Robert Rickard read a tract of the Texas and Pacific Railway that puffed the money that could be made by families who went west; he then moved his family of four to Sherman, Texas, when George was only four. Unable to find work as a millwright or other "means of acquiring wealth with far less labor," the family's covered wagon wheeled into Cambridge a year later, a two-year-old frontier town at the edge of Commanche country. Five of the town's first nine businesses were saloons, and little "Dink" made his money outside one of them shining cowboys' boots.[6]

When Dink was ten the family moved again, this time to neighboring Henrietta, where they lived in a dirt shack, ate corn pone, turnip greens, and sowbelly and settled into "the somber melancholy of poverty." At eleven, Dink left home for good and became a hired hand at a grown man's wage of ten dollars a month on a neighboring ranch, where the youth was schooled in "thinking big" about the cattle business. Within a year his father died, and the rancher who had taken him in was shot and killed in a saloon fight. This was how Rickard learned to "set his face grimly" at the first sign of trouble. A thirty-dollars-a-month cowhand while still a teen, he lost a friend on the trail to Honeywell, Kansas, and sat guard all night fending off wolf attacks against the corpse.[7]

By the age of nineteen, Rickard was a six-foot, straight-backed, dark-eyed veteran trail driver, making fifty dollars a month on his last roundup. He had a self-confidence born of many emergencies and hardships, such as surviving prairie fires, blizzards, and the necessity of sitting in a saddle for forty-eight hours at a time. He turned down an offer to hold up a mail train, and unlike the others who did, lived to tell about it. He returned to Henrietta, where he became town marshal. He was better at drawing a full house than a gun. He married Leona Bittick, who died soon after. In 1895, the year of Jack Dempsey's birth, Rickard found that flour sold for $1 a pound in the Klondike. Bitten by the gold bug, he took a one-month leave from his job in depression-ridden Texas. He planned to "make a lot of money, get me a stake, and buy 1,000 yearlings." He never returned.[8]

For fifteen months, Rickard experienced uninterrupted insolvency as a $20-a-day bartender, faro dealer, and front man in a variety of Dawson City saloons. His pay in gold dust barely covered personal losses in faro and cards. He sat at the foot of six-foot, three-inch Wilson Mizner, a twenty-one-year-old aristocratic pitchman turned medicine show spieler, who taught Rickard the art of making money with your mouth. When he got a few dollars ahead in the fall of 1898, Rickard decided to open a saloon of his own in Rampart, at the edge of the Arctic Circle. There he promoted his first fight, along with Rex Beach, the Michigan-born lawyer who was soon to become a best-selling author of Alaskan adventures. The well-attended bout ended when one of the fighters was knocked cold with a head butt.[9]

Hearing of a gold strike on Cape Nome, Rickard took a steamboat to St. Michael and parlayed a $21 bankroll into a half share in Nome's Great Northern Saloon. The business made $100,000 its first year, and half a million dollars during Rickard's four years in Nome, a time that saw more than $30 million in gold mined from the Seward Peninsula. Jack Kearns was called "kid" as one of Rickard's gold weighers, and Rickard's saloon, from the day it opened its doors in May 1900, was Nome's bank. Miners kept pokes behind the bar without benefit of a receipt. Six bartenders staffed the Northern twenty-four hours a day beneath crystal chandeliers, amidst the whirl of roulette, blackjack, and twenty-one. Their boss declined an offer to run for mayor but agreed to serve on the city council.[10]

Rickard put on fight cards at the Standard Theater in Nome. They required little promoting. Fight fans came free and paid combatants by passing the hat. One memorable night Paddy Ryan, a heavyweight the *Police Gazette* had promoted into a title tilt with the Great John L., took on a jilted bridegroom at the Standard, and they simultaneously knocked one another out. Miners were happy to pay for their pleasure. By this time, sour mining leases and gambling losses had whittled Tex's take to $15,000. He sold his interest in the Northern for $50,000 more, hoping to buy a Texas ranch. Stopping off in

Seattle, he heard about a secret diamond mine in South Africa. By the time he got to San Francisco by way of the Cape of Good Hope, he was busted.[11]

Tex hunted up former heavyweight champion James Corbett, hoping to promote a fight.[12] Failing that, he made a modest salary as a San Francisco faro dealer and married Edith Mae Myers, an eighteen-year-old who had played piano in the Great Northern. His Seattle saloon failed when he refused to pay protection money. By 1906, with wife and adopted daughter in hand, he headed for the Nevada gold fields thinking it his "last chance to make a fortune."[13] Settling in Goldfield, situated between salt marshes and mud flats at the mouth of an extinct volcano, Rickard rebuilt his gambling business. As a one-man chamber of commerce, he fielded ideas on how to stimulate investor interest in local mining stocks. One idea was to create a beer-filled lake; another was to build a track and race camels. Instead, Rickard promoted a fight for the light-weight championship between Battling Nelson and Joe Gans. When eastern papers ignored the announcement, Rickard arranged a wire service stunt by placing the fight's $30,000 guarantee in $20 gold pieces in his saloon front. In mock anger, Rickard told reporters, "When Goldfield says something, we mean it."[14]

Rickard's powers of promotion made the September 3, 1906, fight a sporting and mining stock success, covered by an unprecedented four rows of ringside reporters representing papers from Chicago, Denver, New York, San Francisco, Helena, New Orleans, and points in between. The Associated Press wire report was read in round-by-round summaries to crowds gathered in front of the *San Francisco Examiner's* building at Market, Kearney, and Third streets. The paper's publisher, William Randolph Hearst, had been an early convert to boxing's ballyhoo and promoted his papers in fight coverage ghostwritten for Corbett and other former champs. In Fresno, accounts of the forty-two-round struggle were announced by megaphone from a balcony at Ryan's Saloon at Tulare and F streets. Gans, having the better of it, was butted and elbowed by Nelson in the fifteenth, the round in which Gans broke his right hand. Gans fought the rest of the fight left-handed and won when Nelson, nearly blinded in the battle, fouled with what was judged a deliberate blow below the belt.[15]

With the $13,000 he made from the fight, Rickard built his family Goldfield's first all-brick home and furnished it with imported Circassian walnut furniture. But any thought of settling down ended as Goldfield's mines began to play themselves out. Rickard sold his saloon and with the money promoted the heavyweight championship bout between Jack Johnson and Jim Jeffries by publicizing his guarantee of $101,000, plus two-thirds of the movie rights. It was nearly twice as large as any guarantee ever given for a fight. Johnson had deeply offended many whites when he knocked out Tommy Burns on December 26, 1908, in Sydney, Australia, to become the first black heavy-weight champion. Novelist Jack London spoke for many when he implored retired champion Jim Jeffries "to emerge from his alfalfa farm" in Southern California and "remove that golden smile from Jack Johnson's face."[16]

Rickard didn't have to make the most of racial differences before the bout. Jeffries did it for him by telling his supporters "I realize full well just what depends on me. I am not going to disappoint the white race that has looked to me to defend its athletic superiority."[17] Rickard grabbed more attention when he announced he would referee the fight. The *New York Evening Sun* believed the pre-fight publicity meant the Jeffries-Johnson would mark "a new era in pugilism." Current Literature noted that the fight, scheduled for Independence Day 1910 in San Francisco, was "casting its shadow over a palpitating world." Editorial cartoons showed Jeffries and Johnson dominating the public mood while thrusting Theodore Roosevelt and William Howard Taft to the sideline. Typical of the pre-fight sentiment was the comic strip that appeared in the *Boston Globe*. "Mr. Sambo Remo Rastus Brown," alias Jack Johnson, was shown as a bumbling fool, and certainly no match for the "Great White Hope."[18]

With a new stadium built and $300,000 worth of tickets sold on the eve of the fight, California Governor James Gillett bowed to political pressure and blocked the bout. A protest by California churchmen had gained national impetus by mid-June, leading key congressmen to threaten a cutoff in federal funding for the proposed Panama-Pacific Exposition if San Francisco went ahead with the controversial contest. San Francisco's Mayor, Pat McCarthy, sided with Rickard and favored the fight, anticipating losses to the city of more than a million dollars if the fight was moved elsewhere. But Gillett would not be moved, leading Rickard to cut a deal with Nevada's congenial governor, Denver S. Dickerson, for a Fourth of July fight date in Reno. Rickard made the most of the controversy, grabbing front-page headlines for himself by pleading "great personal suffering" at the hands of "those who desire to injure me."[19]

Johnson's fifteen-round knockout of the previously unbeaten "surly bear of the Sierras" provoked race riots around the country. Street fighting erupted in Kansas City and Norfolk. Whites set fires to black tenements in New York City's San Juan Hill District and reportedly attempted to lock the residents inside. In Mounds, Illinois, a black constable was shot and killed. A black was gunned down in Roanoke, Virginia. S. I. Sawyer, a white actor who took the part of a black in a play, was attacked by a crowd of whites in St. Joseph, Missouri. Streetcars were held up in black sections of Pittsburgh. When Charles Williams, a black man in Houston, was "a little too vociferous in announcing the fight's outcome" on a streetcar, a white man slashed his throat from ear to ear. Three blacks were killed outside Augusta, Georgia. Two blacks were lynched outside Charleston, Missouri, and a third lynching was promised by a white vigilante group. John Rankin was rescued from a lynch mob in Covington,

Kentucky. And Frank Clark, a Negro painter in Kansas City, was beaten up when seen reading a newspaper account of the Jeffries-Johnson clash.[20]

An armed guard protected Johnson from death threats as his "victory train" left Reno. Before it arrived in Chicago, Indiana's Governor Thomas Marshall banned the showing of the fight's film in his state. Legislatures in Louisiana, Virginia, Arkansas, Wyoming, and Georgia quickly followed his lead. City showings were banned in Buffalo, Boston, Baltimore, and Toledo. But Portland Mayor Joseph Simon didn't see the difference between press reports on the fight and a film about it. The mayor of St. Joseph, Missouri, said he was anxious to see the fight film and would take his sons with him. The controversy culminated in a federal law prohibiting the interstate shipment of fight films.[21]

More important than the revenue Rickard lost in the banning of the fight film was the outpouring of public opposition to the fight game. State and city legislators moved to ban boxing. Editorials predicted "the passing of the prize fight," fearing "the triumph of the black race in the ring will be permanent." Others claimed the fight's result "in no way demonstrated the superiority of the black race in athletics." Pugilism was now portrayed in the *Chicago Tribune* as "an ignoble pursuit" that no longer interested "the white portions of this free republic." The *Nation* deplored "the disgusting exhibition." Former President Theodore Roosevelt, one of professional boxing's biggest backers, wrote in the *Outlook* that commercialized boxing no longer taught "courage, hardihood, endurance, and self-control." That was why he had turned from its "warm advocate" to its opponent.[22]

Rickard had learned in his boom and bust days that "there is a time to get in and a time to get out." The moratorium on professional boxing in the United States sent him packing to Paraguay, where he lost what was left of his shirt raising cattle on a five thousand-acre ranch. Rickard intended his beef for the Allies, but the Kaiser's supporters in Asunción made sure the steak never got there.[23] Rickard's return to the ring, however, was at hand. He opened his April 6, 1915, morning paper to see a wire service photo of a prostrate Jack Johnson, shielding his eyes from the one-hundred-degree Havana sun, with the towering Jess Willard standing over him. The champion was counted out in the twenty-sixth round of a controversial hour and forty-four-minute fight that Johnson insisted he had thrown. The publicity tended to tarnish Willard's claim to the title and fed the claims of critics that fixed fights made boxing a "national disgrace."[24]

Rickard now saw and seized his opportunity to get back into boxing. Returning to the States, he borrowed $10,000 from New York ticket broker Mike Jacobs and parlayed it into the promotion of Willard's first title defense. Willard made $42,500 and Rickard $42,000 in Willard's ten-round decision over fighting Frank Moran on March 25, 1916, in Madison Square Garden. The battle brought a $152,000 gate, the largest in sports history for an indoor attraction, even without the press support Rickard had become accustomed to.

For once the press appeared to be behind the learning curve. Editorials deplored the spectacle of a fixed "blood sport." Even Hearst's self-consciously reformist *New York Journal* deplored the "ghastly and demoralizing" drama that left "female spectators spattered in blood." But Rickard knew what circulation-starved publishers would soon discover. With a black fighter out, and a white fighter in, boxing was back in business, and so was he.[25]

That Rickard could make Madison Square Garden a paying proposition was certainly the conviction of the New York Life Insurance Company, which held the mortgage on the building. When the company announced it was converting the Garden, which had never made money as a sports emporium, into an office complex, Rickard won the backing of circus magnate John Ringling to execute a ten-year contract at $200,000 for rental of the facility. It assured Ringling a seasonal venue for his circus and led Rickard to search for the "killer" who would put fans in their seats.[26]

The resolute Doc Kearns claimed he was offering Rickard such an opportunity. Months before, Dempsey had been the least known and least experienced of the major contenders for Willard's crown. But by the fall of 1918, Dempsey had been cunningly built up to a point where he might be promoted into a "killer" contender. The war's end and a white champion persuaded Rickard that fight fans were in a mood to "bust loose." All that was required was the spinning of a story worth shouting about.[27]

Rickard's astute powers of promotion transformed the heavyweight title fight between Jack Dempsey and Jess Willard into a mass-mediated spectacle generating a record-setting gate. Their Independence Day encounter, ballyhooed as a celebration of American fighting spirit, was fought between two fighters who assiduously avoided military combat. The irony was obscured by three veterans of life's wars, partners united in their abiding respect for the power of promotion. Jack Dempsey, Doc Kearns and Tex Rickard were men of the West who came East to make their millions. They would do so by playing upon what postwar Americans liked to believe about the West, transforming Dempsey into the very image of the fast-receding wilderness, in all of its physical threat and quaint nostalgia.

A contemporary historian observed that the closing of the frontier signaled the rise of sport as the principal safety valve for a restless and excitable generation.[28] The cultivation of Dempsey as the embodiment of America's frontier spirit well suited a culture newly committed to play. Leisure industries, like professional boxing, would reemerge after the Great War with strategies designed to stimulate the public imagination. Defenders of middle class probity inside and outside journalism, who saw professional boxing as a sign of society's surrender to the values of conspicuous consumption, found themselves on the defensive. Increasing numbers of Americans were preparing for a good time. A pioneering people who had known work, want, and hardship now found that they had evenings on their hands. Amusing them would prove to be serious business, for if audiences did not see themselves implied in Dempsey's fights, Rickard would find a way to place them there.

The first to feel Rickard's promotional push were, as always, his friends in the press. He struggled to have them take seriously his contention that Dempsey had a legitimate shot at the title. Ring Lardner, who wrote that Dempsey wouldn't last three rounds, spoke for a lot of fellow reporters when he complained of the "Toledo Blues" on the eve of the Independence Day 1919 fight between Willard and Dempsey. The Eighteenth Amendment had been ratified six months before to go into effect in January 1920, but Ohio chose to enforce Prohibition six months early. After six successful years as columnist for the *Chicago Tribune,* Lardner's coverage of the championship fight was his first for the 150-newspaper Bell Syndicate. But the heat of Maumee Bay, combined with the first bitter taste of Prohibition, had taken the edge off a fight he and others saw as terribly one-sided. Lardner wrote, "I guess I've got those Toledo Blues. About this fight I simply can't enthuse. I don't care if Dempsey win or lose, owing to the fact I've got Toledo Blues."[29]

His sentiment was shared by golf-playing partner Grantland Rice, now of the *New York Tribune,* but late of the *Stars and Stripes,* where he had reported the first Army advance on St. Mihiel, the battle for Mount Sec, and the thirty thousand killed in the Argonne Woods. The four hundred reporters who had gathered in Toledo to generate half a million words on the fight struck Rice as testimony to Tex Rickard's sixth sense of "how to get a gate," but poor tribute to the nation's recent dead. Self-consciously he wrote, "Here they come—nut and bum, Banker, Yeggman—all the nation, file by file of varied style in one vast conglomeration; picking Jess or backing Jack, doping out the bloke who'll win it where the atmosphere is black with a million words a minute. If Tex promotes another bout I hope they'll call the army out."[30]

Rice's editor, Stanley Walker, saw two competing camps of sports writers emerging in the immediate postwar period, with reporting on the Willard-Dempsey fight their first expression. The "Gee Whiz!" crowd, which outnumbered its competition, created "pasteboard heroes" out of average pugs by writing "overblown sagas" that stretched the average reader's imagination if not credulity. Despite his reservations, Rice would emerge as one of the leaders of the self-promoting reporters who saw a certain cultural significance in the squared ring, or at least wrote as if they did.[31]

Ring Lardner was a leader of the "Aw Nuts!" school of sports writers which denigrated the "fine fetish" of playing sports to the limit. He saw little glamour in the supposedly sweet science and even less social significance. "The ones who succeed in the game through their ability to 'take punishment,'" Lardner wrote, "die as a rule before reaching old age, as a result of the 'gameness' that made them 'successful.' There is a limit to the number of punches one can 'take' and retain one's health."[32]

An "invading army" of two hundred thousand fight fans, freeloaders, and some crooks came to Toledo in the sweltering days leading up to the big fight, swelling the city's suddenly unfortunate population by double. Some came to see the fighters train; some to make a quick buck; others to do both, if possible. An estimated $2 million dollars would be bet on the fight. Crowded hotel lobbies saw "men running around with checkbooks and fountain pens in hand, yelling out their offers on the fighters." The *New York Times* observed that Toledo "has never seen such a revelry of finance." The *Chicago Tribune* sensed the city was "bulging to the cracking point."[33] Even the taciturn Lardner was getting in on the five-to-four odds favoring Willard. He told his readers, "I don't know nothing that you don't know," and promptly proved it by putting down $600 on Willard. "I don't care if he win or lose," Lardner said of Dempsey, "only I kind of figure that he can't."[34]

Toledo's twenty-five-thousand hotel beds were reserved weeks before the bout, with reporters sleeping eight and nine to a room. The overflow was accommodated on cots put up in the city's vacant office buildings and stores. Those out of luck there built a tent city outside Toledo. At twilight it was almost impossible to move indoors or out "at anything other than a wiggling, dodging gait." The city police chief warned that anyone driving an automobile more than fifteen miles an hour to or from the fight would be jailed. That was why many fans were planning to make the trip to the arena by river launch. On the eve of the fight, an Associated Press reporter noted that "near to a hundred thousand damp pilgrims swarm around and hang on to the rims of Toledo tonight." Even though it was uncomfortably crowded, Toledo's money men thought it a small price to pay for such service to "the city's treasury."[35]

The Dempsey-Willard title fight was hardly Toledo's first big battle. Years before, the governors of Michigan and Ohio had called out the militia and prepared to wage war for the right to claim Toledo. This was after the site had passed from Indian, to French, to British hands, with raids launched from Fort Industry finally finishing Indian claims to the mouth of the Maumee. The arrival of the first steamboat in 1818, and the first railroad eighteen years later, set the stage for a generation of canal building, coal loading and industrial expansion. By 1919, German and Irish settlers were joined by a French community in East Toledo, and immigrants from Poland, Bulgaria, and Southern Europe who made their living in the mills and factories of a peculiarly progressive town. The administrations of Samuel "Golden Rule" Jones and Brand Whitlock carried out a plan of proportional representation and labor conciliation that became a model for other cities considering home-rule, nonpartisan, anti-monopoly government.[36]

Toledo's other side was seen when Willard fought Dempsey. Like much of the nation, it was a city grown weary with reform and appeared ready for a little self-promoting excess. Dempsey remembers it as "a haven for prominent gamblers and hustlers who were on the lam." Doc Kearns thought Toledo a "friendly" place, determined to "grab a lot of newspaper space" and its share of the profits. There was no boxing law in Ohio and the governor of the state, James M. Cox, a former newspaper man preparing for a run at the presidency, knew well the power of publicity in promoting his own political ambitions. His meeting with Rickard and Kearns produced a $25,000 pledge from Rickard to Cox's campaign chest, which the governor rejected, while promising he would do nothing to interfere with the fight.[37]

Cox had made his reputation as a progressive newspaper publisher who had learned in Dayton and Springfield, and later in Miami and Atlanta, the fine art of combining public service and self-promotion. He had built a career as two-term Ohio congressman, governor, and presidential contender by identifying himself with liberal causes, labor, and honing his image as a fighter of political corruption. That meant he saw no inconsistency in Toledo's progressive past and providing a spectacle for its "sports-loving public." Rickard helped move matters along by guaranteeing that 7 percent of the gate would go to help Toledo's poor.[38]

Rickard's partners in the Toledo title match saw the possibility of making a tidy profit as well as a name for themselves. Addison Q. Thacher, a salvage operator and athletic club director, used his association with the big bout to promote himself into becoming Toledo's mayor. Money from Frank Flournoy, a Memphis-based cotton broker and bank president, brought Willard into the ring with a $100,000 guarantee. The thirty-seven-year-old Pottawatomie Giant was scheduled for an Independence Day title defense in an 80,000-seat stadium built especially for the contest. Rickard estimated that the fight's proximity to major population centers of the East and Midwest assured an $800,000 gross. Willard liked the calculation. While making movies and appearing in Buffalo Bill's Wild West Show since winning the title in 1915 had made Willard a fair income, he realized age left him probably one more big payday. That was why he agreed in January 1919 to fight anyone Rickard said at any location chosen for the bout. The financially scrupulous Willard served as his own manager and press agent for the fight. This gave Kearns and Dempsey a decided publicity edge before the first punch was thrown.[39]

Signing Dempsey for the fight was transformed by Rickard and Kearns into a made-to-order media event. Rickard called reporters to New York's Claridge

Hotel for a "major announcement" on Willard's next title defense. Kearns, Dempsey, and a lavish buffet greeted sports writers on their arrival, plus an unexpected plot twist. Rickard and Kearns feigned an impasse over the size of Dempsey's end of the purse. Their spirited discussion distressed even Dempsey, who hadn't been brought in on the act. Rickard insisted he couldn't afford more than $15,000. Kearns claimed Dempsey wouldn't fight for less than $50,000. James Dawson, the boxing writer for the *New York Times*, remembers "strongly resenting" the "unreasonableness" of Kearns, whom he and other New York writers considered "a Johnny-Come-Lately trying to impose his will against the better judgment" of the sport's "outstanding promoter."[40]

With Rickard insisting upon a $25,000 guarantee and Kearns holding out for $30,000, the issue was turned over to a jury of reporters. Voting were Bill "Slim" Farnsworth, sports editor of the *New York Evening Journal;* Robert Edgren, sports editor of *New York World;* Dawson of the *Times;* Gene Fowler of the *New York American* and that paper's syndicated columnist Damon Runyon; Nat Fleischer of the *New York Telegram;* Grantland Rice of the *New York Tribune;* along with veteran sports writers Rube Goldberg, Hype Igoe, Ed Curley, and Fred Keats. They decided to compromise the difference and vote Dempsey a $27,500 guarantee and that's what he got. Dempsey remembers getting a knowing wink from Runyon, suggesting if he won, there'd be plenty more where that came from. Rickard's scheme netted a boatload of free publicity on the bout and made some of the country's most widely syndicated bylines willing partners in promotion.[41]

Dempsey began training in Toledo weeks before Willard did, allowing Kearns to corner the market on pre-fight publicity. He had Dempsey whipping Willard in the first round and challenging French fighter Georges Carpentier to an inter-oceanic showdown. When Willard arrived in Toledo on the eve of the fight without manager, trainer, promoter, or adequate sparring partners, Kearns breached security at Willard's Maumee Bay camp, calling him "a 300 pound stiff." Kearns was certain the strategy would unnerve his opponent, while grabbing headlines for his fighter. He offered to fight the "fat boy" himself and won headlines when Willard promised to "fix him good" while winning by first-round knockout. When Willard's camp notified the press that the champion "would do more heavy work" before the bout, Lardner remarked he was "unaware the big fellow had yet done any."[42]

On the eve of the fight, Lardner was certain too many sports writers were coming to believe their own ballyhoo on Dempsey. After watching the challenger train, Lardner thought Dempsey an overrated pug who had been built up in the press by Kearns. But Grantland Rice, one of Dempsey's leading cheerleaders, thought Willard was not taking his opponent "seriously enough" and bet on Dempsey. Damon Runyon liked the ten-to-one odds that Dempsey would knock Willard out in the first round. So did Kearns, who bet $10,000 he'd scraped together by charging customers fifty cents apiece for the privilege of seeing Dempsey spar. It was nearly even money on the eve of the bout that Dempsey would win, testimony to Kearns's cunning in making Willard's condition and not Dempsey's inexperience the conventional wisdom on the fight. It had been nearly a decade since a fight had been held on American soil in which there was a reasonable chance the heavyweight title would change hands. Lightweight champion Benny Leonard, reporting the battle for the *San Francisco Examiner* syndicate, picked Dempsey. So did Battling Nelson, infamous for the Goldfield foul, who reported this fight through a ghostwriter for the *Chicago Daily News*.[43]

Down on his luck and "a bit eccentric as a result of his ring adventures," Nelson overcame Toledo's housing shortage by pitching a pup tent at the edge of Dempsey's camp at the Overland Club. Fellow writers pulled the pegs on Nelson's home away from home one night as Nelson slept soundly inside. Nelson had the last laugh when he beat the heat the night before the fight by bathing in a vat of lemonade. Rickard ordered Nelson out of the camp and paid the concessionaire for his trouble. The concessionaire pocketed the money and sold his stock on the day of the fight, and there was no record of any complaint.[44]

Nelson was the least of Rickard's problems. Rickard's press agent Ike Dorgan had over-promoted the phony claim that good seats were going fast. The media latched on to the story predicting an eighty thousand attendance and boxing's first million dollar gate.[45] The effect was to discourage fight fans from coming. Lardner was among those writing that Toledo was ill equipped to host a spectacle of this magnitude. "The first thing a man has to do when you land in Toledo is look for a bed," he wrote, "and they're about as plentiful here as a beer garden." If "80,000 cuckoos come to the big disagreement," he warned, "60,000 of them besides being blood thirsty will be hungry for sandwiches."[46] Special excursion trains to Toledo were canceled by Washington in advance of an anticipated nationwide rail strike. Of the more than fifteen special trains scheduled to run between New York, Chicago, Cincinnati, and Toledo, only one made it. Combined with stories of pre-fight price gouging by Toledo's hotels and restaurants, the effect was to keep the paid attendance to twenty thousand, a quarter of earlier estimates.[47]

Before leaving his dressing room on the eve of the fight, Dempsey received well wishes from many of the men who had helped bring him to this moment. Among them were Otto Floto and Damon Runyon, perhaps the earliest sportswriters on the Dempsey bandwagon, along with Scoop Gleeson from the *San Francisco Bulletin*. They were followed by Grantland Rice, Nat Fleischer, Robert Edgren, Rube Goldberg, and Hype Igoe, the scribes who had set his guarantee. Ring Lardner also came to shake the hand of the man he was certain would be knocked out by the third round. Conspicuous by their absence were Bat Masterson and Wyatt Earp. The mustachioed Masterson with his trademark cane and the balding Earp had given themselves the highly visible job of "official collector" of all spectators' knives and guns. In his younger days Masterson had been a buffalo hunter, scout, card dealer, and lawman, and Earp a part-time lawman and boxing referee. Masterson had promoted wrestling matches with Floto before becoming his archenemy as boxing writer for the *Denver Morning Telegraph*. Since Floto was one of Dempsey's biggest boosters, it was not surprising that Masterson would back "my big boy" Willard. Dempsey, he assured his reader, "hadn't had a square fight in a year." Kearns, Masterson charged, had padded Dempsey's record with "set-ups and fakes." That was why Dempsey would "be lucky to leave Toledo alive."[48]

Waves of heat greeted Dempsey as Kearns aggressively cleared his way to the ring. The sea of straw boaters and white shirt sleeves that parted before his deeply bronzed body strained for a look. He presented the very image of the snarling, ferocious heavyweight Kearns had cultivated for more than two years. He stood in his corner beneath a blistering sun, shaded by a beach umbrella bearing advertisements that Kearns had sold to local merchants at $25 a foot. A fleshy-looking Willard arrived in the ring a few minutes after four with what many ringsiders considered "a look of boredom" on his face. He turned his back to Dempsey as Kearns massaged Dempsey's neck and shoulder muscles. "This is it," Dempsey could hear him say. Dempsey looked down at the canvas nervously, hoping a three-day-old stubble of beard might mask his emotions. "Everything outside the ropes of the ring disappeared," he remembered. "I was actually going to fight for the heavyweight championship of the world."[49]

Rickard, serving as fight judge, looked over to Warren Barbour, the official timekeeper, who was having a hard time ringing the bell to start the fight. Barbour would later build his reputation into becoming a United States Senator. But he was no bell ringer. The bell was finally rung for him and the fighters immediately circled one another in the center of the ring, with Dempsey crouching and Willard towering over him, standing bolt upright, his hands at his sides.

For the first thirty seconds, Willard was the only one throwing a punch, missing left-right combinations and straight rights, before connecting with a right uppercut to the head that forced Dempsey to clinch. During the next thirty seconds Dempsey began working on Willard's belly and ribs to no apparent effect. Willard launched a left-right combination at one minute of the first round, forcing Dempsey to cover up in Willard's corner. Until the midpoint of the first round, Willard was clearly the aggressor, taking the attack to Dempsey, who seemed tentative, defensive, and determined to use his superior speed to glide out of the big man's reach.

Then, at 1:32 of the first round, it happened. Coming out of a clinch in the center of the ring, Dempsey feinted with his left, Willard swung a left and Dempsey, crouching, countered with a vicious left hook to the head, and a right-left combination that sent Willard crashing to the canvas for a six count. Willard got up swinging but missed a left. Dempsey connected with a left and a solid right to the jaw and then another left which sent Willard toppling against the top rope, coughing up blood and teeth. Dempsey bore in with a straight right and another right for which he wound up. Two final lefts landed before Willard fell to his hands and knees.

As Willard began to rise at the count of three, referee Ollie Pecord attempted to push Dempsey out of the way to let the champion stand, but Dempsey avoided his grasp and launched another flurry of lefts and rights that dumped Willard for a count of six. As he began to rise, Dempsey struck him from behind with a left and a right, dropping Willard for a count of four. Pecord, an inexperienced ringman, failed to separate the fighters as Willard attempted to regain his feet. Dempsey connected with three roundhouse rights, a right-left combination, and a flurry of punches which pried Willard loose from the ropes and crumpled him for a fifth knockdown at 2:20 of the first round. Willard somehow managed to scramble to his feet, limply swinging a right and left of his own, as the arm-weary Dempsey swung lefts and rights and two successive rights that sent Willard stumbling across the ring with Dempsey in hot pursuit. A right-left-right combination and two more rights had Willard's head through the ropes. He held the middle rope with his left hand before a shattering right sent him to his right knee.

The end of the round was near and Willard, amazingly, was getting to his feet at the count of four, yet holding to the middle rope, his head and shoulders parallel to it. It was then that Dempsey tagged him with three terrific lefts, snapping Willard's head into the turnbuckle, and leaving him seated, stooped, and apparently unconscious in a neutral corner. When Pecord reached the count of four, Willard's second slid his stool into the ring and began to enter it, thinking he'd heard the bell. Pecord hesitated, confused. In the pandemonium, Pecord hadn't heard the bell and resumed his count. As he reached ten, Kearns was bolting through the ropes and into the ring, raising Dempsey's hand high over his head and hustling his man out of the ring. As they approached the press table, Barbour's whistle could be heard above the mob. The round had ended at the count of seven. Kearns had lost his $100,000 bet. Dempsey was ordered back into the ring or he'd be disqualified.

The next two rounds were anticlimactic. Willard, with broken ribs and a shattered cheekbone, spattered in his own blood, looked like a gargoyle but gamely fought on for two more rounds. At the start of the fourth, he was unable to leave his stool. When his seconds threw in the blood-spattered towel, it was finally over. Willard was greeted with hoots and jeers and shouts of "quitter" as he struggled blindly to his dressing room, once falling against the barbed wire of the "Jenny Wren" section, where women were seated for the fight. As an exultant mob carried Dempsey from the ring, Charles MacArthur, then a twenty-three-year-old cub reporter for Hearst's *Chicago Herald and Examiner* reached Willard, who mumbled through cracked and swollen lips, "I have $100,000 and a farm in Kansas."[50]

Press reaction to Dempsey's victory was anything but muted. Otto Floto observed that "the penetrating power of a super punch" made Willard "grovel" before "a great man's feet." His paper took the occasion to castigate competitors for favoring Willard. Bat Masterson's prediction of the day before got a two-column replay in the competing *Post*, which wondered why anyone would read any other paper to get "the straight dope" on "where the big things are doing."[51] "Squatting on the stool in his corner," Damon Runyon wrote, "a bleeding, trembling, helpless hulk, Jess Willard, the Kansas Giant, this afternoon relinquished his title of heavyweight champion of the world. The end came just as the bell was about to toss him into the fourth round of a mangling at the paws of Jack Dempsey, the young mountain lion in human form, from the Sangre de Cristo Hills of Colorado."[52] Runyon's page-one account of the contest, carried nationwide by the Hearst syndicate, became a classic and helped to establish for years to come the image of Dempsey as his generation's man killer.

In an era of mass-mediated spectacle and personal publicity there are winners and losers besides the two men who fight in a squared ring. The fans who associate themselves with the values and qualities projected onto the fighters risk much in the outcome of such contests. But so do the sports writers and editors who carefully cultivate or resist cultivating these images. During the jazz age, the payoff was immediate.

To reward Runyon and Gene Fowler for their early and active backing of his star pupil, Kearns began feeding the New York American a series of "exclusives" designed to further promote the new champion. Dempsey was eager to oblige. Fowler had been a friend since high school and the taciturn Runyon a constant supporter since those first dark days in New York. Runyon's sports writing was governed by the conviction that all readers "are children at heart." That had meant stylizing characters in ways that readers could easily grasp from his earliest days as a reporter on the *Pueblo* (Colorado) *Chieftain*. His depiction of Dempsey appreciated his generation's appetite for heroic figures and was sketched after hours of active listening to the future champ. It left Dempsey reassured that "if ever I fell I could safely land on Runyon or Fowler." Other papers might resent Dempsey's intimacy with the American and the Hearst syndicate, but Kearns promised there'd be color enough for everyone eventually.[53]

The night that Jack Dempsey won the heavyweight championship of the world, he dreamed he had lost it. He awakened "from a strange sort of nightmare" uncertain whether he had been "knocked out." Failing to get to sleep again, he dressed and went out into the street. Newsboys were still hollering their extras. He called to one of them and asked who won the fight. The boy looked at him and said, "Aren't you Dempsey? You ought to know." Dempsey fumbled in his pocket for a coin and the boy interrupted, "That's okay, Champ." Dempsey took the paper back to his room and read its account of the fight three or four times "convincing myself I was really the champ."[54]

It took the press to persuade Jack Dempsey of something that for years seemed unimaginable. At long last he was the heavyweight champion of the world. For many years he had desperately sought media attention and now it took the media to finally certify and authenticate that he was somebody. It began to "sink in" that he was the champion of the world and all that might mean. Kearns saw only dollar signs and prepared to hustle his man killer into highly profitable personal appearances. But the elevation from anonymity to sudden celebrity would not be without cost. The next few months would be "the most miserable" of Dempsey's life, as the media gaze brought into its harsh relief parts of Dempsey's painful past that now became public property.

As jazz-age readers acquainted themselves with the daily details of the ring's newest celebrity, a doughboy recently returned from the war began to imagine himself a future champion, just as Dempsey did when reading the pages of the *Police Gazette*. Jack Dempsey now stood in Gene Tunney's way just as Jess Willard had stood in Dempsey's. And though it would be seven years before they'd finally meet, Tunney began to construct an elaborate plan to win what Dempsey had won. The design that he fashioned inevitably involved winning a hearing in the nation's press and among its sports writers. In an era of personal publicity, rhetorical warfare preceded the first physical blow struck. But where Dempsey had Kearns, was easy to like, and determined to please, Tunney had none of these. It made his journey to their championship meeting a complicated search for public identity in a time of national nervousness and private opportunity.

Tunney, Dempsey, Sports Writers, and Readers

T he month after Jack Dempsey won the heavyweight title and signed a $15,000 weekly contract to tour the Pantages vaudeville circuit, Gene Tunney was an unemployed New York shipping clerk with two bad hands searching for a fight. He had been mustered out of the U.S. Marines without enough money to buy a decent training outfit and borrowed $100 from a friend to begin his seven-year stalk of the heavyweight title holder. Boxing writers found it funny that the little known and lightly regarded light heavyweight had set his sights on the twentieth century's greatest fighting machine, but to Tunney winning the title was simply a matter of rigorous self-discipline and cold calculation. Its logic was born on the day Tunney talked to company corporal Edwin H. McReynolds, a peacetime sports writer for the *Joplin Globe,* while the two sailed down the Rhine River as members of the American Expeditionary Force. That would be one of the few times "the fighting marine" had the press in his corner.[1]

On the surface, Tunney had many of the qualities that appeared perfect for puffing in the jazz-age press. He was good looking, clean living, a former marine if not a war hero. He was an Irish Catholic kid from Greenwich Village, whose family took its religion seriously. Young Tunney had worked his way up from West Side smokers to shipping clerk, took correspondence courses and consciously carried himself like a character out of Frank Merriwell.

There were those in the press who seized on these qualities and portrayed the blonde bomber as an all-American boy worthy of a title shot. Tunney's fan following never approximated Dempsey's, but there were those who saw in "the fighting marine" what they wanted to see, and what certain sports writers helped them to see—a fierce competitor within the urban landscape who rises to the top through the force of intellect, training, and strategy, whose elevation served as symbol for the rewards of solid citizenship and the evidence of social progress.

The trouble with this representation of Tunney was that it failed to satisfy a nervous generation's need to see in its heavyweight champion a man of metaphorical majesty, whose knockout punch served as solace for the deprivations experienced in the daily drama of industrial living. Dempsey cooperated with this construction by his physical destruction of Willard, but more importantly, he cooperated with sports writers in giving the public the Dempsey it wanted. This made his cultural significance far greater. Jack Kearns made sure that Dempsey could be colored. Sports writers soon learned Dempsey was good copy. He could be depicted as an "everyman, fighting our battles," in the words of Paul Gallico, sports editor of the jazz age's leading circulation-getter, the *New York Daily News.* The reading public, which paid a penny or two each day to meet "the people's champion," sought to know Dempsey "better than a member of their own family."[2]

Reporters, however, found Tunney an infinitely pretentious man, who ironically resisted the prevarications of the press that were making Dempsey a household name. Although he was not above occasionally buying sports writers to keep his name before the public, Tunney seemed to lack a one-two punch, a strategy outside the ring with reporters to match his cunning inside it. Reporters who were drawn to Dempsey's natural charm were often struck by Tunney's "artificiality." Tunney's background no less than Dempsey's would have qualified him for working-class hero, but unlike Dempsey, his every utterance seemed to suggest pretensions distancing him from the followers of the fight game. The word on Tunney was that he was "a tactless youth," "a social climber," whose greater crime than arrogance was that he was unspectacular in an era demanding its heroes written large.[3]

Gene Tunney was no stranger to press portrayals of men of action. Where Jack Dempsey's early tastes ran to the *National Police Gazette,* Tunney turned to the *New York Evening World,* Joseph Pulitzer's experiment in people's journalism that featured the nation's first sports department.[4] The first thing the young James Joseph (Gene) Tunney ever remembered reading was Robert Edgren's column in the sports pages of the *World.* He based his early fighting style on Edgren's illustrated columns and practiced his left-right combination on an inflated turkey crop tied to a transom in the Greenwich Village home of John and Mary Tunney. When the carcass gave out, Gene tried Edgren's com-

Jack Dempsey trains in Great Falls, Montana, for his 1923 title fight with Tommy Gibbons. In the absence of Tex Rickard's promotional skill, this fight was a money loser. Dempsey's narrow win over Gibbons and Gene Tunney's knockout over the same challenger set the stage for the Dempsey-Tunney showdown in Philadelphia in 1926. Pictured from left to right are Jerry Luvadis, Dempsey's trainer; Billy Wells, an English welterweight; Dempsey; Joe Benjamin, a West Coast lightweight; Harry Drake, a heavyweight; Johnny Dempsey, the champion's brother; Jack Burke, a heavyweight; and George Godfrey, another of Dempsey's sparring partners. Photograph courtesy of Lyle Whiteman.

bination out on brothers or classmates at Saint Veronica's Parochial School, generously giving and receiving a swollen nose, broken lips, "and a terrific headache" for his trouble. Edgren's celebration of "scientific cleverness" as opposed to "brute strength" found an earnest audience in the skinny young scrapper, as well as Edgren's assertion that attention to detail and a "good business sense" were as crucial in the "new American style of boxing" as the ability to hit while making your opponent miss.[5]

Tunney's tendency toward brittle hands and broken knuckles made him a defensive fighter, who emphasized speed, footwork, and ring agility in fending off opponents. He saw himself as a latter-day James J. Corbett, whose defeat of the imperious John L. Sullivan was the result of careful calculation and a "healthy regard" for the other fellow's fists. Tunney embraced Corbett's technique of mental dexterity and delicate planning in pursuing a ring championship, but he ignored Corbett's words of warning that cultivating good relations with the press and public were fundamental to any fighter's success. Tunney's disdain for the fight crowd extended to most sports writers. He resented their depiction of him as a "prig" and they, in turn, mocked his associations with the literati. Will Rogers spoke for many when he observed that Americans favored heavyweights "with less Shakespeare and more wallop."[6]

Dempsey's rootless childhood with pioneering parents in the West stood in marked contrast to Tunney's upbringing on New York City's West Side. His father was a longshoreman by day and fight fan by night, who frequented Owney Geaghan's boxing club in the Bowery, where, as he liked to tell it, he once fought the house pro to a standstill. Gene's mother, born at Castle Bar in County Mayo, was devoutly religious, and hoped that one of her three sons would become a priest.

Gene's education at De La Salle Academy under the Christian Brothers included organized sprints around Central Park. On warm summer nights Tunney could be seen jogging up Fifth Avenue behind big green double-decker buses. He liked to swim off the pier at West Tenth Street and frequently dove from barges and transatlantic steamers into the Hudson River. One "soldier dive" lead to a concussion. Tunney played center in the local basketball league, liked foot racing and broad jumping meets with competing parochial school students at New York's Clason Point Military Academy, and enjoyed a good game of handball with parish priests. His passion for self-discipline led him to marathon running and a plan to enter the annual "ankle excursion" from city hall to the Bronx. But he reluctantly gave it up when he found "there was no money to be made in it."[7]

Boxing was as much a part of Tunney's teen years as "breathing," even though there was precious little money to be made in fighting. Tunney found that scuffling with rivals in the Gophers and Hudson Dusters for West Side bragging rights taught him valuable lessons "in the manly art of self-protection" and cautioned him to "look out before rushing in."[8] Tunney emulated "Handsome" Jack Goodman, a Greenwich Village light heavyweight, and imitated his short, snappy stride. At home, his fetish for self-improvement included several strategies. He would daily push himself from a wall with each finger five hundred times to strengthen weak hands. He would also stand on a bedroom chair to a count of five hundred to expand his powers of concentration. The point was to have a plan that anticipated your success.[9]

In his middle teens, Tunney fought nearly nightly in West Side smokers for the price of ginger ale and a stale ham sandwich. An early tussle with Leonard Ross failed to impress. The promoter of a competing club found Tunney earnest but "awkward." Owners of the Ocean Steamship Company liked his steadiness and paid the fifteen-year-old office boy five dollars a week, doubling it a year later when he became mail clerk. Promotion to freight classifier made the seventeen-year-old seventeen dollars weekly and gave him the hope he might one day rise to the rank of dock superintendent. He applied himself through correspondence courses in business, mathematics, and English and began carrying himself like a character out of Frank Merriwell.[10]

He became enthralled with the easy optimism of after-dinner speaker and captain of industry Chauncey Depew, a pre–Civil War Yale graduate, whose long public life celebrated "our sacred, scientific and social progress." To Tunney, no American captured the requirements of everyday living as did Depew. To be a "living" human being meant "enjoying the work by which you live." The twentieth century offered "limitless opportunities" for those "vigorous enough to solve its problems and set its records." Depew was convinced that "athletic pursuits are the handmaidens of good habits and solid citizenship." A healthy mind had to have a healthy body, and the two in combination were "necessary partners for intellectual and material triumph."[11]

The youthful Tunney was persuaded the world "might be full of roses" but it was not so on Perry Street, where he grew up. The gloomy garrets that hovered over Little Bohemia's saloons and coffee houses gave refuge to Eugene O'Neill, John Masefield, Lincoln Steffens, Louisa May Alcott, Edna St. Vincent Millay, and George Bellows, men and women of artistic temperament who gathered at Washington Square or within the corridors of the Lafayette Hotel, imagining an end to their own anonymity.

Tunney shared their enthusiasm and added his own pretensions. He would later lecture the press on his conviction that "there are thorns and thistles in every garden," while freely giving advice to "all ambitious young men" that "has served me in good stead." One had to be "ready mentally and physically to face the world and fight for our daily bread." And in this struggle, one must look the part if you expected to be taken seriously by the people who made a difference. So Tunney put on airs, sports writers wrote, by cultivating "the outward appearance and manner of a Park Avenue drawing room blue blood," while he searched out "the ways of the wealthy."[12]

One of those ways, he reckoned, might be boxing, but his first encounter at the age of sixteen with a professional fighter left him so badly battered he resolved "never to fight a professional again." But the monotony of office work for a youth who imagined himself "going places" proved too much. During breaks, he would spar with junior clerks by pushing desks and file cabinets out of the way to provide ring space. Soon he was making the fight club circuit in the evenings, a "rough and tumble" world "where nearly anything went."[13]

Tunney's first fight as a professional came in 1915 when he was a 140-pound eighteen-year-old. He received $18 from the Sharkey Athletic Club, later popularized in the paintings of George Bellows, to fight Bobby Dawson. Unlike the haylofts and firetraps Tunney would frequently fight in, Sharkey's was one of New York's best-known and more widely publicized boxing arenas. Tom Sharkey never promoted respectability as a feature of his saloon club and actively nurtured a reputation for being meaner than most of his competitors. It gave him an appeal that crossed class lines. That is what made Tunney's seventh-round dispatch of Dawson a good start on what would be a long trail to the top.[14]

Four fights quickly followed Tunney's ring debut: a draw and three wins, two by knockout. By the time he was twenty, Tunney was a six-foot, one-inch, 150-pound fighter of "careful" habits. He had learned to counter punch, feint, sidestep, and to time his deliberate attacks. His caution extended to career choice. The steamship company paid better than boxing and he had hopes of promotion. American participation in the Great War gave him a third option, but Tunney failed his induction physical because of an elbow injury. He worked the summer of 1917 as a lifeguard in Keansburg, New Jersey, hoping the sun and exercise would heal his condition. By June of the following year he was on a troop ship bound for France.[15]

While later billed as "The Fighting Marine," the only action Tunney saw as a marine with the American Expeditionary Force was in the squared ring. His talent as a ring marksman became apparent during basic training at Parris Island off the Carolina coast. Thereafter, the choice of guard duty or participating in an elaborate competition to crown the light heavyweight champion of the combined services was not a difficult one. The idea for a tournament was born in the negative publicity generated by the Army's experiences on the Mexican border in 1916. Unstructured off-duty hours led to barroom brawls and bordello imbroglios that produced headlines and a War Department inquiry. Yale's Walter Camp and Princeton's Raymond Fosdick were brought in to organize camp competitions on the Ivy League model of athletics. Their goal was to improve discipline and morale within the service and to provide for good citizenship afterwards.[16]

The signing of the Armistice on November 11, 1918, found two million Americans in France and prompted the seven-month run-up to the Inter-Allied Games, a fifteen-day sports festival involving fifteen hundred athletes from eighteen participating nations. The event was Tunney's first taste of the media gaze that would be given sports coverage in the postwar world. General John J. Pershing's expanding appreciation of the powers of positive publicity led to the creation of a Publicity Department whose mission was to promote the games.[17] The Press Section sent daily articles to publications in all participating countries and was linked to wire services from its command center adjacent to the 25,000-seat Pershing Stadium. Half a million people attended the twenty-six-sport competition, with American media playing up stories of "the sons and brothers who have been called to the colors, who risked life and limb for their country."[18]

Tunney's powers of concentration were sorely tested during the Inter-Allied Games. He had broken a knuckle in a semifinal bout in Tours, his small right hand swelling "to the size of a ham." Fitted with a special boxing glove, he went into the ring against Ted Jamison, the United States amateur light heavyweight champion, whose overhand right made him an imposing opponent. Their championship bout brought into play all the elements that Tunney would use in his seven-year struggle to take the title from Dempsey. Winning was first "a state of mind" in which one "methodically mapped in advance" all movements in the ring. He staged and endlessly rehearsed every counter punch he would need to keep Jamison at a distance and to avoid his deadly right. Tunney grew certain that "the application of rational planning" could make up for fighting this fight essentially one-handed. His victory was testament to his powers of preparation and made him light heavyweight champion of the Inter-Allied Games. The date was July 5, 1919, less than twenty-four hours after Jack Dempsey, half a world away, had slugged Jess Willard to a shiny red pulp to become boxing's heavyweight champion.[19]

Although Tunney was now champion of his weight class, observers found, and Tunney himself agreed, that he had "never been very impressive as a fighter." His defensive style in the ring and failure to follow the fight crowd outside it made him neither a press nor fan favorite. To skeptics, he seemed to cultivate a certain regal bearing and rhetorical style singularly out of place in the violent world of the ring.[20] For all his public confidence that he would one day achieve his destiny as heavyweight champion by whipping Jack Dempsey, he was privately not so sure.

Returning to New York, he tried to get his old job back as shipping clerk. Finding it filled, he strongly considered going to Yale and landing a spot on the football team. He mulled over his future by placing five hundred match sticks end to end, then repeated the process over again. He had welcomed the many disciplines of military life. The ambiguities of being a civilian seemed unsteadying and strange. Greenwich appeared to have lost its pre-war familiarity. At the edge of his unexpected malaise may have been the great nagging fear of failure. After several weeks of uncertainty, he "humiliated" himself by borrowing $100 to buy a training outfit. He would take his chance as a boxer after all.[21]

For two years Tunney made slow if not insubstantial progress through the light heavyweight ranks. His nine knockouts during the spring and summer of 1920 helped him "frame out" of his mind "the possibility of defeat." He trained at the New York Athletic Club on West Fifty-fourth Street, and there he befriended various captains of industry and mass merchandising who had begun to embrace boxing as a manly, leisure time activity. Among these men was Bernard Gimbel, who helped promote Tunney into the undercard of Jack Dempsey's much ballyhooed championship bout with French war hero Georges Carpentier at Boyle's Thirty Acres in Jersey City, New Jersey, in July 1921.

However, Tunney's technical knockout of Canada's Soldier Jones in a preliminary bout did little to advance his name before the public, and it was all but ignored in the aftermath of Dempsey's four-round demolition of Carpentier in boxing's first million dollar gate. Of the more than two million words filed on the Dempsey-Carpentier fight, which Tex Rickard promoted as a grudge match between a French war hero and an American "slacker," barely a paragraph or two noticed Tunney's painful triumph over the lightly regarded Jones. Tunney realized he "had no business" on the fight card if not for his record as a service boxer. His chronically sore hands exaggerated his defensive style and were hardly a crowd-pleaser. The payoff came as he watched Dempsey dispatch Carpentier and realized how far he would have to come before he faced the "man killer" in the ring.[22]

Tunney desperately tried "to keep my name before the public," reluctantly paying 5 percent of his meager earnings to two New York newspapermen in exchange for favorable publicity. The arrangement began to pay off during the fall and winter of 1921, when he fought three matches in New York City; two were at Tex Rickard's Madison Square Garden. His second-round technical knockout of Pittsburgh's Jack Burke was witnessed by Dempsey and persuaded Rickard that aggressive promotion might overcome Tunney's tendency toward ring passivity. Rickard's staging of a light heavyweight championship match between Tunney and Battling Levinsky, whose only defeats had been to Dempsey and Carpentier, drew a capacity crowd of 14,428 to the Garden. Tunney's twelve-round decision in January 1922 generated polite respect, if not overwhelming adulation, in a press still uncertain whether Tunney's limited punching power would long keep him champion.[23]

Their critique seemed substantiated when Tunney lost his title later that year to Harry Greb. The beating Tunney took from the "Pittsburgh Windmill," better known for his late night carousing than training techniques, left him blinded and out on his feet at the end of the fight. To be beaten by a fighter who was five inches shorter and fifteen pounds lighter, while an eight-to-five favorite, stigmatized Tunney as a fighter with limited tools. The former champion had to be assisted by seconds to his dressing room, where he collapsed. Sports writers began to write Tunney off as a courageous if somewhat ordinary boxer. The studiousness with which he approached each match appeared to make him a "synthetic" fighter, one lacking in the brute instinct seen as so essential for success in the ring.[24]

Forty-eight hours after his mauling, Tunney appeared before the New York Athletic Commission to post a $2,500 bond for a return match with Greb. Almost to a man, sports writers agreed with Commissioner William Muldoon that Tunney was "way out of his class in asking for more."[25] Even Tunney's father feared he would be killed. What these men didn't know was Tunney's remarkable capacity for self-detachment. He had fought the final five rounds of his first Greb fight as if he were a spectator. His mind was already rehearsing the feints and starts and footwork that he would use when they met again. Although he lacked the energy to execute his plan and appeared badly beaten by the final bell, he was confident that in a rematch he'd win.[26]

Four fights with the pesky Greb followed. The first two were fought on February 24, 1923, and December 23, 1923, before capacity Madison Square Garden crowds, and while technically they were draws, reporters in each case gave Tunney close decisions. The brutal contests won Tunney a new measure of respect, demonstrated his capacity to take a punch and give two in return, and persuaded Tex Rickard, who had promoted the bouts, that Tunney had overcome his former timidity and could draw a good crowd under the right conditions.[27] Rickard's promotional touch was sadly lacking in return bouts between Tunney and Greb staged in Cleveland on September 17, 1924, and St. Paul on March 25, 1925. The matches generated local publicity, but were largely ignored in the national press. This was a missed opportunity, because each contest was a one-sided Tunney win, with the final clash as damaging to Greb as the first had been to Tunney.[28]

Tunney fought only twice more as a light heavyweight—against Italian champion Ermino Spalla, at Yankee Stadium in June 1924, and against Georges Carpentier at the Polo Grounds one month later. Each fight ended in controversy, casting doubt on his claim he was a legitimate contender for Dempsey's heavyweight title. Rickard's promotion of the first fight promised a hefty donation to Mrs. William Randolph Hearst's Milk Fund to assist American veterans and their families. Spalla and Tunney had known each other as allies in France, but their reunion proved an embarrassment for Spalla, who was disqualified in the sixth round when, staggered and bloodied, he refused to break a clinch.[29] The clash with Carpentier proved equally unsettling. The "Orchid Man" had been driven to the canvas at the end of the fourteenth round by what his seconds insisted was a low blow. At the bell for the final round, they pushed the stricken Frenchman to his feet, but Tunney refused to take the fight to his helpless foe, and the referee was forced to step in amidst the bedlam and award the fight to Tunney on a technical knockout.[30]

The outcome of the Carpentier encounter infuriated Tunney for a second reason. The gate had been good. A crowd of 31,133 paid $136,681 to see the bout. It suggested Tunney was becoming, at least in his native New York, a drawing card when well matched. But in an effort to solidify his standing with society friends, Tunney had signed with Jimmy Johnston and the Cromwell Athletic Club to promote the fight. Carpentier got $45,000 of the fight's $118,000 net. After the athletic club had deducted its share for staging and publicizing the match, less the cost of preliminaries, sparring partners, training expenses, and other incidentals, it left Tunney a measly $3,000 share of the receipts.[31] For a man interested in keeping up appearances, it was difficult for the press to take Tunney's insistence on a title shot fully seriously. Tunney had lost but one of his first fifty-one fights, yet could command only pocket change compared to the earnings of Jack Dempsey, the man he insisted on being measured against.

After six years of steady fighting, only one man seemed to stand between Gene Tunney and his shot at the title. Tommy Gibbons was a crafty light heavyweight who had bulked up to fight Dempsey to a fifteen-round standstill at Shelby, Montana, on July 4, 1923. His narrow defeat was his only loss in more than one hundred ring appearances dating back to 1911. Gibbons shared Tunney's enthusiasm for scientific fighting and had made Dempsey look awkward and hopelessly outclassed before giving way to fatigue and the aggressive body work of a far larger opponent.[32]

That Gibbons was the first of Dempsey's opponents to go the distance with the champion raised questions on whether Dempsey might be slipping. Commentators wondered if sudden celebrity and a soft life in Hollywood, where he made movies, had reduced Dempsey from man killer to mere mortal. Media disappointment in Dempsey's less than lethal showing in Shelby was reflected in the writing of *New York Times* boxing expert James P. Dawson, who noted disapprovingly of Dempsey's inability to dominate an opponent "not his equal in size, weight, or strength." For the first time, Dawson observed, Dempsey "was not the reliable death dealing hitter we expected." The narrow victory over Gibbons recast Dempsey's conquest of Carpentier. Reports circulated that Dempsey must have tagged the challenger's "fragile chin" two years before. Now Dempsey seemed "as wild as a March hare," leaving sports writers to long for "the day of the lightning-line bone crunching punch" that spelled opponents' doom and Dempsey victories.[33]

For two years Tunney had avoided Gibbons and the Irishman's insulting demands that the two men meet in the ring. During that time, Tunney had studied Gibbons's elusive style in fight films and had sparred with men who had sparred with Gibbons. He rehearsed Gibbons's pattern of feints and leads and planned to counter with a short right to the left eye when Gibbons used his double feint and followed with a left hook. The June 5, 1925, match at the Polo Grounds attracted nearly fifty thousand fight fans and was billed as the bout to decide who would challenge Dempsey for the title. Dempsey, who hadn't fought in two years, endorsed the ballyhoo and promised to fight the winner. That would be Tunney, whose meticulous execution of his fight plan made him Gibbons's master throughout the contest. Tunney capped the evening off by doing something Dempsey had failed to do. His right to the chin put Gibbons on his back for a count of seven in the twelfth round. When Gibbons got to his feet, Tunney unloaded another right, and for the first time in his career, Gibbons was counted out.[34]

Finally, it was Tunney's turn to make a little money. He was rushed into the production of *The Fighting Marine*, and although the feature did mediocre box office nationwide, it was a hit with New York City audiences. Tunney had emerged as Gotham's first fighter to challenge for the heavyweight title. But while Tunney was a favorite to fight for the heavyweight championship, he was hardly the favorite of New York City sports writers. The reasons had to do with both style and substance. Dempsey had become transformed from a frightened frontier kid to his generation's most idolized sports hero for an urban reading public far removed from the realities, but not the myths, of frontier living. This incarnation drew upon a ring style, perfected by Doc Kearns, that swept Dempsey from his corner, bobbing and weaving, with an unshaven smirk upon his lips, and what commentators felt certain was blood lust in the eyes. This had made Dempsey sometimes the heavy, sometimes the hero, but always the giant killer turned millionaire who teased the public imagination.

Tunney's elevation from obscurity to the man in line to fight for the heavyweight championship inevitably aroused the publicity mill in sports departments across the country. However, even from the outset Tunney fought the promotional war at a distinct disadvantage. It was not only his sense of estrangement from the fight crowd and the sports writers who wrote the stories working-class readers liked to read. Tunney's other problem was that his portrayal in the press inevitably served as foil for the better-known and more passionately loved, or occasionally loathed, Dempsey. If Dempsey had been the apotheosis of the American pioneering spirit as the self-made man who felled the far larger Willard, many felt betrayed when his failure to serve in the Great War later came to light. It was because so many felt they had a stake in Dempsey, and that he was one of them, that the story of his life, as told by the press, seemed such a human one. And it was the perception of Tunney's self-satisfied distance from the fight crowd and conscious recreation of the juvenile fictional hero that served to separate him from the images of stark ferocity that the reading public liked to associate with gladiators of the squared ring.

The decision of how to play Dempsey and Tunney in the nation's press on the eve of their long-awaited championship fight also illustrates journalism's jazz-age jitters over the kind of society America was becoming and journalism's role in reflecting and shaping that society. Self-conscious defenders of journalistic respectability deplored the trend towards self-culture in postwar society and saw the celebration of fighters and the myth-making that surrounded them as an unfortunate form of civic spectacle in which the nation's press played a dubious role. Their objections were vigorously opposed by eager young men and women who had recently come to journalism for the same reason Tunney and Dempsey had taken to boxing—they were trying to become somebody. This clash within jazz-age journalism is an interesting subplot and consequence of the impact of Jack Dempsey on the popular culture of the twenties.

That sports reporters had a vested interest in the fighting legend they had helped to create was never more apparent than in the last fight Dempsey would have before facing Gene Tunney. His first-round slugfest with Argentinian challenger Luis Firpo, before 88,000 fight fans in the Polo Grounds, produced eight knockdowns and one of the most extraordinary moments in the history of sports. Firpo came off the canvas for a seventh time, nailing Dempsey with a desperate overhand right that drove the champion to the ropes, followed by a series of rights that sent Dempsey through the ropes and crashing on to the press table.

As the referee began his count, a startled Jack Lawrence of the *New York Herald Tribune,* pushed an equally flabbergasted champion off his damaged typewriter, and assisted by Western Union operator Perry Grogan, helped catapult Dempsey into the ring at the count of nine. After Dempsey's second-round knockout of the "Wild Bull of the Pampas," half a dozen members of the media and a dozen more from the worlds of entertainment and high finance claimed credit for coming to Dempsey's aid. They included Frank Menke of International News Service, who insisted Dempsey's fall broke his typewriter, even though everyone knew he wrote with a pencil; noted columnist Walter Winchell; boxing's premier painter George Bellows, who was covering the fight for the *New York Evening Journal;* and comedian Milton Berle, who wasn't within twenty yards of the ring.[35]

At the height of the pandemonium, benches set up for the fight on the Polo Grounds infield toppled over and led to a donnybrook in which Babe Ruth, baseball's "Sultan of Swat," took a widely reported swing at welterweight boxing champion Mickey Walker. The excitement was not lost on W. K. Vanderbilt and L. H. Rothschild, whose connections won them ringside seats. They stood spellbound for the fight's entire four and a half minutes. So did Archibald and Kermit Roosevelt, A. J. Drexel Biddle, junior and senior, and Nobel Peace Prize winner Eliahu Root, whose art of diplomacy was insufficient to stem the mayhem. The bout evoked for many Dempsey's heart-stopping slaughter of Jess Willard four years before, but was made all the more urgent by Dempsey's near defeat. Ethel Barrymore spoke in behalf of those who witnessed the fight that night by announcing she "couldn't imagine anyone beating the Dempsey I saw tonight."[36]

The million-dollar gate for the Dempsey-Firpo fight, the second in ring history, reflected the degree to which boxing had become big business in jazz-age America and the role of mass media in promoting that leisure industry. The *New York World* observed that Tex Rickard's "skillful publicity campaign, day after day, beating up interest" had transformed Firpo from an unknown, oversized Latin fighter with an antipathy toward training, into the "Wild Bull of the Pampas." *The Brooklyn Eagle* concurred. One could only wonder, the paper remarked, "what might have happened to the Monroe Doctrine if Firpo had won." The criticism, however, did little to dampen the enthusiasm of either paper in playing the contest with multi-column headlines that brought a record press run.[37]

In five years, Dempsey had fought thirty-nine rounds, totaling three min-

Dempsey knocks down Luis Firpo for one of seven times in their famous September 1923 championship fight in the Polo Grounds. For "sheer ferocity," ringside reporters considered it the greatest slugfest of the twentieth century. Concurring in this opinion was James J. Corbett, seated at ringside in this photograph, wearing glasses. Corbett had taken the championship thirty-one years before from John L. Sullivan and now made a living as a celebrity fight reporter. Photograph courtesy of Lyle Whiteman.

utes less than two full hours. His total earnings of $1,257,000 during that time prorated to $32,230.74 a round, $10,743.59 a minute, $179.00 a second. For the pleasure of sending Firpo back to Buenos Aires, he made $100,000 a minute.[38]

The Firpo fight restored Dempsey to a public image he and Rickard and Kearns had worked carefully to cultivate. A messy divorce and an indictment by a federal grand jury in February 1920 for evading the draft forced West Coast studio Pathe to shelve Dempsey's fifteen-episode serial *Daredevil Jack*. A not guilty verdict did little to placate veterans groups or editorial writers offended by a "warrior" who left to others "the real fighting." The war against Dempsey's war record was waged in the nation's press when his former wife wrote the *San Francisco Chronicle* a letter claiming Dempsey had lied about supporting her to evade the draft. The negative publicity threatened to kill the big money Dempsey and Kearns had hoped to make out of the championship and only subsided when Kearns "persuaded" Maxine Cates to recant her story with a handsome buy out.[39]

Firpo is counted out in the second round of his fight with Dempsey after the champion was catapulted back into the ring by reporters after a Firpo haymaker landed on Dempsey's chin. The fact that a boxing novice like Firpo could knock Dempsey down twice in their championship bout further convinced Gene Tunney, then fighting as a light heavyweight, that Dempsey could be had. Photograph courtesy of Lyle Whiteman.

Tex Rickard saw before Dempsey and Kearns did that "hatin' is as good for box office as lovin'" and used the strategy in promoting a million dollar gate in Dempsey's July 1921 title defense against French war hero Georges Carpentier.[40] The success solidified Rickard's certainty that New York City would support a new Madison Square Garden. The $11 million building, backed by a banking syndicate, was a tribute to the business of sports and its marriage of convenience with the nation's sports-writing establishment. From his paneled office, the former cowpuncher now oversaw a twenty-member support staff and a high-salaried publicity department that would have been the envy of any major corporation. The mounted boxing gloves of Battling Nelson were a reminder of how far Rickard and the sport of fives had come.[41]

Dempsey's old insecurities prevented him from enjoying the role of badman, even if it was profitable. Though he played the part of "the rich and famous" with unabashed enthusiasm, he was haunted by the fear his new life would be taken away from him. It made him "sweat at night" and led to fears he would "wind up in the gutter" like so many fighters had before him.[42] As a result he tried to please, whether it was by signing an autograph, giving an "exclusive" to a member of the press, or by fighting well-publicized exhibitions for veterans aid groups. The effort led many in the press and public to forgive his failure to fight for his country, passing it off as "a very serious mistake" of youth which Dempsey had lived down through "modesty and good behavior."[43] The public act of repentance made Dempsey appear all the more endearing. Finally, it was President Coolidge's decision to honor Dempsey at the White House in February 1924 that irrevocably placed the imprimatur of national hero upon him.[44]

The press had played its part in legitimizing both boxing and Dempsey and this greatly disturbed some of its most respected and senior members, who launched a national organization of newspaper editors in 1923 to stem the abuses of jazz-age journalism that threatened in their minds the reputation of the profession. They argued that the tendency of the "Typhoid Marys of Journalism" to "continuously distort the news in the interest of undiluted entertainment," including "playing sports to the limit," only fed "a craving for stimulation" that characterized American public opinion since the end of the Great War.[45] Paul Bellamy, editor of the *Cleveland Plain Dealer* and one of the founders of the American Society of Newspaper Editors, observed that "since the war the public mind has been highly excited. The national nerves have not returned to normal." This had put a great many editors in an untenable position. Since "the public exercises over us the power of life and death each day," the pressure was to "fill our pages with boot legging, jazz-dancing, automobiles, moving pictures, radio and sports to get ourselves read." Editors complained that they could not remember a time in which public taste was more determined to find stories of celebrity and civic spectacle.[46]

The creation of mass-mediated sports celebrities struck many of the nation's senior editors as "the great fake of American journalism." They praised the example of the *New York Herald-Tribune's* city editor Stanley Walker who banned "maudlin balderdash" from appearing on the paper's sports pages. Walker had his publisher's support in disdaining the "overblown sagas" of sports heroism produced by sports writers who lacked "all sense of proportion." The paper's sports editor, Stanley Woodward, gave strict orders that writers avoid "godding up" professional athletes. The "temptations" of making a little "dishonest money" by boosting a fight were so great, that the paper made certain reporters were "honest" and "hard-boiled" before they were given the sports beat.[47]

Malcolm Bingay, the irascible managing editor of the *Detroit News,* was convinced "somebody was getting something" in Tex Rickard's "circus-like" promotion of Jack Dempsey. The promoter's frank admission that "sugaring" sports writers was "a routine business expense" prompted a probe by the American Society of Newspaper Editors into the murky relations between sports writers and promoters. It found that promoters annually paid $24,000 to get a good press on their fights. This included making sports writers and editors silent partners in the staging of fights, having them ghost articles and books under the signature of fighters, and making them judges in fight decisions.[48] Bingay, who admitted he was trying to "live down" the fact he had been sports editor at the *News* when only nineteen, called the cozy relations between sports writers and promoters "the rottenest condition in American journalism." Joined by Willis J. Abbot of the *Christian Science Monitor* and other senior editors, Bingay urged the end of "fanning interest in foolish fights for the sake of journalism's reputation."[49]

The Bingay faction found that the "ungodly union" of sports writers and circulation managers meant that three-quarters of all sports editors sent their copy directly to the composing room, bypassing seasoned copy editors whose blue pencils assured the standardization and uniformity that veteran editors associated with the highest ideals of the profession. This freedom had led to a 50 percent surge in sports coverage in the last generation alone, buoyed by readership surveys that showed one reader in four now listed the sports page as the most important reason they read the paper.[50] Circulation managers welcomed the 50 percent readership gain on the eve of a Dempsey title defense, but managing editors and city editors saw the demand for "more and more sport" a threat to their authority. They deplored storytelling based on "box office receipts" and urged a return to journalism's traditional role of "educating the youth of America to the wholesome benefits of amateur athletics." The Bingay faction argued that it was the responsibility of every editor to direct every boy and girl "to put their heart and soul into clean fine sports." This would allow newspapers to serve their cities and "build circulation on a permanent and profitable basis" rather than playing into the "poisonous" world of professional promoters.[51]

Bingay's old guard was vigorously opposed by defenders of "a higher pragmatism" who argued the jazz age required a new sports page to chronicle it. Their leading spokesman was Marvin Creager, managing editor of the *Milwaukee Journal,* who believed it was his responsibility "to print the news as it happened," including "the fundamental human instinct of being interested in conflict." Creager's liberal education at the University of Kansas and work as feature editor at the *Kansas City Star* persuaded him that "the glamorous and sensational have their place" in newspaper work.[52] Creager was joined by younger editors in urging journalism's senior citizens "to face actualities" and realize "the millennial age" would not be delayed by editors satisfying reader interest in the fight game. An interest in sports was "the most striking social phenomenon since the war," they were certain, with sports selling more papers than "any other classification of news." For that reason, editors who ignored prizefights invited their own "suffering."[53]

Implicit in the debate over Dempseymania was a struggle between competing visions of journalism's future. On one side were those who saw the surge in daily newspaper readership—twenty-eight million in 1920 and thirty-four million five years later—as a signal that efforts to rationalize the newspaper "business" through syndication and chain ownership was working. Roy W. Howard, a partner in the nation's second-largest newspaper chain, argued that the deaths of journalism's great "public-minded men"—Horace Greeley, William Cullen Bryant, Charles Dana and Henry Watterson—enabled "organization and management to do its stuff where genius formerly functioned, and the results are better." To the *Herald-Tribune's* Ogden Reid, that meant "collaboration" and "conformity" would characterize journalism's future.[54]

But it was precisely an "emotional commitment to conventionality" that struck press critics and sports writers as what was most wrong with journalism. Heywood Broun, a columnist and long-time sports writer for the *New York World*, became one of the decade's highest-paid story-tellers" by bucking "the standardization of the copy desk." Sports writing, like any other writing, Broun observed, wasn't any good unless it had "the power of imagination" behind it.[55]

It was in the self-interest of sports writers to write "high and wide" if they could get away with it. Despite the flourishing of journalism schools and the creation of a national association dedicated to cultivating "the highest ethical standards of the profession," the job paid poorly and required long hours. The $25 a week a reporter earned was what reporters made a generation before, and it was a smaller wage than the salaries of many of the skilled and semi-skilled workers the reporter wrote for.[56] While the work week in non-agricultural industry averaged forty-five hours in 1920, a full six-day schedule remained standard for most reporters, with no days off when a story was "breaking." While 60 percent of the average American's salary went to basic necessities in 1900, barely 50 percent of income went for that purpose in 1920. These trends helped create a $31 billion recreation and amusement industry, absorbing one-quarter of the national income. Jazz-age journalists chronicled a rapidly changing world without having the resources to fully participate in it.[57]

The tendency towards the standardization of America's 1,250 newspapers, which had been accelerated by syndication, the wire services, and chain ownership, struck many sports writers as precisely the kind of thing jazz-age journalism needed to avoid.[58] "The newspaper game has been reduced to a mechanical reaping and binding like the preservation of wheat," wrote one defender of journalistic enterprise. As journalism was strengthened "as a mechanical business proposition," it was weakened as a force for social transformation, critics argued. The reporter who tried to "inject personality into the drab events of the day" would have his best work deleted by the "disillusioned editors" of the copy desk. A New York reporter noted that "the fundamental principle of metropolitan journalism is to buy white paper at three cents a pound and sell it at ten cents a pound."[59] In this claim the jazz-age journalist was evoking the same rejection of bureaucratic alienation that appeared to prompt many an urban office-goer into sports-page searches for stories on their beloved and "beautiful" Dempsey.

The sports page, argued advocates of playing sports to the limit, offered solace and excitement and a form of reassurance to readers whose workweeks were increasingly characterized by the cheerlessness of service as corporate cogs. The rhythm of building up competitors and having them clash for periodic championships in which, at least rhetorically, much appeared at risk, imposed a certain order of expectation onto a social scene that seemed to be fragmenting everywhere.[60] A culture remarkably untutored in what to do with "free" time now turned to the media on evenings in which it had "nothing to do." The rise of a leisure culture required the creation of heroic figures to stand above a strangely leveled landscape.[61]

Surveys showed that men and women of all ages preferred reading the newspaper and looking at its funny pages beyond any other leisure activity. The thirty-five million Americans who daily read newspapers in 1926 were supplemented by the fifty million who weekly went to the movies, the thirty million who listened to radio, the fifteen million who played phonograph records, and the fifteen million who read a popular monthly magazine.[62] The phrase "killing time" became part of the American vocabulary. For some, mass media served as an antidote to boredom, a stimulation needed to navigate the "great emptiness" and sudden uncertainty of leisure living. For others, it permitted vicarious participation in a public world far more exciting than the private sphere.[63]

Although Americans did a considerable amount of playing during the 1920s, commentators noted that "for the first time the chair has invaded the realm of recreation." Bertrand Russell observed that more and more men and women were coming to realize that their work only involved "altering the position of matter at or near the earth's surface relative to other such matter or telling other people to do so."[64] The Labor Department tended to support Russell's hypothesis, finding that three of every five American workers tended a machine or cleaned up after someone who did. The press provided these working-class readers with a crash course in how to make meaning of leisure.[65] Cultural commentators might disparage America's preoccupation with fighters and other forms of civic spectacle as "a case of arrested spiritual development" in which "the instinct of workmanship demands purposeful action," but the exaggerated accounts of a hero whose name became synonymous with laying a man low with a punch played well to readers whose lives seemed far less certain or satisfying.[66]

In 1900, when readers were asked to choose "the Hall of Fame for great Americans," not a single sports personality made the list. The moral seriousness of latter-day Victorians celebrated past builders of the rational order—the rulers and statesmen, inventors and educators, preachers and philanthropists, authors and editors, businessmen and soldiers, who in their eyes had made the nation great.[67] Less than a generation later, mass media's careful cultivation of leisure industries had changed much. "Yes, We Have No Bananas," the biggest hit of the middle-twenties, was sung more often than "'The Star-Spangled Banner' and all of the hymns in all of the hymnals put together." Readers hoped "to fill their minds with the color of romance" to "relieve our dullness, to furnish us with jokes, to give us something to talk about."[68]

Ring Lardner, who had made his literary reputation by sneering at the public enthusiasm for sports heroes he had helped to create, considered "Dempsey worship" a "national disease" informed by "blissful asininity" and "anile idolatry." He mocked the crowds that closed in on Dempsey at every public appearance, "hoping a drop of divine perspiration might splash on their undeserving snout." In his three years away from the ring following his Firpo fight, Jack Dempsey made millions in movies and personal appearances. He became aware of what "star quality" meant. Men and women would pay money to shake his hand and seemed perfectly content just to be in his presence. Reporters now vied with one another for access to Dempsey, and he obliged with diminishing enthusiasm, despite the obvious value in "keeping my name before the public."[69]

Dempsey was in no hurry to return to the ring. His romance with Estelle Taylor, a beautiful though fast-fading silent film actress, briefly revived her career and led to their highly publicized February 1926 wedding. Her determination to soften the public perception of Dempsey as American savage led to his cosmetic surgery, a nose job, and an end to his long partnership with Doc Kearns. Kearns complained that Tex Rickard had knifed him in the back in hopes of getting a bigger piece of the Dempsey bandwagon, but it was Taylor's determination to manage Dempsey for their "mutual benefit" that prompted the breakup. Developments in Dempsey's life seemed to sour him on the success he had fought so long and hard for. Kearns, he was now certain, had tried to make him his "chattel." He admitted his former manager had "helped pilot me to the championship," despite his habit "of saying the wrong thing at the wrong time." Dempsey told reporters that he would follow Jess Willard's example, convinced "I can handle my own affairs as well as any manager."[70]

Behind Dempsey's bravado lurked the thinly disguised fear that the fate that befell all boxers awaited him. "They call you a bum before you get to be champion," he remarked. "And they call you a bum after someone slaps you out of the title." That someone, he suspected, might be Gene Tunney.[71] The countdown for the Dempsey-Tunney fight would be orchestrated by Rickard across three cities—Chicago, New York, and finally Philadelphia—with jazz-age editors dividing on the meaning of the melee and the prominence it should be given in their papers. The much ballyhooed bout became a cultural text in words writ large by sports and editorial writers for the benefit of their reading publics. The story they spun might have been time-tried hokum, but that made the passion it prompted no less real nor revealing.

Hearst, the Colonel, Ochs, and the Captain: Four Publishers Bid for the Fight

Hosting Jack Dempsey's long-awaited return to the ring struck Tex Rickard as something the nation's largest cities and newspapers might fight over. Gone were the days when John L. Sullivan and Jake Kilrain fought their great fight in an open meadow far from the gaze of process servers and the law. And only dimly remembered was California's last-minute decision to block Rickard's patriotic slugfest between Jim Jeffries and Jack Johnson in 1910 on grounds that Independence Day was no time to promote a business controlled by "crooks, sharpers and disreputable tricksters." California's repudiation of Rickard and the fight intensified speculation that boxing was "one of the dying sports," not because of its brutality, but because it had been "so completely corrupted by the scramble for the almighty dollar."[1]

Rickard and a cooperative press, each for their own reasons, worked together in the years that followed to repair this image, and while both admitted "fakes, frauds, and skin games" still corrupted the sport, they well understood that "that portion of the race that reads newspapers" took personally stories "of who could lick the other guy."[2] Holding court at Chicago's Blackstone Hotel, in the very room where four years before senior newspaper editors had plotted a professional organization to combat the "abuse" of the reading public by papers with "no sense of civic responsibility," Rickard told reporters the big bout between Dempsey and Tunney would go to the highest bidder, and that appeared to be Chicago. Beneath his trademark fedora hat with its snap brim turned down and sporting a straight, gold-headed Malacca cane and the inevitable cigar, Rickard promised the city's sports-minded public that there was no place he'd rather stage "the most anticipated fight" of the postwar period than in Chicago.[3]

If some of Chicago's sports writers didn't take Rickard fully seriously, it was because of his open courtship with members of New York's Boxing Commission to stage history's first $2 million fight in their city. It struck commissioner George Mower as "only natural" that Dempsey's title defense should be staged in "America's first city," a direct dig at Chicago's secondary status, and while Rickard felicitously played civic pride and public passion in each city against the other, he faced major obstacles in both. Tammany Hall wanted Dempsey to fight a black in hopes of courting Harlem's votes. And the Windy City's reform mayor didn't know if Chicagoans were yet ready for the "flare, blare, and hokum" of a heavyweight championship match.[4] Amidst this uncertainty, Rickard's widely publicized arrival at Union Station aboard the Twentieth Century Limited created an opportunity for Chicago's intensely competitive press and its deeply divided constituencies to settle old scores on who spoke in behalf of the city on matters of symbolic significance. While for some, the staging of a civic spectacle of the magnitude of a Jack Dempsey fight meant "all eyes would be on the city" and "millions will be made," to others, the promoter's flirtation with the city's sporting press and its city fathers was a lesson in communal credulity, if not venality, during America's jazz age.[5]

The prairie poet Carl Sandburg, for one, didn't know who would win the heavyweight championship if it were held in Chicago, and didn't really care. Tex Rickard was generating front-page headlines by promoting the title match for Soldier Field in September 1926, with part of the proceeds going to widows and orphans of slain Chicago policemen. Sadly, Sandburg was certain there would be no shortage of candidates for the money. The city's violent past seemed mirrored in Tunney's latest movie, Sandburg wrote as drama critic of the *Chicago Daily News*. The poet feared that a city which took its violence seriously might not find Tunney fully persuasive as "the fighting marine" who "shakes off and knocks down heavies" while "keeping a straight face." Sandburg found Tunney "a better actor" than Dempsey, but didn't think Dempsey's rough ring manners required much acting.[6]

Sandburg's "Shee-caw-go" had been a mud flat at the foot of a vast inland ocean, the place of the skunk and the wild onion smell, when incorporated in 1837, the year of the Great Panic, as a frontier town of four thousand hearty if anxious souls. Canal and rail construction made the city a mid-century mecca for the shipment of wheat, meat, and lumber and stimulated a surge in immigration that placed Chicago's population at half a million on the eve of the Great Chicago Fire of 1871.[7] The city's $187 million in losses primed a massive rebuilding effort, illustrating the resilience of its immigrant population and the chronic avarice and unfailing rapacity of its political leadership.[8]

Chicago's immigrant working class, who inhabited a world of tool chest and timecard, were "independent as a hog on ice" in Sandburg's view, and "whistled ragtime" over the dull "monotony of the punch clock." But when it came to superintending the reigns of power that ruled the city, newcomers to democracy proved "dead from the neck up."[9] Reformers found that Chicago's settlement pattern facilitated the worst in ward politics, with little regard and less consensus on what was good for the city as a whole. They found Progressive-era Chicago criminally open, commercially brazen, socially bankrupt, and lacking political consciousness. The requirements of everyday living had led working-class Chicagoans to surrender their city to a greedy handful who saw "good government" as "nobody's business" but their own. The painful result, Lincoln Steffens observed, was that in Chicago "everybody was for himself and none was for Chicago."[10]

On the eve of the Dempsey-Tunney fight, two Chicagos had emerged. The first was a thin line of academics, publishers, and social pioneers working assiduously to cultivate a "conscience" for the city. Against them were arrayed the competing and divergent interests of the city's multi-ethnic communities, who all too often received their marching orders from "the motley crew of saloon keepers, proprietors of gambling houses and undertakers" who ran the city. The city's five-term mayor Carter H. Harrison noted that nowhere was the public life of "a great, growing, energetic city" so dominated by "a low-browed, dull-witted, base-minded gang of plug-uglies, with no outstanding characteristic beyond an unquenchable lust for money" as was the fate that befell Chicago as it entered the postwar era.[11]

The circulation wars between William Randolph Hearst and Medill McCormick set the tone for the municipal violence that was to give Chicago an international reputation. Hearst had come to Chicago hurriedly, launching the *American* on July 2, 1900, after only six weeks preparation in an old warehouse "unventilated since the death of Queen Victoria." The building on West Madison Street was so decrepit that Hearst, in Chicago for an inspection of his new property, refused to set foot in it. The purpose of the paper was to further the interests of the Democratic Party in Chicago and Hearst's interests in the party. It followed the Hearst formula of reaching "the great middle class" with "gee-whiz emotion" and led to a clash with the *Chicago Tribune* company when Hearst moved into the morning field with the *Herald and Examiner.* A major turf war erupted when Hearst hired toughs to make room for his papers in Chicago newsstands. The *Tribune's* notorious circulation manager Max Annenberg was deputized by the sheriff's department to meet violence with violence. When shots fired at *Examiner* delivery trucks failed to prove persuasive, shoot-outs followed, leaving twenty-seven dead and scores wounded.[12]

Neither the *Tribune* nor the *Herald and Examiner* reported the rough stuff surrounding their fight for circulation. A series of articles by the *Daily Socialist* eventually forced a grand jury investigation, but the *Tribune*'s intimate ties with State Attorney Charles Wayman and his successor Maclay Hoyne and Hearst's "friendship" with police chief John McWeeney meant the charges would never come to trial.[13] The blasting underscored the certainty of the civic-minded that a "crisis in authority," deeply rooted in the impermanence and anonymity of the industrializing city, threatened its future.[14] Crime Commission and Civil League reports portrayed a city whose citizens were alternately appalled and enthralled by the unholy alliance of underworld and city administrators, who split an estimated $60 million in annual pre-Prohibition revenues and marked the occasion with a well-publicized festive ball at the city's Coliseum attended by fifteen thousand.[15]

While Dempsey was winning the heavyweight title during the summer of 1919, Chicago was erupting in racial violence. Thirty-eight people were killed, 543 were injured and $2 million in black homes and neighborhood businesses went up in smoke. *The Chicago Defender* saw the destruction springing from "Chicago's appetite for lawlessness," which had seen black homes bombed in Hyde Park and young blacks victimized by white youth gangs in the precincts along Wentworth Avenue.[16] The city's "sizzling mix of human chemicals" had other flash points. When Dion O'Bannion, a thug from the Hearst Press, was gunned down in 1924 inside his flower shop, it was the beginning of a bootlegging war between North Side Irish and South Side Italians.[17] A history of violent relations had seriously estranged labor and management.[18] On the eve of the city's chance to host the Dempsey-Tunney fight, a citywide survey saw Chicago as a composite of communities in transition. Everything was "loose and free" which made "everything problematic." In a city where thirty or more tongues were spoken, one could not trust one's neighbor "to act for the common welfare." It produced a metropolis of four and a half million united "by networks of mass media" and separated by "the impersonal relations of industrial organization" in which merit was defined by money.[19]

It may have been "hard to tell the difference between gangsters and reporters in this city," as one jazz-age observer saw it, but it is equally true that Chicago journalists often fought for reform by articulating a vision for the city that surpassed purely private interests. The *Daily News* was launched by Victor Lawson in the ashes of the Great Chicago Fire in the hope that the force of mass communication could encourage the development of communitarian notions of interdependence and identity.[20] While long an advocate of Chicago's corporate culture, *Tribune* publisher Joseph Medill was elected mayor of the city in 1871 to supervise its post-fire reconstruction. He returned to the paper in 1874 determined to make it "an articulator of common sense" in its "advocacy of political and moral progress."[21] His great editorial campaign won Chicago the right to host the quadrennial celebration of Columbus's encounter with America and led to the construction of Daniel Burnham's "White City," a neoclassical wonderland carved along seven miles of swamps and marshes south of the city's center. The Columbian Exposition was a self-conscious affirmation of the power of civic planning and sustained in its elegant urban imagery a unified vision for the city's future.[22]

In the aftermath of the Columbian Exposition, the city's homeless moved into its precincts, fires were built against the cold, buildings burned, the city's mayor was assassinated, and the effort of civic reformers to redeem the promise of the "White City" awaited the ascension to City Hall of Judge William Dever in 1923.[23] With the strong backing of the *Tribune* and *Daily News*, Dever went after the city's racketeers, bringing thirty-eight indictments, and rooted out corrupt public officials who kept the city's fifteen thousand speakeasies thriving. The health department was expanded. Alleyways that served as breeding grounds for rats and flies were cleaned. Communicable disease rates went down. Recreation centers were built. A civic commission was established to encourage development of the arts. The Board of Education was quarantined from political interference. Dever had hardly created a "White City," but the Chicago Tex Rickard visited in July 1926 to sell on a heavyweight championship bout, was going through an unexpected and exhilarating period of reform.[24]

Chicago had long been unsure of staging a professional boxing bout. The excitement of the Dempsey-Willard match had stimulated passage of a boxing bill in Illinois, only to have it vetoed by Gov. Frank Lowden. The *Daily News* supported the ban, following the instruction of publisher Victor Lawson who likened boxing to "banditry and bank robbery." The paper's sports editor, Fred Hayner, argued that boxing was becoming "a cold, commercial proposition benefitting no one but promoters." That had long been the opinion of the *Tribune*'s founder Joseph Medill, who considered his sports page the favorite reading of "gamblers." Medill's irritation with professionalizing sports once led him to fire his sports department en masse. His vitriolic campaign against horse racing forced the cancellation of the American Derby at Sixty-first Street and Cottage Grove Avenue. But his greatest animosity was reserved for boxing. He considered it "a barbaric affair, where one brute pounds another for the benefit of a gang of other brutes."[25]

The *Tribune* was under the new management of Medill's grandson, Col. Robert McCormick, when Rickard came to the city to sell it on the idea of hosting the Dempsey-Tunney title tilt. The "Colonel" was receptive. McCormick had just returned from the World War and saw fighting as moral instruction. "Boxing," he was certain, "breeds a stout hard race and a fearless one." A champion fed "the human imagination" with images of excellence and a journalism that promoted public interest in "boxing spectacles" performed a positive public service. It gives our "fat citizens," he argued editorially, a taste of the "lean, hard sacrifice" required of all Americans.[26]

A boxing bill was passed by the Illinois legislature and signed by Lowden's successor in April 1926, apparently paving the way for a Dempsey-Tunney fight. In a trial run, twenty thousand rain soaked fans watched Sammy Mandell of Rockford wrest the light heavyweight title from Rocky Kansas of Buffalo in a ten-round decision at Comiskey Park on July 2, 1926, while scores more watched from rooftops along Wentworth Avenue. The Hearst press thought the city was becoming "quite a sports center" and marked the "historic occasion" with front-page banner headlines.[27] The death of Victor Lawson had muted the *Daily News's* opposition to professional boxing. The paper's editor Charles H. Dennis, a forty-five-year veteran of the Chicago newspaper wars and a founder of the American Society of Newspaper Editors, still thought it best "to advance amateur sports." But there was no denying public interest in prize fighting and the *Daily News* did not "create" an interest by covering it. "It is an elemental feature of life and people will have it," Dennis believed. "Fighting is central to our existence, an indication men are still red-blooded."[28]

Mayor Dever "did not care to be quoted" when the *Tribune* asked his official blessing on Rickard's planned September spectacle. The city's ministerial association was predictably up in arms. The Rev. Kirk Robbins, representing the city's Methodists, urged city hall to stop the "brutalizing" show, but the *Tribune* gave far more attention to athletic club, park commission, and business community representatives who were certain the fight would make a "ton" of money for the city. The *Tribune* was also sensitive to the argument of William Veeck, president of the Chicago Cubs, as well as other city sportsmen, who were certain "staging a heavyweight championship fight in Chicago will be another step in the process of making this city the all around sports center of the country."[29]

Col. Robert McCormick, the silver spoon-born publisher of the "World's Greatest Newspaper," was certain that any public event that stimulated the circulation of his newspaper while promoting the commercial interests of the city made good "business" sense. Maintaining a newspaper's "independence" meant assuring its "profitability." That had led to a significant expansion of the *Tribune's* sports section under McCormick's leadership. Its seventeen-member sports department was supplemented by a small army of syndicated correspondents and a nationwide stringer network of reporters in the major college towns. Their charge was to give "a detailed, accurate account of all sports" in an "individual style each reporter should strive to perfect." McCormick wanted his sports section to be "one of the best written in the country" and the hiring of Ring Lardner and Westbrook Pegler added to the paper's reputation of taking its sports coverage and sports reporters seriously.[30]

The *Tribune*'s self-confidence and dedication to "personal service" helped assure leadership in the city's nasty circulation wars. By the start of 1926, the paper boasted a daily circulation of seven hundred thousand, the largest of any morning newspaper in the nation and a Sunday circulation of 1.1 million. The "quality" of that readership helped generate one hundred thousand columns of advertising for the previous year and supported construction of the paper's new home, a thirty-six-story castle on the Chicago River, complete with Gothic gargoyles, grotesques, and tower. The four thousand people who worked within its half-acre of floor space were one-quarter the population of Chicago when McCormick's grandfather had helped found the struggling paper seventy-nine years before.[31]

McCormick's personal taste in sports ran to polo and fox hunting. He liked to practice his polo shots while astride a mechanical horse on the roof of Tribune Tower. As a member of the Chicago Athletic Club, he developed a distinct distaste for the club's sports star, William Hale Thompson, the city's future mayor. McCormick's public reputation had been built as a reformer. While studying law in the practice of Robert Todd Lincoln, son of the former president McCormick's grandfather had helped elect, McCormick represented his Gold Coast district in the city council. His arrival at council meetings in polo costume and riding boots designated him as one of the city's eccentrics. His association with Chicago's professional class made the *Tribune* an ally of good government campaigns, if a self-promoting one.[32]

Perhaps it was the passion of the rivalry between the McCormick and Hearst press, but anything the *Tribune* endorsed, the *Evening American* and the *Herald and Examiner* sought ways to deprecate. That was the case with the proposed Dempsey-Tunney title fight. While Hearst had alternately supported and opposed professionalized boxing as it suited his political ambitions, he was content by the 1920s to attend each of the Dempsey title defenses and used his nationwide network of newspapers and magazines, which reached into the homes of one in four American families, to vigorously promote the sport. Hearst was a pioneer in seeing the relationship of sports reporting to readership and had quadrupled the size of the *New York Journal*'s sports section when locked in a circulation war with Joseph Pulitzer. The war of words and sports-page budgets culminated in Hearst's unprecedented training camp coverage of James J. Corbett's title defense against Charlie Mitchell.[33] Sports reporting always reflected Hearst's determination to reach "the great middle class" with "undiluted entertainment" and made him anathema to journalism's self-respecting establishment. Critics charged that no man in the history of journalism had so "debased" the profession by "gathering garbage from the gutters of life" as had Hearst. Even those who deplored Hearst's methods often imitated his techniques in hopes of replicating his record circulations.[34]

The Hearst press appeared to initially embrace a Dempsey-Tunney title fight in Chicago. Hearst editor Arthur Brisbane's signed page-one editorial claimed New York ring officials were now "writhing in jealousy" because Chicago had "taken their bread and butter" with a projected $2 million fight gate, the biggest in history. The *Herald and Examiner,* sounding very much like the *Tribune,* gave three columns to Rickard's pledge to move his operation to Chicago, making the city "the country's new fight mecca." In boldface, the paper even congratulated itself on "exclusively announcing" Rickard's fight plans, despite the fact that Rickard "exclusives" had been given to each of the city's major dailies. The *Tribune* had run its announcement with word that Rickard, widowed the year before, was to remarry. Pictures of the bride, "a former actress," and groom were given prominent play on a back page. The *Daily News* ran the story under a picture of the dapper promoter posing by a telephone. His "hot" news was that Chicago would get the big fight and an ice hockey team too.[35]

The city's black press would have nothing to do with promoting a "white man's fight between white men," and when the magnitude of the *Tribune*'s ballyhoo became apparent, the Hearst press also opposed the spectacle. Many of the city's one hundred thousand blacks had supported Dempsey since his first days as champion, in part because they liked his heavy hitting, but also because he had beaten the man who had beaten Jack Johnson, a South Side legend, whose Cafe de Champion at 42 West Thirty-first Street had been a meeting place and watering hole for the city's notorious and its sports-minded. But Dempsey's determination to draw the color line and his refusal to fight black champion Harry Wills had soured the black community on the champion. "Jack has been out of the game for sometime, dodging Wills," the *Defender* noted, predicting he was primed for a fall.[36]

The *Examiner* seized on Dempsey's widely publicized break with Jack Kearns to oppose the fight. The acrimonious end to their long partnership, prompted by quarreling between Kearns and Dempsey's new wife, Estelle Taylor, gave Hearst sports editor Warren Brown the opening he was looking for. The Hearst press began running pieces signed by Kearns detailing his past association with Dempsey and Rickard and "the lack of gratitude" by both. The columns threatened "one big lawsuit" if the proposed fight came off without Kearns getting his "cut of the cake." Brown embraced Kearns's claim that Rickard was simply trying to "use" Chicago to force New York to hold the fight. The *Examiner,* in the interests of "public service," editorially argued that Chicagoans, new to professional boxing, were not yet ready to host its championship. The city's two Hearst papers assured their one million readers that "people in the know" thought the rival *Tribune* a trifle "premature" in thinking the fight a done deal.[37]

The *Tribune* would have none of Brown's "sour grapes." Sports writer

Walter Eckersall, who had made his reputation as a star running quarterback on Amos Alonzo Stagg's University of Chicago football team, argued that the city shouldn't fumble its chance to become the nation's fight capital. Westbrook Pegler wrote that the "grand ballyhoo" over whether Rickard or a local promoter had a right to stage the spectacle was nothing for Chicagoans "to get a ruddy inflammation over." Pegler reported the "refined" Tunney "left grammarians fainting" with unexpected straight talk Chicagoans could appreciate. "I'll bounce him around so bad," Tunney told Pegler, "the boys will be saying he laid down." The pre-fight promise presumably had the city in a "lather." *Tribune* cartoonist John T. McCutcheon expressed fan sentiment in a July 25 edition. Promoters and politicians are pictured in the ring. Fight fans are seen shouting, "Throw the bums out! Bring on the cauliflower!"[38]

The *Tribune* did a quick about-face a day later when Rickard hastily pulled out of Chicago and told reporters from the back platform of the Twentieth Century Limited that the fight was moving to New York. Eckersall's lead beneath the inevitable eight-column headline acknowledged "the Chicago bout is off" and "the bluff is ended," then, amazingly, he added, "just as the *Tribune* indicated it would be." Pegler implied that Chicago, in the midst of reform, had become inexperienced in "bribe-taking," so Rickard decided "to pay the ice bill" in New York. Sports editor Don Maxwell, whose byline was changed to "W. Donald Maxwell" when McCormick made him the paper's city and managing editor, charged that Rickard must have thought Chicagoans "nit wits" to believe he could "kid Chicago into helping Tex." Every newspaper in town, Maxwell pointed out defensively, had printed "in good faith" Rickard's pledge to hold the fight in the city "although some have forgotten that now."[39]

The Hearst press would have none of the *Tribune*'s revisionist history. Brown boasted that "educated observers" could see that Rickard would be forced "to take the air." That others had failed to "report the facts" was another reason to read the Hearst press. "The *Herald and Examiner* was the first and only paper in Chicago," it noted in a self-promoting postscript, to recognize what was "obvious" all along. Brown reminded readers that he knew Rickard "more intimately" than "average reporters at another newspaper" who had failed to let their readers in on "the real score." It was comforting for one million Chicagoans to know, he supposed, that they were reading a "newspaper in the know" and "unafraid" to tell what it knew.[40] Walter Howey, a Hearst editor soon to be immortalized as the irascible editor of *The Front Page,* could not contain his glee. A former $9,000 a year editor at the *Tribune,* he danced around *Her-Ex*'s newsroom and into its dimly lit lobby with managing editor Ashley De Witt, where they freely mingled with the prostitutes, pimps, and policy writers that had given Chicago and *Her-Ex* their unique reputations. The paper had "put one over" on its hated competitor and done its bit to position itself as a "faithful defender of reform in forcing Rickard to find some other place to stage his civic spectacle.[41]

Tex Rickard came to Chicago in the summer of 1926 certain he could sell a championship fight. Late Victorian opposition to the fight game was fast fading. The sport was on its way to social sanctioning. Dempsey hadn't been in the ring in three years, but that hadn't stopped the public from following his Hollywood wedding and messy breakup with Jack Kearns in its daily press. Rickard had hoped to promote this public preoccupation into boxing's first $2 million gate. What he failed to anticipate was the city's brief brush with reform and lingering ambiguity over the fight game that the Hearst press fanned as a way of settling an old score with a cross-town rival. The *Tribune*'s business-minded ballyhoo in staging the Dempsey-Tunney extravaganza in Chicago had given Hearst a heaven-sent opportunity he couldn't pass up. He urged readers to decide who Chicago's true civil servant was, and which paper had favored the fight as a way of promoting purely personal profit.

Carl Sandburg's *Daily News* had viewed the bare-knuckle brawling between Hearst and the *Tribune* with nearly as much relish as the gloved contest Rickard now took to New York. Barely ten days before, the New York promoter had come to Chicago promising big and delivering small. Now, photographed on the same Twentieth Century Limited that had brought him out from Gotham, he claimed himself ready to return to the mouth of the beast. The *Daily News* had deplored Dempsey's refusal to face black challenger Harry Wills and saw with unusual prescience that Harlem's voters would feel the same way.[42]

Tex Rickard's experience in Carl Sandburg's "Shee-caw-go," the place of the skunk and the wild onion smell, would find its parallel in America's self-proclaimed "first city." It was there the wily Rickard received his second lesson in as many months on the symbolic significance of a Dempsey championship fight and how the civic spectacle he had helped to create could be used by others for their own purposes and to settle old scores. It was because Jack Dempsey had come to represent so much to so many that his return to boxing became enmeshed in political constraints extending far beyond the squared ring. Rickard's cold calculation that city fathers and the press in Chicago and New York could be made to see the money that could be had in promoting the Dempsey-Tunney title fight missed the symbolic purposes others might attach to the contest. Tammany's politically sensitive boxing commission was no more anxious to put on the game than the Dever administration had been if it meant weakening the Harlem vote on the eve of a major election. And while the city's self-respecting and self-promoting press shared a mutual interest in backing a bout that stimulated circulation, they were equally eager to be seen serving not their interests but those of the city.

Adolph S. Ochs, the sixty-eight-year-old Tennessee-born publisher of the

New York Times, was several days short of his thirtieth anniversary with the nation's most self-respecting newspaper when it published the "startling" page-one news that Jack Dempsey would fight Gene Tunney for the heavyweight championship on September 16, 1926, at Yankee Stadium. Ochs had sent the paper's circulation soaring from less than 10,000 to more than 350,000 by cultivating the *Times*'s reputation as "a clean newspaper of high and honorable aims" among New York's socially approved readership.[43] But editorial page editor Garet Garrett thought that Ochs's ambition "to produce a highbrow newspaper for intellectuals" was guided by his working-class background and innate sense of "crowd consciousness."[44] This had led to thirteen pages of coverage when Dempsey knocked out Georges Carpentier in July 1921 and the fighter's symbolic emergence in the *Times* as the embodiment of the frontier spirit. Two years later, *Times* ace reporter Elmer Davis anointed the champion "an Assyrian king" when he whipped Tommy Gibbons in Shelby, Montana.[45]

In resuscitating the *Times* from the brink of bankruptcy in 1896, Ochs had amplified the paper's sports coverage. Ivy League sports and the country's bicycling craze crashed the paper's front page with Ochs resisting the signed columns and circus makeup that marked the "yellow" press of Hearst and Joseph Pulitzer. Ochs scrupulously avoided taking sides in the cutthroat competition between Pulitzer's *World* and Hearst's *Journal* that used staged sports spectacles to stimulate circulation. As the conservative son of a Civil War soldier, Ochs lacked both the resources and inclination to risk "the goodwill and confidence of intelligent readers" for the sake of short-term circulation gains.[46] So he continued old management's policy of space pay for sports writers, leading one writer to wonder how he could survive on "thirty-five cents for a summer's work."[47] Ochs's determination to market the *Times* as a "clean paper" for "pure-minded people" led to the methodical enlargement of those sections of the paper that attracted the carriage crowd, even as he expanded the paper's appeal to working-class readers who sought to be seen reading the *Times.*[48] The strategy proved successful. Within months, Ochs had sealed up the paper's $1,000-a-day operating losses and, by dropping the paper's price to a penny, helped triple its circulation.[49]

By the 1920s, Ochs's careful stewardship of the *Times* had demonstrated the value of news as a sales asset. His marketing also benefited from the paper's scrupulously clean makeup and the widest-ranging photographic service of any newspaper in the country. Ochs had learned the importance of the composing room as a printer's devil in Knoxville and, although work prevented a high school education, he surrounded himself with men and women whose intellectual horizons pushed the paper beyond New York's commercial class.[50] Honorary degrees from Yale, Columbia, and New York universities affirmed Ochs's celebrity status, and the awarding of the first Pulitzer Prize to the *Times* for "journalistic excellence" seemed to sanction Ochs's long held certainty that the *Times* was the closest thing America had to a national newspaper. In the jazz-age struggle over journalistic respectability, no paper stood taller than the *New York Times* with its self-proclaimed responsibility to serve as the nation's newspaper of record by printing "all the news that's fit to print."[51]

Ochs's boxing editor James P. Dawson observes that the postwar transformation of prize fighting from "outcast to major fixture on the entertainment calendar" greatly facilitated a 40 percent increase in the size of the *Times* sports section. The *Times* came to consider boxing "a manly endeavor" that now appealed "to the best people." The portrayal of Dempsey as "Tiger Man," whose "savage instinct and terrible fists wrecked men," played well to a *Times* readership that liked its sports heroes "aggressive to the point of recklessness." Tex Rickard's "Midas touch" at promotion encouraged the public fascination with the "lean, scowling, black-browed" champion.[52] The paper's determination to celebrate "the ordinary virtues" and what it perceived as the "median in cultural values" combined with Ochs's "congenital conformity" to make the *Times* an eager player in the ballyhoo over a Dempsey-Tunney title bout in New York. The paper claimed the city's "serious-minded" citizens supported Boxing Commissioner George E. Brower's observation that a fight "of this magnitude" could only be staged by the nation's "leading showman" in America's "first city."[53]

Rickard's effort in early August to generate public pressure to force the New York licensing board to back the bout received opposition from a most unexpected source. The *New York Daily News,* which had been in Rickard's corner during its seven-year climb to becoming the nation's largest circulation newspaper, favored Dempsey defending his title against black champion Harry Wills. The paper's twenty-eight-year-old sports editor Paul Gallico, who won his job by sparring with Dempsey in advance of his title defense against Luis Firpo, wrote that a Dempsey-Tunney fight would signal "a colored man may not try for the heavyweight championship of the world."[54] Tunney's open letter to the *Daily News* charged Tammany-backed state commissioners with "incompetency" and "politics" in blocking his bid for the title and soured Gallico still further on the fight. "The fighting marine," with a penchant for "75 cent words," Gallico wrote, had "attacked the dignity of the state of New York" by "giving a swift kick to its athletic commission." Tunney retorted that "only a knave or a fool" would believe a "crackpot" like Gallico. Gallico, warming to the challenge, wrote that Tunney was a "tactless snob," which was why the "nice people" might like Tunney, while "everyone else wanted to see Dempsey knock the book-reading dude back to Shakespeare."[55]

The verbal sparring between Gallico and Tunney played well to the working-class readership of the *Daily News,* a tabloid targeting first- and second-generation Smiths and Cohens, Mullers and Nelsons and LaVoies who lived on

New York's Lower East Side, in Upper Manhattan, Brooklyn, the Bronx, and Staten Island. Nearly 40 percent of metropolitan New York's six and a half million residents read the *Daily News* in 1926, a monument to its publisher's capacity to pick stories working-class readers liked to read.[56]

By birth and training, Joseph Medill Patterson, the founder of the *New York Daily News,* seemed ill suited for the role of public servant. His namesake and grandfather was Joseph Medill, a strong-minded Scotch Irishman who founded the often imperial *Chicago Tribune* and gave it its vaulting self-confidence.[57] Patterson's father was Robert Wilson Patterson, the tall and taciturn son of a noted Presbyterian minister, who gave up a career in law to become a reporter at the *Tribune.* Patterson's marriage to Medill's daughter Elinor led to his being named editor of the paper at Medill's death in 1899. By that time, Joseph Medill Patterson was a twenty-year-old graduate of Groton whose studies at Yale were soon interrupted to report the Boxer Rebellion for the Hearst Press.[58] After graduating, Patterson split his time between his mother's thirty-room mansion on DuPont Circle in Washington and his father's Superior Street mansion on Chicago's Gold Coast. Patterson married heiress Alice Higinbotham, won a seat in the Illinois House of Representatives by opposing traction magnate Charles Yerkes, and became the reform-minded commissioner of public works for the city of Chicago. After the money panic of 1907, he castigated the "desolute" values of the idle rich and shocked his family by converting to socialism. Plays and books followed, as Patterson used his wealth and energy to ridicule the "over-refinement" and "inanimateness" of a "dead aristocracy," while publicizing the coming of a socialist state.[59]

Patterson became chairman of the Chicago Tribune Company in 1911, one year after his father's death, and maintained editorial control of the paper while his cousin Robert McCormick ran the paper's business operations. Patterson's genius in features and syndication brought an immediate surge in the *Tribune*'s Sunday edition, producing a seven hundred thousand circulation and more than a million dollars in operating profits. Patterson's extraordinary sense of what ordinary people wanted to read made the *Tribune* a colossus among dailies at the outbreak of the Great War and was rooted in his conviction, perfected at the *Daily News,* that "we can't make things too clear and easy for our readers."[60]

Patterson served with distinction as a battery commander for the Forty-second Rainbow Division, under Gen. Douglas MacArthur, in the battles of Champagne-Marne. While convalescing from wounds and a gassing at Mareuilen-Dole, Captain Patterson met with his cousin, now a colonel, to consider publishing plans after the war. Patterson's conversation in London with Lord Northcliffe, publisher of the highly successful *Daily Mirror,* had persuaded him that America might be ready "for a new kind of newspaper," one that "thought visually" and accommodated "the rush in big city living" by "telling each story in a flash." It would be a paper built by men and women "who think in terms of pictures" and who knew how to inject "romance and drama" in the stories they wrote.[61]

The *New York Daily News* was launched in a squared corner of the old *Evening Mail* office on June 26, 1919, at a rental cost of $166.67 a month. The newcomer "scratched and scrambled for a living every day" with a bare-bones staff and borrowed presses. While Patterson and McCormick thought a tabloid picture daily would be a sure-fire success, their mothers—Joseph Medill's daughters—did not, and they, not their sons, controlled the parent Tribune Company's purse strings. The result was the cash-starved stepchild nearly strangled in its cradle. A daily circulation of 83,000 won by the first issue had collapsed to barely 10,000 three weeks later, with more than three in four newsstand editions going unsold.[62] Patterson was undaunted and urged his editorial staff to "lay emphasis on romance and print pictures of New York girls involved in romance." The paper's crime coverage was expanded and included daily pictures of crime scenes. Editors were urged to "hit it harder" and "make it snappy, make it local, make it news."[63]

By the fall of 1919, Patterson's plan appeared a failure. Circulation was barely half of peak summer levels and seemed stagnant. The paper's single-man advertising and circulation operations were notified in early 1920 that the paper's $1 million debt would likely force suspension of the enterprise. Critics carped that there weren't enough "office boys" and "stock girls" to support such "common pandering to the meretricious tastes of the masses." The paper's core readership were women from seventeen to thirty years of age, who were struck by the paper's emphasis on contests, serials, and its depiction of a fantasy world of romance and excitement. A publicity campaign directed to "letting people know that the *News* is on the earth and what it really is" failed to move circulation forward. Patterson was told "the New York newspaper field is not easy to conquer" and was encouraged to cut the *Daily News* back to sixteen pages to reduce losses. Scrimping led Patterson's general manager to write on the back of three-by-five cards rather than buy new ones as the thirty-five-member staff awaited word from Chicago that the end had come.[64]

Patterson, who ran the paper from Chicago, came to New York to find out what was wrong. He took an early morning subway tour to see what riders were reading. He had begun the *Daily News* hoping to emulate British tabloids in trapping women readers with tall tales of romance and mystery. But on the eve of Jack Dempsey's title defense against the pesky Billy Miske, set for Benton Harbor, Michigan, on September 7, 1920, he was struck by how commuting males of all classes had their papers opened to the sports page. His fear had been that his shoestring operation couldn't "compete with other papers in sports anymore than we can with the stock market." This particularly meant steering clear of prize fight pictures that would "shock refined women and make them ashamed of being seen with the paper." As an experiment, Patterson authorized the paper's extensive photographic department to "take better and more pictures of this fight" than any in history and to publish them "before anyone else." *Daily News* photographer Lou Walker fit a twenty-four-inch lens on a five-by-seven Graflex camera and got a telescopic view of Miske on the canvas. An airplane rushed the photo to the *News* with three other pictures that the paper plastered on its front and back pages. Hearst's *American,* Patterson was certain, copied Walker's pictures from that evening's eleven o'clock edition, but the effect was "as black as mud." The result was a record press run for the *News* and the establishment of "picture scoops" that played well to celebrity-seeking male and female audiences.[65]

In the wake of the Dempsey-Miske fight, Patterson began his search for a fight reporter. John B. Foster was promptly hired and quickly fired because Patterson charged "he writes like a foot."[66] Harry Newman was his "high class" substitute and took on Patterson's idea of "kidding the life out of the idea of a Willard-Dempsey rematch," then being floated in the Hearst press.[67] Willard's return to the ring, elaborately staged by Hearst to combat circulation gains by the *Daily News,* was treated by Patterson with kid gloves over the objections of his new managing editor Philip Payne. Payne thought the fight "a lot of hogwash designed to build another setup for Dempsey to knock over." But Patterson, noting the contest was for charity, told Payne "to be cordial," to get him two properly publicized ringside seats, and to do Hearst one better by having *Daily News* readers pick Dempsey's next opponent in a write in poll.[68]

The paper's expanded sports coverage, cleaner look, and increased reliance on pictures and contests boosted circulation to 275,000 by the end of 1920. A Sunday edition was launched three months later and within three years shot to a million circulation, the nation's largest.[69] Five thousand posters strategically spaced throughout the city teased readers with photo stunts and hot-pink headlines promising "the latest on Dempsey." Soaring circulation had made Patterson an unabashed Dempsey backer. He wrote his editor that "great men resemble their mas" and Dempsey was a classic "case in point." A special plane hired to take pictures from the Dempsey-Carpentier fight in Jersey City, New Jersey, landed on the Hudson River at the foot of the *Daily News* office building, enabling its six o'clock edition to beat the town with Dempsey's licking of the French champ. The paper's "bulldog edition" immodestly asked its audience in a full-page headline "How Does the *Daily News* Do It?"[70]

Patterson pushed for a highly visual sports page and wondered how much sports coverage his paper could take without alienating its female reader. Staff photographer Harry Olen modified photographic plates, making them more light-sensitive, and created the most vivid boxing stills ever made in capturing

Dempsey's defeat of Bill Brennan at Tex Rickard's Madison Square Garden. Full-page sports pictures became a standard part of the *News*'s back page, with Dempsey's face the most prominent. John Alcock was brought in from the *Tribune* to brighten the paper's sports writing.

Subway tours now showed businessmen were hiding copies of the disreputable *Daily News* inside their morning *Times*. Advertisers who argued the *Daily News* "wasn't good for selling anything but corsets" realized that the paper offered an expanding male audience also. Emmet J. Gordon, the paper's advertising make-up man, who for a year had "nothing to do" suddenly needed a support staff. When pressure came in April 1925 to expand the paper's sports section beyond its customary six-to-eight pages, Patterson urged holding the line against making the paper "any heavier."[71]

Competitors watched the paper's progress warily. Hearst editor Arthur Brisbane threatened to launch a competing tabloid when Patterson refused to sell the *News* to Hearst. Hearst later did, but failed. Ochs hoped readers who teethed on the *Daily News* would one day be trained to read a truly "serious" paper, namely his. In the meantime, Ochs hoped to reach those readers by advertising in the Sunday *Daily News,* and Patterson reciprocated by privately praising Ochs and his "great" paper.[72] Ochs's managing editor Carr Van Anda was less disparaging about the "people's daily" than his boss. He predicted that Patterson's "picture paper" would reach a circulation of two million. That estimate was not far off. When Patterson moved to New York in 1925 to personally supervise the paper, he could be seen walking west on Forty-second Street, eating his Eskimo Pie and wearing rumpled, washed-out trousers and a short-sleeve shirt open at the neck, appearing anything but the city's most successful newspaper publisher. He cultivated the look of a people's editor so well he was one day denied access to the *Daily News* building at Forty-second Street and Third Avenue because the doorman took him for a bum.[73]

Patterson's chief weapon on the sports page was a recent college graduate he had fired as movie critic. Paul Gallico was the only child of Paolo Gallico, a pianist with the New York Philharmonic. After graduating Columbia, where the six-foot, three-inch Gallico had been oarsman on the university rowing team, he married Alva Taylor, a Radcliffe girl who was the daughter of *Chicago Tribune* columnist Burton Lester Taylor and a piano student of Gallico's famous father. Gallico fancied himself a writer too, but the only job he could get was movie censor for the National Board of Review. That got him a job as movie critic on the *Daily News* even though he "didn't like movies." When his reviews made that apparent, Patterson fired him. Managing editor Philip Payne "hid" Gallico in the sports department where he was reduced to copywriting and paste-ups. After "serving my time," he was allowed to write "color, crowd stuff" and an occasional feature for the Sunday predate edition that was circulated across the country. Gallico was schooled in the art of writing that made readers "an eye witness to the big news of the day."[74]

Sometimes the news was manufactured, like the series Gallico did on the "perfect athlete," in which photographic doctoring completed the composite professional with the eyes of Babe Ruth, the wrists of Bill Tilden, the arms of Bobby Jones, and the torso of Jack Dempsey. "God liked the idea," Gallico was told, when Patterson caught wind of the project. God liked even better Gallico's idea to do a feature on Dempsey by boxing with the champion. Though "scared stiff," Gallico arrived for the exhibition at Dempsey's Saratoga Springs training site in trunks, headgear, and college rowing shirt. Three thousand spectators paid a dollar apiece to watch Dempsey lay out three sparring partners before a reluctant Gallico entered the ring. At the bell, Dempsey came in bobbing and weaving and walked into Gallico's left. As Gallico flicked a jab, a Dempsey left sailed purposely over his head with Harry Olen's camera capturing the moment for *Daily News* readers. Flushed with his success, Gallico dropped his guard, stabbed with his left and Dempsey answered with a left to the chin. Somehow Gallico got up at the count of eight. Dempsey clinched and whispered in his ear, "hang on, kid, til your head clears." It never did. Six rabbit punches floored Gallico again. When he regained his senses half an hour later he felt "a building had fallen on me." A bloody lip and "terrific headache" did not deter him from making the morning editions.[75]

When Patterson read the piece, he "laughed his head off." The next day Gallico had a byline and two months later was made sports editor. Patterson was "a very rugged guy" who "admired physical courage" and "liked people who had ideas." Gallico repeated his boxing stunt by catching Benny Friedman's passes, Herb Pennock's curve, and Dizzy Dean's fastball, by riding with speedboat driver Gar Wood and swimming with Johnny Weismuller, by racing with Cliff Berege at the Indianapolis Speedway, by playing tennis with Helen Wills, golf with Bobby Jones, and by flying acrobatics with Al Williams. *Daily News* circulation continued to soar. The paper staged swim races featuring "girls in tight bathing suits" as a promotion. Eighty thousand attended its water circus at Jones Beach. Coupons encouraged readers to pick winners of weekend college football games. Two hundred fifty thousand entries were turned over to advertisers who were encouraged to do business with the *Daily News*. For these efforts, the business-minded Patterson gave Gallico a hefty raise and urged him "to stay with the *Daily News* as sports editor as long as you stay in the newspaper business."[76]

Gallico freely admitted his pen was "dipped into the sheerest heliotrope hysteria" and "an appalling amount of purple ink," but his job was to "impress and excite the reader." To his generation of "gee-whiz" sports writers, athletic competition was "played for high drama." Particularly in buildups for big fights, "everything went. Storytellers told readers we were going to war. It was our side against theirs." Although the war had bred its share of cynics, Gallico found his readers remarkably ready for "the delicious idiocies" and "passionate devotions" that went with jazz era sports writing. He remembers writers and readers alike embraced the easy logic and "essential psychological simplicity" of the sports page with "a marvellous callowness." Tall-tale telling came easily in an era in which athletes could be made the most visible part of the nation's shared experience. The adulation of these heroes, Gallico found, "to the point of almost national hysteria" reflected a postwar generation's appetite "for alter egos that lifted us above our humdrum lives."[77]

For many of the three hundred thousand Jews, seventy-five thousand Italians, and scores of Irish, Germans, Poles, Chinese, Greek, Spanish, and Egyptians who packed one and three-quarters square miles on the city's Lower East Side, reading the *Daily News* seemed a practice for passing citizenship.[78] The paper's Sinclair Dakin found this target market had "surplus income" and was "looking for ways to spend it." Garment workers made $18 to $60 weekly. Cutters could make as much as $200. Some East Side salesmen earned $80 a week, but the average was $35 to $40. Pushcart peddlers averaged $126 gross. Rents of $27 a month for a three-room flat left East Siders with enough purchasing power to afford a $5 shirt and accompanying Stetson. There were more imported English carriages on the East Side than Park Avenue, as well as Paris fashions, $400 pianos, and forty bank and trust companies to report the working man's ascent.[79]

Readers of the *Daily News* drove trucks, belonged to trade unions, sold goods, and ran businesses. Three in four of them married, and Dakin found, "believed in God, the United States and life insurance." They respected education "and wanted their kids to have plenty of it." They wanted "grapefruit for breakfast, to own their own home, to have money in the bank, and a better future for Sweeney juniors."[80] This made them prime candidates for the consumption culture cultivated in the pages of the *Daily News* and raised to the level of civic spectacle by its coverage of Dempsey's bouts in its sports pages.

Implicit in the one thousand words Paul Gallico wrote weekly for *Daily News* readers was the rich delight that puffing paid. Barely a generation before sports writers were seen as "stumblebums," who offered their services to fight managers and boxing promoters for walking around money. Now sports writers were no longer "tramps and lushes" in a pecking order "barely above the office cat."[81] The decade had made both athlete and sports writer stars, and while the former came and went, the latter could finally "afford to drive a motorcar and to have a home in the country." If perpetrating "sentimental tosh" made the sports writer the bane of the serious-minded, it commended him to office boys and circulation managers who saw "poetry" in playing sport to the limit. If boxing was not altogether respectable, at least its chroniclers persuaded themselves that a newspaper's most uninhibited, and best writing, was found in its sports pages.[82]

The possibility of a Dempsey-Tunney title fight in Gotham stimulated the city's fight fans and celebrity watchers to fever pitch. Dempsey's long journey east, his triumphal arrival at Grand Central Station, and motorcade to the state's licensing board was covered by the *Times* and the *Daily News* in a manner befitting a president. Beneath a five-column picture, the *Daily News* reported that "pandemonium gripped the fight mob" when Dempsey's car arrived at the Flatiron Building. "Frenzied sportlovers, craning necks to catch a fleeting glimpse of the Utah mauler" were held back by "perspiring bluecoats swinging clubs to make a path for Jack's car." The *Times* was persuaded that the thousands who greeted the champ had cast their vote with the *Times*, in urging state commissioners to hurriedly sanction the big bout.[83]

New York Democrats, fearing the loss of votes in Harlem, balked in backing the bout. James A. Farley, chairman of the state athletic commission and future party boss, joined hands with John J. Phelan, the colorful colonel on the state licensing board, to block the contest. The reason given was that Dempsey had violated rules requiring he defend his title every six months. The decision outraged octogenarian William Muldoon, the self-proclaimed "Iron Duke of Athletics," who had made his reputation as John L. Sullivan's trainer. As the Republican voice on the state athletic commission, he publicly deplored "political interference" in staging the title match. Phelan, a little known National Guardsman and underwear importer, loved the media gaze as much as mixing it up with Muldoon. Purposely prolonging the drama for maximum political effect, he told reporters in characteristic confusion, "There's no man alive who can accuse me of being honest."[84]

The *Times* could see "no good reason" to delay the Dempsey-Tunney fight. Their boxing writer James Dawson charged the Tammany-controlled licensing authority had been "overzealous" in insisting Dempsey fight Wills first. "Having waited quite a few years to see something happen," Dawson wrote, the public could be forgiven for thinking commissioners "lost in a fog." He noted with approval the ruling by Republican Attorney General Albert Ottinger that Phelan had "exceeded his authority" in barring the bout. It was only "common sense," the *Times* observed, that since a Dempsey-Wills match could not be made, that a Dempsey-Tunney fight be staged. Failure to act harmed the future of boxing in the Empire State, while costing the city millions.[85]

The *Daily News* predicted "no serious depression in New York State" when Phelan finally announced on August 16 that there would be no Dempsey-Tunney fight. Gallico argued that fight fans might have benefited if commissioners on opposite sides of the issue had settled matters with padded fists. Failing that, the paper would not "join the crusade in public print seeking the scalp" of commission members who simply acted in behalf of "the common man." The paper understood the irritation of those who felt Dempsey had "betrayed the brotherhood by ducking fights and going Hollywood." Gallico saw no harm in Dempsey's widely publicized threat he would "never again ply his trade in the State of New York." The business of eking out a living for readers of the *News* would "proceed apace."[86]

The surprise announcement by Tex Rickard on August 18, 1926, that he was abandoning plans of pressing a court suit against the state athletic commission and would instead be staging the championship bout in Philadelphia struck the *Times* as "a major blow" to boxing interests in New York City and a slap in the face to its many fight fans. Dawson wondered whether, on such short notice, Philadelphia would be able to successfully promote a title fight that rightfully belonged to the people of New York. Describing Tunney as "a nice young man" upon whom "the oracles smiles," the paper deplored the fact that New Yorkers would have to travel one hundred miles to watch a native son fight for the first time for the heavyweight championship of the world. As far as the *Daily News* was concerned, New Yorkers could save their money. Tunney was a pretender to the throne, "a no account clerk in an arrow collar," "a tactless youth" who had been artificially elevated into a title shot over worthier contenders, namely Wills.[87]

The battle of New York followed Chicago's pattern. The bastion of self-respecting journalism in the city went all out in its endorsement of a Dempsey-Tunney title extravaganza, while its tabloid competitor, portraying itself as civil servant, fought the match in behalf of the "people." Both cases showed how self-interest guided sentiment in the storytelling function of jazz-age sports writers and their editors, and the symbolic significance politicians and the public now attached to the civic spectacles stimulated by Jack Dempsey's return to the ring. Tex Rickard's troubled summer had found that the Dempsey-Tunney title fight meant more to readers than even he had bargained for. In an era that took its heroes seriously, the meaning of the upcoming battle was subject not only to those who staged it, but those who saw, sanctioned, and chronicled it.

Nowhere was the struggle to define the many meanings of the Dempsey-Tunney title fight more painful than in the city to which it was now taken. The City of Brotherly Love, already gagging on a sesquicentennial celebration that had helped divide the city against itself, was now asked to swallow whole a heavyweight championship extravaganza. Rickard might be warmly welcomed in Philadelphia by city fathers anxious to make a quick buck, but he found there bitter communal quarreling that exposed a populous uncertain of its past and bitterly divided over its future. It was a division depicted and deepened by its competing newspapers, who spoke in behalf of contending constituencies. This ensured that the plan to finally hold the championship fight in Philadelphia would lay bare old wounds, and before it was over, would open new ones.

The Philadelphia Fight

The announcement by Tex Rickard that Jack Dempsey would fight Gene Tunney on September 23, 1926, at the Sesquicentennial Stadium for the heavyweight championship of the world was the second body blow sustained by self-conscious defenders of Philadelphia's "communitarian past" in a week. A spring- and summer-long controversy over the efficacy of staging a seven-day sesquicentennial to revive public interest in the flagging festival had led to a Sunday baseball game between the Athletics and the White Sox, the first in Philadelphia history. Sabbatarian threats to arrest the players were blocked by a court injunction in what was depicted as "a victory for the masses." The level of communal quarreling intensified with news that city hall had secretly brokered the deal bringing the fight to Philadelphia. Presbyterian, Baptist, Methodist, and Lutheran clergymen decried the "sophistry" implied in sanctioning "a bloody contest in which fighters are paid to disfigure one another." They passed a resolution "regretting beyond words injury to the city's fair name" and charged that the forces of modernity that gave the city Sunday baseball and a secular centennial were out to "debase" a patriotic celebration of the nation's one hundred fiftieth birthday by supporting a "blood sport."[1]

With the big bout in Philadelphia's 100,000-seat Sesquicentennial Stadium barely two months off, Tunney prepared to open camp in East Stroudsburg and Dempsey planned to move his from the racing country of Saratoga to the bathing-beauty, postcard, dance-band, boardwalk capital of the world, Atlantic

City. Sixty miles to the west, the solid and sober citizens of the City of Brotherly Love were appalled by what they saw. The spectacle of a Dempsey-Tunney fight further confirmed their own humiliation. A celebration of the nation's one hundred fiftieth anniversary, sold to them as a way of commemorating the city's sacred role in the country's spiritual life, had been "stolen" from them by secularists simply out to make a buck. The nostalgia these Philadelphians felt for the city's past was rooted in their belief that the city stood for something singular in the nation's one hundred fifty year history. The distance Philadelphia had traveled from its central role in civilizing America was all too painful for those who remembered the proud part the city had played in the nation's centennial celebration of 1876.

Philadelphia was well positioned to lead the national euphoria in America's one hundredth year. The city had survived the Civil War and the Panic of 1873 with its financial institutions and reputation for conservative change intact. Its lack of primary industries and availability of cheap land made what was then the nation's second-largest city a community of single-family homes for skilled and semi-skilled workingmen. The city's wealth and prominence in manufacturing, commerce, banking, and transportation encouraged a mood of civic optimism and complacency. This sustained a Republican political machine that emphasized "order and cohesion" while marginalizing Election Day 1871 clashes that left three blacks dead and scores wounded. The *North American* thought "safe, prudent, moderate" Philadelphia the perfect site for America's centennial celebration, and the million people attending evangelistic crusades by Dwight L. Moody and Ira Sankey at the Pennsylvania Railroad Depot during the winter of 1875–1876 seemed to signal that the city would lead the nation's second century through a spiritual rebirth.[2]

Five hundred seventy-five church bells rang out the morning of May 10, 1876, as 186,272 people, including President Grant, gathered in the largest crowd ever assembled on the North American continent to celebrate the opening of the nation's centennial exposition. More than ten million people would tour the festival's two hundred buildings, including a central exhibit hall covering twenty-one-and-a-half acres, making it the largest building in the world. The "progress of one hundred years" was underscored by the appearance of Alexander Graham Bell's telephone, Thomas A. Edison's quadraplex telegraph, George Westinghouse's air brake, and George Pullman's palace car. The star of America's first national fair, however, was the Corliss engine, "an athlete of steel and iron" that powered eight hundred humming machines in Machinery Hall. Fairgoers could view the whole of Philadelphia from the lofty heights of Fairmount Park, clearly seeing elaborately restored Independence Square and the newly constructed city hall in a vista that seemed to substantiate the city's claim as the patriotic, moral, and material capital of a new nation.[3]

No communal consensus, however, was to emerge in the months preceding the city's sesquicentennial celebration. Instead, the exposition created a self-defining forum for a city divided by income, race, and religion, while mired in machine politics. The struggle over the sesquicentennial and the staging of a heavyweight championship fight pierced Philadelphia's self-portrait as America's "prototypical city," while exposing an urban wilderness privatized by competing constituencies who lacked a meaningful community life.[4] A seven-day sesquicentennial and a major prize fight became the pretext for revisiting old and abiding antagonisms within the city's estranged communities. To Protestants, caught in the intractable rancor between modernists and fundamentalists, the sesquicentennial was portrayed as an opportunity to commemorate the country's "deeply religious roots" and the contribution of the church to "human advancement."[5] To the 750,000 Catholics in Greater Philadelphia, the sesquicentennial was sold as a means of affirming civic patriotism and the "central" Catholic role in the fight for personal freedom amidst contemporary claims by the Ku Klux Klan and other hate groups that "America should be for Americans."[6] For the city's two-hundred-thousand-member black community the sesquicentennial was a unique chance to overcome the racial stereotyping of "Jim Crow side shows" that had characterized previous international expositions and to strike a blow against "the curse of racial discrimination and race hatred that tainted American democracy."[7] For Philadelphia's business community, the sesquicentennial would promote their city as "an industrial and commercial center." To the working class, the celebration promised jobs in the construction trades, and would serve as a symbol of their struggle against "the forces of capital" while functioning as "a gathering place for fellow workers from across the country."[8]

From the outset, Philadelphia's sesquicentennial celebration was plagued with problems. Piles were driven for the Sesquicentennial Stadium, the "crown jewel" of the event, in April 1925 while work crews made slow headway in draining surrounding marshland south of the city. Streets, sewer and water service, and mosquito abatement were more than four hundred contracts funneled through William S. Vare's political organization with the alleged complicity of city treasurer Harry A. Mackey. Civic reformers saw "Boss" Vare as the symbol of Philadelphia's retreat from moral authority and the very embodiment of corruption and criminality "so rooted as to defy removal."[9] Construction delays and chronic budget problems led to the resignation of the sesquicentennial's manager on October 29, 1925. Over the strong objection of city auditor E. L. Austin and members of the city council, Mayor W. Freeland Kendrick vowed on November 22 to open the exposition as scheduled. The move stemmed from his certainty that after his years of faithful service as Imperial Potentate of the Lu Lu Temple, tens of thousands of Shriners would come to Philadelphia to open the sesquicentennial in May, setting the stage for a $35 million windfall for the city. Kendrick's calculation left only six months to construct the city's sports stadium as well as the eighty-three buildings that would rise to either side of the sesquicentennial gladway.[10]

On the eve of the sesquicentennial's opening, event organizers bravely predicted fifty million visitors would attend the seven-month spectacle, quadrupling the turnout of world's fairs in St. Louis in 1904 and nearly doubling throngs at Chicago's White City in 1893. The sesquicentennial's high-powered publicity apparatus, led by former city reporter and political writer Odell Hauser and Edward A. Foley, a former city editor of the *North American*, brought two hundred newspapermen and women to Philadelphia for a tour of the sesquicentennial. Kendrick claimed the spectacle would "tell the nation's glorious story" and pitched the sesquicentennial stadium as "the most colossal building ever built," while avoiding any mention of the fact the festival's 84,000-seat, $3 million "crown jewel" was $1 million over budget. Press releases puffed the festival as "a door that will lead to untold wonders" and as "the city of brotherly love's hearty handclasp to our glorious nation," when the sad truth was the sesquicentennial was barely half finished when opening day arrived.[11]

The summer was beginning badly for both Tex Rickard and sesquicentennial organizers. While Rickard's entourage was casting about from Chicago to New York in search of a place to stage his promotion, Philadelphia's festivities were faring no better. By the second week of the fair's operation, the city was well on its way to spending $15 million in loans and $8 million in taxpayers' money that had been allocated for the event. Its operating deficit was already $2 million, still a fraction of what Rickard estimated the city would net in staging the Dempsey-Tunney title fight. The sesquicentennial's controller, who had been badly beaten up in the press, appeared ailing and on his way out. City auditor Austin was rushed in to take his place under orders to make the sesquicentennial "a paying proposition." Austin's decision to suspend Philadelphia's 132-year-old "Blue Laws" and keep the sesquicentennial open Sundays, combined with his secret negotiations with Rickard to lure the title fight to Philadelphia, only succeeded in splitting the fragile coalition and the establishment press that had been the earliest backers of the exposition.[12]

The desecration of the Sabbath in holding a seven-day sesquicentennial had been bad enough. A major fight on top of that, privately negotiated away from the gaze of public participation, was worse still. To evangelical and conservative Protestants particularly, a seven-day sesquicentennial with its bloody championship bout were a painful object lesson in what had gone terribly wrong in America, and it stood as a symbol of the clash between modernity and tradition that was splitting the church into rival camps. Many of the city's Presbyterians, Methodists, Moravians, and Congregationalists, joined by fundamentalist Baptists, Reformed Episcopals, and evangelical Lutherans, saw the command to honor the Sabbath as an integral part of a Godly standard "upon which the whole moral, social and civil life of Christian civilization rests." Noting that two-thirds of three-million colonists at the outbreak of Revolution were Calvinists, these groups claimed "the establishment of the American Republic was an achievement of Calvinism," and a celebration staged to honor them "while breaking faith with them" was "a violation of God's law" and their memory. The Lutheran saw the argument in terms of the effect of growing secularism on the country's uncertain future. "When an automobile runs down a hill at a much too rapid rate, wisdom would indicate that the brake be used instead of the accelerator."[13]

The debate turned ugly in the days leading to a June 27 vote by the Exposition Board on Sunday openings. Episcopal and Lutheran ranks divided. Modernists saw the fight as a battle between "rich Pharisees" determined to legislate morality against "poor publicans." The *Philadelphia Daily News*, a self-conscious defender of "workers' rights" and the city's first tabloid, agreed. Sabbatarians were "narrow-minded fanatics," a "lunatic fringe" who practiced "class warfare" by denying workers access to the sesquicentennial on the only day that many could make it. A positive vote by the forty-member board was a foregone conclusion since it had been hand-picked by Kendrick, Vare, and the city's Republican machine. The only member of the sesquicentennial board to oppose Sunday openings told a packed protest rally that Kendrick had "stacked" the commission with "rich men" who put business interests ahead of the will of the "common people." The *Philadelphia Evening Bulletin,* published by seventy-four-year-old William McLean, perhaps the most respected man in Pennsylvania journalism, agreed. A seven-day sesquicentennial was "an offense to the people of Philadelphia," the *Bulletin* charged, that "degraded the city's celebration of the birth of American independence." The paper concluded that "the law and tradition of Pennsylvania" required event organizers to "keep faith" with Philadelphia history and "honor the sabbath."[14]

McLean's solid support for the Sabbatarians lent legitimacy to their growing protest and sprang from his sense of how deep a divide the sesquicentennial's secularism was creating in Philadelphia's diverse readerships. McLean knew the city's newspaper readers well, having begun his career in the circulation department of the *Pittsburgh Leader* before becoming business manager of the *Philadelphia Press* when he was only twenty-six. Seven years later he purchased the *Bulletin,* the oldest afternoon newspaper in the state, and in less than half a year he managed to increase its circulation fivefold. On the eve of the Dempsey-Tunney title fight, the paper's daily circulation was approaching five hundred thousand, almost one hundred times what it had been when he bought the paper, making it the third largest selling daily in America.[15]

McLean's paper and those of his competitors became the forum through which each side advanced its case and sought converts in "the fight for the future of Philadelphia." The symbolism of a seven-day sesquicentennial beginning July Fourth was all too poignant. Forty local organizations joined by more than one hundred area churches petitioned Gifford Pinchot, the state's reform governor, urging state action "to save the city's reputation." The *Philadelphia Record*, a Democratic paper, joined the protest over "commercializing the sabbath." It argued that Sunday openings would soon be followed by Sunday baseball and Sabbath-breaking movies. Its compromise suggestion of operating the fair free on Sundays was embraced by city Quakers and initially by Mayor Kendrick, who hoped to maintain good relations with the city's evangelical voter. But Austin's plea that free-admission Sundays only deepened the sesquicentennial's soaring debt won the day along with his admonition that "anyone who loves the city" should back its sesquicentennial and stop "temporizing" Sabbatarians.[16]

The *Record* was offended by the smugness of event organizers who claimed to exclusively speak in behalf of "the people's interests." A protest rally opposing Sunday openings held July 2 at the Bethany Presbyterian Church at Second Street and Bainbridge had special significance for the paper. The church was founded by department-store millionaire John Wanamaker, an early agitator for a sesquicentennial celebration, whose son Thomas had published the *Record*. The Wanamakers had long been active in church and charity work in Philadelphia and were firm Sabbatarians. John Wanamaker was president of the Philadelphia Young Men's Christian Association for thirteen years and had been the central figure in bringing D. L. Moody to the city. Just as important as his outspoken moral leadership was the advertising revenue Wanamaker, his heirs, and like-minded conservative businessmen could bring or withhold from newspapers that opposed the Sabbatarian cause.[17]

Sabbatarians could look to other people in high places for more than moral support. The state attorney general and Philadelphia's Methodist Men's Committee of One Hundred each filed suit against the sesquicentennial board. Austin was arrested and convicted of violating the city's blue laws. That decision was reversed on appeal when city solicitor Joseph P. Gaffney argued that a $100 million investment would be lost, the city "humiliated," and the nation "embarrassed" if the sesquicentennial failed to succeed. When a state judge decided for the Sabbatarians, the city appealed the verdict, extended its line of credit, and borrowed to keep the debt-ridden fair open. The argument became personal and knew no middle ground. Members of the sesquicentennial committee on religion resigned in protest, charging Kendrick had "dug his political grave." They urged their churches to boycott the exposition. Paid admissions to the fair did not reach one million until August 7, a small fraction of projected estimates. By that time the sesquicentennial was $8 million in the hole and losing $1 million a month. Creditors were restless. More than six hundred of them threatened suits to recover their losses. At several events "ushers outnumbered paying customers." Amid the finger pointing nearly everyone agreed fair attendance was "a scandalous disgrace."[18]

The *Philadelphia Inquirer* and the *Philadelphia Public Ledger*, with strong ties to city hall, saw no evil in Sunday openings, marginalized the growing protest and continued to claim that supporting the sesquicentennial was everyone's "patriotic duty." The *Inquirer*, with a reputation as the Republican Bible of Pennsylvania, editorially castigated "the malicious and ignorant organized opposition" who "knocked the exposition." The paper's president and publisher, Col. James Elverson, Jr., who cultivated an enthusiasm for yachts, stamps, and antique clock collecting, argued that opposition to the sesquicentennial was "a burning shame and disgrace" for those "who would be better served getting the sesqui habit." The paper blamed unnamed "self-serving individuals" and not the board's Sunday opening policy for dividing the city.[19]

The *Public Ledger,* published by Cyrus H. K. Curtis, fumed that Philadelphia's "honor and good name" were at stake in the sesquicentennial controversy. The city could not allow "the depreciation of a few to defeat the Exposition and tarnish Philadelphia's reputation as the trustee of the nation." Curtis had built a $100 million national publishing empire through his *Ladies Home Journal* and *Saturday Evening Post* with a dedication to "romanticizing the accomplishments of American business" and by aggressively soliciting "the most intelligent and progressive readers," who were the "backbone of the community's buying power." Curtis was certain reasonable men would agree "to put aside differences" to make sure "the sesquicentennial went down in history as worthy of the city of the Declaration."[20]

As Rickard opened talks with the sesquicentennial authority to move his twice-jilted prize fight to Philadelphia, the city's struggle over its sesquicentennial became even uglier. Protestants who associated "desecrating the sabbath" with "the breakdown and passing of American civilization" included three thousand of Philadelphia's small and prominent businessmen who saw Sunday opening as a symbol of America's flirtation with "European forces" that were pushing that continent into anarchy. This fear was nourished by Ku Klux Klan members who passed out literature at the close of protest rallies demanding "America for Americans." The decision of Mayor Kendrick to prevent Klansmen from marching to the fairgrounds while welcoming the Knights of Columbus was exploited by nativists who charged Jews and Catholics were "gaining control of American institutions" while rewriting the nation's history. One Presbyterian pastor received a two-minute ovation when he charged "there is not a single outstanding Protestant" in Kendrick's administration and that the mayor was "under the control" of solicitor general Joseph Gaffney, a Catholic.[21]

The Sabbatarians' moral tone and fellow travelers alienated leaders of organized labor and many of Philadelphia's Catholics, blacks and Jews. The executive committee of the Allied Building Trades endorsed Sunday openings, charging workers "would not be dictated to by capital." Patrick Cardinal O'Donnell, primate of all Ireland, personally toured the sesquicentennial and told reporters it was "a strong factor for peace." The city's archdiocese ridiculed those who claimed America "a Protestant nation." Sixty percent of all Americans did not go to church, the *Catholic Standard and Times* reported, and of the remaining 40 percent who did, half were Catholics. Such was the "pathetic breakdown" of "the Protestant family." Dennis Cardinal Dougherty sent the word to Philadelphia's 150 parishes, representing the area's 750,000 Catholics, that a minimum 150,000 Catholics should march to the fairgrounds "in a public act of faith and patriotism" to show their support for "the one city in America that from the very beginning of its existence has permitted an unrestricted freedom of conscience to her Catholic citizens." The nation's sesquicentennial provided "striking proof of Catholic loyalty to America," Dougherty was certain, and served notice on "evil men undermining many dumb minds" that Catholics were "determined to safeguard our religious freedom."[22]

While many leaders in Philadelphia's black community sympathized with Sabbatarian regard for "the moral climate of the city," they saw the celebration of American independence as incomplete so long as blacks faced "hatred, prejudice and segregation." Chris J. Perry, who had published the *Philadelphia Tribune* since its founding in 1884, thought "colored Americans face an impending crisis" because of racial intolerance. Black lynchings and hate group demagoguery meant "America has reached a point where it is impossible to think clearly on the issue of race." Perry charged that the money that the city spent to revive its failed fair or to boost a heavyweight bout would be better spent "assuring the rights of coloreds to vote." While Kendrick's decision to bar half a million "hooded haters" from marching to the sesquicentennial encouraged black support, his failure to appoint a committee "celebrating the important part the Negro has played in America" did not. Belatedly, such a committee was established, but it did not stop exhibitors from featuring a watermelon patch, complete with Negro hut and pickaninnies. This left the city's blacks estranged from both sesqui supporters and opponents. "After 150 years of freedom," Perry told his readers, the sesquicentennial showed "the white man is still not ready to give you yours."[23]

By the time the city captured the Dempsey-Tunney title fight, Philadelphia's celebration of the one hundred fiftieth anniversary of American independence had devolved into a costly and embarrassing civic struggle over the meaning of that celebration and the role of the city's disparate communities in defining Philadelphia's past and the nation's future. The exposition sharpened divisions between communities and within communities and locked the city in protracted court fights, appeals, and endless boycotts. The effect was devastating. Barely two million of a projected fifty million people had bothered to see the show, disillusioned sesqui creditors had filed their suit against the city, the peak tourist season was ending, and the city cast desperately about to resuscitate the situation.

The city administration saw Tex Rickard as just such a resurrectionist when he came to the city for a second time to seal the deal on the fight. Sesquicentennial opponents lost a powerful ally in the press at that moment. Just before the sesquicentennial opened, local promoters Herman Taylor and Robert H. Gunnis had failed to persuade city fathers to sanction a Dempsey title bout against Harry Wills. Kendrick boasted such a fight was "inconsistent" with Philadelphia's cultural past. The real objection, however, was the fear the fight would cut into the sesquicentennial gate. But by mid-August, city hall was anxious to reconsider. And they would have a unified press on their side. Even those papers who had supported Sabbatarians on Sunday openings saw no evil in using a championship fight to promote the city. They were not unaware that the promotion would do wonders for circulation. Charges the Dempsey-Tunney fight would "debase" the city and transform its sesquicentennial into "a commercialized game of graft, fakery, and greed" fell on deaf ears.

The *Record* and the *Evening Bulletin* parted company with festival opponents and quickly joined the *Inquirer* and the *Public Ledger* in backing the bout. The *Inquirer* set the pre-fight standard in hyperbole, exulting that "the greatest crowd ever" would attend "the greatest boxing event ever" on the grounds of "the greatest international exhibition ever conceived." The *Daily News* concurred. "The subterranean knocking of the sesquicentennial had kept thousands away," the paper charged, but the Dempsey fight would make Philadelphia "the focus of the nation."[24] When statewide Presbyterians and Methodists sent a letter to Governor Pinchot demanding he stop the bout "in the interest of public order and civil decency," Pinchot, who helped legalize boxing in Pennsylvania three years before, refused. Instead, he received front-page headlines when he rationalized the contest as "a test of courage and endurance which are so necessary in the battle of life."[25]

Politicians who feared alienating constituencies in the Sunday-closing fight hoped to win votes by associating themselves with values projected onto the fighters. Pinchot, who was considering an independent run for the U.S. Senate, was photographed at Tunney's Stroudsburg training site, where he told reporters "the battling marine" was "a clean cut chap" Americans would do well to emulate. Pinchot promised to be ringside the night of the fight "pulling for my man Tunney." The colorful Kendrick got into the act when he and Tunney rode the shoulders of marines gathered on the sesquicentennial grounds to "honor America by honoring its noble youth Tunney."[26] Philadelphia's press cooperated in building up the fight by touting the relatively unknown Tunney. He was portrayed as "the fitting hero of America's sesquicentennial year," a man "sharpened by a life so remarkably clean and wholly American as to be beyond belief." Flappers reportedly "wondered whether the good-looking Tunney was married." The *Public Ledger* thought him "a man of destiny." "Business men, newsboys, trolley men, police, and women of all ages" presumably sought the elusive Tunney's autograph. The challenger's face began appearing with regularity in Philadelphia's newspapers. One caption read "Tunney's smile." A tight shot of his clenched fist promised "Waiting for Jack's Jaw." Dempsey, however, needed little building up, even though his "killer spirit" was daily magnified in the story of his life that appeared in the pages of Philadelphia's press. City fathers noted that the impassable crowds that thronged Dempsey's highly publicized visit to Sesquicentennial Stadium sparked record interest in the fair. The Sunday before the September 23 fight, sixty-five-thousand people arrived at the fairgrounds. Many were looking for the seats they would occupy for the fight that was being billed as "the greatest in the history of the heavyweight division."[27]

The sesquicentennial's publicity department, castigated for failing to overcome civic quarreling in promoting the fair, supplied more than five hundred photographs to ten thousand newspapers nationwide on preparations for the fight. The expansion of stadium seating to 130,000 made headlines across the country and was followed up by mailings from the Chamber of Commerce to 250 targeted organizations nationwide, who were urged "there is no better time to visit the sesquicentennial." Sesquicentennial president Philip H. Gadsden estimated that each person seeing the fight would pour an average of one hundred dollars into the local economy. Posed pictures with Dempsey and Mayor Kendrick in a harmonica duet and the champ arm-in-arm "with the youth of America" at his Atlantic City training site kept the fight before Philadelphians and the nation even when no news was being made.[28]

Just as a seven-day sesquicentennial served as a touchstone for conflicting cultural values, the images created by Tex Rickard and cultivated by Philadelphia's press for the coming "battle of the century" reflected the jazz age's uncertainty over self-identity. Readers were told "two modern gladiators," one a "cave man," the other "a student," would test the limits of "brute force" and "brains." The fight was pitched as a struggle between "primitive man" and his "modern counterpart." Publicity on the fight relentlessly portrayed each fighter as a "type." Dempsey is described to working-class readers as "a Neanderthal with the backward sloping brow of the man born to be a fighter." Tunney is puffed to his suburban supporters as an upwardly mobile challenger having "a full and well-developed forehead—the head of a student and scholar." Readers concerned with America's "moral direction" were told "the cause of culture might be materially advanced if mind were to triumph over matter."[29]

Press coverage in the days preceding the championship fight served the dual purpose of building circulation while rescuing the sesquicentennial from financial collapse. The strategy used to achieve both goals was to symbolically pit competing visions of American society against one another in the personifications of Dempsey and Tunney. The night they fought in a pounding rain, the illumination of 157 floodlights and the equivalent of seventeen full moons, cast an exaggerated brightness on the bodies of two fighters whose struggle served as metaphor for an uncertain and nervous generation. More than two hundred stories would be filed on the fight by Philadelphia's leading dailies in an outburst of "patriotic service" not lost on Mayor Kendrick, who boasted the promotion had earned the city $5 million. Critics charged that the wet weather was "God's justice on a sordid affair," but event organizers pointed to box office receipts as a sign from on high that the city had done the right thing.[30]

For the record-setting 130,000 spectators who saw the contest and the millions more who listened in at communal outposts across America, the first Dempsey-Tunney fight was a civic spectacle in which it meant something to be present. Though separated by many miles and divided by ethnic, religious, and psychic differences that spanned the uncertainties of the jazz age, these crowds simultaneously witnessed one of the era's greatest dramas. They came, dressed in their Sunday best, and gathered earnestly if playfully before loudspeakers, bullhorns, and bulletin boards, to see how Dempsey was doing. Much seemed implied in the result, and that this was so owed much to the cultivation of public personality by mass media and the power of public imagination. For the story these witnesses came to see and record was one written by an unsurpassed promoter and a self-promoting press who succeeded in creating a vision of reality that fed the appetites of a newly emerging leisure class, nervous for heroic figures to stand above the leveled landscape of industrial living. That was why much could be implied and appeared at risk in Dempsey's return to the ring, a struggle that could be shaped to absorb the attention of thirty-nine-million listeners, the largest number of Americans to ever simultaneously witness the same event in the country's history.

Those fortunate few who had radios became neighborhood listening outposts on the evening of the sesquicentennial fight. Their extended families were never so large as they were on the night of the fight, but few seemed to mind. The Philadelphia fight was, for nearly everyone, necessarily a shared experience. The overwhelming majority who witnessed it did so publicly in the early fall air in cities across the country, in parks, and storefronts, in town squares, theaters, bowling alleys, and before newspaper offices, all determined to get within "earshot" of the action. Many wore suits, as befitted a public occasion, appearing to be on their way to church. What they didn't know and couldn't see was that earlier in the day, when Jack Dempsey and Gene Tunney arrived in Philadelphia for their title fight, each appeared deathly ill but for different reasons. Tunney had decided to stage psychological warfare by flying to Philadelphia from his training site at Stroudsburg eighty miles away. Photographers waiting for the overdue flight at Philadelphia's navy yard thought the challenger emerged a little ashen looking after pilot Casey Jones lost his way in heavy weather over the Poconos. Early editions captured a bravely smiling ex-Marine carefully extricating himself from the stunt plane's passenger seat despite having lost his stomach somewhere over the Delaware Water Gap.[31] Tunney had hoped the flight would confirm that he was fearless in the face of danger, but the strategy only strengthened the betting odds on Dempsey when word got back from the weighing-in ceremony that the three-to-one underdog was "green with fright" and "scared to death" of his evening meeting with the Manassa Mauler.[32]

Tunney's tactic was born of inner necessity as much as public relations. Behind the brave front was the fear he might lose the fight he had spent six years preparing for. Daily readings in the pre-fight press of Dempsey's "invincibility" and Tunney's "not having a chance" helped undermine his confidence on the eve of the bout. Press predictions of his own knockout became vivid in his mind. "I saw myself down—dazed—getting to one knee—rising at the count of nine— my nose broken and bleeding—mouth open, eyes glassy, the ring whirling." All his nightmare could see was "Dempsey, the killer, stepping out from behind the referee with another murderous punch." That sent him "down again—this time on my face, the crowd on the backs of the seats cheering and shouting." The vision of defeat and humiliation left Tunney "trembling." He resolved "to read no more newspapers" until after the fight. He determined to "cultivate the faculty of will" and enter the ring "better psychologically fit" than the champion.[33]

The fear of failure that gripped Dempsey before finding Doc Kearns now hounded him in his first fight with Kearns no longer in his corner. A feud between Kearns and Dempsey's new wife, silent film actress Estelle Taylor, forced Dempsey to reluctantly dissolve their professional partnership. The separation was acrimonious. Kearns filed a series of lawsuits to recover hundreds of thousands of dollars he argued Dempsey owed him. Process servers swirled around the Atlantic City dog track where Dempsey trained, and he surrounded himself with bodyguards to keep them out. Sheriff's deputies attached the Rolls Royce that Taylor was driving, forced her to get out, and walk back to camp.[34] As she was steaming, Kearns was sitting in Philadelphia's best hotel, dressed in a pink smoking jacket, exultantly telling reporters he was "softening Dempsey up for Tunney." In his daily column in the Hearst press, he lectured Dempsey on "ingratitude" and told the story of how he had been "the man who made Jack Dempsey." Without Kearns, the good doctor was certain, "Dempsey isn't there and never will be again."[35]

Dempsey saw Kearns's "pen and ink" campaign as a calculated effort to make him "a wreck by the time of the fight." It was working. A week before the bout his skin began to blister and break open in what doctors called dermatitis brought on by nervous strain. Dempsey told reporters and a chancery court that Kearns was an "ex-con" who had made a fortune watching Dempsey "take it on the chin" while "misappropriating" half a million dollars Dempsey never saw.[36] Inwardly, Dempsey knew that at thirty-one he was not the fighter he had once been. His twenty-four fights on the way to the title had taken their toll. He was struck by the irony that many in the media considered him impregnable now though he was well past his peak, while the same writers said he was little match for Willard when, in his mind, winning seemed assured. Such was the nature of the "man-killing myth" that Kearns had so carefully cultivated.[37]

Boxing writers who saw Dempsey swing and miss in training remained "blinded by our own ballyhoo," according to Paul Gallico of the *New York Daily News.* Dempsey remained "our boy" even though the telltale signs were everywhere that the champ was slipping.[38] Kearns claimed Dempsey's "punch and power" were gone and that he trained "like a man burned out." He argued sports writers were in love "with Dempsey's reputation, the reputation that I put on legs and in motion."[39] Otto Floto, an early and eager Dempsey backer, acknowledged the champion's three-year layoff "hasn't done him any good," but was certain the title contest would be a "cakewalk." James P. Dawson of the *New York Times,* saw it similarly. Dempsey was "the near unanimous choice of followers of the fight game" because of "an inherent fighting instinct" that made him "sturdy as an oak and as dependable and destructive as a fieldpiece." Even sports writer Robert Edgren, whose reports on the manly art Tunney had diligently read while a Greenwich Village youngster, picked Dempsey. The champion had not met "a worthy challenger in seven years," he admitted, but would be more than a match for a defensive fighter like Tunney.[40]

It took Grantland Rice, long a booster of "the greatest attacking machine I've ever seen," to note that something was wrong with the champion. It wasn't simply Kearns's lawsuits. "Dempsey is now in the frame of mind where he believes the entire world is against him." Dempsey knew the crowd would favor the marine over the shirker, the all-American underdog against a liver of the good life. That this was so owed as much to Tex Rickard's promotional genius as it did the storytelling function of sports writers, Dempsey's three-year absence from the ring, and public ambivalence over the highest-paid star in sports. Without Kearns, there was no one to fight this publicity war for Dempsey. Gone for reporters was the wide open training camp, the long talks, and card games that helped ingratiate Dempsey to those writers during his rise to the top. Dempsey's newfound nervousness left Rice wondering whether Dempsey "will hold up if the fight goes the distance."[41]

When Dempsey's train pulled in to the Broad Street Station on the morning of the fight, Jack was sick to his stomach. As his party headed for the stadium, they stopped several times "so I could jump out and vomit my guts out." Dempsey felt emotionally spent and physically exhausted. He "couldn't stop retching." A day-long drizzle began to fall, mirroring his mood. He wondered "how many more times I would be sick" and had to be helped up the steps of his dressing room. He remembered feeling "absolutely empty." He couldn't take off his street shoes "for fear of falling down." He half considered canceling the fight but was prevented by pride and Rickard's announcement the contest would draw a $2 million gate.[42]

The daily press had already cranked up special editions before the first punch was thrown at the Sesquicentennial Stadium. The *New York Daily News* "pink edition" sold a million and a half copies with a headline claiming "Fight Fans Battle Police." But there was no "onrushing mob" as the picture paper reported when the stadium gates opened at three, only the advanced guard of what would grow to become the largest sporting public in the nation's history. They took their seats in an intermittent mist on half a million feet of lumber spaced at distances of twenty-five to six hundred feet from the action. There they waited through the preliminary bouts while looking through binoculars for the twenty-five-hundred millionaires Rickard had promised would be present. Charlie Chaplin was quickly spotted. And Tom Mix. And Norma Talmadge. Al Jolson. Will Rogers. Bill Hart. Three members of the Coolidge cabinet. Many of the nation's political leaders, its congressmen, governors, mayors. And leading publishers, too, were there, including William Randolph Hearst. As the stadium began to fill, Rickard remarked to fiancée Maxine Hodges, "I never seed anything like it." The same was said by several scalpers who reported getting five hundred dollars for ringside seats, a price rivaling the entire gate Rickard got in promoting the Gans-Nelson title fight in Goldfield, Nevada, twenty years before.[43]

Rickard's Philadelphia spectacle might have "belonged to everyone," as the *St. Louis Post-Dispatch* editorially claimed, but the promoter was doing everything to keep it "a private show." Royal Typewriter Company paid $35,000 for exclusive rights to the nationwide broadcast, with Rickard barring newspapers from broadcasting wire reports of the bout. Newspapers argued that "one man should not have the privilege of telling the world" an event of such public magnitude. Some speculated Rickard's determination to "out-Barnum Barnum" would lead to the "commercialization" of other sports promoters who might sell their shows to "the highest bidder."[44]

Newspapers hoped to overcome the embargo by offering their readers something radio could not. For days they ran front-page ads announcing plans to stage fight parties at editorial offices across the country with blow-by-blow coverage relayed by megaphone and loudspeaker. The purpose was to promote the newspaper as a sports authority while providing readers with a shared experience. It worked. Tens of thousands of Denver fight fans packed Welton Street sidewalk to sidewalk, from Seventeenth to Eighteenth streets, to cheer *Denver Times* sports editor Ed Lyons and his call of the contest. Over on Champa Street, the *Denver Post* printed a full-page picture to support its claim that "the greatest crowd ever gathered in Denver" had come to the newspaper office to hear Tod Sloan's call of the contest. "The mammoth crowd," the paper noted, "proved the *Post* was the pacesetter" in bringing the most important news to its readers—a point, the paper observed, that would not be lost on its advertisers.[45]

Denver's example was repeated elsewhere. In Salt Lake City, thousands of fans gathered before the Main Street office of the *Deseret News,* to hear an "iron lunged caller" recreate the fight over megaphone from an Associated Press wire. It seems Rickard was breaking his embargo for a small fee and the continuing good wishes of his friends in the press. The switchboard of the Mormon-owned *Deseret News* became jammed with calls from men and women new to the fight game, one wanting to know if a Dempsey loss meant that "Tunney was de vinner?"[46] The *Salt Lake Tribune* had the city's chief of police and Utah Light & Traction assure the safety of the twenty thousand fight fans who jammed Main Street between First and Second South to catch "the electric thrill" of Earl Glade's public address report of the fight. The largest crowd in the history of the intermountain region, captured in a self-promoting eight-column picture beneath the masthead, had come to hear "their native son, the unconquerable Dempsey" defeat "this prancing marine." The local Pantages Theater interrupted the evening showing of "Blarney," a "bare-fisted romance of the old-time prize ring," with telegraph reports of the fight. That was also the case at the Bluebird dance club where Adolph Brox and his orchestra punctuated each round's report with a drum roll.[47]

Kansas City Star readers were certain the Pleiades itself looked on as Dempsey, "a man of monstrous disproportions," entered the ring at a quarter to nine Kansas City time. The Star's radio station, WDAF, broadcast the fight from loudspeakers opened to the plaza from the *Star's* south face, where "ninety-nine in one hundred" of the assembling throng were certain Tunney stood no chance. Others gathered in hotels, clubs, drug stores, garages, radio shops, restaurants, and the Kansas City armory to hear the encounter. The *Kansas City Times* produced fight extras that blocked traffic on Twelfth Street. Beneath car dome lights, drivers eagerly read of the contest. In one Lincoln sedan, four of the five passengers could be seen with newspapers. While some deplored a battle that would place Dempsey "in the financial class with the Rockefellers," few could be found to bet that he wouldn't win. Those who did made headlines. "Big" Bill Meyers, a lieutenant in the Kansas City police department, had become a local celebrity by claiming to have given the champion meal money during his long climb to the top. But on the eve of the Philadelphia fight, Meyers thought the champion was punched out and read a press release predicting that "Dempsey will go where the woodbine twineth and the lion roareth and the whangdoodle mourneth for his first born."[48]

Contemporaries saw the Dempsey-Tunney title fights as a sociological phenomenon, marking a new era in the professionalization and commercialization of sports spectacles. Avery McBee observed in the *Baltimore Sun* that the $700,000 Dempsey would be making for a maximum thirty minutes in the ring was ten times the salary President Coolidge would earn "for fulltime work in the whole of twelve months." The era gave rise to a new species, the "physically famous," who capitalists cultivated through moving pictures, the stage, radio, magazines, and most of all the nation's daily press, making them personalities "everyone knows." A consistent lightweight boxer, given star treatment, now made more money than most governors, while the promotion of Dempsey's reputation was a "gold mine" for all who labored in the prize fighting industry, whether it was the champion, his manager, or boxing's many promoters in the media.[49]

The Radio Corporation of America used its broadcast of the Dempsey-Tunney title match to take out full-page advertisements in newspapers nationwide announcing the creation of the National Broadcasting Company. The network had been made possible by the million dollar acquisition of New York station WEAF, which would send the signal of the fight to as many of the five million American homes equipped with radio that could be made to receive it. RCA publicists predicted public reaction to fight coverage would enhance the respectability of radio, convincing many that "the day has gone when the radio receiver set is a plaything." Instead, Americans would realize radio was "an instrument of service" that would one day bring "every event of national importance to every home in America."[50]

Newspapers that owned radio stations had two reasons to promote the new network's cause. A successful title fight stimulated circulation while boosting listenership. That's why the *St. Louis Post-Dispatch*, which had decried Rickard's selling broadcast rights of the fight when it feared it would not get those rights, now cheerfully admitted that those who tuned in to KSD would get a "ringside seat" for the drama. Radio coverage meant communities could simultaneously experience the same event in a shared "realism" that "left little to the imagination," and the next day's *Post-Dispatch* could cheerfully announce that a special edition on the fight sold a record fifty thousand copies "in a matter of minutes."[51]

The *Detroit News* and *St. Paul Pioneer Press* saw matters similarly. The *News* placed front-page ads touting broadcast of the fight on its own WWJ and eagerly reported the thousands who stood in the rain in Grand Circus Park and Cadillac Square for the Graham McNamee and J. Andrew White call of the contest. The paper reported that Detroit was "fight mad" with the whole of the city gathered in their homes, clubs, lodges, fraternal organizations, and in stores, restaurants, and billiard halls, everywhere a radio set could be found, to participate in the public spectacle.[52] The *Pioneer Press* reported the money and passion stirred by a single fight showed "that in 1926 Americans are so fond of prize fights that they will pay well if they have to." On the eve of the battle, the paper admitted "surrendering unconditionally to the spirit of the occasion." WCCO, the paper's "gold medal station," promised to take the fight to private parties for those who couldn't find room at the paper's party on *Dispatch* corner.[53]

In Chicago, two thousand fight fans packed the Auditorium Theater at a dollar a piece for the experience of "hearing the fight while it is being fought," and thousands more descended on Hartman Auditorium at Wabash and Adams to hear the fight for free after enduring selections from the Hartman Orchestra and a sales pitch from Hartman himself on the need for every home to have a radio of its own. The denizens of John Johntry's fistic rialto at Cermak Park on Twenty-sixth Street and Kostner Avenue suffered no such sales talk and began arriving at 6:30 local time to "hear the heavies do their duty." William Dever, the reform-minded mayor who helped block the bout in America's second city, claimed to be only "mildly interested" in the outcome, but most Chicagoans echoed the observation of George Halas, organizer of the upstart National Football League's Chicago Bears, that it would be "Dempsey by a touchdown." The *Chicago Tribune's* radio station WGN broadcast the fight from its studio atop the Drake Hotel while the paper's sixteen special operators simultaneously opened fifteen keys each to answer forty-eight-thousand calls on the fight.[54]

In New York, scheduled games between the Cardinals and Giants at the Polo Grounds and the Cubs and the Dodgers at Ebbets Field were canceled "to afford players and fans an opportunity to see the fight." Some claimed to see the glow in the southwestern sky from the 34-arc lamps trained on the fighters as they entered Sesquicentennial Stadium. In Annapolis, Navy's football practice was canceled. Its coaches had gone to Philadelphia to cheer on Tunney. Most sportsmen, however, were of the opinion Tunney stood little chance. Babe Ruth arrived in Philadelphia expecting "Dempsey to murder the bum." A *New York Times* sampling of celebrity opinion supported the view of Ethel Barrymore who "couldn't imagine any man on earth beating the man I saw beat Firpo." Detroit's American League batting champion Harry "Slug" Heilmann gave Tunney "four rounds tops before Dempsey finishes him." Tunney had his supporters within respectable society, but they lacked the courage of their convictions. New York Judge E. C. Smith indicated he'd "like to see Tunney win," but was "afraid that Dempsey is too much for him."[55]

The *Times* carefully detailed the five auto routes that would be taken by fifteen thousand motorists from New York to Philadelphia, for many their first trip west of the Hudson River. The paper included maps of Philadelphia, seating patterns at its stadium and walking paths for rail passengers who would be arriving in Philadelphia via forty filled "Tex Rickard Specials." Every hotel room in Philadelphia was booked for fight night and every available cot taken. Private homes opened their doors to the overflow and emergency shelters like the armory took the rest. The forewarned made reservations on sleeping cars of the New Jersey Central and planned to pass the night in Reading Terminal before an early morning run back to New York.[56]

Rickard had "never seen so many people claiming to be reporters" and seeking passes to a championship fight. After accommodating the first three hundred of them, several hundred more from smaller cities and towns and foreign duchies too small to have papers were encouraged to "find seats as best as you can" in the stands. More than two million words would be filed on the fight, a record for any sporting event in the nation's history, on more than one hundred wires installed by Western Union. Perched precariously forty feet north of the ring were platforms for motion picture crews and still photographers. Each was supported with a single post and everyone who crowded onto them was urged to stay put. Carpenters could not guarantee that the platforms would not topple down if men began rushing around to catch the perfect picture.[57]

Paul Gallico of the *New York Daily News* arrived early for the big event. Like others who had seen Dempsey's lackluster training, it crossed his mind that Tunney might "hand the experts the greatest shock of their careers by winning." But his personal antipathy towards Tunney and the strength of Dempsey's man-killer reputation, which he had helped to create, put him in Dempsey's corner. "Every person I spoke to prayed fervently that Dempsey would knock his block off. Tunney's strutting, his blowing, his vain parading have aroused a longing in the breasts of many to see his still form stretched beneath the white lamps." Tunney's problem with the press, noted Gallico's colleague at the *News,* Marshall Hunt, was that many found him "a sanctimonious master," built up by "clever publicity." What they disliked about him was that he came to believe his own clippings. The "manufacture" of Tunney as "fighting marine" and "scientific challenger" was "cultural nonsense" that made a good story and stimulated circulation, Hunt wrote. But Tunney would have to "lay aside his cap and gown" and "fight like hell" to beat Dempsey. And there were few in the press who thought he would or could.[58]

Minutes before the big bout, several hundred self-avowed candy and peanut hawkers tried to ease their way past a police cordon at the southern edge of Sesquicentennial Stadium. They were stopped by an advanced guard of four thousand of Philadelphia's finest, whose orders were to make sure only ticket holders got within fifty yards of the stadium. Disgruntled, the confederates drifted away in the falling mist before finding shelter and hot coffee at a police booth, where a patrolman with a patriotic name, John Adams, gave them round-by-round results he heard over the radio. They joined other Americans listening to the fight in the most unexpected places. Riders of the Broadway Limited en route from New York to Chicago crowded the club car for summaries of the fight that came on the quarter hour. That was the pattern for every club car of the Pennsylvania Railroad operating during the fight. The radio call of the contest was beamed to veterans hospitals on the order of the Secretaries of War and the Navy. Even the deaf, standing in the street outside the *Jacksonville* (Illinois) *Journal,* made arrangements for an interpreter to sign them the Associated Press running account of the contest.[59]

Radio extended the range of witnesses to Philadelphia's civic spectacle to crowds that gathered in Mexico City's Plaza de la Constitution, the cabarets of Montmarte, and aboard the ocean liners Belgenland and Berengaria in the North Sea. Each assembly strained through the static of General Electric's short wave signal to hear an account of the contest beamed their way from Schenectady, New York. In Argentina, Brazil, Panama, and the Philippines it was the same. In Cape Town and Johannesburg, pajama-clad radio fans sat until three in the morning, "listening for the sound of the gong and the roaring crowd." Worldwide, crowds stirred uncertainly before primitive radio amplifiers, many for the first time, to participate in an event thousands of miles away. They bent their elbows in the pubs of County Mayo, alternately toasting Tunney and quieting one another, as their "boy" stepped into the ring. Across the Irish sea, the Prince of Wales leaned into the palace radio. He told reporters he was pulling for Dempsey. On the Continent, the Crown Prince of Belgium was touting Tunney. Only President Coolidge and members of New York's beleaguered boxing commission claimed neutrality in the moments before the main event, even though the former reportedly listened, and the latter were seventh row center.[60]

"It is a ten-round bout for the championship of the world," announcer J. Andrew White could be heard suddenly saying, as three stenographers from the State Law Reporting Company, working in relays, took up their pencils and began recording each of radio's words for the next edition of the *New York Times*. "The introductions have been completed," they were writing. "The dramatic moment has arrived." Before the bell Tunney appeared to smile and bow his head. Dempsey sat scowling, unshaved, a towel over his shoulder. Around the fighters, *Time*'s omniscient narrator wrote, rose the crowd, "united in a common consciousness," like cells in a single brain, "burning inward and downward" at two men in a white ring, amidst the rumble of thunder and distant lightning, on a violet night. "They are ready for the gong," White was saying. And then above his voice the clang could be clearly heard. Crowds everywhere became strangely silent. "There it goes," the shorthand writers wrote. "The battle is on. The heavyweight championship."[61]

Although the fight went the distance and Dempsey fought gamely, he never appeared to recover from a first-round right Tunney landed to his head. It was a punch Tunney had been planning after a careful review of Dempsey's fight films. He had noticed that Carpentier nearly knocked the champion out with a straight right counter to Dempsey's dangerous looping left in their 1921 title fight. When Dempsey characteristically charged from his corner at the beginning of the first round, Tunney fled. Tunney's strategy was to make Dempsey think he was in for "a hoofing match." Tunney backpedaled again from Dempsey's second rush, stepping outside a left hook lead. The two fighters circled the referee at the center of the ring, Dempsey leaning forward on his toes, the sound of rain in his ears, the air dull and heavy. Tunney sensed Dempsey was thinking about lengthening his left and feinted Dempsey into throwing it. As he did, Tunney dug his right heel into the slippery canvas for a firm foothold and nailed Dempsey high on the cheek with "the hardest right I've ever thrown."[62]

Dempsey did not go down but ringside observers saw him stop and his knees sag. Some in the crowd were shouting "Dempsey's done." The champion fought on furiously but to little effect as Tunney piled up points. Dempsey couldn't catch Tunney, and when he did, Tunney beat him to the punch. White told the country "this is not the Dempsey we are accustomed to seeing. Tunney's winning by a mile." At the sound of the bell ending the first round, Dempsey searched for his corner. The side of his face was swollen, much as Willard's had been, because of the blows he had taken. All he could hear was the rain coming down and the clicking of typewriters and the muted roar of the crowd. Among the many faces he knew that "Doc was somewhere out there" and that Kearns knew what the nation was now finding out—Dempsey didn't have it anymore.[63]

The ninth round was typical of the eight before it—Dempsey was taking a beating. The champion opened the round, desperately behind in points, and swinging two roundhouse lefts at Tunney who easily danced away. Dempsey attempted to cut off the ring and stooped low to burrow into his opponent, hoping the body work would force Tunney to drop his guard. But Tunney tied Dempsey up and then beat him to the punch out of the break with two straight lefts. Dempsey pressed matters in the middle of the ring but badly missed a long, looping left. Tunney was comfortable counterpunching and clinching and dropped his guard, confident Dempsey was just about done. Dempsey responded with a long, lunging left and Tunney countered with a sharp right and then a right-left-right combination. Out of a clinch, Dempsey seemed out on his feet with little movement, there for the taking if Tunney had pressed matters. When another Dempsey left missed, Tunney scored with an overhand right to Dempsey's head. The champion, blinded by rain and exhaustion, his face swollen and cut up and his right eye closed, fought instinctively, attempting to cut off Tunney's retreats by moving right. For his trouble, Tunney doubled him up with a left-right-left combination that had Dempsey on the ropes. Tunney followed a clinch with a right-left-right combination that had Dempsey on the ropes again. At the break, Dempsey walked blindly into a left hand lead, and grabbing hold of Tunney, tried to fight under the challenger's guard but only got laces in the face for his effort. At the bell, Tunney was stalking Dempsey in the center of the ring and Dempsey, bending low, appeared in search of his target.[64]

The ten-round pounding Dempsey took in a drenching rain was witnessed with a curious mix of shock, pity, and some contempt by fans who felt let down by the champion's performance and by those anxious that he be brought down. The spectacle of Dempsey rushing out of his corner at the beginning of the tenth round and "tearing in" only to be beaten up and humiliated by Tunney made him a courageous if pathetic figure in the eyes of ringside announcer Graham McNamee. It was a "sorrowful sight" to see his generation's greatest fighting man made to look "like a novice." Before the final bell Dempsey was out on his feet, staggering under a wave of Tunney combinations, his face grotesquely mottled and cut to pieces. Driven to the ropes, Dempsey took a terrific right under the heart, fell into a clinch, and in separating instinctively stepped forward trying to cut Tunney off while delivering a single punch that might reverse the inevitable result. But there would be no rally. "Dempsey is gone," White could be heard saying as the crowd came to its feet. Dempsey lunged and threw an overhand right Tunney easily dismissed and the bell sounded. The fight was over.[65]

Some of the sports writers who had helped build Dempsey up into a cultural icon attempted to blame their hero's defeat on others. Otto Floto of the *Denver Post* was "dumbfounded" by the bad advice of Dempsey's new handlers. Instead of the "slashing attack" of "the old rip-tearing man killer," Dempsey "boxed" himself out of a title to a man much his inferior. Paul Gallico of the *New York Daily News* thought Dempsey "too cocky and self-assured" for a man on a three-year layoff from fighting. Westbrook Pegler of the *Chicago Tribune* thought movie acting, marriage, and the good life had transformed Dempsey from "man killer" to "timid, pawing, second rater." Damon Runyon, writing for the Hearst syndicate, thought months of court fights with Kearns had taken its toll on the champion. Ring Lardner preferred believing Dempsey had thrown the fight because "the title wasn't worth a dime to him." Lardner's view was that "there was nobody else for Dempsey to fight" that the public would take seriously. Lardner privately wrote friend F. Scott Fitzgerald that "the thing was a very well done fake, which lots of us would like to say in print, but you know where newspapers are where possible libel suits are concerned." Grantland Rice, the elder statesman of the "gee whiz" sports-writing crowd, was too drunk to file any story on the fight, though his readers never knew it. Lardner, still irritated at the loss of a $500 wager on the fight, mimicked Rice's reporting style, by describing how "the challenger hammered the champion's face almost out of shape" until "it was like nothing human when the tenth round ended." Then Lardner filed the story under Rice's name for the *New York Tribune* syndicate.[66]

Doc Kearns took little satisfaction in Dempsey's loss, a sentiment soon shared by many of those once eager for Dempsey's downfall. The sight of Dempsey's "once unbeatable face a mass of blood and swollen flesh" made him "sick at heart." From his seat at the press table he felt the urge to climb into the ring and tell his champion to "pull up your socks and smack the big bum down." At one point he had to be restrained from going to Dempsey's corner and making the point. The sight of Dempsey "stumbling to the center of the ring" when the decision was announced "and throwing his arms around the man who had whipped him" made Kearns "physically ill."[67] When the badly battered former champion, towel over his head and tears in his eyes, was blindly led to his dressing room, he seemed to many more human than his vaguely strutting conqueror. Julia Harpman of the *Chicago Tribune* heard Tunney tell interviewers he had "realized my ambition" by beating Dempsey, but Harpman felt much more moved by Dempsey's simple summary of his loss. When asked by his wife what went wrong, the fallen champ reportedly replied, "Honey, I forgot to duck." Even veterans' groups who had castigated Dempsey for ducking the draft had to admit nothing Dempsey had done since he won the title so honored him as the way in which he lost it.[68]

Crowds "larger than Caesar's army" began leaving Philadelphia and public squares all over America with many not precisely sure what they had witnessed. The most publicized and best-known athlete of his generation had gone suddenly stale. Dempsey's dreadful performance in Philadelphia's rain seemed somehow inscrutable to fight fans who had worshipped the image of the all conquering hero, while simultaneously envying and loathing a media-made man now seen as sadly softened by the good life their patronage had made possible.[69] It was not simply that Dempsey, their "beautiful" Dempsey, had disappointed them, but that his great destructiveness was irretrievably lost. That was Kearns's conclusion when he wrote the spectacle at the Sesquicentennial Stadium only confirmed the hard truth that "they don't come back."[70] That was why White's closing comment on the night of the fight was all the more disturbing. "Dempsey is gone," many heard him saying as crowds nationwide reluctantly went to their homes.[71] If Dempsey was done, they would have to find or make another.

The year that followed proved remarkable. The Dempsey that fans and many in the media had counted out in Philadelphia would rise again to try and reclaim his heavyweight title. These critics knew little of the fear of failure that informed his Philadelphia defeat. But Dempsey did. And that was why fighting again was not only a way of proving the critics wrong but restoring his personal honor. As Tunney disappeared from public view to intensify his courtship with the heir to a Connecticut fortune, Dempsey cast about for a way of reviving the image shattered at the Sesquicentennial Stadium.

Not surprisingly, Tex Rickard had such a strategy. The two decided to stage an elimination tournament of contending fighters for the right to challenge Tunney to the heavyweight title. Rickard portrayed the promotion as a test of Dempsey's ability to come back. The press played it as high drama. It proved a terrific story. The gritty comeback effort of a fallen champ made him more popular then he had ever been when riding high and at the top. Working-class readers who might have wondered if money and success had gone to Dempsey's head, admired his determination to "even the score" with Tunney. The new champion played his part in the drama as well, disdaining interviews and public appearances that had helped market Dempsey as people's champion. The remaining chapter in the public romance with Jack Dempsey would end in his eventual return bout with Gene Tunney in the most famous fight in the history of the ring, a fight that offered the most breathtaking moment, arguably, in the history of sports. This scenario owed much to the power of personality, Dempsey's personality, and its careful cultivation in the press, as well as the passionate embrace of that image by a leisure culture which took its heroic symbols seriously—and none more so than Jack Dempsey.

The Comeback, the Chicago Fight, and Its Aftermath

There might never have been a second Jack Dempsey–Gene Tunney fight if the former champion had had his way. The beating Dempsey had taken at the Sesquicentennial Stadium seemed to confirm his growing fear he was a "has been," and an awkward post-fight meeting with reporters in which he hastily announced his retirement seemed to assure the Manassa Mauler was finished fighting. Reading press reports had persuaded Dempsey seven years before that he really had taken the title from Jess Willard. Now, as he and Estelle waited at Philadelphia's Broad Street Station to return to California, reading the paper made it "sink in" that Dempsey wasn't the champ anymore. Reporters in Chicago, receiving a wire from Tex Rickard that Dempsey would be passing through, came to the station to greet him. But the session seemed stillborn. No one knew what to say. Dempsey sensed "they seemed to want to get the interview over with so that they could get on with other news."[1] A solitary atmosphere enveloped Dempsey's life in Los Angeles. Fifteen years before, he had begun training in hopes one day he might "be somebody." When he returned to roadwork and gym workouts in the spring of 1927, it had been with the idea of simply "staying in shape." He chopped trees in the mountains near Ojai, just as he had years before outside Seattle. Slowly, he could feel his old energy returning. The absence of reporters and a stalled movie career allowed him to punch the heavy bag in the Ventura

Hills "to see if there was anything left." There was. Sparring seemed to prove the point. The idea of returning to the ring, even if he got his "brains beat in," seemed better than living the life of a "forgotten man."[2]

Dempsey came back not only to prove something to himself but to his public. The further readers went from the evening in which Jack Dempsey surrendered his heavyweight championship to Gene Tunney, the more inscrutable the loss seemed. So indestructible had been the Manassa Mauler's mass-mediated image that even those irritated over his war record, Hollywood marriage, and Dempsey's self-indulgent life on Easy Street found it difficult to understand how Tunney could possibly beat him. The film of the fight played to disillusioned audiences across America. The ghostly figure crouching low and lunging wildly in the middle of the ring was Dempsey in name only. Postmortems on the contest emphasized not what Tunney did to Dempsey, but what Dempsey had done to himself. That the generation's greatest fighting machine should end his career in the driving rain out on his feet at the hands of what many saw as a second-rater seemed inconceivable. After a brief interlude of stunned silence, demands arose that Dempsey not retire from the ring. The call to make a comeback reflected the public's abiding romance with its fallen hero, an affection deepened in Dempsey's defeat, not only because he took his public humiliation without complaint, but because many readers could understand well the story of personal failure and determined comeback.

The press played the fable of the fallen hero for all it was worth. The way the story ran was that the great victimizer had been victimized. That explained why the real Dempsey failed to answer the bell at the Sesquicentennial. Allegations simultaneously surfaced in syndicated columns of Robert Edgren, Hype Igoe, and Grantland Rice, which Dempsey and Rickard sagaciously did not deny, that the champion had been drugged the day of the Philadelphia fight "by agents of gamblers" who "penetrated his training camp in Atlantic City."[3] As the story spread to local columnists, Dempsey became a prisoner of the hyperbole. In an open letter to Warren Brown, sports editor of *Chicago Herald and Examiner,* Dempsey demanded Tunney "make it clear to the public" if there was "a gambling plot" to fix the Philadelphia fight. The charge that the truth "might give the folks a somewhat different idea" of what had happened in Sesquicentennial Stadium was given front-page play in the Hearst press and its competitors, casting a rhetorical shadow over the Philadelphia fight and intensifying demands for a rematch.[4]

Tunney's open letter to the press followed. It thought Dempsey's "very cheap appeal for public sympathy" the work of a "sore loser" and Tunney promised to "ignore it." Tunney made much of the fact that he had written his letter while Dempsey hadn't his.[5] The superciliousness of Tunney's statement struck many sports writers as precisely the reason Dempsey needed to dispatch him.

Referee Dave Barry calls Dempsey and Tunney to the center of the ring moments before their historic "Long Count" fight in Chicago on September 22, 1927. This view is a good deal closer look than many of the 105,000 attending the historic contest enjoyed. The fighters were so far away that some in the fight crowd didn't know who had won. Photograph courtesy of Lyle Whiteman.

Paul Gallico, writing for many of his colleagues, admitted he "would appreciate it enormously if Dempsey should get in a lucky one and stretch him out." Westbrook Pegler thought Tunney's "unconscious overvicariousness" had turned "nearly everyone off." Even Tunney backer W. O. McGeehan admitted the new champion's bouts of condescension made him "an unlikely hero in the manly art of modified murder."[6]

When a photo of a smirking Tunney striking an exaggerated boxer's pose, fists out and legs bowed in 1890s style, crossed the wire and was nationally syndicated, former champ Jack Johnson had seen enough. He wished "a million times over" Dempsey would put an end to Tunney's posturing. Will Rogers, who only knew what he read in the papers, thought if Dempsey fought "in the right frame of mind" that Tunney's "comeuppance" would be certain. So did new national hero Charles Lindbergh, who would pass through ticker-tape parades following his transatlantic flight before urging his hero to kindly "knock the other fellow for a loop."[7]

Lindbergh's North Atlantic crossing may be best remembered by cultural historians as the defining moment of the jazz age, but Chicago's Dempsey-Tunney title clash, fought nearly a year to the day after their first meeting, created the greater splash. Fifty million Americans listening on NBC's sixty-four-station radio network eagerly followed that second fight, as well as several million more from the ninety million people in fifty-seven nations within range of radio's signal. Half the country's adult population would be listening and nearly three of every four men.[8] Western Union installed more than one hundred wires at ringside in Soldier Field on Chicago's lakefront to accommodate the fourteen hundred members of the press who were expected to file as many as five million words on the fight. That exceeded by 60 percent the word hole of national nominating conventions which often lasted a week, and easily surpassed the two most celebrated stories of the period, the Snyder-Gray murder trial which lasted sixteen days, and the Hall-Mills murder case which lasted twenty-three days.[9]

Dempsey's decision to return to the ring, a four-month story played by Rickard and sports writers for all it was worth, was praised by publishers and advertisers alike. Joseph Medill Patterson, publisher of the nation's most widely circulating daily, the *New York Daily News,* made sure his cousin, Robert "Bert" McCormick, publisher of the *Chicago Tribune*, arranged for "twenty-five of the best seats you can find" for the Dempsey-Tunney return engagement in Chicago. The *Tribune's* board of directors meeting would be rescheduled to accommodate plans for the contest. Patterson and McCormick thought the Chicago fight the "perfect occasion" to show appreciation to advertisers who had made the papers the most profitable in America.[10]

Rickard had come to Chicago prepared to pay the "ice bill" himself. That meant he would work with local newspapers that had radio stations anxious to broadcast the bout and to win advertising revenue doing it. When Rickard authorized WEBH, the Hearst-owned radio station in Chicago, to broadcast the fight live, it was only a matter of time before competing Chicago papers demanded and received the same preferred treatment for their radio stations. McCormick's *Tribune* made much of the fact its own WGN would be broadcasting the battle for those fight fans who favored "accuracy" to rhetorical extravagance. The *Chicago Daily News* promised its WMAQ would tell listeners "who's who" at the big bout and began by boosting Rickard for bringing the fight to Chicago. The *Chicago Evening Post* urged Chicagoans to save the $5 to $40 for a ticket to the fight and listen instead to WGES.[11] The suggestion that "wise fans" should stay home and "avoid swelling Rickard's income tax" was a bit too much for Tex to take. Six Chicago stations were broadcasting the fight for free and had cut the estimated gate to $2.5 million. He wondered how "a fellow can make any money" by "giving away something for nothing." Privately, however, he knew to "put a festival like this over" a promoter needed the cooperation of the local press, and he was quite prepared to pay it.[12]

The circulations achieved through the second Dempsey-Tunney fight smashed anything that newspapers nationwide had ever known before. Typical was the *Chicago Daily News* which hit the street with extra editions throughout fight night, sometimes within eight-minute intervals. Two hundred men laboring in the paper's composing room assembled special editions of one hundred thousand copies, tying them in bundles of one hundred, with the paper selling them out within minutes of hitting the street.[13] The exhilaration over Dempsey's comeback was producing five- to ten-thousand fan letters a day and kept Dempsey's correspondence secretary Leonard Sacks and his staff working overtime sending the former champion's photo to his many admirers.

The excitement had been stirred by Dempsey's July 21 seventh-round knockout of the highly regarded Boston sailor Jack Sharkey in their million dollar bout before 82,000 in Yankee Stadium. The bout was billed as an "elimination tournament" by Rickard to determine who would fight Tunney for the championship.[14] It produced a record gate for a non-title fight and made a small fortune for speculators who made five times their investment on $27.50 ringside seats. Reporters filed a million words on Dempsey's training in Saratoga Lake in the weeks leading up to the fight and more than a million more the evening of the bout. Graham McNamee and Phillips Carlin's call of the contest was promoted by NBC as "the largest network of radio listeners to ever hear a single broadcast."[15] Newspapers did just as well. Coverage of the Dempsey-Sharkey fight gave the *Chicago Tribune* and other papers their largest weekday circulations in history. It told jazz-age editors what they already knew, that there was no better story than Jack Dempsey.[16]

If Gene Tunney had had his way there would never have been a Dempsey-Sharkey fight, and if Sharkey had fought smarter there would likely never have been a Dempsey-Tunney rematch. Tunney was too busy to talk to United Press reporter Henry Farrell on the eve of the fight, but released a statement saying while he didn't dispute Rickard's "sagacity" in making the match, it might cost Tunney millions, should Dempsey lose.[17] And that seemed likely. Dempsey entered the ring a seven-to-five underdog against Sharkey, and for the first six rounds he fought like one. Graham McNamee told radio listeners that Dempsey was "groggy" and appeared to be "going" after a Sharkey barrage in the first, the third, and again in the sixth. James Dawson of the *New York Times* reported that Sharkey had "badly outboxed Dempsey," leaving the former champion to "flounder around the ring, flat-footed, bewildered, and staggering like a blind man feeling his way." By the end of the second, Westbrook Pegler wrote, "it looked as though Dempsey had fired all he had" and "would never go to his own corner under his own power." The *Chicago Tribune*'s Harvey Woodruff considered Dempsey "finished" in the fourth and a "gory sight." Paul Gallico wondered "how many times the tired old man could pile back in again."[18]

Dempsey's determination to bore in on the quicker Sharkey, ringside re-porters wrote, when each rush was met with the same shattering result, "com-manded the admiration" of those who saw plainly that he was "a shell of the former great fighting machine." The hopelessness of his effort as he entered the seventh, his face smeared with blood from gashes to the nose, mouth and right eye, revealed "the extent to which Dempsey had disintegrated" since To-ledo in everything but "his fighting heart." Many watching from roof tops and water towers and billboards above Ruthville, where the great Bambino liked to launch his homers, and from subway trains stalled beyond the reach of Rickard's three-dollar seats feared by the start of the seventh that Dempsey was primed for a knockout. The sixth had seen Sharkey crossing a right to Dempsey's jaw, leaving the people's choice rocked and apparently ready to go.

But the seventh was different. Dempsey appeared "to draw upon the past for power" as he bore in under the deadly blows that had wrecked him for much of the fight. He had Sharkey on the ropes and tore into his opponent's midsection with a short left and a lethal right-left-right combination. Their arms were locked as they wrestled to the center of the ring when Dempsey got his right hand free and dug it to the pit of Sharkey's stomach. Sharkey leaned left in the direction of referee Jack O'Sullivan and opened his mouth to claim a foul when Dempsey caught him with a terrific left to the point of the chin.[19]

"Sharkey is knocked cold!" McNamee exclaimed to the fight's estimated fifty million listeners. "They are counting over Sharkey and he is out!" "Eighty thousand are on their feet," Gallico wrote. Sharkey had fallen flat on his face and was out, reduced to "a quivering, unconscious jelly." Grantland Rice ar-gued the fatal blow had been "eight inches below the belt." Dawson thought so too. Damon Runyon agreed the blow "seemed low," but Robert Edgren, who had seen as many fights as any of them, didn't think so.

Morning papers were filled with the debate, and it lasted for days after-wards. It made good copy. Dawson was certain Sharkey could have won the fight if he'd kept his distance and outboxed Dempsey, but the lure of "making a name for himself" by knocking out the Manassa Mauler proved too great a temptation. Other reporters agreed.[20] Dempsey was asked to repeat his con-troversial solar plexus punch for photographers and happily obliged, landing it higher and higher with each recreation until it appeared headed toward the sternum. Pegler thought there was something "supremely satisfying" in the spectacle of Dempsey standing above the fallen foe. Editorials asserted the thirty-two-year-old Dempsey had taken "a punch at the old gentleman with the white whiskers" for everyone. Critics considered it insipid to attach such sentiment to a sport that had all the romance of "bubonic plague." But Rickard could see the "figgers." His gamble had paid off. Dempsey had dispatched

Sharkey and he expected Chicago to pay $3 million to find out if Tunney would be next on Dempsey's historic comeback trail.[21]

Dempsey's defeat in the Philadelphia rain and his courageous showing against Sharkey helped humanize him even to detractors. Walter Trumbull of the *New York Evening Post* thought the jazz age had grown up and comfortably older with Dempsey. Dempsey was no longer "the lean and vicious youngster" of Toledo. But there remained "something of the tiger about him." No savage blow had ever "bruised or broken him." If anything, the comeback made him seem "bigger, stronger" and more "fighting man" than ever before, as close as his generation had come to producing a Greek god. Robert Edgren of the *New York World* thought the affection for the former champion stemmed from the fact he "never quit, he never stept back, or ran around the ring," but remained, even with diminishing skills, the fighter his generation most remembered "for emphatic, headlong fighting." The transformation of the "itinerant laborer" and draft dodger, who looked "the part of a bum," and even threw a fight for meal money to the fighter who seemed to symbolize the power of personality for a nervous generation, struck Dawson of the *Times* as a parable of his times.[22] That was why Grantland Rice wrote Dempsey would be "a sentimental favorite in Chicago." The simple storytelling of "sporting commentators" had "romantacized" Dempsey to the point where the real man and his mass-mediated confederate were inseparable in the public imagination, Heywood Broun observed. "Descendents of a fallen Adam" who embraced "the fine splendor and moral lessons of quick jabs and uppercuts" found their Paraclete of "triumphant warfare" in Dempsey. They saw themselves in his newly won vulnerability and could be heard to earnestly shout, "Go on in, Jack. The bum can't hurt you."[23]

While Dempsey dominated headlines in the weeks following the Sharkey fight, Tunney seemed to scrupulously avoid the public gaze. Tunney was handling his own business affairs and felt free as champion to welcome or ignore opportunities for publicity as the mood suited him. While Dempsey appeared to kid the press "in the mood of a friendly polar bear," reporters noted that Tunney appeared "more coldly aloof" with each passing day. If losing the title had humanized Dempsey, winning it helped transform Tunney from all-American challenger to "arrogant" victor.[24] When he admonished the press for calling him a "fighter" and not a "boxer," friends urged him to avoid comments that made it appear he was "high-browing the public." Nat Fleischer of the *New York Sun* thought Tunney's problem was that he didn't think "he owed anything to the press" and didn't mind showing it. Tunney admitted an aversion to the fight crowd and "amusement" when he considered sports writers. He "never saw the necessity" of "standing for" the "inaccuracies" of promoting himself to the public nor the violation of privacy that went with it.[25]

Behind Tunney's arms-length relationship with the press and the public was his "intense anxiety with crowds." The star status that went with celebrity in jazz-age America wearied him. His cool and calculated preparation for Dempsey in the ring was quite useless outside it. It was the "unknown quantity" that truly frightened him. He didn't doubt that he could beat Dempsey again. What he did doubt was his "ability to get up and face that mob of people without trembling." In his infrequent meetings with reporters, he expressed the certainty that "fate" was directing him "to an ending pre-ordained before birth." But as the night for the Chicago fight approached, it was apparent that the new champion remained very much in the shadow of the old one. Damon Runyon found reporters who gathered for pre-fight predictions at Chicago's Morrison Hotel hoping almost to a man that "one good swat from Dempsey would knock Tunney bowlegged." Fans felt the same way. Chicagoans, Gene Fowler wrote, were a lot like most Americans, except more so. They would welcome a little "fistic crotchkicking" in which "nothing less than homicide" would do.[26]

The promotional skill of Tex Rickard, the personality of Jack Dempsey, and the self-interest of sports writers and editors had helped transform boxing from illegal sideshow to civic spectacle and lucrative business. Paul Gallico of the *New York Daily News* was among those noting how much things had changed. "In the old days there was a purse for the winner and a frightful beating for the loser," he observed. "Hunger and need drove men to struggle long after exhaustion and humanity demanded that they stop." Now boxing was a business in which everyone, losers included, stood to make a mighty profit. Tunney would be making a million dollars for the Chicago fight, simply because it was Dempsey he was fighting. Before he fought in Philadelphia the most Tunney had ever earned for a single fight was $12,000. Now he prepared to join Dempsey as the sport's second millionaire fighter. Like Dempsey he strove to become a corporate fighting legend.

Dempsey could remember when he and Doc Kearns had played poker with reporters covering training camp to fill free time. Now reporters needed to navigate through social secretaries, accountants, bankers, lawyers, publicists, real estate developers, representatives of advertising agencies, mayors, civil servants, and the professionally civic-minded to find out where Dempsey was. The assiduous cultivation and projection of his personality had brought celebrity status and the responsibilities of running his own corporation. Training now took its place with conferences, business luncheons, and small receptions with various intimate and interested parties. A reporter, frustrated with his inability to see the great one, asked for a photo of Dempsey instead. He took it with him to his typewriter, gave it a long look, and wired his editor, "Saw Dempsey today. He looks great."[27]

Not all Chicagoans shared his enthusiasm. Four members of the Chicago City Council, heeding the call of the American Legion and other veterans groups, opposed staging the Dempsey-Tunney return match in Chicago's war memorial stadium. Fortieth Ward Alderman John Chapman thought it a "travesty" for a draft dodger to profit in a stadium dedicated to servicemen. But Chapman's argument was met by Fifth Ward Alderman Bert A. Cronson, an ally of Chicago Mayor "Big Bill" Thompson. Cronson noted that "if Dempsey ain't an ex-serviceman, Tunney is." The "Fighting Marine" had been a dollar-a-day man while in uniform. For a night's work in Chicago he would be earning $25,000 a minute, $1 million for a maximum thirty minutes work, making him the country's 208th million dollar man.[28] *Chicago Tribune* publisher Col. Robert McCormick argued proceeds from the stadium's rental could go to fund "a fitting memorial to our soldier dead." Editorial writers agreed. Dempsey had "come clean" with his war record. He'd admitted he'd "made a mistake" and "taken the heat for it." Now it was time to "get on with the show." Rickard put the matter to rest by noting "that war stuff about Dempsey is old news anyways."[29]

Civic reformers and evangelical Protestants, who received an eager hearing from Mayor William Dever a year before when they opposed Rickard's flirtation with the city, received a deaf ear from Thompson. The Boston-born wheeler dealer was a bootlegger's dream, a "political Barnum" who campaigned on doing "big things" for Chicago, even if newspaper attacks proved "experts" were paid many times the cost of construction. To allies in the Hearst press, his win over Dever was "a victory for the people." For Al Capone and other hoods who had fled to neighboring Cicero until the heat lifted, it meant business would now return to normal. To critics he was a caricature of "arrested development," a symbol of twenties rapacity, a "striking example of Chicago's moral amnesia" and "the potency of demagoguery."[30]

Thompson recruited George Fulmer Getz, a man who made his millions as a coal dealer, to head a three-hundred-member businessmen's committee to "do something big for Chicago." Getz fancied himself a big game collector and liked sailing to Africa to stock his private zoo in Holland, Michigan. His first catch as chairman was Tex Rickard and the Dempsey-Tunney rematch.[31] The deal had been cut before Jack Sharkey had been carted from Yankee Stadium. Rickard would be able to charge $40 as a top ticket price to Chicago's 150,000-seat lake front stadium. In exchange, Rickard would be responsible for certain "incidental" expenses. This included contributions to the mayor's favorite "charities," Westbrook Pegler playfully wrote, particularly "the fund for aged and indigent building inspectors, the fund for the relief of starving aldermen, and, most importantly, the precinct committeemen's Christmas fund."[32]

The city's surrender to the flare, blare, and hokum it had ambivalently resisted the year before, when boxing was first legalized in the state, was all but complete. The *Chicago Defender*, the city's black-owned newspaper, which in true Chicago immodesty advertised itself as "the world's greatest weekly," railed against Rickard's failure to release a diagram of stadium seating. The paper reported that some "ringside seats" would be five blocks or more from the fighters. Cultural critics noted Chicago's staging of the spectacle reminded one of "the decadent days of Rome," where "citizens clamored for bread and circuses." Nowadays, the *New Republic* noted, "we seem willing to omit the bread." Witnesses to the September 22 walloping, the *New York Evening Post* reported, were "playing the world's greatest lottery" by not knowing where they'd be seated with no hope of refund. "The democracy of fandom," one critic wrote, now "exalted to an idolatrous rite" the "release of pent up emotions of the cave man type."

A changing world had taken boxing to its bosom, with "the sedulous art of publicity" boosting a bit of barbarity to the level of a "stabilized and standardized industry."[33] Fights once fought at remote sites for fear they'd be stopped by the law were now held under bright klieg lights before a vast team of reporters and broadcasters intimately connected to a promotional apparatus that helped make such extravaganzas civic statements as hyperbolic as storytelling and public passion permitted. Cities that once shunned such a spotlight now vied for the privilege. New York's boxing commission, in what struck Chicago civic planners and sports writers as a fit of "comic opera," were now telling Rickard that "all was forgiven." He could hold the fight in New York after all. Philadelphia, Rickard told reporters, felt the same way. The sesquicentennial was over but the need to pay for it wasn't. As usual, Rickard made the most of the situation. In separate "exclusives" with the Chicago press, the newly remarried Rickard showed off his much younger bride, and admitted "promoting is a funny racket" while promising his heart and the fight to Chicago.[34]

The second Dempsey-Tunney fight grew to become larger than the cumulative reputations and efforts of those absorbed in selling it, from the fighters and Chicago city fathers to the promoters, reporters, broadcasters, and advertisers who stylized the event as social tableau and media tome. Anyone associated or thought to be associated with the spectacle became embedded in the narrative of its daily chronicling. A man calling himself "Tom Rickard" from Champaign, Illinois, made the wire services when he came to Chicago seeking tickets to the fight from his "long lost cousin." Tex Rickard's ticket manager, Walter Fields, made the papers when he received a scratch in a traffic accident between two taxis north of the city's Loop. Carolyn Bishop arrived in the Windy City, "ash blonde, eighteen, and as pretty as any girl has a right to be." The press reported that "Dame Rumor has it" that Tunney was "absolutely crazy" over the flapper's "patrician carriage," despite what went unreported—they had never met.[35]

One could be somebody by being bound up in the mythology of the fight. A twenty-year-old bride of four months, Margaret Coale, made the wire services when she drank poison rather than accompany her husband to Chicago for the fight. Canton, Ohio, Police Chief Jiggs Wise made the national wire when, on his way to the fight, his car overturned north of Lima and he was killed. Salt Lake City newlyweds R. R. Scott and Janet McMurrin made headlines when they received two tickets to the fight as a wedding present. Minnie and Anna Cook of Bloomingdale, New Jersey, were postponing their double wedding at Rev. Charles Waldron's Methodist Episcopal Church to hear the radio call of the contest. Mary Lozzi from South Chicago went into labor with twins just before the big battle and promised to name her boys Jack and Gene. Thirteen-year-old Frankie Barone of 4015 Lowerre Place in the Bronx made the papers when he stole $120 his father Pasquale had hidden in the closet and made his way to Chicago for the fight. Twenty-two-year-old John Brennan tried to make a similar escape from Sing Sing but was captured "smelling fearfully" in a garbage can of coffee grounds, potato peelings, and decaying cabbage leaves. Even death could not separate some Americans from the spectacle. Two condemned murderers at San Quentin received permission and publicity when they asked to hear the fight hours before their scheduled executions.[36]

One hundred forty-five thousand miles of Associated Press–leased wires were brought on line to transmit the fight to twelve hundred newspapers, the most for any event in the organization's history. Every available printer was trucked in to composing rooms of member papers to save a few seconds of transmission time in getting the story from editors to Linotype operators. Sixty newspapers prepared to broadcast the progress of the fight through radio stations they owned or leased. This was in addition to the nationwide network NBC had arranged for the fight and a still unspecified number of stations being organized by the infant Columbia Broadcasting System.[37] CBS had hired J. Andrew White away from NBC to broadcast fight coverage and bolster its lofty claims that it was the nation's newly emerging radio network. White's flight to Chicago was a stunt designed to publicize the broadcasting upstart and left Rickard fuming. CBS was claiming rights to the broadcast through its Chicago affiliate WMAQ, the station owned by the *Chicago Daily News*. Rickard's threat to bar WMAQ's transmission of the fight bemused CBS representative Stuart Rogers, who argued the air waves belonged to the public not any individual.[38]

CBS's self-promoting strategy was a dose of Rickard's own medicine. He had become a millionaire by cultivating the power of public imagination and the ability of mass media to shape and stylize events to nourish that imagination. Now he told reporters the Chicago fight was to be his "crowning achievement." The thirty-two-year-old Dempsey could not go on forever, he admitted, and with his passing, the ring would be reduced to men who lacked his "color" and "passion."[39] Rickard's musings may have been part promotion and part merchandising, but also an equal part nostalgia. On the twenty-first anniversary of when he placed $30,000 in $20 gold pieces in his Goldfield saloon front to boost the lightweight championship between Battling Nelson and Joe Gans, he placed two gold-embossed, seven-color ducats, bigger than a dollar bill, in the shiny Fifth Avenue showfront of Thomas Cook & Son, the company conducting the airline tours to Chicago for the big bout. Twenty large passenger planes left New York, Boston, and Philadelphia the day before the fight, with each patron paying $575 for hotel accommodations, meals, a ringside seat, and a pep talk from Rickard. The lobby of Chicago's grandest hotel, the Palmer House, became ticket headquarters for the big event. High rollers seeking seats in the glass-enclosed, partially heated Soldier Field press box dealt directly with Rickard. To the last, he reported a "spirited bidding" for the privilege. Rickard's Madison Square Garden shareholders mightily approved of the show, sending the corporation's stock to an all-time high.[40]

There was no doubt that the draw was Dempsey. When George Getz introduced him at home plate at Wrigley Field, a capacity crowd stood and cheered. Police chief Michael Hughes made him an honorary cop. According to Dempsey publicist James De Tarr, one fanatical fan "cut his hand to pieces" by thrusting it through a car window in hopes of shaking the former champ's hand. Another begged Dempsey to "give him a lump" he could show all his friends, while another wrote he had bet his home Dempsey would win. Dempsey's training sessions were now covered live by WLS, a Sears Roebuck, *Chicago Evening Post* station. Special editions gave blow-by-blow summaries of Dempsey's sparring.[41] Veteran sports writer John Kieran noted that Dempsey's resurrection from fallen hero to cultural icon was facilitated by the way Tunney held the title. America knew Dempsey as the fellow who "crawled out from under a freight car and became a millionaire by knocking over every one who got in his way." But all the boosting in the world "couldn't color Tunney. It came out in the wash." Kieran observed how "no riotous mob of well-wishers" clung to Tunney and perhaps in his reticence he preferred it that way. Tunney "would never get across" to most Americans, Warren Brown wrote on the eve of Tunney's title defense, and what was worse he didn't seem to care if he did. Dempsey "loved the approval of the crowd" as much as he did the fame that went with the crown, several veteran sports writers observed at a testimonial dinner to Dempsey at the Morrison Hotel on the eve of the battle.

Dempsey's suggestion he might retire from the ring following the fight created a sense of urgency within the nostalgia. A *New York Times* reporter thought the end of Dempsey's career would likely make the upcoming contest "the greatest sports spectacle of all time." Ralph Gannon of the *Chicago Daily Journal* saw the drama's central irony. More than 100 million men and women worldwide would witness an event staged in a field memorializing America's war dead in which the generation's most notorious shirker and one of its better-known war heroes would fight to the finish. Yet it was the slacker, the "mixed breed enigma," whom "everyone wanted to win" with an intensity formerly found only in the Great War itself.[42]

Garage men estimated that $250,000,000 in cars descended on Chicago, its lakefront, and sports stadium the day before and of the fight. There were accommodations for fifty thousand of them, barely a third of the number of people planning to come to the city. Chicago's thirty thousand hotel rooms had been booked weeks before. All that remained through the Chicago Hotel Men's Association was routing to private rooms that went for five dollars a night. The Pullman Company reported that for the first time in its history every private car in its service had been placed in operation. People accustomed to drawing rooms and compartments were happy to get an upper berth. The same was being reported by the Twentieth Century, the Broadway Limited, and the Baltimore and Ohio. Specials were being run by nearly every railroad in America—the New York Central, the Illinois Central, the Rock Island, the Michigan Central, and the Northwestern. Officials at local and regional airdromes and landing fields were reported in a panic. Planes were arriving in unprecedented numbers, but pilots were not wiring ahead their plans.[43]

Fight fans clogged Michigan Avenue, spilled out into Grant Park and trod underfoot Burnham Gardens, named in honor of the architect who had fashioned the great White City for the Columbian Exposition. Along the lakefront looking north, they could see the gargoyles and grotesques of Tribune Tower rising above the Chicago River where Marquette and Joliet began their inquiry into the upper Mississippi. A visitor standing here would have his back turned to the Doric columns of the war memorial stadium within which a twenty-foot squared ring waited for its "knuckle-dusting spectacle" with a security detail of twenty-eight-hundred police officers and an undisclosed number of Prohibition agents to keep order. It was all fight talk now. Nest eggs and fortunes were won and lost in the most heavily wagered event in American history. It was estimated that between ten and fifty million dollars would change hands, with bookies admitting they had "never seen anything like it." A last minute surge in smart money, buoyed by reports of Dempsey's determined training, made him a slight favorite. It was the first time many could remember a heavyweight champion entering the ring as an underdog.[44]

Although crowds gathered in municipal parks, storefronts, taverns, hotel lobbies, athletic clubs, and before newspaper offices to witness the fight, many went home to listen privately. At the Radio World's Fair, which opened in Madison Square Garden on the eve of the fight, Gov. Al Smith observed that radio more than any other technology was "bringing the peoples of the world together." But when Dempsey fought Tunney a second time, this was certainly not true. Communal witnessing of the fight now competed with spectatorship in the privacy of one's home. Consumers had two thousand receiving sets to choose from. Thirty percent of them could be plugged into a light socket, and in 1928 the number would rise to 50 percent. The signal they received was more certain, the work of the Federal Radio Commission in minimizing interference and the work of patents developed under the Radio Corporation of America to improve transmission. Ads taken out in most metropolitan dailies argued the big fight was the perfect reason to buy a radio. Even Dempsey seemed to approve. A full-page ad taken out by Wurlitzer showed the former champ looking natty in a three-piece suit with sweater vest, argyle socks and spats seated next to his "Wurlitzer Championship Radio."[45]

When everyone was assembled, Dempsey came out from among them, cutting his way to the ring and appearing to Grantland Rice "lean, hard, ready" and determined "to get the man who got him" in Philadelphia. All James Dawson sitting beside him could see was "a solid sea of faces" rising in serried rows into the darkness, "yelling themselves hoarse" as the saddle-colored Dempsey in a white bathrobe entered the battle platform and its "pool of white light." For the $5 patrons, who sat beneath American flags rippling at the top rim of the stadium, the ring was more than seven hundred feet away. Some brought binoculars, others opera glasses, and a few had telescopes. Many could be seen gathered around their radios. Just before ten, the voice of Graham McNamee, the nation's best-known baritone, was heard to say, "Good evening, ladies and gentlemen of the radio audience. This is the night."[46]

At six minutes past ten local time, W. O. McGeehan of the *New York Herald-Tribune* looked down at his watch. Both fighters were in the ring, had taken their gloves from an incongruous box tied with "pretty blue ribbon," and were waiting for the bell. It was then Damon Runyon sensed that the crowd became "strangely silent." Tunney seemed to be smiling slightly, a confidence that infuriated Dempsey as much as his ploy to keep the former champion waiting before climbing through the ropes.

The action was duly noted by the country's most famous cousins, Robert McCormick and Joseph Medill Patterson, who sat side by side at ringside, and William Randolph Hearst, who sat with his entourage several rows away. The artists colony included Charlie Chaplin, John Barrymore, Douglas Fairbanks, Mary Pickford, Harold Lloyd, Gloria Swanson, Buster Keaton, Fatty Arbuckle, and film czar Will Hays, pulling for fellow thespian, Jack Dempsey. Dempsey was also the choice of Broadway envoys George M. Cohan, Al Jolson, Florence Ziegfeld, and David Belasco, who had backed the former champ in a play. Ringside watchers wanted to know how financier Bernard Baruch had bet the action, or how David Sarnoff felt watching a fight that would seal the reputa-

Tunney is down from a Dempsey shove and a slip. Dempsey's strategy of boring in and working the body during the first half of the Chicago fight still had him behind on points going into the fateful seventh round. At thirty-two, Dempsey was game but not the fighter he had been in dispatching Jess Willard and Luis Firpo. His only hope was a knockout over the quicker Tunney. Photograph courtesy of Lyle Whiteman.

tion of his newly emerging radio network, or what Albert Lasker and John Ringling thought of the spectacle as a promotion. Tex Rickard sat taking it all in under a gray fedora and brought a cigar to his mouth as the uncertain sound of the opening gong was struck. As near to Dempsey's corner as he could get, Doc Kearns set aside a green beard he wore to the fight as both gag and disguise. He was going to "pull hard" for Dempsey and "bet big" that way.[47]

John Kieran of the *New York Times* remembers that the bout began with a burst of "several thousand flashbulbs" from three photographers' nests sixteen feet above the action. Fight films clearly capture Dempsey rushing out and leading with a long left. Tunney clinched and circled left. Dempsey bore into the body. Tunney counterpunched and circled left away from Dempsey's hook. His pre-fight publicity predicted Dempsey would tire if forced to chase and that Dempsey "would be beaten by his own legs." For the first six rounds that seemed to be the case. Rice saw Tunney "run and dance away" from Dempsey's "wild and flailing fists." Edward Niel of Associated Press reported Dempsey "worked furiously" with little sustained effect and took two blows for every one he gave. In the "bowl of the battered noses," Gene Fowler wrote in the Hearst press, the crowd clamored for Dempsey for every blow he struck and with every blow by which he was struck. By Paul Gallico's count Tunney had won the last three rounds and five of the first six, but Dempsey had won the crowd with his determination to "keep stalking" regardless of cost. Just before the end of the sixth round, McNamee thought he saw something. A right-left combination fired at close range got through Tunney's guard and made "the ring tremble" above McNamee's head. At the bell, veteran ring reporter Nat Fleischer saw it too. For the first time Tunney was "bothered" and "breathing heavily." Frank Getty of United Press wired he had glimpsed "a vision of the Dempsey of old."[48]

The seventh round of the Chicago fight, the most famous in the history of the ring, began not with the old Dempsey but the new Tunney forcing the action. Tunney's tendency to attack when attacked led him to uncharacteristically force the fight as the round opened. With Dempsey bobbing and weaving and circling right in a low crouch, Tunney stood bolt upright at the center of the ring, abandoning the movement that had him the fight's prohibitive leader in points. Tunney launched a left, a right, and a left that Dempsey easily avoided before clinching. Dempsey ducked a right-hand lead to the head that exposed Tunney's chin and followed with three light lefts to the face. Dempsey feinted with a right that Tunney blocked.

And then it happened, the most famous moment in the history of sports. Dempsey connected with a looping left-hand lead and fired a right that took Tunney to the ropes. A left caught Tunney on the chin as he sprang from the ropes and a right on the button had him going down. He crumpled under a right-left-right barrage, his left arm dangling helplessly against the middle rope, his seat on the canvas, his eyes glazed over, as Dempsey circled behind him. "Tunney is down," McNamee seemed to be saying. "Tunney is down," he appeared to be repeating, as a hundred thousand throats filled the uncertain space that followed. Referee Dave Barry was pushing Dempsey toward a neutral corner and Dempsey, not understanding or not wanting to, stood in the corner nearest his fallen foe. Robert Edgren looked at his watch. Timekeeper Paul Beeler was on his feet counting Tunney out and Hype Igoe of the *New York Journal* was counting with him. McNamee's voice fell silent. There was confusion in the ring and pandemonium around it. Fleischer had picked up Beeler's count at four, but Barry hadn't. "The fight is going on," was all McNamee could think to say, "and they are counting," as Dempsey scurried to a neutral corner and Barry turned to face Tunney. It was 10:34 Chicago time. "Six . . . seven . . . eight . . . ," McNamee seemed to be saying, but whose count he was recounting remained obscure. Barry began the count at one, ignoring Beeler's call as photographers flashed the image of Dempsey standing with his

For a generation of fight fans, this was the moment they'd never forget. Tunney is floored by a lethal Dempsey combination at the midpoint of the seventh round as several hundred ringside reporters rose to their feet. Referee Dave Barry attempted to steer Dempsey to a neutral corner. Dempsey's initial failure to go bought Tunney six important seconds. Fight extras would report the number of men who died from heart attacks during Barry's long count. They never knew Tunney was able to regain his feet. Photograph courtesy of Lyle Whiteman.

massive arms on the corner ropes and Tunney seated across the ring beneath Barry, dazed and down.[49] At the count of three, Tunney lifted his head and looked at Barry. At the count of six he looked at his corner. At nine he was on his feet.

"Tunney is up," McNamee was heard by some to say, "and now they are at it again." But ten fight fans in six states never heard the outcome. They died of heart attacks during the "long count" and two more died just after it, one of them, fifty-four-year-old factory worker James J. Dempsey, was stricken while defending his namesake in a heated argument. Publicizing their passing became, like the long count itself, an inextricable part of the civic spectacle scrupulously cultivated and carefully chronicled in Chicago on that day and for many years afterwards.[50]

The confusion over the count had given Tunney time to clear his head and consider his options. He had no recollection of the final combination that sent him to the canvas for the first time in his ring career. Instead, he noticed the distance between his eyes and the canvas seemed short and realized reluctantly that he must be sitting. "It felt good," he thought, as his cornermen "wild-eyed" pleaded with him to get up again. He calculated that he could clinch when he rose but Tunney had seen Dempsey paralyze men with a close-in chop to the back of the neck. Tunney considered launching a haymaker with Dempsey carelessly coming in, but in seventeen rounds, Dempsey had shown he could take whatever Tunney dished out. That left escape the only survival strategy, so Tunney decided to backpedal. Dempsey launched two looping lefts and Tunney danced to the left evading them. Dempsey bore in but Tunney retreated diagonally away. The brush with defeat seemed to energize Tunney as much as the nearness of victory appeared to exhaust Dempsey. Later in the round he fired a left-right-left combination and had Tunney on the ropes but couldn't finish him. Tunney backpedaled out of harm's way and Dempsey appeared spent.[51]

That was when the coda for the long count fight occurred, a moment as rich in simple symbolic significance in its first telling as in its many retellings. It was near the end of the seventh round. Tunney was back on his bicycle, retreating to the left. Dempsey attempted to cut off his escape, but Tunney avoided his left again. Dempsey stopped in the middle of the ring, motioned to Tunney, and reportedly said, "Come on and fight." But Tunney was too sensible for that. In so doing, he escaped the fate that befell Sharkey. Tunney retrieved the situation in the eighth when an exchange with Dempsey had the former champion down for the count of one. Just as characteristically, Dempsey refused to take the nine count that had saved Tunney in the seventh, later telling reporters "I wanted to kill the bum." The result was that Dempsey took a beating in the ninth and took matters into his own hands when he wrestled Tunney to the canvas at the start of the tenth. At the bell it was apparent Tunney would win the fight by decision, but that was not the decision sports writers and their readers and the fight's 100 million worldwide witnesses had come to.[52]

"We was robbed," said Dempsey's manager Leo P. Flynn, a sentiment shared by Dempsey's previous manager Doc Kearns, who blamed Flynn for not taking Dempsey from the ring as he had done in the first round of the Willard fight. "The Chicago count," Paul Gallico wrote, had saved "King Gene the First" even if public opinion made Dempsey his conqueror. The romance of sports writers and readers with Dempsey, Damon Runyon wrote, soured them to a successor as "serenely colorless" as Tunney. He appeared a new kind of champion, the first to emerge from a business culture that brought marketing and merchandising "to the manly art of busting beezers." Tunney's trouble with the fight mob had always been that he wasn't Dempsey. Now he had defeated their beloved Dempsey for a second time while admittedly on the deck for more than fourteen seconds. For the "sluggish human stream that flowed with glacierlike slowness" from Soldier Field down Michigan Avenue in the direc-

Dempsey went down for a one count in the eighth round. Tunney had taken a nine count the previous round, coldly calculating what to do when he arose. But Dempsey shot back up as quickly as he fell. That was what reporters and the public liked about the way Dempsey fought. The former champion was dogged, but in the fight's final two rounds he was beaten to the punch and failed to land the knockout blow. Photograph courtesy of Lyle Whiteman.

tion of Chicago's honeycombed skyline, the experience of the fight had been an exercise in nostalgia, pitting "marionettes," as one writer put it, against one another in a passion play linked in the cultural imagination to "when the world was young again" and "we lived for a brief moment in the valley near the cliffs." If it was true, as Kearns later claimed, that "they don't come back," no one had given it a better show than Jack Dempsey, nor left his fans with more garish memories.[53]

The Chicago fight showed the power of tall-tale telling in creating civic spectacles that stylized the uncertainties of a nervous generation. The publicity apparatus that united the daily press and newly emerging radio networks in the promotion of sports and the creation of celebrity had "put Chicago on the map," in the words of Big Bill Thompson. It had stimulated the circulation of the city's many newspapers to record levels, served as a windfall for area hotels and restaurants, and contributed to the campaign coffers of Thompson and his fund for overaged aldermen. The implication seemed clear. Similar rewards would come to those cities smart enough to claim their slice of the consumption culture. The *Christian Century* thought it time to admit the fact that the pyramiding interest in prize fights was not the result of a few men who admired seeing other men "pummeled into pulp." Rather, hosting and promoting a prize fight had become as socially sanctioned and infinitely more profitable than "hosting an Elk's convention." Indeed, no sooner had the fight ended than the controversy surrounding it began to build. Rickard doctored the films of the Chicago fight, extended Tunney's time on the canvas, and inserted a training-camp picture of an unmarked Dempsey. This message seemed a certain winner. Dempsey had been had. Rickard saw a $4 million rematch on his horizon with many cities bidding on it and launched a distribution company to put the fixed film of the Chicago fight into every home in America.[54]

The historic irony of the Chicago fight was that it was as much an end as it was a beginning. The civic spectacles carefully crafted for public consumption by Kearns and Rickard and Dempsey and a cooperating mass media during a prosperous decade would soon be finished. Dempsey, fearing blindness, resisted Rickard's angling and the public/press clamor for an immediate rematch. He had made nearly a million dollars in his last two fights and knew he would never be the fighter he once was, nor the noble savage the press and an adoring public had imagined him to be. Tunney told reporters he would never retire undefeated and then proceeded to do precisely that after a title defense against the equally colorless Tom Heeney in 1928 cost Rickard a fortune. There were few calls for his return. Rickard was suddenly left without a heavyweight worth promoting. As he huddled with Dempsey to "figure it all out," time was about to run out on the wily promoter and the golden decade he had helped to create.

When Dempsey fought Tunney at Soldier Field on the evening of September 22, 1927, memories were made for many of the nearly 102,460 people present, and a great many more who were not there, that would last a lifetime. Lieutenant Carl Ekman of the Evanston police department locked up his friend, brick maker Rudy La Bohn, when La Bohn announced he was going to wager his $10,000 bond on a Tunney triumph. Ekman, a Dempsey diehard, "couldn't bear" to see his friend lose the money and only released him when the bout was over. La Bohn, enraged, got drunk, and was arrested for driving under the influence. Associated Press did not note whether Ekman was also the arresting officer.

Thirty-four-year-old Duff Lewis, of 935 Sunnyside Avenue in Chicago, was arrested by police when he got to seat twenty-five in the eighteenth row of the thirtieth section of Soldier Field. His ticket had been stolen from an insurance office safe in Davenport, Iowa. Police were checking his story that he had purchased the ticket from a sidewalk scalper. Warden County jailer Edward J. Fogarty had such a poor seat he "didn't see a blow struck." That didn't stop him from saying Dempsey was the "clear winner" and from wishing he had "stayed at home and gotten the returns over the radio." The "five dollar boys"

An estimated seventy million Americans, gathered in private homes, parks, theaters, public squares, and before newspaper offices across the country, simultaneously received the news that Gene Tunney, his arm raised in this photograph, had beaten Jack Dempsey in their return match. Dempsey's decision to accept the controversial verdict further endeared him to fight fans. After an unspectacular title defense, Tunney retired. The death of Tex Rickard one year later marked the end of boxing's "golden era," a period members of the mass media had worked so hard to cultivate. Photograph courtesy of Lyle Whiteman.

sitting at the rim of the stadium had a better view of a fight between "a bum in a brown hat" and "a bum who wasn't wearing one" who insisted on standing on their seats to see the ring. But as the "binocular brigade" left the stadium and crossed Grant Park on their way home, they could be heard to wonder aloud "how one fellow could knock the other fellow flat and still lose the fight."[55]

Pittsburgh's Bridget O'Brien wired Dempsey that she had bet her house and only son on him and was certain he had won. So was a Montana rancher who remained convinced the Manassa Mauler could tame Tunney and his wildest horse on the same evening. The 750 citizens of Salt Lake City who signed a twenty-two-foot telegram reminded Dempsey he would always be their champ. Four young men who had been living in Soldier Field's Doric columns for four days prior to the fight to assure a "good view" of their man Dempsey missed their chance when security found them but claimed "it was worth it anyway." A fan who carried a .45 Colt on his hip to the fight "just in case they said Tunney won" was relieved of his firearm and left powerless to reverse the result he had feared. Gene Fowler, who had begun his career as sports writer when Jack Dempsey had begun his as a fighter, observed that the open end of the emptying stadium faced the Field Museum of Natural History with its plaster casts of Neanderthal and Piltdown. These were the "patron saints of primitive fighting" just as Dempsey and Tunney and Tex Rickard and Doc Kearns were the founding fathers of boxing as big business, mass spectacle, and civic celebration.[56]

Rickard's wife of only a year had worn a white fox fur to an occasion that drew together the Vanderbilts and Harrimans, the Morgans and the Mellons, and the Insulls and the Chryslers in the socially approved event of the season. They sat beside more than one hundred governors, mayors, cabinet officers, and congressmen in a gathering of America's first families at the height of their powers in the nation's prosperity decade. The press, however, played their presence as a part of the country's ultimate democratizing event. Nowhere else, reporters noted, "had so many cross sections of America been assembled in one place at one time. Culture and "commonality" rubbed shoulders. And if their dress gave social class away, their cheering did not. The "veneer of civilization" fell before "the tumult and the shouting," the event uniting "highbrow" and "roughneck," cosmopolitan, sophisticate, and prodigal in an enduring public memory of jazz-age America. It wasn't enough that the nation had listened in and witnessed the event. Now much was being made of the dictaphone technique developed by Westinghouse to preserve "for all time" Graham McNamee's call of the historic contest.[57]

The long count lingered as the sustaining image of the Chicago fight, while Rickard and sports writers worked assiduously to keep it that way, hoping for another big payday. Pseudo-scientific explanations were given for Dempsey's refusal to go to a neutral corner when the championship appeared his. "Auto-intoxication, caused by Dempsey's frenzied, venemous rage," one ring judge told reporters, produced a chemical reaction called "toxine poisoning" that made it impossible for him to move when the referee ordered it. Furthermore, Dempsey's "wild fury" left him almost as weak as "the man he had just floored" and prevented him from finishing Tunney off. It was reasoned that while it only took ten pounds of pressure behind a punch to floor a man, Dempsey hit with fifty. That meant "in his mad desire to annihilate his opponent," Dempsey burned up "unnecessary energy." Experts could be found to argue that Dempsey remained Tunney's "physical master" and that only the long count by a "Tunney leaning referee" was responsible for the result. In short, it was hard to imagine and even more difficult to accept that Dempsey was through and with him the spectacular saga of the squared ring that had been meticulously built up around him.[58]

The class with which Dempsey handled defeat in the Philadelphia rain and the Chicago long count further endeared him to his generation. After abandoning plans to appeal the decision, Dempsey told reporters it was simply "the breaks of the game." Dempsey no longer needed to fight to make money. In an era of personal publicity he had helped to launch, Dempsey was a celebrity simply by appearing. He starred with wife Estelle in The Big Fight, produced by David Belasco, and premiered to enthusiastic audiences during the summer of 1928 in Philadelphia.[59]

Denied another million dollar payday, Tunney faced New Zealand heavyweight Tom Heeney in a July 1928 title defense staged by Rickard in New York which was remarkable for the lack of interest it generated. Soon after that sluggish victory, Tunney announced plans to retire from the ring and marry Mary Josephine (Polly) Lauder of Connecticut, heir to the Carnegie estate. He had become a millionaire through boxing Jack Dempsey and would make a second fortune as a corporate executive. He traveled extensively, made friends with George Bernard Shaw, Thornton Wilder, and other members of the literary community and even lectured on Shakespeare at Yale. He had lost but one of sixty-three recorded bouts, but when he retired from the ring, there was little of the nostalgia and gloom that marked Dempsey's passing. His ascendancy had briefly been interpreted as a Horatio Alger success story, but his "unspectacular efficiency" inside the ring and "bookish social climbing" outside it failed to touch, as Heywood Broun put it, "the heart of America" as Dempsey had and did.[60]

After the $400,000 bath he took on the Tunney-Heeney affair, efforts were underway behind the scenes to ease Rickard out of his job as head of the Madison Square Garden Corporation. He left for Miami to launch an elimination tournament for the vacated heavyweight championship with promotional help coming from his old pal Jack Dempsey. The idea was to pit Dempsey against the winner of the Young Stribling–Jack Sharkey fight, scheduled for February, even though Dempsey had retired from the ring. But on January 2, the afternoon of his fifty-eighth birthday, with Dempsey en route from New York, Rickard underwent emergency surgery for a ruptured appendix. The promoter's sinking medical condition made front-page headlines in the days that followed and was played in the press like one of his great fights. William J.

Mayo of the Mayo Brothers Clinic, a friend of Rickard's and a fight fan, was summoned to Florida on the evening of January 5, as Rickard weakened. Newspapers quizzed specialists on what they would do in Rickard's case as rumors swirled that he was dead. Rickard reportedly faced "a battle for life grimmer than any of his battles of the century." His every word, real and imagined, was faithfully reported as the press kept final vigil. When a grim-faced Dempsey left Rickard's room, the promoter, who was by then unconscious, was quoted as saying, "Jack, I've got this fight licked."[61]

The end for George L. (Tex) Rickard came at 8:37 in the morning on January 6, 1929, at a Miami Beach hospital with Jack Dempsey at his bedside. Meeting reporters afterwards, the former champ was pale. "I have lost the best pal I ever had," he told them, "and not only myself but the whole sporting world has lost its best friend." What followed was an unprecedented tribute to the fallen promoter in news and sports pages across the country from sports writers, men in public life, and the very men and women whose support for boxing Rickard had so long and carefully cultivated. Many sensed Rickard's death and Dempsey's retirement had irrevocably closed the first chapter in an era of personal publicity each had helped to create.[62] Reports chronicled Rickard's days on the Texas plains and in the Klondike. "Windy Joe" McDowell reported how he would have died from exposure if Rickard hadn't pulled him inside the Overland Limited after the hobo clung to the steps of a Pullman car bound for Reno in the dead of winter. And a sailor recalled for wire service reporters a steamship that sailed from Seattle during the Klondike gold rush and an "above board roulette player" he fondly nicknamed Tex. Rex Beach, who remembered him from his Dawson City days, thought of him as "a fine, straight-shooting fellow," whose life made for pulp fiction and social history. Tunney, reached in St. Moritz, expressed his "inexpressible shock." Dempsey, who helped arrange Rickard's very public wake at Madison Square Garden, confided to a friend he was "through fighting for good."[63]

A crowd of twenty thousand filed past Rickard's silver bronze casket, breathing in the enigmatic aroma of narcissi, roses, and orchids that mixed with the stale scent of cigarettes, cigars, and an occasional pipe. This was a corrupted Eden. Palm trees nine feet high touched above the bier, and as the Garden's lights were dimmed Dempsey could be seen standing there, as he had so many times in the past, beneath Box 80, the crepe-draped luxury box from which Rickard had looked out at the building that Jack built. He had been urged to succeed his friend as head of Madison Square Garden, and while he promised "to carry on as Tex would have wanted," he felt "the bottom dropped out" of his passion for the ring with Rickard's passing. A death mask of the dead promoter was taken at Woodlawn Cemetery for a bronze bust ordered by the Board of Directors of the Garden Corporation. It was to be housed in a "prominent place" within Madison Square Garden while plans were drawn to construct a mausoleum at Woodlawn "befitting the man whose business sense" helped rationalize the spending patterns of a leisure culture by staging "spectacular exhibitions" for a "pleasure-loving public." His achievement struck editorial writers and social critics as "one of the most magnificent, and for some, appalling success stories of our time."[64]

Within months of Rickard's death, the collapse of the stock market and the onset of the Great Depression signaled the end of the prosperity decade and the beginning of a new round of financial problems for Jack Dempsey. When society writers linked him to a Broadway babe he had never met, his wife Estelle, whose career had lapsed when sound came to film, noisily announced she had had enough. A costly divorce and $3 million in Florida real estate losses had the former champ all but bankrupt. His efforts to land a sports commentator job at NBC were kindly rebuffed.[65] In 1931, at the age of thirty-six, he embarked upon a series of boxing "exhibitions" designed to build him up for another title shot. The effort was cut from the same cloth that Doc Kearns had fashioned for Dempsey when he was an up-and-comer fourteen years before. With Estelle out of the picture and Kearns managing middleweight champion Mickey Walker, the two old friends had let bygones be bygones. Losing Rickard's leading made a settling of scores with Kearns all the more necessary for Jack.

He was, however, hardly the same man that had bailed Kearns out of an Oakland barroom brawl when barely twenty-two. His legs were gone and much of his punch along with it. The heart beat proudly in the man they still called "champ," but there was little left. The media had helped make him an icon to millions, a hero even in defeat. Dempsey's portrayal of the primitive inside the ring and his unaffected presence outside it had helped endear him to a generation that liked its heroes larger than life while always accessible. But a four-round exhibition with top-ranked heavyweight Kingfish Levinsky in Chicago Stadium finally persuaded Dempsey to end the pretense. In the city where he and Doc Kearns first won sports writers to their side in a publicity campaign to corner Jess Willard, it was over. The city of the legendary long count was finally where the people's champion realized there was no future for him in boxing.[66]

As occasional actor and part-time wrestling referee, Jack Dempsey kept a roof over his head during the Great Depression and felt he redeemed his reputation by joining the Coast Guard while in his middle forties during the Second World War. By that time, the jazz age seemed a long way away and the cultural memory of Dempsey as slacker had been displaced by the affection with which old time fighters are regarded when they and their generation enter middle age. For years thereafter, he would take a familiar seat at his Broadway restaurant and greet the many who came to shake his hand beneath the fighting photos of his ring years. Before the restaurant closed in 1974 to make way for a fast-food chain, Dempsey had swapped many a story with adoring sports writers and had, with Kearns by his side, recreated a past in which the two had never really been at odds at all.

The passing of Kearns in 1963 and Tunney fifteen years later left only Dempsey of the boxing men whose personalities and performances elicited the tallest of tale-telling by sports writers and editors in the interwar era. The nervous generation of the twenties had been superseded by the yuppies of the eighties, who read with vague interest front-page accounts on June 1, 1983, of the passing of "the legendary champion." An obituary by Red Smith appeared in the *New York Times,* even though Smith, like nearly all of the sports writers who had covered Dempsey, was now himself dead. Smith recalled a breakfast he had shared with Dempsey in Chicago twenty-two years after the long count fight and the day before Ezzard Charles and Jersey Joe Walcott were to fight for the title left vacant by the retirement of Joe Louis. A stranger passing by the table recognized the old champion. "Jack Dempsey!" he said, offering his hand. "Oh, boy, Jack, do I remember you! Do I remember how you gave it to Jack Willard back there in Toledo!" Leaning forward he whispered, "I hope you beat the hell out of that guy tomorrow night." Speechless, Dempsey watched as the man turned away. "I'll be damned," he said, shaking his head slightly. "He still thinks I'm champ."[67]

When Gene Tunney died, Jack Dempsey told reporters he felt "like part of me is gone." The statement was an acknowledgment that, fifty years after their fights, they remained intimately linked in the public consciousness as inseparable parts of the most famous moment in sports history. Their connection owed as much to the power of publicity as personality, and to the peculiar circumstances of a prosperity decade when a nervous generation turned to newspaper and broadcast accounts of prize fights as both a refuge and as a means of exploring, defining, and signifying personal and cultural preoccupations over individual autonomy and communal security during America's mad dash to modernity.

Although Dempsey had outlived most of his idolaters, his seventy-fifth birthday, staged at Madison Square Garden in June 1970 to hype attendance for a Jerry Quarry–Mac Foster heavyweight bout, packed the house and led to his being serenaded with a rousing and affectionate birthday chorus. When Dempsey was waked at the Campbell Funeral Home on Madison Avenue and Eighty-first Street before his burial on Long Island, Theodore Mann, a middle-aged art director, stopped by to pay his respects. As a boy of eight, he had shaken Dempsey's right hand. Now, even in death beneath a single spotlight in a coffin draped by an American flag, it remained the "biggest" hand he had ever seen. That was why it wasn't hyperbole when Ronald Reagan, like Dempsey a well-known thespian, and now acting president, read a good line when he lamented,

"Our attachment to America's colorful past is weakened by the passing of Jack Dempsey."[68]

When Jack Dempsey fought Gene Tunney, the largest crowds to ever gather on the North American continent could be found before radio receivers and men who spoke through megaphones in public squares across the country. Many had gotten out of work early, eaten dinner quickly, dressed for the occasion, and hurried to the place where fight returns would be read or broadcast. It was as important to get a good spot as it was to be present. As the hour-long fights went on, no one minded standing. The announced rally of either fighter was a cause for celebration or desolation, depending on one's point of view. When the two men had finished fighting and the decision was read, there were few anxious to rush home. One's tendency was to linger at the spectacle and extend the shared experience. Differing points of view were passionately argued for a fight all had witnessed but none had seen. Mass communication had connected these communities, if only for the evening.

The Dempsey-Tunney fights, however, were an end as much as a beginning. The time was fast approaching when one could follow a favorite fighter through a radio receiver in the privacy of one's own home. When that time came, there was no lack of appetite for heroes. Mass media would cultivate celebrity as anxiously for Depression-era audiences as jazz-age writers had when Dempsey fought Tunney. But future personalities would never be witnessed in precisely the same public way. A consumption culture's early and eager embrace of leisure was above all a public romance in America's jazz age, made possible through a newly emerging communication network that tied the country's disparate communities together in civic spectacles that helped define and shape the era.

Notes

INTRODUCTION

1. *St. Paul Pioneer Press,* Sept. 24, 1926, 1.

2. *Kansas City Star,* Sept. 24, 1926, 1, 2.

3. *Denver Post,* Sept. 24, 1926, 1, 28. *Rocky Mountain News,* Sept. 24, 1926, 1, 9.

4. *Salt Lake Tribune,* Sept. 24, 1926, 1. *Deseret News,* Sept. 24, 1926, 7.

5. *New York Times,* Sept. 19, 1926, 5; and Sept. 27, 1926, 1, 4. *Detroit News,* Sept. 21, 1926, 1; and Sept. 23, 1926, 1. For NBC's promotion of its coverage of the Dempsey-Tunney fights, see the press release, "Tex Rickard's Boxing Bouts to Be Broadcast on NBC," in NBC Papers (1927), correspondence, box 2, folder 61, State Historical Society of Wisconsin, Madison.

6. Stanley Woodward, *Sports Page* (New York: Simon & Schuster, 1949), 38.

7. The apocalyptic words are those of Willa Cather and George Santayana. See William E. Leuchtenburg, *The Perils of Prosperity, 1914–1932* (Chicago: Univ. of Chicago Press, 1958), 158–77, 269–73. Also, Henry F. May, introduction to *The End of American Innocence: A Study of the First Years of Our Time, 1912–1917* (New York: Knopf, 1959), 363–98. For an excellent summary on the literature portraying the 1920s as a "nervous" generation, see Roderick Nash, *The Nervous Generation: American Thought, 1917–1930* (Chicago: Rand McNally, 1970), 5–32.

8. Lewis Mumford, *The City in History: Its Origins, Its Transformations, and Its Prospects* (New York: Harcourt, Brace & World, 1961), 8–10, 531–43, 575. Lewis Mumford, *The Culture of Cities* (New York: Harcourt, Brace, 1938), 4–5. See also Sam Bass Warner, *The Private City: Philadelphia in Three Periods of Its Growth* (Philadelphia: Univ. of Pennsylvania Press, 1969), xi, 194, 202, 222–23. Bruce M. Stave, "A Conversation with Sam Bass Warner, Jr.: Ten Years Later," *Journal of Urban History* 11 (1984): 85.

9. The controversy within the newly organized American Society of Newspaper Editors over alleged press excesses in covering the Jack Dempsey–Gene

Tunney 1926 title bout is described in *Problems of Journalism* (Washington: American Society of Newspaper Editors), vol. 5 (1927): 96–111. The scope of record-setting fight reporting is described in *Chicago Tribune*, Sept. 24, 1926, 1. *Detroit News*, Sept. 21, 1926, 1. *New York Times*, Sept. 13, 1926, 27. Randy Roberts, *Jack Dempsey: The Manassa Mauler* (Baton Rouge: Louisiana State Univ. Press, 1979), 188. An early analysis of America's enthusiasm as sports spectator with "a passion for looking on and reading about athletic sports" is found in James Bryce, "America Revisited: The Changes of a Quarter Century," *Outlook*, Mar. 25, 1905, 738–39.

10. The debate over conventionality and personal enterprise in 1920s journalism is captured in "Personal Journalism Is Coming Back—Broun," an interview with Heywood Broun in *Editor and Publisher*, Mar. 15, 1924, 7; and "Ogden Reid Says Public Is Best Served by Fewer But Better Papers," an article by Matthew Pew in *Editor and Publisher*, Mar. 29, 1924, 1. See also remarks by Paul Bellamy, editor of the *Cleveland Plain Dealer* in *Problems of Journalism*, vol. 2 (1924): 114–15; and Paul Gallico, *Farewell to Sport* (New York: Knopf, 1940), 103–7. The charge that corporate interests now guided newspapers is found in Ernest Greuning, "Can Journalism Be a Profession? A Study in Conflicting Tendencies," *Century*, Sept. 1924, 693–97; and "Sell the Papers! The Malady of American Journalism," by an anonymous newspaper man, in *Harper's*, June 1925, 1–9. An early expression of this sentiment is Max Eastman, *Journalism vs. Art* (New York: Knopf, 1916), 67–73, 89. See also Charles T. Sprading, *Ruled by the Press* (Los Angeles: George Rissman Publishing, 1917), 2–11. Thomas A. Lakey, *The Morals of Newspaper Making* (Notre Dame: Univ. Press, 1924), 70–73.

11. See John William Ward, "The Meaning of the Lindbergh Flight," in *Red, White, and Blue: Men, Books, and Ideas in American Culture* (New York: Oxford Univ. Press, 1969), 21–37. Also, Lawrence W. Levine, "Progress and Nostalgia: The Self-Image of the 1920's," in *The Natural Temper: Readings in American Culture and Society*, ed. Lawrence A. Levine and Robert Middlekauff (New York: Harcourt Brace Jovanovich, 1972), 287–302.

12. The observations of Paul Bellamy, a senior editor with the *Cleveland Plain Dealer* and an early leader within the American Society of Newspaper Editors, can be found in the 1924 and 1927 proceedings of that organization. *Problems of Journalism*, vol. 2 (1924): 111–26; and *Problems of Journalism*, vol. 5 (1927): 152–56. See also Bellamy's postscript on the period in his letter to Mrs. James O. Peale, dated Dec. 4, 1954, in the unprocessed papers of the Marvin H. Creager Collection, State Historical Society of Wisconsin, Madison. Bellamy's view was that the press simply reflected the confusion of the interwar era. The press "faithfully mirrors the life of its time," he noted, and it can only lead "in such a manner the public can follow."

For tension and uncertainty as central, sustaining metaphors in describing the jazz age, see Frederick Allen Lewis, *Only Yesterday: An Informal History of the 1920's* (New York: Harper & Row, 1959), 73–101. Isabel Leighton, ed., introduction to *The Aspirin Age*, (New York: Simon & Schuster, 1949). Burton Rascoe, *We Were Interrupted* (Garden City, N.Y.: Doubleday, 1947), 1–11, 220–42. A contemporary critique supporting this imagery is Edmund Wilson, *The Twenties: From Notebooks and Diaries of the Period* (New York: Farrar, Straus and Giroux, 1975).

13. See Lee R. Coleman, "What Is American: A Study of Alleged American Traits," *Social Forces* 19 (1941): 492–99; and John Higham, introduction in *New Directions in American Intellectual History,* ed. John Higham and Paul Conkin, (Baltimore: Johns Hopkins Univ. Press, 1979); and Warren I. Susman, "Personality and the Making of Twentieth Century Culture," in *New Directions,* ed. Higham and Conkin, 221–26. Also, Rowland Berthoff, introduction in *An Unsettled People: Social Order and Disorder in American History* (New York: Harper & Row, 1971). Russell Jacoby, "A New Intellectual History?" *American Historical Review* 97 (1992): 405–24. For the current crisis in intellectual history see Dominick LaCapra, *Soundings in Critical Theory* (Ithaca, N.Y.: Cornell Univ. Press, 1989), 197–99; and Robert Darnton, "Intellectual and Cultural History," in *The Past Before Us: Contemporary Historical Writing in the United States,* ed. Michael Kammen, (Ithaca, N.Y.: Cornell Univ. Press, 1980), 326–27.

14. Victor Turner, *Schism and Continuity* (Manchester: Manchester Univ. Press, 1957), 92. Victor Turner, *Dramas, Fields, and Metaphors* (Ithaca, N.Y.: Cornell Univ. Press, 1974), 32–33. John J. MacAloon, *Rite, Drama, Festival, Spectacle* (Philadelphia: Institute for the Study of Human Issues, 1984), 3–10. Clifford Geertz, *The Interpretation of Cultures* (New York: Basic Books, 1973), 447–48.

15. George H. Sage, *Power and Ideology in American Sport* (Champaign, Ill.: Human Kinetics, 1990), 26–29. Barry McPherson, James E. Curtis, and John W. Loy, *The Social Significance of Sport: An Introduction to the Sociology of Sport* (Champaign, Ill.: Human Kinetics, 1989), 7–23. Pierre de Coubertin, *The Olympic Idea: Discourses and Essays* (Stuttgart, Germany: Olympischer Sport-Verlag, 1967), 99–118. John J. MacAloon, "Olympic Games and the Theory of Spectacle in Modern Societies," in *Rite, Drama,* 266–70. Chris Rojek, *Capitalism and Leisure Theory* (London: Tavistock, 1985), 51–60. Emile Durkheim, *The Elementary Forms of Religious Life* (New York: Free Press, 1965), 427–28, 475–76. Johan Huizinga, *America: A Dutch Historian's View from Afar and Near* (New York: Harper & Row, 1972), 113–16.

16. Donald J. Mrozek, *Sport and American Mentality, 1880–1910* (Knoxville: Univ. of Tennessee Press, 1983), xv–xx, 230–34. Orrin E. Klapp, *Heroes,*

Villains and Fools (Englewood Cliffs, N.J.: Prentice-Hall, 1962), 27–28. Bruce Kuklick, *To Every Thing a Season: Shibe Park and Urban Philadelphia, 1909–1976* (Princeton: Princeton Univ. Press, 1991), 11–30. David Glassberg, *American Historical Pageantry: The Uses of Tradition in the Early Twentieth Century* (Chapel Hill: Univ. of North Carolina Press, 1990), 201–27. Benjamin Lowe and Mark H. Payne, "To Be a Red-Blooded American Boy," *Journal of Popular Culture* 8 (1974): 383–91. In the same volume, see Christian Messenger, "Tom Buchanan and the Demise of the Ivy League Athletic Hero," 402–10. See also John R. Tunis, "Changing Trends in Sports," *Harper's,* Dec. 1934, 78. Alan Woods, "James J. Corbett: Theatrical Star," *Journal of Sport History* 3 (1976): 174–75. Robert Goldman and John Wilson, "The Rationalization of Leisure," *Politics and Society* 7 (1977): 185–86. Allen Guttmann, "Who's on First?, or, Books on the History of American Sports," *Journal of American History* 66 (1979): 353–54. Benjamin G. Rader, "The Quest for Subcommittees and the Rise of American Sport," *American Quarterly* 24 (1977): 368–69.

17. For the growth of sports during the 1920s see Harry Edwards, *Sociology of Sport* (Homewood, Ill.: Dorsey, 1973), 32–34. Also, *Problems of Journalism,* vol. 5 (1927): 84–85. For Dempsey as a product of sports promotion see Jack Kearns and Oscar Fraley, *The Million Dollar Gate* (New York: Macmillan, 1966), 84–85, 98–99, 117–19. Jack Dempsey and Barbara Piatelli Dempsey, *Dempsey* (New York: Harper & Row, 1977), 28, 42–45, 58–59, 68–73. Jack Dempsey and Myron M. Stearns, *Round by Round: An Autobiography* (New York: Whittlesey House, 1940), 133, 145, 215–16. Bob Considine and Bill Slocum, *Dempsey: By the Man Himself* (New York: Simon & Schuster, 1960), 56–59. Nat Fleischer, *Fifty Years at Ringside* (New York: Fleet, 1958), 108–9. Nat Fleischer, *Jack Dempsey* (New Rochelle, N.Y.: Arlington House, 1972), 39–40, 59–60, 67, 78–79.

For early press accounts of Dempsey-media relations see Grantland Rice, "The Golden Panorama," in *Sport's Golden Age: A Close-up of the Fabulous Twenties,* ed. Allison Danzig and Peter Brandwein (New York: Books for Libraries, 1948), 2–3. Grantland Rice, *The Tumult and the Shouting* (New York: A. S. Barnes, 1954), 116–37. Paul Gallico, "The Golden Decade," in *Sport U.S.A.: The Best of the Saturday Evening Post* ed. Harry T. Paxton (New York: Thomas Nelson, 1961), 3–29. Gallico, *Farewell to Sport,* 13–29, 92–107. Jerome Holtzman, *No Cheering in the Press Box* (New York: Holt, Rinehart and Winston, 1974), 62–72. Roger Burlingame, *Don't Let Them Scare You: The Life of Elmer Davis* (Philadelphia: J. B. Lippincott, 1961), 95–96.

For background, see Roberts, *Jack Dempsey,* 16–19. Randy Roberts, "Jack Dempsey: An American Hero of the 1920's," in *The Sporting Image: Readings in American Sport History,* ed. Paul Z. Zingg (Lanham, Md.: Univ. Press of America, 1988), 267–80.

18. For the response of wire services to the growth of the sports industry in general and Dempsey's popularity in particular, see *Problems of Journalism*, vol. 5 (1927): 97, 101, 108; vol. 6 (1928): 12–15; and vol. 7 (1929): 26. Woodward, *Sports Page*, 35–38. Stanley Walker, *City Editor* (New York: Frederick A. Stokes, 1934), 115–33.

19. The American Society of Newspaper Editors was launched by *St. Louis Globe-Democrat* editor Caspar Yost to enhance "the integrity of the profession" in the face of published criticism that journalism's only commitment was to "entertainment" and "profits." See minutes of ASNE's first organizational meeting, held at Chicago's Blackstone Hotel on Apr. 25, 1922, American Society of Newspaper Editors Archive, Newspaper Center, Reston, Va. Yost's action followed a scathing critique of the profession found in Frederick L. Allen, "Newspapers and the Truth," *Atlantic Monthly*, Jan. 1922, 44–54. For Yost's hope that ASNE would restore the "dignity" of the profession, see his letter to his wife, Anna Yost, dated Apr. 25, 1922, from New York City, where Yost claims creating ASNE might be "the greatest thing ever done for journalism." My thanks to Robert W. Yost of Webster Groves, Mo., for a copy of that letter. See also *Problems of Journalism*, vol. 5 (1927): 98–100; and *Problems of Journalism*, vol. 6 (1928): 12–15.

20. The self-conscious efforts of ASNE's senior leadership to enhance the "integrity of the profession" focused on the promulgation of a Canon of Ethics that they hoped would take "a bulldog grip on the minds of the nation's editors." See "Our Faith and Action," *Editor and Publisher*, Feb. 23, 1924, 44; and "Editors Mean Business," *Editor and Publisher*, May 3, 1924, 26. But the code of ethics proved non-binding on members and had little impact on stemming the impact of tabloid values on the newspaper industry. See Silas Bent, *Ballyhoo: The Voice of the Press* (New York: Boni and Liveright, 1927), 44, 111, 131–33, 211, 241. Nelson A. Crawford, *The Ethics of Journalism* (New York: Knopf, 1924), 186–239. Caspar S. Yost, preface to *The Principles of Journalism* (New York: D. Appleton, 1924), and 152–56. Leon N. Flint, *The Conscience of a Newspaper: A Case Book in the Principles and Problems of Journalism* (New York: D. Appleton, 1925), 292–99. See also *Problems of Journalism*, vol. 2 (1924): 114–15. *Problems of Journalism*, vol. 4 (1926): 99–100. *Journalism Bulletin* 2 (Jan. 1926): 30–31.

21. *New York Daily News*, July 31, 1926, 20; and Aug. 3, 1926, 28. Gallico, *Farewell to Sport*, 29, 81–82. *Philadelphia Evening Bulletin*, Sept. 2, 1926, 27. *The Nation*, Oct. 6, 1926, 311.

22. Paul Gallico, *The Golden People* (Garden City, N.Y.: Doubleday, 1965), 99.

23. Pierce Egan, *Boxiana or Sketches of Ancient and Modern Pugilism from the Days of the Renowned James Figg and Jack Broughton to the Heroes of the Late Milling Era* (London: The Folio Society, 1976), 14, 16. Egan advertised box-

ing as "far more benign than the stiletto or the stone" and certain "to educate youth, to strengthen the body, to dissipate all fear, and to infuse with manly courage." See also A. J. Liebling, *The Sweet Science* (New York: Viking 1956), 10–12. Egan's publicity in behalf of "pugilistica crossed the Atlantic and helped to create an audience for "the bunch of fives" in America. See John Rickards Betts, "Public Recreation, Public Parks, and Public Health Before the Civil War," in *Proceedings of the Big Ten Symposium on the History of Physical Education and Sport at Ohio State University, Columbus, Ohio on Mar. 1–3, 1971,* ed. Bruce L. Bennett (Chicago: The Athletic Institute, 1972), 34–35.

24. Typical of British interest in the fight is the account in *Saturday Review,* Apr. 18, 1860, 1, that admires "the resource pluck and bottom of fighters." See also the fight's appreciation in *Punch,* Apr. 28, 1860; and Sayers's letter to the "great British public" thanking them for their patronage in *The Times* of London, May 7, 1860. For a rich, textured background on the Sayers-Heenan fight see Alan Lloyd, *The Great Prize Fight* (New York: Coward, McCann and Geohegan, 1977), 153–81.

25. *Supplement to the Police Gazette of New York,* Feb. 18, 1892, 1. Fox's enmity toward Sullivan stemmed from a personal insult. In the spring of 1881, Sullivan, then twenty-two, refused to walk across Harry Hill's Dance Hall and Boxing Emporium, just off the Bowery, to shake Fox's hand. That was a slight not to be forgotten by "the most influential figure in America's sporting world." See James A. Cox, "Mr. Jake vs. the Great John L.," *Smithsonian,* Dec. 1984, 157–61.

For background on Fox and the success of sports promotion by the *National Police Gazette* in stimulating circulation, see Walter Davenport, "The Nickel Shocker," *Collier's,* Mar. 10, 1928, 26, 28, 38, 40; and Walter Davenport, "The Dirt Disher," *Collier's,* Mar. 24, 1928, 26, 30, 52–53. Fox's circulation-building schemes included steeple climbing, oyster opening, haircutting, one-legged dancing, sculling, and female boxing. He also offered trophies to the man who could balance a ferris wheel on his chest and to another man who could balance a block of iron on his while someone repeatedly struck the iron with a sledge hammer.

On the importance of Fox and his abrasive relationship with the equally colorful Sullivan in building interest in boxing, see W. O. McGeehan, "The Last Gladiator," *Saturday Evening Post,* Sept. 28, 1929, 37, 149–50, 153. William Muldoon, *The Modern Gladiator: Being an Account of the Exploits and the Experiences of the World's Greatest Fighter: John L. Sullivan* (St. Louis: The Athletic Publishing Company, 1889), 353–54. John L. Sullivan, *Life and Reminiscences of a 19th Century Gladiator* (Boston: James A. Hearn, 1892), 41–48. Stephen Hardy, *How Boston Played: Sport, Recreation, and Community, 1865–1915* (Boston: Northeastern Univ. Press, 1982), 171–73. Michael T. Isenberg, *John L. Sullivan and His America* (Urbana: Univ. of Illinois Press, 1988), 379–84.

26. Gallico, *Farewell to Sport*, 28. Gallico, *Golden People*, 73. Grantland Rice, "The Golden Fleece," *Collier's*, Sept. 17, 1927, 9, 44.

27. Gallico, *Farewell to Sport*, 13–14, 25, 97, 103. Gallico, *Golden People*, 76–77.

28. Gallico, *Farewell to Sport*, 16–18, 27–29.

29. For the perceived threat to individual autonomy as a result of the industrializing workplace, see Daniel T. Rodgers, *The Work Ethic in Industrial America, 1850–1920* (Chicago: Univ. of Chicago Press, 1978), 121–22, 233–34. For the effect of increasing bureaucracy on the notion of self and its relationship to the rise of sports and leisure, see Joe L. Dubbert, *A Man's Place: Masculinity in Transition* (Englewood Cliffs, N.J.: Prentice-Hall, 1979), 167–87. Dale A. Somers, "The Leisure Revolution: Recreation in the American City, 1820–1920," *Journal of Popular Culture* 5 (1971): 125–42.

30. For an interesting discussion on the significance of boxing to preindustrial America, see Elliot J. Gorn, "Gouge and Bite, Pull Hair and Scratch: The Social Significance of Fighting in the Southern Backcountry," *American Historical Review* 90 (Feb. 1985): 18–43. In a culture where gouged-out eyes or snapped-off noses were viewed as trophies, "natural men" settled disputes through direct action that certified their honor.

31. Horace Gregory, "Dempsey, Dempsey," in *The American Writer and the Great Depression*, ed. Harvey Swados (Indianapolis: Bobbs-Merrill, 1966), 349–51.

32. George Santayana, "Philosophy on the Bleachers," *The Harvard Monthly*, July 1894, 181–90.

33. On the relationship of sports, leisure, and freedom in the evolution of modern consciousness, see John Higham, "The Reorientation of American Culture in the 1890's," in *The Origins of Modern Consciousness*, ed. John Weiss (Detroit: Wayne State Univ. Press, 1965), 25–40. Peter N. Stearns, "Modernization and Social History: Some Suggestions, and a Muted Cheer," *Journal of Social History* 14 (Winter 1980): 191–95. John Kelly, *Leisure Identities and Interactions* (London: George Allen and Unwin, 1983), 5–18.

34. The apocalyptic literature on major media effects that argues the "American mind" is powerfully shaped by the "myth-making power" of media includes the "narcosis" effect described by Marshall McLuhan, *Understanding Media: The Extensions of Man* (New York: New American Library, 1965), 51–56. For a summary of this literature see Daniel J. Czitrom, *Media and the American Mind: From Morse to McLuhan* (Chapel Hill: Univ. of North Carolina Press, 1982); and *Communication in History: Technology, Culture, Society*, ed. David Crowley and Paul Heyer (New York: Longman, 1991).

For the "decivilization perspective" that sees media as a prime shaper of the "psychoculture" that guides human behavior and social experience, see Willard D. Rowland, Jr., foreword to *Communication in History*, vii–x. Also

Media, Consciousness and Culture: Explorations of Walter Ong's Thought, ed. Bruce E. Gronbeck, Thomas J. Farrell, and Paul A. Soukop (Newbury Park, Calif.: Sage, 1991), 105. Walter J. Ong, *Interfaces of the Word: Studies in the Evolution of Consciousness and Culture* (Ithaca, N.Y.: Cornell Univ. Press, 1977), 315.

For a critique on the claims of the major effects school and its misreading of the "American mind" see James L. Baughman, "Television in the Golden Age: An Entrepreneurial Experiment," in *Media Voices: An Historical Perspective,* ed. Jean Folkerts (New York: Macmillan, 1992), 417. Joli Jensen, *Redeeming Modernity: Contradictions in Media Criticism* (Newbury Park, Calif.: Sage, 1990), 10–13, 178.

35. For a review of the literature on the West and its place in the American imagination, see Gerald D. Nash, *Creating the West: Historical Interpretations, 1890–1990* (Albuquerque: Univ. of New Mexico Press, 1991), 223–32. Henry Nash Smith, *Virgin Land: The American West as Symbol and Myth* (New York: Vintage Books, 1957), 99–135. Roderick Nash, *Wilderness and the American Mind* (New Haven: Yale Univ. Press, 1967), 67–83. Also, Robert G. Athearn, *The Mythic West in Twentieth Century America* (Lawrence: Univ. Press of Kansas, 1986), 249–75. And William Cronon, George Miles, and Jay Gitlin, "Becoming West: Toward a New Meaning for Western History," in *Under an Open Sky: Rethinking America's Western Past,* ed. William Cronon, George Miles, and Jay Gitlin (New York: W. W. Norton, 1992), 3–27.

Well-known western historian Earl Pomeroy found the American West to be surprisingly urban and highly imitative of eastern city structures. See Michael Malone, "Earl Pomeroy and the Reorientation of Western American History," in *Writing Western History: Essays on Major Western Historians,* ed. Richard W. Etulian (Albuquerque: Univ. of New Mexico Press, 1991), 311–34. Also, Michael Malone, "Toward a New Approach to Western American History," in *Trails Toward a New Western History,* ed. Patricia Nelson Limerick, Clyde A. Milner, Charles E. Rankin (Lawrence: Univ. Press of Kansas, 1991), 140–59. Donald Worster, *Under Western Skies: Nature and History in the American West* (New York: Oxford Univ. Press, 1992), 23–28.

For Turner's articulation of his frontier thesis, see Frederick Jackson Turner, *Rise of the New West, 1819–1829* (New York: Harper & Bros., 1906); and *The Frontier in American History* (New York: Henry Holt, 1920), 1–38. For the impact of Turner's thesis on his generation of scholars, see Frederic Logan Paxson, *The Last American Frontier* (New York: Macmillan, 1910); and Paxson's application of the frontier as safety valve for urban excesses in his "The Rise of Sport," *Mississippi Valley Historical Review* 4 (Sept. 1917): 143–68. For an early critique of the Turner/Paxson hypothesis, see Mody C. Boatright, "The Myth of Frontier Individualism," *Southwestern Social Science Quarterly* 22 (1941): 14–32.

36. *Creede Candle,* June 22, 1918, 3; and June 21, 1919, 8.

37. *Leadville Carbonate Weekly Chronicle,* July 7, 1919, 4.

38. For an analysis of Dempsey and his relationship to the fight crowd which saw him as their hero, see Orrin E. Klapp, "Hero Worship in America," *American Sociological Review* 14 (Feb. 1949) 53–62; and Benjamin G. Rader, "Compensatory Sports Heroes: Ruth, Grange and Dempsey," *Journal of Popular Culture* 16 (Spring 1983): 18–21.

39. Dempsey endorses the story of his mother reading John L. Sullivan's autobiography shortly before Jack's birth. It presumably was payment by a peddler for something to eat and a place to sleep. See Dempsey and Dempsey, *Dempsey,* 7–8.

CHAPTER 1
DEMPSEY AND THE DOCTOR

1. Jack Dempsey and Barbara Piatelli Dempsey, *Dempsey* (New York: Harper & Row, 1977), 16. James A. Cox, "Mr. Jake and the Great John L.," *Smithsonian,* Dec. 1984, 157. Walter Davenport, "The Nickel Shocker," *Collier's,* Mar. 10, 1928, 26, 28, 38, 40. Walter Davenport, "The Dirt Disher," *Collier's,* Mar. 24, 1928, 26, 30, 52–53. For Fox's increased reliance on boxing as a circulation stimulator, see also Richard D. Mandell, *Sport: A Cultural History* (New York: Columbia Univ. Press, 1984), 185.

2. See Jack Dempsey's foreward to *Muldoon: The Solid Man of Sport, His Amazing Story as Related for the First Time by Him to His Friend,* by Edward Van Every (New York: Frederick A. Stokes, 1929), vii. On Sullivan's domination of the fighters of his day, see Lester Bromberg, *Boxing's Unforgettable Fights* (New York: Ronald Press, 1962), 3–5, 10–13.

3. Davenport, "The Nickel Shocker," 26, 28. Cox, "Mr. Jake," 156–58. Jeffrey T. Sammons, *Beyond the Ring: The Role of Boxing in American Society* (Urbana: Univ. of Illinois Press, 1988), 6–10. Dale Somers, *The Rise of Sports in New Orleans, 1850–1900* (Baton Rouge: Louisiana State Univ. Press, 1972), 162–70.

4. *Boston Globe,* Aug. 9, 1887, 1. Stephen Hardy, *How Boston Played: Sport, Recreation, and Community, 1865–1915* (Boston: Northeastern Univ. Press, 1982), 171–74. Michael T. Isenberg, *John L. Sullivan and His America* (Urbana: Univ. of Illinois Press, 1988), 6–7. William H. Adams, "New Orleans as the National Center of Boxing," *Louisiana Historical Quarterly* 39 (Jan. 1956): 92–97. Cox, "Mr. Jake," 166. Davenport, "Dirt Disher," 52.

5. For contemporary coverage of the fight, see *New York Times,* July 9, 1889, 1; and *New Orleans Picayune,* July 9, 1889, 1. For poetic interpretations of the fight's significance in American cultural history, see Vachel Lindsay, "John

L. Sullivan, The Strong Boy of Boston," *New Republic,* July 16, 1919, 357–58. See also Isenberg, *John L. Sullivan,* 13–14. Donna R. Braden, *Leisure and Entertainment in America* (Dearborn, Mich.: Henry Ford Museum & Greenfield Village, 1988), 213, 231. Richard K. Fox, *Life and Battles of John L. Sullivan* (New York: Police Gazette, 1891), 27–32, 62–66. John L. Sullivan, *John L. Sullivan: Life and Reminiscences of a 19th Century Gladiator* (Boston: James A. Hearn, 1892), 43–47. *The Modern Gladiator, Being an Account of the World's Greatest Fighter: John Lawrence Sullivan* (St. Louis: Athletic Publishing, 1889), 23–33, 61–63, 129–64.

6. For the cultivation of Corbett's public and stage persona during his five-year reign as heavyweight champion, see Alan Woods, "James J. Corbett: Theatrical Star," *Journal of Sport History* 3 (1976): 162–75. For the rise and fall of the Ivy League hero, see Christian Messenger, "Tom Buchanan and the Demise of the Ivy League Athletic Hero," *Journal of Popular Culture* 8 (1974): 402–10.

For the role of media-savvy managers in manufacturing public personas for sports stars, see William A. Brady, *Showman* (New York: E. P. Dutton, 1937), 97–108. Corbett says he and Brady netted $150,000 during the first-year run of "Gentleman Jack." See James J. Corbett, *The Roar of the Crowd: The True Tale of the Rise and Fall of a Champion* (New York: G. P. Putnam's Sons, 1925), 207–35.

For critiques of Corbett's work as an actor, see *Cincinnati Enquirer,* Oct. 24, 1892, 5; and *Boston Evening Transcript,* Dec. 6, 1892, 5.

For background, see Alexander Johnston, *Ten and Out! The Complete Story of the Prize Ring in America* (New York: Ives Washburn, 1927), 100–104. Bromberg, *Unforgettable Fights,* 14–19, 46–55. Nat Fleischer, *The Heavyweight Championship: An Informal History of Heavyweight Boxing from 1719 to the Present Day* (New York: G. P. Putnam's Sons, 1949), 105–16.

7. *Rocky Mountain News,* June 25, 1895, 1. *Denver Post,* June 25, 1895, 2.

8. *Rocky Mountain News,* June 25, 1895, 3.

9. *Craig Courier,* June 22, 1895, 4; and June 29, 1895, 4.

10. Dempsey and Dempsey, *Dempsey,* 6, 17, 26. Randy Roberts, *Jack Dempsey: The Manassa Mauler* (Baton Rouge: Louisiana State Univ. Press, 1979), 7–8.

11. *Meeker Herald,* June 29, 1895, 1.

12. *Antonito Ledger,* June 1, 1895, 2.

13. *Steamboat Springs Pilot,* Jan. 5, 1898, 1. *Alamosa Independent-Journal,* Feb. 20, 1902, 2. For studies on the ethos of reciprocity that informed booster journalism in the West, see Sally Foreman Griffith, *Home Town News: William Allen White and the Emporia Gazette* (New York: Oxford Univ. Press, 1989); and Barbara Cloud, *The Business of Newspapers on the Western Frontier* (Reno: Univ. of Nevada Press, 1992). David Fridtjof Halaas, *Boom Town News-*

papers: Journalism on the Rocky Mountain Mining Frontier, 1859–1881 (Albuquerque: Univ. of New Mexico Press, 1981).

Frontier newspapers replaced any pretense of objectivity with the logic of civic boosting and self-promotion. Typical was the observation by the *Alamosa Independent-Journal,* Apr. 30, 1903, 2, that "the great man shines before the population in vain without the newspaper."

For background, see Barbara Cloud, "Establishing the Frontier Newspaper: A Study of Eight Western Territories," *Journalism Quarterly* 61 (Winter 1984): 805–11. Sherilyn C. Bennion, *Equal to the Occasion: Women Editors of the 19th Century West* (Reno: Univ. of Nevada Press, 1990). William Katz, "The Western Printer and His Publications, 1850–1890," *Journalism Quarterly* 44 (Winter 1967): 708–14. Wendell W. Norris, "The Transient Frontier Weekly as a Stimulant to Homesteading," *Journalism Quarterly* 30 (Spring 1953): 44–48. Larry Cebula, "For Want of the Actual Necessaries of Life: Survival Strategies of Frontier Journalists in the Trans-Miss. West" (paper presented at a meeting of the American Journalism Historians Association, Salt Lake City, Oct. 7, 1993).

14. *Leadville Evening Chronicle,* Jan. 3, 1902.

15. *Alamosa Independent-Journal,* Jan. 7, 1904, 1, 2.

16. Dempsey and Dempsey, *Dempsey,* 12–13. *Creede Candle,* Mar. 18, 1916, 2; and *Steamboat Pilot,* Nov. 10, 1897. Typical of frontier greetings was the *Moffat County Courier*'s front-page salutation of Mar. 9, 1911, "extending the right hand of fellowship to the homeseeker to this New Empire."

17. *Moffat County Courier,* July 10, 1919, 1.

18. *Routt County Courier,* Oct. 21, 1909, 1.

19. Dempsey and Dempsey, *Dempsey,* 16–22. Nat Fleischer, *Jack Dempsey* (New Rochelle, N.Y.: Arlington House, 1972), 16–18. Jack Dempsey and Myron M. Stearns, *Round by Round: An Autobiography* (New York: Whittlesey House, 1940), 14–16. Jim Tully, "Jack Dempsey," *American Mercury* 29, Aug. 1933, 398–99.

20. Dempsey and Dempsey, *Dempsey,* 23–31. Roberts, *Manassa Mauler,* 11–12. John Durant, *The Heavyweight Champions* (New York: Hastings House, 1971), 66–68. See also Red Smith's obituary of Jack Dempsey in *New York Times,* June 1, 1983, sec. B, 4.

21. Dempsey and Dempsey, *Dempsey,* 31–36. Nat Fleischer, *Jack Dempsey: Idol of Fistiana* (New York: The Ring, 1929), 10–12. Mel Heimer, *The Long Count* (New York: Atheneum, 1969), 67–69.

22. *Denver Post,* Aug. 5, 1929, 1, 4. *Rocky Mountain News,* Aug. 5, 1929, 1, 2.

23. Jack Dempsey, Bob Considine, and Bill Slocum, *Dempsey* (New York: Simon & Schuster, 1960), 47–55. Heimer, *Long Count,* 68. Dempsey and Dempsey, *Dempsey,* 36–37. Dempsey and Stearns, *Round by Round,* 95–99.

24. Fleischer, *Jack Dempsey,* 36–37. Rex Lardner, *The Legendary Champions*

(New York: American Heritage Press, 1972), 222–23. Heimer, *Long Count*, 69.

25. *New York Press*, June 25, 1916, 8; and *New York American*, June 25, 1916, 12. Also, Fleischer, *Jack Dempsey*, 37–38.

26. *New York Press*, July 9, 1916, 9; and *New York Press*, July 15, 1916, 8. Grantland Rice, *The Tumult and the Shouting* (New York: A. S. Barnes, 1954), 130–32. Gene Fowler, *Skyline: A Reporter's Reminiscence of the 1920's* (New York: Viking Press, 1961), 28–30.

27. Dempsey and Dempsey, *Dempsey*, 49–53. Stanley Weston, *The Heavyweight Champions* (New York: Ace Books, 1976), 101–3. Fleischer, *Idol of Fistiana*, 99–101. Many were certain Dempsey had taken a dive for a fast few bucks. See Jack Kearns and Oscar Fraley, *The Million Dollar Gate* (New York: Macmillan, 1966), 79–80.

28. Dempsey and Dempsey, *Dempsey*, 55–59. Fleischer, *Idol of Fistiana*, 101–6. Lardner, *Legendary Champions*, 223.

29. Kearns and Fraley, *Million Dollar Gate*, 77–78. Weston, *Heavyweight Champions*, 105. Dempsey and Dempsey, *Dempsey*, 60–62. Lardner, *Legendary Champions*, 223. Heimer, *Long Count*, 72. Fleischer, *Jack Dempsey*, 41.

30. Kearns and Fraley, *Million Dollar Gate*, 81–82.

31. Dempsey and Dempsey, *Dempsey*, 25. Roberts, *Manassa Mauler*, 12–13.

32. Just like the second Dempsey, the defeat of the first Dempsey also provoked poetry. On his tombstone in Oregon, the "bravest of the brave" is commemorated with the words: "Forgotten by ten thousand throats that thundered his acclaim, Forgotten by his friends and foes, who cheered his very name. Oblivion wraps his faded form, But ages hence shall save the memory of that Irish lad that fills poor Dempsey's grave." See Tom S. Andrews and C. R. Diegle, *Ring Battles of Centuries* (New York: Tom Andrews Record Book, 1914), 7.

33. The quote by Kearns is from Charles Samuels, *The Magnificent Rube: The Life and Gaudy Times of Tex Rickard* (New York: McGraw Hill, 1957), 198–99. See also Roberts, *Manassa Mauler*, 36–33. An excellent summary of Kearns's early career appears in his *New York Times* obituary on July 8, 1963, 29.

34. Jim Tully, "Jack Dempsey," *American Mercury*, Aug. 1933, 401. Nat Fleischer, *The Heavyweight Championship*, 169–70. Nat Fleischer, *Jack Dempsey*, 40–42.

35. Kearns and Fraley, *Million Dollar Gate*, ix–xi. Samuels, *Magnificent Rube*, 199–200. Kearns's pertinacity as self-promoting con man was "deeply resented" by some sports writers. See James Dawson, "Boxing," in *Sport's Golden Age: A Close-up of the Fabulous Twenties*, ed. Allison Danzig and Peter Brandwein (New York: Harper & Bros., 1948), 49–50. Dawson was the senior boxing writer on the *New York Times* during the 1920s.

36. Kearns and Fraley, *Million Dollar Gate*, 78–79. Dempsey and Dempsey, *Dempsey*, 39. Fleischer, *Jack Dempsey*, 41.

37. Dempsey and Dempsey, *Dempsey*, 64. Kearns and Fraley, *Million Dollar Gate*, 81. Weston, *Heavyweight Champions*, 105. Also, Sammons, *Beyond the Ring*, 51–52.

38. Kearns and Fraley, *Million Dollar Gate*, 81. For background on the Kearns-Dempsey collaboration and the crucial role Kearns played in rescuing Dempsey's faltering career, see Benjamin G. Rader, *American Sports: From the Age of Folk Games to the Age of Spectators* (Englewood Cliffs, N.J.: Prentice-Hall, 1983), 186–89. Orrin E. Klapp, *Symbolic Leaders: Public Dramas and Public Men* (Chicago: Aldine, 1964), 239–41.

39. Kearns and Fraley, *Million Dollar Gate*, xii, xiv. Dempsey and Dempsey, *Dempsey*, 66–67. A. J. Liebling, *The Sweet Science* (New York: Viking, 1956), 67–70. Elliott J. Gorn, "The Manassa Mauler and the Fighting Marine: An Interpretation of the Dempsey-Tunney Fights," *Journal of American Studies* 19 (1985): 36–37.

40. Kearns and Fraley, *Million Dollar Gate*, 81–82. Dempsey and Dempsey, *Dempsey*, 65. See also Jack Dempsey and John B. Kennedy, "They Call Me a Bum," in *Collier's Greatest Sports Stories*, ed. Tom Meany (New York: A. S. Barnes, 1955), 92–96. The piece was originally published in *Collier's* September 1925 issue.

41. Paul Gallico, *The Golden People* (Garden City, N.Y.: Doubleday, 1965), 77–81. Kearns and Fraley, *Million Dollar Gate*, 82–83. Myron M. Stearns, "Champion Ex-Champion," *Harper's*, Sept. 1939, 417.

42. The coverage seems as much a tribute to Meehan's Bay area reputation as Kearns's ability to great press attention. See *San Francisco Chronicle*, July 26, 1917, 6.

43. *San Francisco Chronicle*, Oct. 2, 1917, 7.

44. An account of the Dempsey–"Gunboat" Smith battle appears in *San Francisco Chronicle*, Oct. 3, 1917, 11. For background, see Roberts, *Manassa Mauler*, 38–39. For Dempsey's feelings of inadequacy despite his assiduous promotion in the press, see Dempsey and Stearns, 130–31. For Smith's background and the effect of the fight on Dempsey's conquest of Willard, see Bob Burrill, *Who's Who in Boxing* (New Rochelle, N.Y.: Arlington House, 1974), 55–56, 177, 200–201.

45. The Kearns-Brown connection is described in Kearns and Fraley, *Million Dollar Gate*, 121; and Dempsey and Dempsey, *Dempsey*, 69. Competition between the *Examiner* and the *Chronicle* is described by Edwin Emery, *The Press and America: An Interpretative History of Journalism* (Englewood Cliffs, N.J.: Prentice-Hall, 1962), 417–20; and Ferdinand Lundberg, *Imperial Hearst: A Social Biography* (New York: Equinox Cooperative Press, 1936), 50–51. See also George Everett, "The Age of New Journalism, 1883–1900," in *The Media in America*, ed. William David Sloan, James G. Stovall, and James D. Startt (Worthington, Ohio: Publishing Horizons, 1989), 230–31.

46. See Dempsey and Dempsey, *Dempsey,* 70–71; and Roberts, *Manassa Mauler,* 39–40. *San Francisco Chronicle,* Oct. 16, 1917, 10; and Nov. 2, 1917, 10.

47. An excellent summary of the *Denver Post*'s penchant for tall tale telling is found in Fowler, *Skyline,* 32–37. When Fowler came to work at the *Post* he had faith "in everyone," a view that quickly receded in the face of the *Post*'s circulation stimulating stunts. The self-respecting *Rocky Mountain News* was quick to distinguish itself from its tabloid competitor. See Robert L. Perkin, *The First Hundred Years: An Informal History of Denver and the Rocky Mountain News* (New York: Doubleday, 1959). For a summary of the *Post*'s "bucket of blood" days, see Edwin Emery, *The Press and America: An Interpretative History of the Mass Media* (Englewood Cliffs, N.J.: Prentice-Hall, 1972), 436–37, 457. The sad plight of Agnes Marion is depicted in *Denver Post,* June 26, 1895, 1.

48. The *Denver Post*'s promotion of Jack Dempsey as a proof that it is the "authoritative voice" in the world of sports for the West can be seen in *Denver Post,* Dec. 27, 1917, 8; July 12, 1918, 8; June 24, 1919, 9; July 5, 1919, 8; and Aug. 5, 1929, 1, 4. Floto's place as an early Dempsey advocate is reluctantly acknowledged by the competing *Rocky Mountain News* in its obituary of Floto on Aug. 5, 1929, 1, 2.

49. *Chicago Tribune,* Dec. 18, 1917, 15; Dec. 19, 1917, 21; Dec. 20, 1917, 13; Dec. 22, 1917, 12; Dec. 23, 1917, sec. A, 1; and Dec. 28, 1917, 14.

50. The two men arrived in Chicago as a blizzard was settling over the city, one later described as "the worst storm in the city's history." *Chicago Tribune,* Jan. 7, 1918, 7.

51. *Chicago Tribune,* Dec. 30, 1917, sec. A, 1. Samuels, *Magnificent Rube,* 203.

52. Corbett's account of the Brady treatment and how it contributed to a title fight against John L. Sullivan is found in Corbett, *Roar of the Crowd,* 176–201. Brady's development of Corbett's "highly valuable prestige" is found in Brady, 146–70. That Brady's showmanship served as a model for Kearns is acknowledged in Kearns and Fraley, *Million Dollar Gate,* 87, 118.

53. *Chicago Tribune,* Jan. 6, 1918, part 2, 3. Dempsey and Dempsey, *Dempsey,* 74.

54. *Chicago Tribune,* Jan. 15, 1918, 9. Kearns and Fraley, *Million Dollar Gate,* 87–88. Fleischer, *Jack Dempsey,* 107–38.

55. The claim is made by Roberts, *Manassa Mauler,* 41, on the basis of stories appearing in the *San Francisco Chronicle,* Mar. 18, 1918, 8; and Mar. 26, 1918, 9. Also, the *New York Tribune,* Mar. 26, 1918, 12. Rader points out in *American Sports,* 188, that Dempsey's career knockout record of 61.3 percent was "unexceptional," well below that of Floyd Patterson and Primo Carnera and only slightly above that of Tommy Burns, the man often considered the weakest of the heavyweight champions. See also Benjamin G. Rader, "Compensatory Sport Heroes: Ruth, Grange and Dempsey," *Journal of Popular Cul-*

ture 16 (Spring 1983): 11–22, where Rader argues that Dempsey "assisted the public in compensating for the passing of the traditional dream of success, the erosion of Victorian values and feelings of individual powerlessness."

56. The charge is made by Fleischer in *Heavyweight Championship*, 169–70.

57. *Milwaukee Journal*, Feb. 26, 1918, 12. Burrill, *Who's Who*, 28. Kearns and Fraley, *Million Dollar Gate*, 92. Dempsey and Dempsey, *Dempsey*, 76. Samuels, *Magnificent Rube*, 203–4.

58. Dempsey and Stearns, *Round by Round*, 148–49. See also *St. Paul Pioneer Press*, July 1, 1919, 9; and *Deseret Evening News*, July 1, 1919, 4, which reminded Salt Lake City readers that Willard's fall to Fulton in four rounds and Joe Cox in five showed that he was not "invincible."

59. *New York Times*, July 28, 1918, sec. 2, 5.

60. Dempsey and Dempsey, *Dempsey*, 85. On the sports hero as an "object of adulation," see Garry Smith, "The Sports Hero: An Endangered Species," *Quest* 19 (Jan. 1973): 59–70. Boxing promoters and fans have a storehouse of collective stereotypes from which they draw when casting the "image" of individual fighters. See R. Terry Furst, "Boxing Stereotypes versus the Culture of the Professional Boxer: A Sociological Decision" (master's thesis, Staten Island Community College, 1971). See also Franklin Robert Lloyd, "Big Men and Regular Fellows: Popular Heroes of the 1920's" (Ph.D. diss., Univ. of Iowa, 1975). Lloyd sees interwar heroes as mediators of cultural tensions. For a contemporary account of Dempsey as "the greatest individual drawing card in the history of sport," see Grantland Rice, "The Golden Fleece," *Collier's*, Sept. 17, 1927, 9, 44.

61. Kearns and Fraley, *Million Dollar Gate*, 98–102. Dempsey and Dempsey, *Dempsey*, 90–92. Dempsey was simply following in Willard's theatrical footsteps. Fleischer notes in *The Heavyweight Championship*, 164–65, that Willard had incorporated shortly after winning the title in an effort to freeze out the speculators who had backed him from gaining the profits from his circus and theatrical engagements.

62. Emerson's observation is cited in Dixon Wecter, *The Hero in America: A Chronicle of Hero Worship* (New York: Charles Scribner's Sons, 1941), 476–91. On the nature of hero worship and the search for "great men" in the interwar era, see Orrin E. Klapp, "Hero Worship in America," *American Sociological Review* 14 (Feb. 1949): 53–62; and Orrin E. Klapp, "The Folk Hero," *Journal of American Folklore* 62 (Jan.–Mar. 1949): 17–25.

63. Bruce Bliven, "Worshiping the American Hero," in *America as Americans See It*, ed. Fred J. Ringel (New York: Literary Guild, 1932), 123–29. Roderick Nash, *The Call of the Wild: 1900–1916* (New York: George Braziller, 1970), 1–15. Ralph A. Luce, Jr., "From Hero to Robot: Masculinity in America—Stereotype and Reality," *Psychoanalytic Review* 54 (1967): 53–74.

64. Gallico, *Golden People*, 14.

CHAPTER 2
TEX AND TOLEDO

1. For conflicting versions of the Biltmore meeting between Kearns and Rickard, see Charles Samuels, *The Magnificent Rube: The Life and Gaudy Times of Tex Rickard* (New York: McGraw-Hill, 1957), 205. Mrs. Tex Rickard and Arch Obeler, *Everything Happened to Him: The Story of Tex Rickard* (New York: Frederick A. Stokes, 1936), 270. Jack Kearns and Oscar Fraley, *The Million Dollar Gate* (New York: Macmillan, 1966), 102–10. Jack Dempsey and Barbara Piatelli Dempsey, *Dempsey* (New York: Harper & Row, 1977), 92–95. For background on John "Muggsy" McGraw, and his passion for publicity, baseball, and brawling, see Charles C. Alexander, *John McGraw* (New York: Viking, 1988).

2. See the obituary for Jess Willard in *New York Times*, Dec. 16, 1968, 47. Also, Bob Burrill, *Who's Who in Boxing* (New Rochelle, N.Y.: Arlington House, 1974), 200–201. On Willard's unpopularity and lack of box office appeal, see W. O. McGeehan, "Battles of the Century," in *Sport U.S.A.: The Best from the Saturday Evening Post*, ed. Harry T. Paxton (New York: Thomas Nelson & Sons, 1961), 121. Tim Cohane, *Bypaths of Glory: A Sportswriter Looks Back* (New York: Harper & Row, 1963), 80–82. Randy Roberts, *Jack Dempsey: The Manassa Mauler* (Baton Rouge: Louisiana State Univ. Press, 1979), 50–52. Alexander Johnston, *Ten and Out! The Complete Story of the Prize Ring in America* (New York: Ives Washburn, 1927), 204. Nat Fleischer, *Fifty Years at Ringside* (New York: Fleet Publishing, 1958), 113–15. Nat Fleischer, *The Heavyweight Championship: An Informal History of Heavyweight Boxing from 1719 to the Present Day* (New York: G. Putnam's Sons, 1949), 155–68. Stanley Weston, *The Heavyweight Champions* (New York: Ace Books, 1976), 86–92.

3. Grantland Rice, *The Tumult and the Shouting* (New York: A. S. Barnes, 1954), 134–37. Joe Humphreys, "The Rickard I Knew," *Collier's*, Nov. 9, 1929, 28, 59–60. Jack Kofoed, "The Master of Ballyhoo," *North American Review*, Mar. 1929, 282–86.

4. James Dawson, "Boxing," in *Sport's Golden Age: A Close-Up of the Fabulous Twenties*, ed. Allison Danzig and Peter Brandwein (Freeport, N.Y.: Books for Libraries, 1948), 38–43. Paul Gallico, *The Golden People* (Garden City, N.Y.: Doubleday, 1965), 179–95. McGeehan, "Battles," 121–22.

5. For appreciations of Rickard, see *New York Times*, Jan. 7, 1929, 1, 24, 28. Will Rogers observed that "the world is full of men who do big things, but when you meet 'em they are not outstanding personalities. Pretty near everybody is almost alike. Tex Rickard was a character. I wouldn't a missed knowing him for anything."

6. Samuels, *Magnificent Rube,* 10–13. Rickard and Obeler, *Everything Happened,* 5–13. *New York Times,* Jan. 7, 1929, 24. On the role of wilderness in American mythology, see Roderick Nash, *Wilderness and the American Mind* (New Haven: Yale Univ. Press, 1982), 44–66. On the role of the saloon in frontier society, see Elliott West, *The Saloon on the Rocky Mountain Mining Frontier* (Lincoln: Univ. of Nebraska Press, 1979), 130–49.

7. On the idealization of cowboy culture, see Will James, "Cowboy and Dude Ranches," in *America as Americans See It,* ed. Fred J. Ringel (New York: The Literary Guild, 1932), 61–64. For background, see John Marvin Hunter, *The Trail Drivers of Texas* (Nashville: Cokesburg Press, 1925); and Emerson Hough, *The Story of the Cowboy* (New York: D. Appleton, 1931), 7. Rickard and Obeler, *Everything Happened,* 15–19, 26–28, 39–40. Samuels, *Magnificent Rube,* 17–18. Gallico, *Golden People,* 184. *New York Times,* Jan. 7, 1929, 24. Burrill, *Who's Who,* 162–63.

8. *New York Times,* Jan. 7, 1929, 22, 24, 28, 31; and Jan. 8, 1929, 36.

9. *New York Times,* Jan. 8, 1929, 36. Samuels, *Magnificent Rube,* 52–62. Dawson, "Boxing," 42–43. McGeehan, "Battles," 118. Paul Gallico, *Farewell to Sport* (New York: Knopf, 1940), 92–94. For background on Wilson Mizner, see Addison Mizner, *The Many Mizners* (New York: Sears Publishing, 1932). For Rex Beach's experiences during the Klondike Gold Rush, see Rex Beach, *Personal Exposures* (New York: Harper & Brothers, 1940). For background, see Beach's frontier trilogy, *The Spoilers* (New York: Harper, 1906); *The Silver Horde* (New York: Harper, 1907); and *The Barrier* (New York: Harper, 1908).

10. Samuels, *Magnificent Rube,* 66–74. Kofoed, "Master of Ballyhoo," 282–83. Jack Dempsey, Bob Considine, and Bill Slocum, *Dempsey: By the Man Himself* (New York: Simon & Schuster, 1960), 203–5. For background on the Klondike Gold Rush, see A. S. Harris, *Alaska and the Klondike Goldfields* (Chicago: Monroe Book Company, 1897); Joseph Ladue, *Klondike Facts* (New York: American Technical Book Company, 1897); Ernest Ingersoll, *In Richest Alaska and the Goldfields of the Klondike* (Chicago: The Dominion Company, 1897); Tappan Adney, *The Klondike Stampede* (New York: Harper & Brothers, 1900); and Russell R. Bankson, *The Klondike Nugget* (Caldwell, Idaho: Caxton Printers, 1935).

11. *New York Times,* Jan. 7, 1929, 24. Dempsey, Considine and Slocum, *Dempsey: Himself,* 204–5. Samuels, *Magnificent Rube,* 76–81. Nat Fleischer, *Jack Dempsey* (New Rochelle, N.Y.: Arlington House, 1972), 64–66. A. J. Liebling, *The Sweet Science* (New York: Viking Press, 1956), 1–4.

12. After his loss to Bob Fitzsimmons in 1897, Gentleman Jim turned to baseball. Though a miserable hitter, Corbett was a fine fielder and solid first baseman. See William A. Brady, *Showman* (New York: E. P. Dutton 1937), 182–87.

13. *San Francisco Examiner,* Jan. 7, 1929, 1. *Seattle Post-Intelligencer,* Jan. 7, 1929, 1. Rickard and Obeler, *Everything Happened,* 194. For background on the Nevada gold rush, see Writers Project of the Works Progress Administration in the State of Nevada, sponsored by Jeanne Elizabeth Wier, Nevada State Historical Society, *Nevada: A Guide to the Silver State* (Portland, Oreg.: Binfords and Mort, 1940); and Dan De Quille, *An Authentic Account of the Discovery, History and Working of the World Renowned Comstock Lode of Nev., Including Present Condition of Various Mines Situated Theron, Sketches of the Most Prominent Men Interested in Them, Incidents and Adventures Connected with Mining, the Indians and the Country, Amusing Stories, Experiences, Anecdotes and a Full Exposition of the Production of Pure Silver* (New York: Knopf, 1947).

14. James Chinello, "The Great Goldfield Foul," *Westways* 68 (Sept. 1976): 27–29. Rickard and Obeler, *Everything Happened,* 197–201. Joseph Durso, *Madison Square Garden: One Hundred Years of History* (New York: Simon & Schuster, 1979), 105–6. Dempsey, Considine and Slocum, *Dempsey: Himself,* 205.

15. See page-one accounts of the fight in the *San Francisco Examiner,* Sept. 4, 1906; the *New Orleans Picayune,* Sept. 4, 1906; and the *New York Journal,* Sept. 4, 1906. Also, Chinello, "Goldfield Foul," 30, 88. For background, see Edwin Emery, *The Press and America: An Interpretative History* (Englewood Cliffs, N.J.: Prentice-Hall, 1962), 425–26; and George Everett, "The Age of New Journalism, 1883–1900," in *The Media in America: A History,* ed. William David Sloan, James G. Stovall, and James D. Startt (Worthington, Ohio: Publishing Horizons, 1989), 230–31.

16. Rickard and Obeler, *Everything Happened,* 201, 209. John Lardner, *White Hopes and Other Tigers* (Philadelphia: J. B. Lippincott, 1947), 13–19. Lester Bromberg, *Boxing's Unforgettable Fights* (New York: Ronald Press, 1962), 61–65. John Durant, *The Heavyweight Champions* (New York: Hastings House, 1971), 57–64. Randy Roberts, *Papa Jack: Jack Johnson and the Era of White Hopes* (New York: Free Press, 1983), 69. Al-Tony Gilmore, *Bad Nigger! The National Impact of Jack Johnson* (Port Washington, N.Y.: National Univ. Publications, 1975), 32.

17. For a discussion of racial tensions on the eve of the Jeffries-Johnson fight, see John W. Blassingame's introduction to Gilmore, *Bad Nigger,* 3–7; and Roberts, *Papa Jack,* 90–104. On race and ethnicity in boxing, see William M. Kramer and Norton B. Stern, "San Francisco's Fighting Jew," *California Historical Quarterly* 53 (1974): 333–45; R. Terry Furst, "Boxing Stereotypes Versus the Culture of the Professional Boxer: A Sociological Decision" (master's thesis, Staten Island Community College, 1971); S. Kirson Weinberg and Henry Arond, "The Occupational Culture of the Boxer," *American Journal of Sociology* 57 (Mar. 1952): 460–69; Thomas M. Croak, "The Professionalization of Prizefighting: Pittsburgh at the Turn of the Century," *Western Pennsylvania*

Historical Magazine 62 (Oct. 1979): 333–43; Stephen Hardy, *How Boston Played: Sport, Recreation, and Community, 1865–1915* (Boston: Northeastern Univ. Press, 1982), 19–20, 168–79; and Steven A. Riess, *City Games: The Evolution of American Urban Society and the Rise of Sports* (Urbana: Univ. of Illinois Press, 1989), 115–17, 172–77.

18. Roberts, *Papa Jack*, 90–91. *Leadville* (Colo.) *Evening Journal*, May 17, 1910, 1. Hardy, *Boston Played*, 177.

19. *San Francisco Examiner*, June 16, 1910, 1. Walter Bean, *Boss Reuf's San Francisco* (Berkeley: Univ. of California Press, 1952), 85–88. *Sacramento Bee*, June 16, 1910, 1. *Denver Post*, June 27, 1910, 1. Rickard's presumed personal "suffering" can be seen in *Leadville* (Colo.) *Evening Journal*, June 29, 1910, 1. For Jeffries's version of events, see Hugh S. Fullerton, *Two-Fisted Jeff* (Chicago: Consolidated, 1929). Compare to Jack Johnson, *Jack Johnson in the Ring and Out* (Chicago: National Sports Publishing, 1927), 170–71. Roberts, *Papa Jack*, 94–95. Fleischer, *Heavyweight Championship*, 145–54.

20. *Rocky Mountain News*, July 5, 1910, 1. *New York Times*, July 5, 1910, 1. *Chicago Tribune*, July 5, 1910, 1. *St. Louis Post-Dispatch*, July 5, 1910, 1. *Kansas City Star*, July 5, 1910, 1–2.

21. *Indianapolis Star*, July 7, 1910, 1. *New Orleans Picayune*, July 7, 1910, 1. *Atlanta Constitution*, July 7, 1910, 1; and July 8, 1910, 1. *Seattle Post-Intelligencer*, July 7, 1910, 1. *Boston Globe*, July 8, 1910. *Boston Evening Transcript*, July 9, 1910, 1.

22. Gilmore, *Bad Nigger*, 4–5. Hardy, *Boston Played*, 178–79. *Leadville* (Colo.) *Evening Journal*, July 14, 1910, 1. *New York Times*, Jan. 7 1929, 24. Roberts, *Papa Jack*, 110–13.

23. Rickard and Obeler, *Everything Happened*, 209. Samuels, *Magnificent Rube*, 150–51. Kearns and Fraley, *Million Dollar Gate*, 106–7. Dempsey, Considine, and Slocum, *Dempsey: Himself*, 206.

24. Johnson insisted he had thrown the fight with Willard for a payoff and a government pledge to allow him to return to the United States, where he had been under indictment for violation of the Mann Act. See *New York Times*, Apr. 6, 1915, 1; and Dec. 16, 1968, 47. *Chicago Tribune*, Apr. 6, 1915, 1. *Miami News*, Apr. 6, 1915, 1. Johnson, *Jack Johnson*, 23–26. Roberts, *Papa Jack*, 229–30. Gilmore, *Bad Nigger*, 142–46.

25. *New York Times*, Mar. 26, 1916, 1. *Chicago Tribune*, Mar. 26, 1916, 1. Samuels, *Magnificent Rube*, 186–87. Burrill, *Who's Who*, 200–201. Durso, *Madison Square Garden: One Hundred Years*, 108. Barney Nagler, "Boxing," in *Madison Square Garden: A Century of Sport and Spectacle on the World's Most Versatile Stage*, ed. Zander Hollander (New York: Hawthorn Publishers, 1973), 95–99. *New York Journal*, Mar. 26, 1916, 1.

26. Nagler, "Boxing," 96–97. Durso, *Madison Square Garden: One Hun-*

dred Years, 114–15. Humphreys, "Rickard I Knew," 28, 59–60. Dawson, "Boxing," 46–49.

27. Rickard and Obeler, *Everything Happened,* 271. Kofoed, "Ballyhoo," 284. Gallico, *Farewell to Sport,* 189.

28. Frederic L. Paxson, "The Rise of Sport," *The Mississippi Valley Historical Review* 4 (Sept. 1917): 143–68. See also Preston William Slosson, *The Great Crusade and After, 1914–1928* (New York: Macmillan, 1930), 270–86.

29. Ring Lardner, Jr., *The Lardners: My Family Remembered* (New York: Harper & Row, 1973), 95–96. Lardner's "Prohibition Blues," written for the Broadway show *Ladies First* is more to the point. "I've had news that's bad news about my best pal. His name is Old Man Alcohol but I call him Al. Goodbye forever to my old friend 'Booze.' Doggone, I've got the Prohibition Blues." See also Walter R. Patrick, *Ring Lardner* (New York: Twayne Publishers, 1963), 25–26. Otto Friedrich, *Ring Lardner* (Minneapolis: Univ. of Minnesota Press, 1965), 9–10. Jonathan Yardley, *Ring: A Biography of Ring Lardner* (New York: Random House, 1977), 209–11.

30. *New York Tribune,* July 1, 1919, 15. *New York Times,* June 17, 1919, 17. See also Rice, *Tumult and Shouting,* 118, 134. Roberts, *Manassa Mauler,* 58–59. Emery, *The Press in America,* 598.

31. Stanley Walker, *City Editor* (New York: Frederick A. Stokes, 1934), 123–24. Stanley Woodward, *Sports Page* (New York: Simon & Schuster, 1949), 60–61. Grantland Rice, "Never Another Jones," in *Sport U.S.A.,* 211–16. Grantland Rice, "The Golden Panorama," in *Sport's Golden Decade,* ed. Allison Danzing and Peter Brandwein, 1–7. Warren Susman, "Piety, Profits, and Play: The 1920s," in *Men, Women, and Issues in American History,* ed. Howard H. Quint and Milton Cantor (Homewood, Ill.: Dorsey Press, 1975), vol. 2: 211–12. Frederick W. Cozens and Florence Scovil Stumpf, "The Sports Page," in *Sport and Society: An Anthology,* ed. John T. Talamini and Charles H. Page (Boston: Little, Brown & Co., 1973), 427–31.

32. Ring Lardner, "Sport and Play," in *Civilization in the United States: An Inquiry by Thirty Americans,* ed. Harold E. Stearns (New York: Harcourt, Brace, 1922), 459. Ring Lardner, "The Battle of the Century," *Saturday Evening Post,* Oct. 29, 1921, 12, 84–86. For other instances of Lardner's "aw nuts" brand of sports reporting, see Ring W. Lardner, *You Know Me Al* (New York: George H. Doran, 1916); *Gullible's Travels* (Indianapolis: Bobbs-Merrill, 1917); *The Real Dope* (Indianapolis: Bobbs-Merrill, 1919); "A Variety of Sports," 81–114, and "A Prize Fight," 148–78, in *First and Last* (New York: Charles Scribner's Sons, 1934); and "Champion," 239–57, and "A World's Serious," 578–87, in *The Ring Lardner Reader,* ed. Maxwell Geismar (New York: Charles Scribner's Sons, 1963).

33. *New York Times,* July 4, 1919, 6. *Chicago Tribune,* July 3, 1919, 21.

34. Lardner, *The Lardners,* 96. *Chicago Tribune,* July 4, 1919, 9.

35. *Rocky Mountain News,* July 3, 1919, 11; and July 4, 1919, 1, 2. *Chicago Tribune,* July 2, 1919, 19; and July 4, 1919, 8. *St. Paul Pioneer Press,* July 4, 1919, 8.

36. On Toledo's history as contested prize and progressive city, see Tana Moshier Porter, *Toledo Profile: A Sesquicentennial History* (Toledo: Toledo Sesquicentennial Commission, 1987); and Morgan Barclay and Charles N. Glaab, *Toledo: Gateway to the Great Lakes* (Tulsa, Okla.: Heritage Press, 1982). For Whitlock's platform providing for the initiative, referendum, recall, and direct nominations, see Brand Whitlock, *On the Enforcement of Law in Cities* (Indianapolis: Bobbs-Merrill, 1913); and Brand Whitlock, *Forty Years of It: An Autobiography* (New York: D. Appleton. 1920).

37. There seems little doubt that Rickard offered Cox a bribe to support the fight, although there is some uncertainty where the payoff was offered and who was present. In his autobiography, Cox remembers it as being at a hotel in New York City. Jack Kearns insists it was in Columbus. Kearns gives himself a leading role in smoothing relations between Cox and Rickard. Cox makes no mention of Kearns being present. See James M. Cox, *Journey Through My Years* (New York: Simon & Schuster, 1946), 215–16. Also, Kearns and Fraley, *Million Dollar Gate,* 112–14 and Dempsey and Dempsey, *Dempsey,* 102.

38. Cox had been a reporter and editor on the *Dayton Daily News* before purchasing the paper in 1898 at the age of twenty-eight. For his carefully crafted reputation as progressive publisher, see Emery, *Press in America,* 500, 625, 678, 680–81, 756. See also "James Middleton Cox," *Encyclopedia Americana* (New York: Americana Corporation, 1963), vol. 13: 139–40. *Toledo Blade,* May 6, 1919, 1. *New York Times,* May 6, 1919, 17. Cox, *Journey,* 216.

39. See *New York Times,* Jan. 25, 1919, 8. Dawson, "Boxing," 51. William Cunningham, "No Wonder They Want to Fight!" *Collier's* 74, Sept. 13, 1924, 14, 45. Burrill, *Who's Who,* 200–201. Roberts, *Manassa Mauler,* 50–53. See also Dempsey and Dempsey, *Dempsey,* 102–11. *Rocky Mountain News,* July 3, 1919, 1, 4, 11. *Deseret News* (Salt Lake City), July 2, 1919, 4. *St. Paul Pioneer Press,* July 4, 1919, 8. *Chicago Tribune,* July 2, 1919, 19.

40. Dawson, "Boxing," 49–50. Dempsey and Dempsey, *Dempsey,* 97–98. *New York Times,* Feb. 11, 1919, 8. Kearns and Fraley, *Million Dollar Gate,* 110.

41. Dawson, "Boxing," 50–51. Fleischer, *Jack Dempsey,* 66–69. Dempsey and Dempsey, *Dempsey,* 97–99. Kearns and Fraley, *Million Dollar Gate,* 110–12. Samuels, *Magnificent Rube,* 209.

42. *New York Times,* June 17, 1919, 17; June 18, 1919, 21; June 19, 1919, 21; June 20, 1919, 14; June 21, 1919, 13; and June 22, 1919, 21. *Chicago Tribune,* June 16, 1919, 21; June 17, 1919, 19; June 18, 1919, 19; June 19, 1919, 19; June 20, 1919, 19; and July 2, 1919, 13.

43. *New York Times,* July 4, 1919, 6. Cohane, *Bypaths of Glory,* 80–81. Dempsey and Dempsey, *Dempsey,* 17–18. Kearns and Fraley, *Million Dollar Gate,* 10–19. *San Francisco Chronicle,* July 3, 1919, 8. *Chicago Daily News,* July 2, 1919, 2.

44. Kearns and Fraley, *Million Dollar Gate,* 12. Dempsey and Dempsey, *Dempsey,* 109. Samuels, *Magnificent Rube,* 210–11.

45. *New York Times,* June 25, 1919, 23; and June 29, 1919, 23. *Chicago Tribune,* June 24, 1919, 19. *Rocky Mountain News,* July 3, 1919, 11. *Kansas City Times,* July 1, 1919, 16. *St. Paul Pioneer Press,* July 1, 1919, 9. *Salt Lake Tribune,* July 2, 1919, 4.

46. *Chicago Tribune,* June 22, 1919, sec. A, 1; and June 29, 1919, sec. A, 1. *St. Paul Pioneer Press,* June 22, 1919, sec. 4, 8; and June 29, 1919, sec. 4, 8.

47. *New York Times,* July 2, 1919, 14; July 3, 1919, 10; July 4, 1919, 1 and 6; and July 5, 1919, 5. Samuels, *Magnificent Rube,* 211. *Chicago Tribune,* June 30, 1919, 19; July 1, 1919, 17; and July 3, 1919, 21.

48. Dempsey and Dempsey, *Dempsey,* 114–15. *New York Times,* July 4, 1919, 6. *Denver Morning Telegram,* July 4, 1919, 1,8.

49. Dempsey and Stearns, *Round by Round,* 178–80. Jack Dempsey and Barbara Piatelli Dempsey, "The Destruction of a Giant: How I Beat Jess Willard," *American Heritage,* Apr. 1977, 76–81. Kearns and Fraley, *Million Dollar Gate,* 14. *Denver Post,* July 5, 1919, 8. *Chicago Tribune,* July 5, 1919, 1.

50. "Saturday Sports Showcase: Fifteen Greatest Rounds, Dempsey vs. Willard, July 4, 1919," part 3, TV documentary, NBC, May 12, 1990. Dempsey and Piatelli, "The Destruction of a Giant," 81–82. Samuels, *Magnificent Rube,* 215–16. *Chicago Herald & Examiner,* July 5, 1919, 1, 8.

51. *Denver Post,* July 5, 1919, 8. The *Post* was aiming its barb not only at Bat Masterson and the *Telegram,* but also at the *Rocky Mountain News,* whose E. W. "Dick" Dickerson was certain Willard was "in the pink" and would make short work of Dempsey. See *Rocky Mountain News,* July 3, 1919, 11.

52. *New York American,* July 5, 1919, 1.

53. On Dempsey's friendship with Runyon and Fowler, see Dempsey and Dempsey, "The Destruction of a Giant," 72, 74–75, 77. Dempsey and Dempsey, *Dempsey,* 42–43, 47–48, 102–3, 115, 120, 142, 144, 153, 156, 172, 174–76, 216, 224. Dempsey notes that he "loved Fowler like a brother." Dempsey believed the two "understood each other perfectly." Runyon was "an invaluable friend," who had won his confidence with patient listening. Dempsey claims the exclusives he gave the *American* caused other sportswriters to "deeply resent" Runyon and Fowler, but there is little evidence of that. See interviews with Marshall Hunt and John Kiernan in *No Cheering in the Press Box,* ed. Jerome Holtzman (New York: Holt, Rinehart and Winston, 1974), 29, 43–44. Gallico, *Golden People,* 294. Gallico considered Runyon "the most accurate" of the interwar sportswriters.

Runyon's attitude toward sports writing can be seen in Damon Runyon, "The Crowd Was—," in *Sport U.S.A.: The Best from the Saturday Evening Post,* ed. Harry T. Paxton (New York: Thomas Nelson & Sons, 1961), 90–98; and in Gene Fowler, *Skyline: A Reporter's Reminiscence of the 1920's* (New York: Viking, 1961), 28–31, 44–51, 273–84. Fowler observes that "Runyon's longtime search for a heavyweight of championship potential became a joke among sports writers. He did not like this." Most of Runyon's discoveries, Fowler notes, "ate like lions and fought like lambs."

54. Dempsey and Stearns, *Round by Round,* 185. Dempsey and Dempsey, *Dempsey,* 121. It is interesting to note that in these accounts of the fight, written thirty-seven years apart, Dempsey remembers and emphasizes the incident.

CHAPTER 3
TUNNEY, DEMPSEY, SPORTS WRITERS, AND READERS

1. Jack Dempsey and Barbara Piatelli Dempsey, *Dempsey* (New York: Harper & Row, 1977), 124–25. Rex Lardner, *The Legendary Champions* (New York: American Heritage Press, 1972), 258. Gene Tunney, *A Man Must Fight* (Boston: Houghton Mifflin, 1932), 100–101. Gene Tunney, "My Fights with Jack Dempsey," in *The Aspirin Age,* ed. Isabel Leighton (New York: Simon & Schuster, 1949), 152–53. My thanks to Bill Caldwell, librarian for the *Joplin Globe and News Herald,* in Joplin, Mo., for helping to fix McReynolds' identity through American Legion records and his employment with the *Globe.*

2. Paul Gallico, *Farewell to Sport* (New York: Knopf, 1940), 81–90.

3. For the perception of Tunney as affected challenger, see Paul Gallico, *The Golden People* (New York: Doubleday, 1965), 95–110. John Lardner, *White Hopes and Other Tigers* (Philadelphia: J. B. Lippincott, 1951), 168–71. Nat Fleischer, *The Heavyweight Championship: An Informal History of Heavyweight Boxing from 1719 to the Present Day* (New York: G. Putnam's Sons, 1949), 183–85. Ring Lardner, Jr., *The Lardners: My Family Remembered* (New York: Harper & Row, 1976), 148–49. Grantland Rice, *The Tumult and the Shouting* (New York: A. S. Barnes, 1954), 145.

4. Edwin Emery, *The Press and America: An Interpretative History of Journalism* (Englewood Cliffs, N.J.: Prentice-Hall, 1962), 389. For background on Pulitzer's development of the *World,* see James W. Barrett, *Joseph Pulitzer and His World* (New York: Vanguard Press, 1941); Don C. Seitz, *Joseph Pulitzer: His Life and Letters* (New York: Simon & Schuster, 1924); William Inglis, "An Intimate View of Joseph Pulitzer," *Harper's,* Nov. 11, 1911, 7; and Arthur Brisbane, "Joseph Pulitzer," *Cosmopolitan,* May 1902, 51.

5. Tunney, *Fight,* 7–8. Robert Edgren, "The Modern Gladiator," *Outing,* Mar. 1903, 298–306. *New York Evening World,* Sept. 8, 1892, 1.

6. Gene Tunney, *Arms for Living* (New York: Wildred Funk, 1941), 11–19. James J. Corbett, *The Roar of the Crowd: The True Tale of the Rise and Fall of a Champion* (New York: G. P. Putnam's Sons, 1925), 195–206. "Corbett to Tunney on 'How to Win the Mob,'" *Literary Digest,* Jan. 14, 1928, 55–60. James Dawson, "Boxing," in *Sport's Golden Decade: A Close-up of the Fabulous Twenties,* ed. Allison Danzig and Peter Brandwein (Freeport, N.Y.: Books for Libraries Press, 1948), 72–73. Fleischer, *Heavyweight Championship,* 183–93.

7. Tunney, *Arms for Living,* 12–15. Tim Cohane, *Bypaths of Glory: A Sportswriter Looks Back* (New York: Harper & Row, 1963), 85–87. Ed Van Every, *The Life of Gene Tunney: The Fighting Marine* (New York: Dell Publishing, 1927), 2–6. Tunney, *Fight,* 9–10. For background on the use of physical education as a teaching tool for New York City and Progressive-era America, see Stephen Hardy and Alan G. Ingham, "Games, Structures, and Agency: Historians on the American Play Movement," *Journal of Social History* 17 (Winter 1983): 285–301. Richard Knapp, "The National Recreation Association, 1906–1950," *Parks and Recreation* 7 (Aug. 1972): 48–49. Richard Gruneau, "Freedom and Constraint: The Paradoxes of Play, Games, and Sports," *Journal of Sport History* 7 (Winter 1980): 68–86. Benjamin G. Rader, "The Recapitulation Theory of Play: Motor Behaviour, Moral Reflexes and Manly Attitudes in Urban America, 1880–1920," in *Manliness and Morality: Middle Class Masculinity in Britain and America, 1800–1940,* ed. J. A. Mangan and James Walvin (Manchester: Manchester Univ. Press, 1987), 123–34.

For the physical education and recreation movement as student socializer, see Cary Goodman, *Choosing Sides: Playgrounds and Street Life on the Lower East Side* (New York: Schocken Books, 1979); Dominick Cavallo, *Muscles and Morals: Organized Playgrounds and Urban Reform, 1880–1920* (Philadelphia: Univ. of Pennsylvania Press, 1981); and Guy Lewis, "Sport, Youth Culture and Conventionality, 1920–1970," *Journal of Sport History* 4 (Summer 1977): 129–32.

8. Nat Fleischer, *Gene Tunney: The Enigma of the Ring* (New York: The Ring, 1931), 2–3. Tunney, *Arms,* 11–12. Tunney, *Fight,* 12.

9. Tunney, "My Fights," 154, 162. Lardner, *The Lardners,* 251–52. See also Tunney's introduction to Alexander Johnston, *Ten and Out: The Complete Story of the Prize Ring* (New York: Ives Washburn, 1927). On the relationship of sports to "self-culture" in Progressive-era America, see Joseph F. Kett, *Rites of Passage: Adolescence in America, 1790 to the Present* (New York: Basic Books, 1978), 245–64; and Michael Oriard, *Reading Football: How the Popular Press Created an American Spectacle* (Chapel Hill: Univ. of North Carolina Press, 1993), 157–62. On individual success and its relationship to manhood, see Peter N. Stearns, *Be a Man! Males in Modern Society* (New York: Holmes and Meier, 1990), 155–65. On individual success and its relationship to community, see John G. Cawelti, *Apostles of the Self-Made Man* (Chicago: Univ. of Chicago Press, 1965), 239–48.

For contemporary accounts on the cultivation of self-culture through the crucible of sports, see Maurice Thompson, "Vigorous Men, a Vigorous Nation," *Independent*, Sept. 1, 1898, 609–11. "The Value of College Athletics," *Outlook*, Jan. 27, 1906, 151–52. Walter Camp, "What Are Athletics Good For?" *Outing*, Dec. 1913, 259–72. Frederic Paxson, "The Rise of Sport," *Mississippi Valley Historical Review* 4 (Sept. 1917): 143–68.

10. Tunney, *Arms*, 15–18. Tunney, *Fight*, 13–14. Lardner, *The Lardners*, 148–49. Benny Green, *Shaw's Champions: George Bernard Shaw and Prizefighting from Cashel Byron to Gene Tunney* (London: Elm Tree Books, 1978), 138, 153–55. Mel Heimer, *The Long Count* (New York: Atheneum, 1969), 41–42. For writings on Frank Merriwell as ideal athletic type, see Burt L. Standish, *Frank Merriwell at Yale* (Philadelphia: David McKay, 1903), 257–68, 371–83; and Burt L. Standish, *Frank Merriwell's 'Father': An Autobiography* (Norman: Univ. of Oklahoma Press, 1964), 176–81. Also, George Santayana, "A Glimpse at Yale," in *George Santayana's America: Essays on Literature and Culture*, ed. James Ballowe (Urbana: Univ. of Illinois Press, 1967), 54–55. Robert Boyle, *Sport: Mirror of American Life* (Boston: Little, Brown & Co., 1963), 242–44. Robert J. Higgs, "Yale and the Heroic Ideal, Gotterdammerung and the Palingenesis, 1865–1914," in Mangan and Walvin, *Manliness and Morality*, 160–75. Christian Messenger, "Tom Buchanan and the Demise of the Ivy League Athletic Hero," in *Journal of Popular Culture* 8 (1974): 402–10. Christian K. Messenger, *Sport and the Spirit of Play in American Fiction: Hawthorne to Faulkner* (New York: Columbia Univ. Press, 1981), 180–207. Gregory S. Sojka, "Evolution of the Student-Athlete in America," *Journal of Popular Culture* 16 (Spring 1983): 55–67.

11. On Tunney's affinity for Depew's world view, see *New York Daily News*, Sept. 9, 1926, 31. For the great Republican's view of youth culture, the cultivation of the individual through athletics and his civic responsibility, see Chauncey M. Depew, *My Memories of Eighty Years* (New York: Scribner's, 1922), 5–6, 225–27, 313–32, 401–9. John Denison Champlin, ed., *Orations, Addresses and Speeches of Chauncey M. Depew* (New York: Depew Trust, 1910), vol. 3: 16, 25–26, 36, 58; vol. 4: 285, 302–5; vol. 5: 23–25, 215–17.

12. Tunney's attitude toward self-improvement and athletics as a means of moneymaking is expressed in his interview with *New York Daily News* reporter Jack Farrell, on Sept. 8, 1926, 27. For background on the history of Greenwich Village and its bohemian community, see Henry Wisham Lanier, *Greenwich Village Today and Yesterday* (New York: Harper, 1949); and Fred W. McDarrah, *Greenwich Village* (New York: Corinth Books, 1963). For a contemporary account, see Sarah M. Lockwood, *New York: Not So Little and Not So Old* (Garden City, N.Y.: Doubleday, 1926).

13. *New York Times*, Nov. 8, 1978, 22. *Chicago Tribune*, Nov. 8, 1978, 1, 3. Tunney, *Arms*, 19–20. *New York Daily News*, Sept. 10, 1926, 45.

14. For background on Sharkey's, see Marianne Dozema, *George Bellows and Urban America* (New Haven: Yale Univ. Press, 1992), 80. Dozema notes that the gentry who frequented Sharkey's were encouraged to leave all "noble notions of sportsmanship behind." See also Margaret Breuning, "Bellows in National Gallery," *Art Digest*, Jan. 1, 1945, 22. Emma L. Bellows, *The Paintings of George Bellows* (New York: Knopf, 1929); and Peyton Boswell, Jr., *George Bellows* (New York: Crown Publishers, 1942).

15. *New York Daily News*, Sept. 11, 1926, 24. Fleischer, *Tunney*, 5–6. Tunney, *Fight*, 48–51.

16. Guy Lewis, "World War I and the Emergence of Sport for the Masses," *The Maryland Historian* 4 (Fall 1973): 109–11. Raymond B. Fosdick, *Chronicle of a Generation: An Autobiography* (New York: Harper, 1958), 139–45. Daniel R. Beaver, *Newton D. Baker and the American War Effort, 1917–1919* (Lincoln: Univ. of Nebraska Press, 1966), 218–23. Douglas A. Noverr and Lawrence E. Ziewacz, *The Games They Played: Sports in American History, 1865–1980* (Chicago: Nelson-Hall, 1983), 68–70.

17. For the role of publicity in promoting the Inter-Allied Games, see Lewis, "Emergence of Sport," 112–14. On Pershing's many uses of publicity in furthering war aims and maintaining morale, see James G. Harbord, *The American Army in France, 1917–1919* (Boston: Little, Brown & Co., 1936); and John J. Pershing, *My Experiences in the World War* (Blue Ridge Summit, Pa.: Tab Books, 1989).

18. *New York Times*, July 6, 1919, 17. *Chicago Tribune*, July 7, 1919, 8. *Carbonate Weekly Chronicle* (Leadville, Colo.), July 7, 1919, 4. *Routt County Sentinel* (Steamboat Springs, Colo.), June 27, 1919, 6; and July 4, 1919, 6. *Denver Post*, July 5, 1919, 1. *Deseret News* (Salt Lake City), July 2, 1919, 4.

19. Tunney, *Arms*, 72–78, 82–83. Fleischer, *Tunney*, 6–7. Tunney, *Fight*, 98–99. Heimer, *Long Count*, 43–44.

20. For Tunney's troubles with the press and fight community, see *New York Daily News*, July 29, 1926, 32. Also, Rice, *Tumult and Shouting*, 140–55. Paul Gallico, *Golden People*, 91–111. Gallico, *Farewell* 81–90. Lardner, *White Hopes*, 168–85. William Inglis, *Champions Off Guard* (New York: Vanguard Press, 1932), 284–311.

21. Tunney, *Fight*, 100–104. Tunney, "My Fights," 159–61. Tunney, *Arms*, 101–3. Lardner, *Legendary Champions*, 257–58.

22. *New York Times*, July 3, 1921, 1–5. *Chicago Tribune*, July 3, 1921, 1, 2.

23. *New York Times*, Jan. 14, 1922, 13. *New York Daily News*, Jan. 14, 1922, 30. James Dawson, "Boxing," 67–68.

24. *New York Times*, May 24, 1922, 11. *New York Daily News*, May 24, 1922, 32. Bob Burrill, *Who's Who in Boxing* (New Rochelle, N.Y.: Arlington House, 1974), 84, 188. Trevor C. Wignall, *Ringside* (London: Hutchinson, 1941), 102–5.

25. *New York Times*, May 26, 1922, 13. *New York Daily News*, May 26, 1922, 37. Lardner, *Legendary Champions*, 255. Fleischer, *Heavyweight Championship*, 187–88.

26. Lardner, *Legendary Champions*, 255. Van Every, 215–16. Fleischer, *Tunney*, 15. Dawson, "Boxing," 67.

27. *New York Daily News*, Feb. 25, 1923, 26. *New York Times*, Dec. 24, 1923, 12. Fleischer, *Tunney*, 20–38.

28. *Cleveland Plain Dealer*, Sept. 18, 1924, 12. *St. Paul Pioneer Press*, Mar. 26, 1925, 9. John Durant, *The Heavyweight Champions* (New York: Hastings House, 1971), 76–77. Charles Samuels, *The Magnificent Rube: The Life and Gaudy Times of Tex Rickard* (New York: McGraw-Hill, 1957), 276–77.

29. *New York Journal*, June 27, 1924, 1. Fleischer, *Tunney*, 40–41.

30. *New York Daily News*, July 25, 1924, 37. *New York Times*, July 25, 1924, 15. Lardner, *Legendary Champions*, 259–60.

31. Tunney, *Fight*, 167–70. Lardner, *Legendary Champions*, 259. Fleischer, *Tunney*, 43–46.

32. *St. Paul Pioneer Press*, June 26, 1923, 12; June 27, 1923, 9; and July 5, 1923, 11. Burrill, *Who's Who*, 80. Dempsey and Dempsey, *Dempsey*, 153–55. *Chicago Tribune*, July 5, 1923, 1, 19.

33. *New York Times*, July 5, 1923, 13. *Chicago Tribune*, July 5, 1923, 21. *St. Paul Pioneer Press*, July 5, 1923, 9. *Denver Post*, July 5, 1923, 13.

34. *New York Times*, June 6, 1925, 11. *New York Daily News*, June 6, 1925, 35. Tunney, *Fight*, 170–76. Fleischer, *Tunney*, 47–52.

35. *New York Tribune*, Sept. 15, 1923, 1. *New York Times*, Sept. 15, 1923, 1. *New York Daily News*, Sept. 15, 1923, 1. Frank G. Menke, "Dempsey-Firpo," in *The Fireside Book of Boxing*, ed. W. C. Heinz (New York: Simon & Schuster, 1961), 292. Dempsey and Dempsey, *Dempsey*, 159–61.

36. *New York Times*, Sept. 14, 1923, 2. *New York Tribune*, Sept. 14, 1923, 10. *New York Daily News*, Sept. 14, 1923, 1, 24. *Chicago Tribune*, Sept. 14, 1923, 1, 9. Randy Roberts, *Jack Dempsey: The Manassa Mauler* (Baton Rouge: Louisiana State Univ. Press, 1979), 184–89.

37. "The 'Big Business' of Prize Fighting," *Literary Digest*, Oct. 13, 1923, 60–62. See the Sept. 14, 1923 editions of the *Brooklyn Eagle* and *New York World* for their front-page coverage of the Dempsey-Firpo fight.

38. William Cunningham, "No Wonder They Want to Fight!" *Collier's*, Sept. 13, 1924, 14. Bruce Bliven, "Arc Lights and Blood: Ringside Notes at the Dempsey-Firpo Fight," *New Republic*, Sept. 26, 1923, 115. John R. Tunis, "The Business of American Sports," in *America as Americans See It*, ed. Fred J. Ringel (New York: Literary Guild, 1932), 118–22.

39. See *San Francisco Chronicle*, Jan. 23, 1920, 11. For the running battle between Maxine Cates and Jack Kearns in the pages of the *Chronicle*, see *San*

Francisco Chronicle, Jan. 24, 1920, 9; Jan. 25, 1920, 6; and Jan. 27, 1920, 11. On the fears of Dempsey and Kearns that the negative publicity would make the new champion box office poison, see Dempsey and Dempsey, *Dempsey,* 126–30; and Jack Kearns and Oscar Fraley, *The Million Dollar Gate* (New York: Macmillan, 1966), 120–26.

Negative publicity associated with the draft evasion case can be seen in *New York Times,* Jan. 28, 1920, 8; Feb. 27, 1920, 12; Mar. 21, 1920, 1; and June 16, 1920, 1. *New York Tribune,* Jan. 26, 1920, 10; and June 16, 1920, 1. *Chicago Tribune,* June 16, 1920, 1. *Atlanta Constitution,* June 16, 1920, 14.

40. Mrs. Tex Rickard and Arch Obeler, *Everything Happened to Him: The Story of Tex Rickard* (New York: Frederick A. Stokes, 1936), 280–83. Samuels, *Magnificent Rube,* 230–51. For illustrations of how mass media reproduced and embellished Rickard's representations of Dempsey and Carpentier, see Irvin S. Cobb's widely syndicated page-one account of the fight in *New York Times,* July 3, 1921. This account also appears in George Mowry, ed., *The Twenties: Fords, Flappers and Fanatics* (Englewood Cliffs, N.J.: Prentice-Hall, 1963), 86–88. For the Dempsey-Carpentier fight as the basis of literary invention, see Ring Lardner, "The Battle of the Century," *Saturday Evening Post,* Oct. 29, 1921, 12, 84, 86. See also Paul Gallico, *Golden People,* 191–92.

41. Joseph Durso, *Madison Square Garden: One Hundred Years of History* (New York: Simon & Schuster, 1979), 120–39. Barney Nagler, "Boxing," in *Madison Square Garden: A Century of Sport and Spectacle on the World's Most Versatile Stage* ed. Zander Hollander (New York: Hawthorn Publishers, 1973), 97–98. Joe Humphreys, "The Rickard I Knew," *Collier's,* Nov. 9, 1929, 28, 59–60. Maxwell F. Marcuse, *This Was New York: A Nostalgic Picture of Gotham in the Gaslight Era* (New York: 1969), 238–39. Lloyd Morris, *Incredible New York: High Life and Low Life of the Last Hundred Years* (New York: Random House, 1951), 293–94. Cunningham, "They Want to Fight," 45. "The 'Big Business' of Prize-fighting," 61–62. Jack Kofoed, "The Master of Ballyhoo," *North American Review* 227, Mar. 1929, 285–86.

42. Dempsey and Dempsey, *Dempsey,* 162–63. Jim Tully, "Jack Dempsey," *American Mercury* 29, Aug. 1933, 395–402. Myron M. Stearns, "Champion Ex-Champion," *Harper's,* Sept. 1939, 413–23. Jack Dempsey and John B. Kennedy, "They Call Me a Bum," in *Collier's Greatest Sports Stories,* ed. Tom Meany (New York: A. S. Barnes, 1955), 92–99.

43. *New York Times,* Sept. 8, 1923, 9; and Sept. 14, 1923, 18. *Salt Lake Tribune,* Sept. 19, 1926, 17. *Kansas City Star,* Sept. 24, 1926, 38. *St. Paul Pioneer Press,* June 24, 1923, sec. 3, 1.

44. *Chicago Tribune,* Feb. 23, 1924, 1. *New York Times,* Feb. 23, 1924, 1. *San Francisco Chronicle,* Feb. 23, 1924, 1.

45. A scathing attack on the integrity of jazz-age journalists by Frederick

Allen in the January 1922 issue of *Atlantic Monthly* prompted Caspar Yost, an editor of the *St. Louis Globe-Democrat*, to call a meeting of interested editors, leading to the creation of the American Society of Newspaper Editors. See Frederick L. Allen, "Newspapers and the Truth," Jan. 1922, 44–54; and Alice Fox Pitts, *Read All About It!—Fifty Years of the American Society of Newspaper Editors* (Washington: American Society of Newspaper Editors, 1974), 3. Also, *Problems of Journalism*, vol. 1 (1923): 14–21, and vol. 5 (1927): 101–5. "Our Faith and Action," *Editor and Publisher*, Feb. 23, 1924, 44; and "Editors Mean Business," *Editor and Publisher*, May 3, 1924, 26.

46. See *Problems of Journalism*, vol. 2 (1924): 111–26, and vol. 5: 152–56.

47. "Big Names and Little Stuff," *Editor and Publisher*, Jan. 5, 1924, 36. Stanley Walker, *City Editor* (New York: Frederick A. Stokes, 1934), 120, 133. Stanley Woodward, *Sports Page* (New York: Simon & Schuster, 1949), 163–73. See also interview with Red Smith in Jerome Holtzman, *No Cheering in the Press Box* (New York: Holt, Rinehart and Winston, 1974), 259.

48. *Problems of Journalism*, vol. 4 (1926): 107–8, and vol. 5 (1927): 103. See also Silas Bent, *Ballyhoo: The Voice of the Press* (New York: Liveright, 1927), 131. Nat Fleischer, *Fifty Years at Ringside* (New York: Fleet, 1958), 108–9. William Henry Nugent, "The Sports Section," *American Mercury*, Mar. 1929, 336. Dempsey and Dempsey, *Dempsey*, 42–43. W. O. McGeehan, "Battles of the Century," in *Sport, U.S.A.*, ed. Harry T. Paxson (New York: Thomas Nelson, 1961), 122–23.

49. Background material on Malcolm Wallace Bingay is available through his unprocessed papers at the Detroit Newspapers office in Detroit, Michigan. Bingay entered newspaper work as a printer's devil at the age of fourteen in 1898. He went from boy-messenger at the *Detroit News* to police reporter by the age of seventeen. He became sports editor two years later despite the fact he didn't know how to score a ball game. He became city editor of the *News* in 1910 and managing editor four years later when only twenty-nine. See *Problems of Journalism*, vol. 5 (1927): 98, 103. Bingay's obituary appears in *New York Times*, Aug. 22, 1953, 17. Joining Bingay in deploring the corruption of the fight game and its negative impact on jazz-age youth in addition to Abbot were E. T. Stackpole of the *Harrisburg Telegraph*, Will Owen Jones of the *Nebraska State Journal*, and E. R. Stevenson of the *Waterbury Republican and American*.

50. *Problems of Journalism*, vol. 2 (1924): 114–15, vol. 5 (1927): 97–101, vol. 6 (1928): 18–19. Bent, *Ballyhoo*, 42, 241. Wayne M. Towers, "World Series Coverage in New York City in the 1920's," *Journalism Monographs* 73 (1981): 5.

51. *Problems of Journalism*, vol. 5 (1927): 96–102, 108. An undated Bingay column, appearing in the *Detroit Free Press* shortly after the death of ASNE founder Caspar Yost on May 30, 1941, articulates a paternalistic approach for

newspaper editors who should cultivate "good citizenship on the common ground of high purpose." He and fellow editors saw their fight against an un-bridled sports page as a central part of that mission. See Bingay's unprocessed papers in *Detroit News* and *Detroit Free Press* Archives, *Detroit News* offices, Detroit, Mich.

52. For Marvin H. Creager's journalistic philosophy and its relationship to jazz-age sports reporting, see his unprocessed collection at M62–180, the State Historical Society of Wisconsin, Madison. The collection includes an undated typewritten draft by Creager, titled "The Aim of the News and Feature Depart-ments at the *Milwaukee Journal.*" In the same collection, see Dale Wilson, "Marvin Creager and the Kansas City Crowd," *Historical Messenger* (of the Milwaukee County Historical Society), Sept. 1961, 2–4.

53. "Milwaukee Journal Reflects Its Editor's Character," *Bulletin of the American Society of Newspaper Editors,* Sept. 15, 1926, 1. *Problems of Journal-ism,* vol. 5 (1927): 105–10, vol. 6 (1928): 18, and vol. 7 (1929): 25–28. On Creager's leadership within ASNE see a letter from Paul Bellamy to Mrs. James O. Poole, dated Dec. 4, 1954, in Creager Papers. State Historical Society of Wisconsin. Bellamy writes Creager's daughter that her father's "rare qualities" made him a board member and later a president of ASNE. Joining Creager in justifying press attention to the fight game were Charles H. Dennis of the *Chi-cago Daily News,* William Preston Beazell of the *New York World,* Tom Wallace of the *Louisville Times,* George A. Armstrong of the *Hartford Courant,* and George Hough of the *New Bedford Standard.*

54. *Problems of Journalism,* vol. 2 (1924): 114–15. *Problems of Journalism,* vol. 5 (1927): 211. Marlen Pew, "Ogden Reid Says Public Is Best Served by Fewer But Better Papers," *Editor and Publisher,* Mar. 29, 1924, 1.

55. See "Personal Journalism Is Coming Back—Broun," an interview with Heywood Broun in *Editor and Publisher,* Mar. 15, 1924, 7. Heywood Broun, *The Sun Field* (New York: G. P. Putnam's Sons, 1923), 4, 14, 29–31.

56. The self-conscious hope that a national organization emphasizing the ethics of journalism would "do something great for journalism" is reflected in the letters of Caspar Yost, editor of the *St. Louis Globe-Democrat* who helped found the American Society of Newspaper Editors. His letters, dated Apr. 24, 1922, Apr. 25, 1922, and Apr. 26, 1922, to Anna Yost from New York's Waldorf-Astoria, meeting site of ASNE organizers, were made available to the author by Casper Yost's grandson, Robert W. Yost of Webster Groves, Mo. See also Ameri-can Society of Newspaper Editors Minutes, Apr. 25, 1922, meeting, 2; and ASNE minutes, Oct. 10, 1922, meeting, 6–7. American Society of Newspaper Editors Archives, Newspaper Center, Reston, Va. Also, *Problems of Journalism,* vol. 1 (1923): 18–22.

On journalism's struggle for occupational respectability during America's jazz age, see Thomas L. Haskell, *The Emergence of Professional Social Science: The American Social Science Association and the 19th Century Crisis of Authority* (Urbana: Univ. of Illinois Press, 1977), 1–15. Burton J. Bledstein, preface to *The Culture of Professionalism: The Middle Class and the Development of Higher Education in America* (New York: W. W. Norton, 1976). Talcott Parsons, "The Professions and Social Structure," *Social Forces* 17 (May 1939): 457–67. A. M. Carr-Saunders, *Professions: Their Organization and Place in Society* (Oxford: Clarendon Press, 1928), 3–31. A. M. Carr-Saunders and P. A. Wilson, *The Professions* (Oxford: Clarendon Press, 1933), 284–85.

On the development of schools of journalism to facilitate the professionalization of reporting, see Albert A. Sutton, *Education for Journalism in the United States from Its Beginnings to 1940* (Evanston, Ill.: Northwestern Univ. Press, 1940); Sarah Lockwood Williams, *Twenty Years of Education in Journalism* (Columbia, Mo.: E. W. Stephens Publishing, 1929); and Allen S. Will, *Education for Newspaper Life* (Newark, N.J.: Essex Press, 1931).

57. Joseph S. Zeisel, "The Workweek in American Industry, 1850–1956," *Monthly Labor Review,* Jan. 1958, 23–29. Ted Curtis Smythe, "The Reporter, 1880–1900: Working Conditions and Their Influence on News," *Journalism History* 7 (1980): 1–10. Robert L. Duffus, "The Age of Play," *The Independent,* Dec. 20, 1924, 539. Stuart Chase, "Play," in Charles A. Beard, ed., *Whither Mankind: A Panorama of Modern Civilization* (New York: Longmans, Green, 1928), 338.

58. Elmo Scott Watson, "A History of Newspaper Syndicates in the United States, 1865–1935," Supplement to *Publisher's Auxiliary,* Nov. 16, 1935, 5–21. Walter Swanson, *The Thin Gold Watch: A Personal History of the Newspaper Copleys* (New York: Macmillan, 1964), 87–101. Oswald Garrison Villard, *The Disappearing Daily: Chapters in American Newspaper Revolution* (New York: Knopf, 1944), 57–63. George Britt, *Forty Years, Forty Millions: The Career of Frank A. Munsey* (New York: Farrar and Rinehart, 1935), 165–82. Samuel T. Williamson, *Imprint of a Publisher: The Story of Frank Gannett and His Newspapers* (New York: R. M McBride, 1948), 96–110. See also Clifford F. Weigle, "The Young Scripps Editor: Keystone of E. W.'s System," *Journalism Quarterly* 41 (1964): 360–66. William David Sloan, "Historians and the American Press, 1900–1945: Working Profession or Big Business?" *American Journalism* 3 (1986): 154–66. Dan Schiller, "An Historical Approach to Objectivity and Professionalism in American News Reporting," *Journal of Communication* 29 (Autumn 1979): 46–57. Raymond B. Nixon, "Changes in Reader Attitudes Toward Daily Newspapers," *Journalism Quarterly* 31 (Fall 1954): 21–22.

On the rise of the wire services, see Stephen Vincent Benet, "The United Press," *Fortune,* May 1933, 67–68. Will Irwin, "United Press," *Harper's,* Apr. 25, 1914, 6–7. Richard Edes Harrison, "AP," *Fortune,* Feb. 1937, 89–90. For background, see Joe Alex Morris, *Deadline Every Minute: The Story of the United*

Press (New York: Doubleday, 1957). Victor Rosewater, *History of Cooperative News-Gathering in the United States* (New York: D. Appleton, 1930). Melville E. Stone, *"M. E. S." His Book* (New York: Harper & Bros., 1918). Kent Cooper, *Kent Cooper and the Associated Press: An Autobiography* (New York: Random House, 1959).

59. Robert Benchley's reviews on "The Wayward Press" appeared in *The New Yorker*. A summary of his attack on conventionality in American life and its newspapers appears in Ringel, 331–40. See also John Macy, "Journalism," in *Civilization in the United States: An Inquiry by Thirty Americans*, ed. Harold E. Stearns (New York: Harcourt, Brace, 1922), 35–51. Reuel Denney, *The Astonished Muse* (Chicago: Univ. of Chicago Press, 1957), 146–65. Roy G. Francis, "The Sportswriter," in *Motivations in Play, Games and Sport* ed. Ralph Slovenko and James A. Knight (Springfield: Charles C. Thomas, 1967), 712–17.

60. Henry F. May, "Shifting Perspectives on the 1920's," *Mississippi Valley Historical Review* 43 (Dec. 1956): 405–27. Gregory Stone, "American Sports: Play and Dis-Play," *Chicago Review* 9 (Fall 1955): 83–100. Max Lerner, *America as a Civilization: Life and Thought in the United States Today* (New York: Simon & Schuster, 1957), 805–18. Orrin E. Klapp, "Hero Worship in America," *American Sociological Review* 14 (Feb. 1949): 53–62. Robert Smith, "Heroes and Hurrahs: Sports in Brooklyn, 1890–1898," *Journal of Long Island History* 11 (1975): 7–8.

61. See remarks of Dorothy Canfield Fisher at the University of Kansas, summarized in the *Graduate Magazine* of the University of Kansas, vol. 26 (June 1928): 8–9. Fisher observes that the rise of leisure required a fundamental recalculation of American psychology and values held since pioneering days. A culture schooled by the necessities of "work, want and hardship" now needed to be educated to "the dangers from the lack of material hardships." For background, see Fisher's trilogy on the tensions between tradition and modernity in rural Vermont: *Hillsboro People* (New York: Grosset and Dunlap, 1915); *The Brimming Cup* (New York: Harcourt, Brace, 1921); and *Raw Material* (New York: Harcourt, Brace, 1925).

62. For an analysis by contemporary social scientists of America's awkward encounter with leisure, see Harvey C. Lehman and Paul A. Witty, *The Psychology of Play Activities* (New York: A. S. Barnes, 1927). Also, Chase, *Sound and Fury*, 332–53. See also George Esdras Bevans, "How Workingmen Spend Their Spare Time" (Ph.D. diss., Columbia Univ., 1913), 19–22, 37–43, 65–87.

63. See Aldous Huxley, "Accidie," in *On the Margin: Notes and Essays* (London: Chatto and Windus, 1923); and Foster Rhea Dulles, *America Learns to Play: A History of Popular Recreation, 1607–1940* (Gloucester, Mass.: Peter Smith, 1963, 347–64. Peter R. Shergold, *Working Class Life: The 'American Standard' in Comparative Perspective, 1899–1913* (Pittsburgh: Univ. of Pittsburgh Press, 1982), 3–7, 224–30. Dale A. Somers, "The Leisure Revolution:

Recreation in the American City, 1820–1920," *Journal of Popular Culture* 5 (Summer 1971): 125–47.

64. Herbert Collins, "The Sedentary Society," *The Scientific Monthly* 79 (Nov. 1954): 288–92. Bertrand Russell, *In Praise of Idlenesss and Other Essays* (New York: W. W. Norton, 1935), 12–21.

65. Silas Bent, *Machine Made Man* (New York: Farrar and Rinehart, 1930), vi–vii, 113–15. Chase, *Sound and Fury*, 346–47. Robert M. MacIver, *The Pursuit of Happiness* (New York: Simon & Schuster, 1955), 132–51.

66. Thorstein Veblen, *The Theory of the Leisure Class* (New York: B. W. Huebsch, 1926), 68–82, 246–59, 263, 271. Mark Sullivan, *Our Times, 1900–1925*, vol. 6, *The Twenties* (New York: Charles Scribner's Sons, 1972, 1–13. *The Parade of Heroes: Legendary Figures in American Lore,* ed. Tristram Potter Coffin and Hennig Cohen (Garden City, N.Y.: Doubleday, 1978), xxiii, 52–53.

67. Louis Albert Banks, *The Story of the Hall of Fame, Including the Lives and Portraits of the Elect and of Those Who Barely Missed Election* (New York: Christian Herald, 1902), 13–19, 369–72. Daniel Walker Howe, ed., *Victorian America* (Philadelphia: Univ. of Pennsylvania Press, 1976), 6–20. D. H. Meyer, *The Instructed Conscience: The Shaping of the American National Ethic* (Philadelphia: Univ. of Pennsylvania Press, 1972), 14–31. Christopher Kent, "Higher Journalism and the Mid-Victorian Clerisy," *Victorian Studies* 13, Dec. 1969, 181–98.

68. Sullivan, *Our Times,* 457. Hamlin Garland, *The Son of the Middle Border* (New York: Macmillan, 1917), 134–37.

69. Ring W. Lardner, "Sport and Play," 459–61. Klapp, "Hero Worship," 56–62. Orrin E. Klapp, *Heroes, Villains, and Fools: The Changing American Character* (Englewood Cliffs, N.J.: Prentice-Hall, 1962), 27–29, 98–101. Dempsey and Dempsey, *Dempsey,* 163–77.

70. Dempsey and Dempsey, *Dempsey,* 174–81. Kearns and Fraley, *Million Dollar Gate,* 142–63. Samuels, *Magnificent Rube,* 283–84. Jack Dempsey and John B. Kennedy, "They Call Me a Bum," in *Collier's Greatest Sports Stories,* ed. Tom Meany (New York: A. S. Barnes, 1955), 93–96.

71. Dempsey and Kennedy, "They Call Me a Bum," 93–95. Jack Dempsey and Myron M. Stearns, *Round by Round: An Autobiography* (New York: Whittlesey House, 1940), 228–34.

CHAPTER 4
HEARST, THE COLONEL, OCHS, AND THE CAPTAIN

1. *New York Times,* July 9, 1889, 1. *New Orleans Picayune,* July 9, 1889, 1. *San Francisco Examiner,* June 16, 1910, 1. *Salt Lake Tribune,* June 16, 1910, 1. *Leadville* (Colo.) *Evening Chronicle,* May 24, 1910, 2.

2. *Leadville* (Colo.) *Evening Chronicle*, May 24, 1910, 2; and June 16, 1910, 2. *Rocky Mountain News*, July 4, 1919, 8. *Denver Post*, Sept. 18, 1926, 10.

3. *Chicago Herald and Examiner*, July 7, 1926, 8. *Chicago Evening American*, July 21, 1926, 1. *Chicago Tribune*, July 11, 1926, part 2, 2.

4. *New York Times*, Aug. 17, 1926, 16. *New York Daily News*, Aug. 15, 1926, 29. *Chicago Herald and Examiner*, July 23, 1926, 9. *Chicago Evening American*, July 21, 1926, 1.

5. *Chicago Tribune*, July 11, 1926, part 2, 2, 3. *Chicago Herald and Examiner*, July 7, 1926, 8. *Chicago Evening American*, July 22, 1926, 11.

6. *Chicago Daily News*, July 21, 1926, 1; Sept. 23, 1926, 32. *Chicago Evening American*, July 21, 1926, 1, 11. *Chicago Herald and Examiner*, July 23, 1926, 1. *Chicago Tribune*, July 22, 1926, 13; and July 25, 1926, part 2, 1.

7. Carl Sandburg, "The Windy City," in *Slabs of the Sunburnt West* (New York: Harcourt, Brace, 1922), 3–11. Bessie Louise Pierce, *A History of Chicago* (New York: Knopf, 1937), vol. 1: 3–6. Robert Knight and Lucius H. Zeuch, *The Location of the Chicago Portage Route of the Seventeenth Century* (Chicago: Univ. of Chicago Press, 1928), 17–27. Milo M. Quaife, *Checagou: From Indian Wigwam to Modern City, 1673–1835* (Chicago: Univ. of Chicago Press, 1933), 133–43. Wayne Edson Stevens, *The Northwest Fur Trade, 1763–1800* (Urbana: Univ. of Illinois Press, 1928), 109–15.

8. Henry Justin Smith, *Chicago's Great Century* (Chicago: Univ. of Chicago Press, 1933), 84–101. Milo M. Quaife, *The Development of Chicago* (Chicago: Univ. of Chicago Press, 1916), 123–45. Graham Taylor, "Chicago as Viewed by Its Intimate Friends," *Chicago Theological Seminary*, Jan. 1930, 8–11.

9. Carl Sandburg, "Chicago," in *Chicago Poems* (New York: Holt, Rinehart and Winston, 1916), 3–4. Also, in the same anthology, see, "Masses," "Subway," "The Shovel Man," "Fish Crier," "Working Girls," and "To Certain Journeymen," 4, 8–9, 16,19. Also, "Chicago Poet," in *Cornhuskers* (New York: Holt, Rinehart and Winston, 1918), 22; and "Chicago Baby Boy," in *The Complete Poems of Carl Sandburg* (New York: Harcourt Brace Jovanovich, 1970), 380–81.

10. Lincoln Steffens, *The Shame of the Cities* (New York: Sangamore Press, 1957), 164–65. George W. Steevens, "The Land of the Dollar," in *As Others See Chicago: Impressions of Visitors, 1673–1933*, ed. Bessie Louise Pierce (Chicago: Univ. of Chicago Press, 1933), 400–401.

11. Louise C. Wade, *Graham Taylor: Pioneer for Social Justice, 1851–1938* (Chicago: Univ. of Chicago Press, 1964), 186–87. Graham Taylor, "Developing the American Spirit," in *America and the New Era: A Symposium on Social Reconstruction*, ed. Elisha M. Friedman (New York: E. P. Dutton, 1920), 231–45. Carter H. Harrison, *Stormy Years* (Indianapolis: Bobbs-Merrill, 1935), 79–80. William T. Stead, *If Christ Came to Chicago* (Chicago: Laird and Leer, 1894), 67–82.

12. W. A. Swanberg, *Citizen Hearst* (New York: Scribner's, 1961), 182–83. Jesse G. Murray, *The Madhouse on Madison Street* (Chicago: Follett, 1965), ix, xi, xii and 421. Oliver Carlson and Ernest Sutherland, *Hearst: Lord of San Simeon* (New York: Viking Press, 1936), 49, 174. Joseph Gies, *The Colonel of Chicago* (New York: E. P. Dutton, 1979), 35–37. Jay Robert Nash, *People to See: An Anecdotal History of Chicago's Makers and Breakers* (Piscataway, N.J.: New Century Publishers, 1981), 27–33.

13. For background on the Chicago socialist press and its competition with the city's major dailies, see Jon Bekken, "This Paper Is Owned by Thousands of Working Men and Women" (paper presented at the Midwest Regional Conference of Journalism and Mass Communication Historians, Northwestern Univ., Evanston, Ill., Apr. 7, 1990). See also Nash, *People to See,* 29. Ferdinand Lundberg, *Imperial Hearst: A Social Biography* (New York: Equinox Cooperative, 1936), 147–55. Lloyd Wendt, *Chicago Tribune: The Rise of a Great Newspaper* (Chicago: Rand McNally, 1979), 386–95. William T. Moore, *Dateline Chicago: A Veteran Newsman Recalls Its Heyday* (New York: Taplinger Publishing, 1973), 182–91. Burton Rascoe, *We Were Interrupted* (Garden City, N.Y.: Doubleday, 1947), 12–18.

14. Sam Bass Warner, foreward to *A City Comes of Age: Chicago in the 1890's*, ed. Susan E. Hirsch and Robert I. Goler (Chicago: Chicago Historical Society, 1990), 8–23. Thomas G. Aylesworth and Virginia L. Aylesworth, *Chicago: The Glamorous Years, 1919–1941* (Greenwich, Conn.: W. H. Smith Publishers, 1986), 59–76. Stephen Longstreet, *Chicago: An Intimate Portrait of People, Pleasures and Power, 1860–1919* (New York: David McKay, 1973), 232–54.

15. Chicago Vice Commission, *The Social Evil of Chicago* (Chicago: Chicago Vice Commission, 1911), 25–33, 51–63, 260–74. Virgil W. Peterson, *Barbarians in Our Midst* (Boston: Little, Brown & Co., 1952), 87–93. Lloyd Wendt and Herman Kogan, *Lords of the Levee: The Story of Bathhouse John and Hinky Dink* (Indianapolis: Bobbs-Merrill, 1943), 282–97. Graham Taylor, *Pioneering on Social Frontiers* (Chicago: Univ. of Chicago Press, 1930), 86–89. Herbert Asbury, *Gem of the Prairie: An Informal History of the Chicago Underworld* (New York: Garden City, N.Y. Publishers, 1942), 243–51. Emmett Dedmon, *Fabulous Chicago* (New York: Random House, 1953), 241–64.

16. *Chicago Defender,* July 5, 1919, 20; and July 12, 1919, 20. Dempsey J. Travis, *The Autobiography of Black Chicago* (Chicago: Urban Research Institute, 1981), 35–46. Harold F. Gosnell, *Negro Politicians: The Rise of Negro Politics in Chicago* (Chicago: Univ. of Chicago Press, 1935), 123–28. Stanley Dance, *The World of Earl Hines* (New York: Charles Scribner's Sons, 1977), 93–105. Allan H. Spear, *Black Chicago: The Making of a Negro Ghetto, 1890–1920* (Chicago: Univ. of Chicago Press, 1967), 76–87. Edward Dean Sullivan, *Rattling the Cup on Chicago Crime* (Freeport, N.Y.: Books for Libraries Press,

1971), 67–81. St. Clair Drake and Horace R. Cayton, *Black Metropolis: A Study of Negro Life in a Northern City* (New York: Harcourt, Brace, 1945), 474–82.

17. Lloyd Lewis and Henry Justin Smith, *Chicago: The History of Its Reputation* (New York: Harcourt, Brace, 1929), 440–50. Charles E. Merriam, *Chicago: A More Intimate View of Urban Politics* (New York: Macmillan, 1929), 147–74. Ernest Poole, *Giants Gone: Men Who Made Chicago* (New York: McGraw-Hill, 1943), 189–203. Mark H. Haller, "Urban Crime and Criminal Justice: The Chicago Case," *Journal of American History* 57 (Dec. 1970): 619–35. John Landesco, *Organized Crime in Chicago* (Chicago: Univ. of Chicago Press, 1968), 149–63.

18. Royal E. Montgomery, *Industrial Relations in the Chicago Building Trades* (Chicago: Univ. of Chicago Press, 1927), 17–26. Gordon L. Hostetter and Thomas Quinn Beesley, *It's a Racket!* (Chicago: Univ. of Chicago Press, 1929), 133–45. Graham Taylor, "Between the Lines in Chicago's Industrial Civil War," *The Commons,* Apr. 30, 1900, 1–4. Graham Taylor, "An Epidemic of Strikes in Chicago," *The Survey,* Aug. 2, 1919, 645–46.

19. Robert E. Park, "The Urban Community as a Spacial Pattern and a Moral Order," in *The Urban Community: Selected Papers from the Proceedings of the American Sociological Society, 1925,* ed. Ernest W. Burgess (Chicago: Univ. of Chicago Press, 1926), 9–17. Robert E. Park, "The City: Suggestions for the Investigation of Human Behavior in the Urban Environment," in *The City,* ed. Robert E. Park, Ernest W. Burgess, and Roderick D. McKenzie (Chicago: Univ. of Chicago Press, 1925), 1–17. Also see Robert E. Park, "The Natural History of the Newspaper," in *The City,* 80–81, 97–98. Harvey Warren Zorbaugh, *The Gold Coast and the Slum: A Sociological Study of Chicago's Near North Side* (Chicago: Univ. of Chicago Press, 1976), 1–16, 155–61. Also, see Robert E. Park's introduction to *The Gold Coast,* xiii–ix.

20. David Paul Nord, "The Public Community: The Urbanization of Journalism in Chicago," *Journal of Urban History* 11 (Aug. 1985): 412–14. "Lawson Falls at 75 from Overwork Serving His Great Press Ideal," in *Editor and Publisher,* Aug. 22, 1925, 1, 4. Charles H. Dennis, *Victor Lawson: His Time and His Work* (Chicago: Univ. of Chicago Press, 1935), 111–38. A. T. Andreas, *History of Chicago* (Chicago: A. T. Andreas, 1885), 700–702. See also Lawson's introduction in Melville E. Stone, *Fifty Years a Journalist* (Garden City, N.Y.: Doubleday, 1921). John J. McPhaul, *Deadlines and Monkeyshines: The Fabled World of Chicago Journalism* (Westport, Conn.: Greenwood Press, 1973), 109–10. Doug Fetherling, *The Five Lives of Ben Hecht* (Toronto: Lester and Orpen, 1977), 64–65. Frank C. Waldrop, *McCormick of Chicago: An Unconventional Portrait of a Controversial Figure* (Englewood Cliffs, N.J.: Prentice-Hall, 1966), 86–91. Norma Green, Stephen Lacy, and Jean Folkerts, "Chicago Journalists at the Turn of the Century: Bohemians All?" *Journalism Quarterly* 66 (Winter 1989): 812–21. Nash, *People to See,* 52.

21. John Tebbell, *An American Dynasty: The Story of the McCormicks, Medills and Pattersons* (Garden City, N.Y.: Doubleday, 1947), 205–6. Andreas, *History of Chicago*, 492–95. Philip Kinsley, *The Chicago Tribune: Its First Hundred Years* (New York: Knopf, 1943), vol. 1: ix–x, 378–81. Philip Kinsley, *The Chicago Tribune: Its First Hundred Years* (Chicago: Chicago Tribune Company, 1945), vol. 2: ix, 233–61. Philip Kinsley, *The Chicago Tribune: Its First Hundred Years* (Chicago: Chicago Tribune Company, 1946), vol. 3: viii, 3–7. William T. Hutchinson, *Cyrus Hall McCormick: Harvest, 1856–1884* (New York: D. Appleton-Century, 1935), 316–31. Wendt, *Chicago Tribune*, 141–63.

22. William Dean Howells, "Letters of an Altrurian Traveller," *The Cosmopolitan*, Dec. 1893, 218–32. *Chicago Tribune*, Nov. 1, 1893, 1 and 4. Clarence A. Buskirk, "The Pageant of the Centuries from the Dawn of the New Light to the Triumph of the Full Day: A Vision of Strong Manhood and Perfection of Society in Columbia's Future," a supplement to the *Chicago Inter-Ocean*, Apr. 26, 1893. H. N. Higinbotham, *Report of the President to the Board of Directors of the World's Columbian Exposition* (Chicago: Rand McNally, 1898), 11–15. Reid Badger, *The Great American Fair: The World's Columbian Exposition and American Culture* (Chicago: Nelson Hall, 1979), 113–30. David F. Burg, *Chicago's White City of 1893* (Lexington: Univ. of Kentucky Press, 1976), 112–20, 286–301, 342–48. Charles Moore, *Daniel H. Burnham: Architect Planner of Cities* (New York: De Capo Press, 1968), 31–49. Clinter Keeler, "The White City and the Black City: The Dream of Civilization," *American Quarterly* 2 (Summer 1950): 112–17. Stanley Applebaum, *The Chicago's World's Fair of 1893: A Photographic Record* (New York: Dover, 1980), 103–8.

23. Lewis and Smith, *Chicago,* 170–74. Robert W. Rydell, *All the World's a Fair: Visions of Empire at American International Expositions, 1876–1916* (Chicago: Univ. of Chicago Press, 1984), 64–71. Jane Addams, *Twenty Years at Hull House* (New York: Macmillan, 1910), 310–22. Howard E. Wilson, *Mary McDowell, Neighbor* (Chicago: Univ. of Chicago Press, 1928), 141–48. Hilda Satt Polachek, *I Came a Stranger: The Story of a Hull House Girl* (Urbana: Univ. of Illinois Press, 1989), 68–80, 96–104. Ishbel Ross, *Silhouette in Diamonds: The Life of Mrs. Potter Palmer* (New York: Harper & Bros., 1960), 147–63, 250–54. Graham Taylor, "Vitalizing Chicago," *Journal of Education* 82 (Aug. 26, 1915): 150. George S. Counts, *School and Society in Chicago* (New York: Harcourt, Brace, 1928), 43–73.

24. Lewis and Smith, *Chicago,* 449–51. *Chicago Daily News,* Feb. 10, 1923, 1, and Feb. 19, 1927, 1. Albert Nelson Marquis, *The Book of Chicagoans: A Biographical Dictionary of Living Men of the City of Chicago* (Chicago: A. N. Marquis, 1911), 185. Wade, *Graham Taylor,* 192–93. Nash, *People to See,* 82–83.

25. *Chicago Daily News,* July 3, 1919, 8. McPhaul, *Deadlines and Monkeyshines,* 156–59.

26. *Chicago Tribune,* June 20, 1919, 19; June 21, 1919, 19; June 25, 1919, 17; July 1 1919, 17; and July 7, 1919, 8.

27. *Chicago Evening American,* July 3, 1926, 1, 18. *Chicago Herald and Examiner,* July 1, 1926, 10; and July 5, 1926, 15.

28. *Problems of Journalism,* vol. 5 (1927): 110. Marquis, *Chicagoans,* 183–84. Dennis, *Victor Lawson,* 201–18.

29. *Chicago Tribune,* July 11, 1926, part 2, 2; July 12, 1926, 20; July 14, 1926, 21; July 19, 1926, 21; July 20, 1926, 17; July 21, 1926, 19; and July 22, 1926, 13, 32.

30. "Colonel McCormick Defines a Newspaper," *Editor and Publisher,* Nov. 8, 1924, 4. *Pictured Encyclopedia of the World's Greatest Newspaper* (Chicago: Chicago Tribune Publishing, 1928), 693–701. *The World's Greatest Newspaper: A Handbook of Newspaper Administration, Editorials, Advertising, Production, and Circulation, Minutely depicting in Word and Picture How It's Done by the World's Greatest Newspaper* (Chicago: Chicago Tribune Publishing, 1922), 57–84. Marquis, *Chicagoans,* 438.

31. *Chicago Tribune,* Jan. 3, 1926, 8; and July 18, 1926, 1. Gies, *The Colonel,* 101–3. Wendt, *Chicago Tribune,* 382–86. *Pictured Encyclopedia,* 2–21. McPhaul, *Deadlines and Monkeyshines,* 10–11. James Weber Linn, *James Keeley, Newspaperman* (Indianapolis: Bobbs-Merrill, 1937), 171–88.

32. McPhaul, *Deadlines and Monkeyshines,* 211–13. Gies, *The Colonel,* 103–5. Oswald Garrison Villard, *Some Newspapers and Newspaper-men* (New York: Knopf, 1926), 193–209. Lewis and Smith, *Chicago,* 362–64. Wendt, *Chicago Tribune,* 485–92. Nash, *People to See,* 40–45.

33. William Henry Nugent, "The Sports Section," *American Mercury,* Mar. 1929, 336–38. "In Interview Hearst Speaks Plainly of Policies of His Organization," *Editor and Publisher,* June 14, 1924, 3, 4. Wayne Andrews, *Battle for Chicago* (New York: Harcourt, Brace, 1946), 233–54. Lundberg, *Imperial Hearst,* 149–63.

34. John Tebbel, *The Life and Times of William Randolph Hearst* (New York: E. P. Dutton, 1952), 129–41. Ben Hecht, *A Child of the Century* (New York: Simon & Schuster, 1954), 351. Villard, *Newspapers and Newspaper-men,* 14–41. Oswald Garrison Villard, *Prophets, True and False* (New York: Knopf, 1928), 300–320. Hearst had his defenders. Robert Park, a former newspaper man turned sociologist, thought the Hearst press "a great Americanizer" of the nation's new immigrant. See Park, *The City,* 81.

35. *Chicago Herald and Examiner,* July 7, 1926, 8; July 19, 1926, 11; July 22, 1926, 11; July 23, 1926, 1. *Chicago Tribune,* July 19, 1926, 21; July 20, 1926, 17; July 21, 1926, 19. *Chicago Daily News,* July 19, 1926, 17; July 20, 1926, sec. 2, 1; and July 21, 1926, 1, and sec. 3, 1.

36. Travis, *Black Chicago,* 36–39. *Chicago Defender,* July 5, 1919, 11; July

12, 1919, 11; Sept. 18, 1926, sec. 2, 6; Sept. 25, 1926, sec. 2, 6, 7; and Oct. 2, 1926, sec. 2, 2, 3, 7.

37. The *Herald and Examiner* and *Evening American*'s one million daily circulation placed a Hearst paper in nearly half of all Chicago's households. See *Chicago Herald and Examiner*, July 23, 1926, 9, 11; and July 24, 1926, 6. *Chicago Evening American*, July 3, 1926, 19; July 6, 1926, 15, 16; July 12, 1926, 11; July 13, 1926, 13; July 19, 1926, 10; July 20, 1926, 9, 10; July 21, 1926, 1, 11, 14.; July 22, 1926, 11, 13.

38. *Chicago Tribune*, July 23, 1926, 15, 18; July 24, 1926, 15; and July 25, 1926, part 2, 1, 5. Nash, *People to See*, 147–48. Wendt, *Chicago Tribune*, 359.

39. *Chicago Tribune*, July 26, 1926, 17; July 27, 1926, 17; and July 29, 1926, 15. Wendt, *Chicago Tribune*, 568, 613.

40. *Chicago Herald and Examiner*, July 26, 1926, 9; July 27, 1926, 9; July 28, 1926, 9, 11; July 29, 1926, 9. *Chicago Evening American*, July 27, 1926, 1, 11.

41. *Chicago Herald and Examiner*, June 24, 1926, 6; June 29, 1926, 9, 10; July 30, 1926, 6. Nash, *People to See*, 45–55. McPhaul, *Deadlines and Monkeyshines*, 10–12. Moore, *Daniel H. Burnham*, 86–89. Villard, *Newspapers*, 14–15, 30–31.

42. *Chicago Daily News*, July 24, 1926, 6; and July 27, 1926, 1.

43. "American Newspapers as a Whole Are Clean, Free, Capable and Meet Responsibility Honestly: An Inspiring Interview with Adolph S. Ochs," *Editor and Publisher*, Feb. 16, 1924, 1, 4. Elmer Davis, *History of the New York Times* (New York: New York Times, 1921), 223–26. Meyer Berger, *The Story of the New York Times, 1851–1951* (New York: Simon & Schuster, 1951), 527, 565.

44. R. C. Cornuelle, "Remembrance of the Times: From the Papers of Garet Garrett," *The American Scholar* 36 (1967): 433–34, 443–44. Michael Schudson, *Discovering the News: A Social History of American Newspapers* (New York: Basic Books, 1978), 106–15. Edwin Emery, *The Press and America: An Interpretative History of American Journalism* (New York: Prentice-Hall, 1962), 483–500.

45. *New York Times*, July 3, 1921, 1–10, 13–16; July 1, 1923, 1, 25; July 2, 1923, 10; July 3, 1923, 1, 9; July 4, 1923, 1, 9; and July 5, 1923, 1, 3, 14. Roger Burlingame, *Don't Let Them Scare You: The Life and Times of Elmer Davis* (Philadelphia: J. P. Lippincott, 1961), 95–96. Davis's obituary appears in *New York Times*, May 19, 1958, 1, 25.

46. See obituary to Ochs in *New York Times*, Apr. 9, 1935, 1, 20, 21. See also Silas Bent, *Ballyhoo: The Voice of the Press* (New York: Boni and Liveright, 1927), 44, 150. Frank Luther Mott, *American Journalism: A History of Newspapers in the United States Through 250 Years, 1690–1940* (New York: Macmillan, 1947), 669–70. Jonathan Daniels, *They Will Be Heard: America's Crusading Newspaper Editors* (New York: McGraw-Hill, 1965), 310–19. Nelson A. Crawford, *The Ethics of Journalism* (New York: Knopf, 1924), 111–13.

47. See John Kieran's interview in Jerome Holtzman, *No Cheering in the Press Box* (New York: Holt, Rinehart and Winston, 1974), 42–43. Also, James Dawson, "Boxing," in *Sport's Golden Age: A Close-up of the Fabulous Twenties* ed. Allison Danzig and Peter Brandwein (Freeport, N.Y.: Books for Libraries Press, 1948), 38–40.

48. Gerald W. Johnson, *An Honorable Titan: A Biographical Study of Adolph S. Ochs* (New York: Harper & Bros., 1946), 142–59. Benjamin Stolberg, "The Man Behind the *Times*," *Atlantic Monthly* 138, Dec. 1926, 721–30.

49. Adolph S. Ochs, introduction to *History of New York Times*, viii–xii. *New York Times*, Apr. 9, 1935, 2, 3. Johnson, *Honorable Titan*, 183–88. Berger, *Story of the New York Times*, 116–21.

50. Villard, *Newspapers*, 3–13. Cornuelle, *Papers of Garet Garrett*, 433, 434. Barnett Fine, *A Giant of the Press* (New York: Editor and Publisher Library, 1933), 137–54. F. Fraser Bond, *Mr. Miller of 'The Times'* (New York: Charles Scribner's Sons, 1931), 93–114.

51. George Everett, "The Age of New Journalism, 1883–1900," in *The Media in America: A History*, ed. William David Sloan and James D. Startt (Worthington, Ohio: Publishing Horizons 1989), 232–34. Stolberg, "Man Behind *The Times*," 729–31. Emery, *Press and America*, 488–500. Villard, *Newspapers*, 7–8.

52. Dawson, "Boxing," 38–40. Davis, *History of New York Times*, 381–82. *Problems of Journalism*, vol. 5 (1927): 96–99. Bent, *Ballyhoo*, 41–42. See also Neil MacNeil, *Without Fear or Favor* (New York: Harcourt, Brace, 1940), 413–15. Robert Lipsyte, *Sports World: An American Dreamland* (New York: New York Times Book Company, 1975), 74–75. William Henry Nugent, "The Sports Section," *American Mercury*, Mar. 1929, 336–38.

53. *New York Times*, July 26, 1926, 10; July 27, 1926, 12; July 28, 1926, 1, 13; and July 29, 1926, 13. Stolberg, "Man Behind *The Times*," 721–23. Arthur Hays Sulzberger, introduction to *Story of New York Times*, v–vi.

54. John Chapman, *Tell It to Sweeney: The Informal History of the New York Daily News* (Garden City, N.Y.: Doubleday, 1961), 143–44. See Gallico interview in Holtzman, *No Cheering in the Press Box*, 63–64. See Gallico obituary in *New York Times*, July 17, 1976, 26. *New York Daily News*, July 28, 1926, 26; and July 29, 1926, 32.

55. *New York Daily News*, July 31, 1926, 20 and Aug. 3, 1926, 28. Paul Gallico, *Farewell to Sport* (New York: Knopf, 1940), 85–90, 100–101. Paul Gallico, *The Golden People* (New York: Doubleday, 1965), 97–99.

56. Tebbel, *American Dynasty*, 254–56. Chapman, *Tell It to Sweeney*, 144–45. Rascoe, *We Were Interrupted*, 14–15. Alice Albright Hoge, *Cissy Patterson* (New York: Random House, 1966), 89–90.

57. Kinsley, *Chicago Tribune*, vol. 1: 30–53, 101–11; vol. 2, 236–45; vol. 3, 37–55, 122–41. McPhaul, *Deadlines and Monkeyshines*, 10–11. Wendt, *Chicago Tribune*,

134–55. *World's Greatest Newspaper* (Chicago: Chicago Tribune, 1922), 3–13.

58. Paul F. Healey, *Cissy: The Biography of Eleanor M. "Cissy" Patterson* (Garden City, N.Y.: Doubleday, 1966), 19–27. Hoge, *Cissy Patterson*, 7–9. Joseph Medill Patterson, *The Notebook of a Neutral* (New York: Duffield, 1916), 43–44. See the obituary of Joseph Medill Patterson in *Chicago Tribune,* May 27, 1946, 1, 3, 18.

59. The best example of Patterson's publicity work in behalf of socialism is his novel, *A Little Brother of the Rich* (New York: Reilley and Britton, 1908). Protagonist Paul Porter is a provincial social climber and playboy who drops his true love for a brewery heiress and the values of the "yachting sect." See also the script for *The Fourth Estate,* a play Patterson co-wrote and helped produce, which associates journalism with the power to reform capitalism while fighting "the interests." The play opened on Broadway in 1909 to generally favorable reviews. *Rebellion* and *Dope,* staged during the next two years, marked the high water mark of Patterson's romance with socialism.

60. On Patterson's editorial philosophy, see his correspondence with Arthur L. Clarke, managing editor of the *New York Daily News,* on Dec. 5, 1919, in box 16, folder 6, Joseph Medill Patterson Papers, Donnelley Library, Lake Forest College, Lake Forest, Ill. See also Wendt, *Chicago Tribune,* 373–75, 385–91, 397–405. *Pictured Encyclopedia,* 3–12. Gies, *The Colonel,* 26–28. Villard, *Newspapers,* 194–98. Healy, *Cissy Patterson,* 112–14.

61. Joseph Medill Patterson to S. N. Blossom, Sept. 9, 1922, box 15, folder 3, Patterson Papers. Patterson to Milton E. Burke, acting manager of the *New York Daily News,* May 15, 1922, box 16, folder 1, Patterson Papers. See also "What Is the Lure of the Tabloid Press?" *Editor and Publisher,* July 26, 1924, 7, 34. Walter E. Schneider, "Fabulous Rise of the *N.Y. Daily News,*" *Editor and Publisher,* June 24, 1939, 5. *New York Times,* May 27, 1946, 1, 22, 23. Healy, *"Cissy" Patterson,* 114–20. Jack Alexander, "Vox Populi," *New Yorker,* Aug. 6, 1938, 27–32. Kenneth Stewart and John Tebbel, *Makers of Modern Journalism* (New York: Prentice-Hall, 1952), 12–21.

62. William H. Field to Joseph Medill Patterson, Nov. 1, 1919, box 17, folder 1, Patterson Papers.

63. Patterson to Field, July 8, 1919, box 17, folder 1, Patterson Papers. Field to Patterson, July 9, 1919, box 17, folder 1, Patterson Papers.

64. Max Annenberg to Patterson, Nov. 25, 1919, box 15, folder 1, Patterson Papers. J. W. Barnhardt to Patterson, Aug. 13, 1920, box 15, folder 4, Patterson Papers. See also Chapman, *Tell It to Sweeney,* 13–18. Gies, *The Colonel,* 46, 74–76. *Editor and Publisher,* Feb. 16, 1925, 1, 4. Simon M. Bessie, *Jazz Journalism* (New York: E. P. Dutton, 1938), 19–33. Helen M. Hughes, *News and the Human Interest Story* (Chicago: Univ. of Chicago Press, 1940), 12–22. McPhaul, *Deadlines and Monkeyshines,* 206–9. Tebbel, *Modern Journalism,* 214–15.

65. Burke to Patterson, Sept. 7, 1920, box 16, folder 1, Patterson Papers. Perly Boone to Edward Beck, managing editor, *Chicago Tribune*, copied to Patterson, Sept. 8, 1920, box 15, folder 3, Patterson Papers. Patterson to Burke, Sept. 15, 1920, box 16, folder 1, Patterson Papers. Patterson to Field, Oct. 16, 1920, box 17, folder 2, Patterson Papers.

66. Burke to Beck, Sept. 14, 1920, box 16, folder 1, Patterson Papers. Burke to Patterson, Sept. 14, 1920, box 16, folder 1, Patterson Papers. Patterson to Burke, Sept. 15, 1920, box 16, folder 1, Patterson Papers. Burke to Patterson, Sept. 17, 1920, box 16, folder 1, Patterson Papers. Patterson to Field, Oct. 21, 1921, box 17, folder 2, Patterson Papers.

67. Patterson to Philip Payne, acting manager news editor of the *New York Daily News*, Jan. 8, 1922, box 19, folder 9, Patterson Papers.

68. Payne to Patterson, Feb. 7, 1923, box 19, folder 10, Patterson Papers. Patterson to Payne, Feb. 8, 1923, box 19, folder 10, Patterson Papers.

69. Patterson to Burke, Aug. 10, 1920, box 16, folder 1, Patterson Papers. Patterson to Burke, Dec. 16, 1920, box 16, folder 1, Patterson Papers. Patterson to Burke, Dec. 20, 1920, box 16, folder 1, Patterson Papers. Patterson to Field and Annenberg, Mar. 14, 1921, box 15, folder 1, Patterson Papers.

70. Annenberg to Patterson, June 21, 1922, box 15, folder 1, Patterson Papers. Patterson to Burke, May 13, 1921, box 16, folder 2, Patterson Papers. Burke to Patterson, May 19, 1921, box 16, folder 2, Patterson Papers.

71. Barnhardt to Patterson, Mar. 23, 1921, box 15, folder 5, Patterson Papers. Barnhardt to Patterson, Apr. 19, 1922, box 15, folder 5, Patterson Papers. Patterson to Barnhardt, Aug. 16, 1924, box 15, folder 7, Patterson Papers. Payne to Patterson, Apr. 17, 1925, box 20, folder 3, Patterson Papers. Patterson to Payne, Apr. 20, 1925. box 20, folder 3, Patterson Papers. See also Chapman, *Tell It to Sweeney,* 115–21. Frank Luther Mott, *The News in America* (Cambridge: Harvard Univ. Press, 1952), 147–61. Emery, *Press and America,* 624–26. John R. Brazil, "Murder Trials, Murder and Twenties America," *American Quarterly* 33 (Spring 1981): 163–69.

72. Patterson to Adolph Ochs, Aug. 24, 1921, box 11, folder 8, Patterson Papers. Ochs to Patterson, Aug. 30, 1921, box 11, folder 8, Patterson Papers. Ochs to Patterson, Apr. 15, 1924, box 11, folder 8, Patterson Papers. Patterson to Ochs, Apr. 17, 1924, box 11, folder 8, Patterson Papers. Patterson to Ochs, July 8, 1925, box 11, folder 8, Patterson Papers. Bessie, *Jazz Journalism,* 82–83. "American Newspapers as a Whole Are Clean," *Editor and Publisher,* Feb. 16, 1924, 1, 4; In Interview Hearst Speaks Plainly," *Editor and Publisher,* June 14, 1924, 1, 4; Walter E. Schneider, "Fabulous Rise of the N.Y. Daily News," *Editor and Publisher,* June 24, 1939, 5. Jack Alexander, "Vox Populi," *New Yorker,* Aug. 20, 1938, 38–41. "Joseph Medill Patterson," *Time,* June 3, 1946, 87.

73. Bruce J. Evensen, "The Media and American Character," in *The Sig-*

nificance of the Media in American History, by James D. Startt and William David Sloan (Northport, Ala.: Vision Press, 1993), 281–84. Bessie, *Jazz Journalism,* 83–84. Emery, *Press and America,* 624–25. Emile Gauvreau, *Hot News* (New York: Macaulay, 1931), 22–35. Hughes, *Human Interest Story,* 235–38.

74. Payne to Patterson, Oct. 6, 1922, box 19, folder 9, Patterson Papers. "What Is the Lure of the Tabloid Press," *Editor and Publisher,* July 26, 1924, 7. *New York Times,* July 17, 1976, 26. Gallico interview in Holtzman, *Press Box,* 61–66. Chapman, *Tell It to Sweeney,* 43–44. See also Warren Susman, "Piety, Profits and Play: The 1920's," in *Men, Women, and Issues in American History,* ed. Howard H. Quint and Milton Cantor (Homewood, Ill.: Dorsey Press, 1975), vol. 2: 191, 211. Frederick W. Cozens and Florence Scovil, "The Sports Page," in *Sport and Society: An Anthology,* ed. John T. Talamini and Charles H. Page (Boston: Little, Brown & Co., 1973), 423–27.

75. *New York Daily News,* Aug. 28, 1923, 28; and Sept. 1, 1923, 32. Gallico in Holtzman, *Press Box,* 63–64. Jack Dempsey and Barbara Piatelli Dempsey, *Dempsey* (New York: Harper & Row, 1977), 157–59. Alfred M. Lee, *The Daily Newspaper in America* (New York: Macmillan, 1937), 609–10.

76. Paul Gallico to Patterson, May 21, 1925, box 17, folder 4, Patterson Papers. Patterson to Gallico, May 22, 1925, box 17, folder 4, Patterson Papers. Patterson to Gallico, Sept. 9, 1926, box 17, folder 4, Patterson Papers. Gallico to Patterson, Sept. 10, 1926, box 17, folder 4. Patterson Papers. Patterson to Gallico, Sept. 11, 1926, box 17, folder 4, Patterson Papers. See also Gallico in Holtzman, *Press Box,* 66–68. Chapman, *Tell It to Sweeney,* 45–46. Paul Gallico, "The Golden Decade," in Harry T. Paxton, ed., *Sport U.S.A.: The Best from the Saturday Evening Post* (New York: Thomas Nelson and Sons, 1961), 172–80. John R. Tunis, *Sports Heroics and Hysterics* (New York: John Day, 1928), 13–14.

77. *New York Times,* July 17, 1976, 26. Gallico, in Holtzman, *Press Box,* 71–72. Gallico, *Golden People,* 22–29. Gallico, "The Golden Decade," 172–74.

78. Irving Howe and Kenneth Libo, *How We Lived: A Documentary History of Immigrant Life in America, 1880–1930* (New York: Richard Marek, 1979), 85–90. Irving Howe, *World of Our Fathers* (New York: Harcourt Brace Jovanovich, 1976), 524–34. Moses Rischin, *The Promised Land: New York Jews, 1870–1914* (Cambridge: Harvard Univ. Press, 1962), 126–27, 158–67. Ronald Sanders, *The Downtown Jews: Portrait of an Immigrant Generation* (New York: Harper & Row, 1969), 217–19, 434–36, 452–53. Ronald Sanders, *Shores of Refuge: A Hundred Years of Jewish Immigration* (New York: Henry Holt, 1988), 165–68. Isaac Metzker, ed., *A Bintel Brief* (New York: Ballantine, 1977), 118–19. See also Harry Golden's annotation to *The Spirit of the Ghetto* by Hutchins Hapgood (New York: Funk and Wagnalls, 1965); and John Higham's preface to *The Rise of David Levinsky* by Abraham Cahan (Gloucester, Mass.: Peter Smith, 1969). Bruce J. Evensen, "Abraham Cahan," in *A Sourcebook of Ameri-*

can Literary Journalism: Representative Writers in an Emerging Genre, ed. Thomas B. Connery (New York: Greenwood, 1992), 91–100.

79. Chapman, *Tell It to Sweeney,* 136–41. *Printer's Ink,* Jan. 1923, 40–41. Park, *The City,* 113–34. Melech Epstein, *Profiles of Eleven* (Detroit: Wayne State Univ. Press, 1965), 76–83, 99–109. Rufus Learsi, *The Jews in America: A History* (New York: World, 1954), 188–91. Daniel Walden, "Urbanism, Technology and the Ghetto in Novels by Abraham Cahan, Henry Roth and Saul Bellow," *American Jewish History* 23 (Mar. 1984): 296–300. Morris Hillquit, *Loose Leaves from a Busy Life* (New York: Macmillan, 1934), 15–25.

80. Rascoe, *We Were Interrupted,* 13–15. Chapman, *Tell It to Sweeney,* 142–44. Hutchins Hapgood, *The Spirit of the Ghetto: Studies of the Jewish Quarter of New York* (New York: Funk and Wagnalls, 1965), 183–86. Jacob Riis, *How the Other Half Lives* (New York: Irvington, 1972), 108–11. Boris D. Bogen, *Born a Jew* (New York: Macmillan, 1930), 36–41, 78–81. Abraham Cahan, *Bleter Fun Mein Lebe, Leaves from My Life* (New York: Forward Association. 1926), 114–21.

81. Gallico, *Golden People,* 22–28. Gallico, *Farewell,* 278–81. Chapman, *Tell It to Sweeney,* 45–46. *New York Times,* July 17, 1976, 26. Gallico in Holtzman, *Press Box,* 71–72.

82. Gallico, "The Golden Decade," 175–79. Gallico, *Golden People,* 193–95. Gallico in Holtzman, *Press Box,* 78–80. John R. Tunis, *The American Way in Sport* (New York: Duell, Sloan and Pearce, 1958), 15–18. Steven A. Riess, "In the Ring and Out: Professional Boxing in New York, 1896–1920," in *Sport in America: New Historical Perspectives,* ed. Donald Spivey (Westport, Conn.: Greenwood, 1985), 122–24. "Personal Journalism Is Coming Back—Brown," *Editor and Publisher,* Mar. 15, 1924, 7.

83. See particularly *New York Daily News,* Aug. 11, 1926, 1, 28, 33; and *New York Times,* Aug. 8, 1926, sec. 1, 1; and Aug. 11, 1926, 16. Also, *New York Daily News,* July 28, 1926, 1, 26; July 29, 1926, 32, 33; July 30, 1926, 34; July 31, 1926, 20, 21; Aug. 2, 1926, 25; Aug. 3, 1926, 28–29; Aug. 4, 1926, 29; Aug. 5, 1926, 1, 28; Aug. 6, 1926, 37; Aug. 7, 1926, 21; Aug. 8, 1926, 53; Aug. 9, 1926, 1, 25; and Aug. 10, 1926, 33, 39. *New York Times,* July 28, 1926, 1, 13; July 29, 1926, 13; July 31, 1926, 7; Aug. 1, 1926, sec. 9, 5; Aug. 2, 1926, 14; Aug. 3, 1926, 15; Aug. 4, 1926, 13: Aug. 5, 1926, 14; Aug. 6, 1926, 9; and Aug. 7, 1926, 13.

84. *New York Times,* Aug. 14, 1926, 14; Aug. 15, 1926, sec. 9, 1, 7; Aug. 16, 1926, 13; Aug. 17, 1926, 16; Aug. 18, 1926, 16; and Aug. 19, 1926, 1, 17. *New York Daily News,* Aug. 12, 1926, 32; Aug. 13, 1926, 34, 36; Aug. 14, 1926, 21; Aug. 15, 1926, 29; Aug. 16, 1926, 24, 25; Aug. 17, 1926, 1, 28; Aug. 18, 1926, 28; Aug. 19, 1926, 1, 32. Also, John Lardner, *White Hopes and Other Tigers* (Philadelphia: J. B. Lippincott, 1951), 172–80. Gene Fowler, *Beau*

James (New York: Viking, 1949), 97–107. Edward Van Every, *Muldoon: The Solid Man of Sport* (New York: Frederick A. Stokes, 1929), 355–62. James A. Farley, *Behind the Ballots: A Personal History of a Politician* (New York: Harcourt Brace, 1938), 45–48. Lester Bromberg, *Boxing's Most Unforgettable Fights* (New York: Ronald Press, 1962), 165–66.

For an obituary on William Muldoon, see *New York Times,* June 4, 1933, 32. For an appreciation of James Farley, see *New York Times,* June 10, 1976, 1, 53; June 11, 1976, 22; and June 13, 1976, 1, 42.

85. *New York Times,* Aug. 13, 1926, 13; Aug. 16, 1926, 13; Aug. 17, 1926, 16; and Aug. 18, 1926, 16.

86. *New York Daily News,* Aug. 18, 1926, 28; Aug. 19, 1926, 1; Aug. 20, 1926, 35; Aug. 22, 1926, 53; and Aug. 24, 1926, 32.

87. *New York Times,* Aug. 18, 1926, 16; Aug. 19, 1926, 1, 17; Aug. 20, 1926, 12; Aug. 21, 1926, 6; and Aug. 22, 1926, sec. 9, 1, 7. *New York Daily News,* Aug. 24, 1926, 32, 33; Aug. 25, 1926, 29; Aug. 26, 1926, 33; and Aug. 27, 1926, 36.

CHAPTER 5
THE PHILADELPHIA FIGHT

1. *Philadelphia Evening Bulletin,* Aug. 20, 1926, 1. *Philadelphia Record,* Aug. 23, 1926, 1; and Sept. 14, 1926, 1. *Philadelphia Daily News,* Aug. 21, 1926, 1; Aug. 23, 1926, 13; and Sept. 23, 1926, 13.

2. Dorothy Gondos Beers, "The Centennial City, 1865–1876," in Russell F. Weigley, *Philadelphia: A 300-Year History* (New York: W. W. Norton, 1982), 417–70. Stewart A. Stehlin, "Philadelphia on the Eve of the Nation's Centennial: A Visitor's Description in 1873–1874," *Pennsylvania History* 44, 1977, 25–36. Frank B. Evans, *Pennsylvania Politics, 1872–1877: A Study of Political Leadership* (Harrisburg, Pa.: Pennsylvania Historical and Museum Commission, 1966), 13–15. Nicholas B. Wainwright, *History of the Philadelphia National Bank: A Century and a Half of Philadelphia Banking, 1803–1953* (Philadelphia: Philadelphia National Bank, 1953), 129–31. Ira V. Brown, "Pennsylvania and the Rights of the Negro," *Pennsylvania History* 28 (1961): 52–54. *Philadelphia North American,* Feb. 14, 1876, 1. Lefferts Loetscher, "Presbyterianism and Revivals in Philadelphia since 1875," *Pennsylvania Magazine of History and Biography* 69 (1944): 57–58.

3. Robert W. Rydell, *All The World's a Fair: Visions of Empire at American International Expositions, 1876–1916* (Chicago: Univ. of Chicago Press, 1984), 9–37. Beers, "Centennial City," 459–70. John Maass, *The Glorious Enterprise: The Centennial Exhibition of 1876 and H. J. Schwarzmann, Architect in Chief* (Watkins Glen: American Life Foundation, 1973), 94–96. For background, see

J. S. Ingram, *The Centennial Exposition, Described and Illustrated, Being a Concise and Graphic Description of This Grand Enterprise Commemorative of the First Centennary of American Independence* (Philadelphia: Hubbard Brothers, 1876), 680–711; and Dorsey Gardner, ed., *United States Centennial Commission: International Exhibition, 1876, Grounds and Buildings of the Centennial Exhibition, Philadelphia, 1876* (Philadelphia: Lippincott, 1878), 141–56.

4. See Sam Bass Warner, *The Private City: Philadelphia in Three Periods of Its Growth* (Philadelphia: Univ. of Pennsylvania Press, 1968), ix–xii. Sam Bass Warner, *The Urban Wilderness: A History of the American City* (New York: Harper & Row, 1972), 190–91. Bruce M. Stave, "A Conversation with Sam Bass Warner, Jr.: Ten Years Later," *Journal of Urban History* 11 (Nov. 1984): 109. Anselm L. Strauss, *Images of the American City* (New Brunswick, N.J.: Transaction Books, 1976), 23–26. Theodore Hershberg, ed., *Philadelphia: Work, Space, Family, and Group Experience in the Nineteenth Century* (New York: Oxford Univ. Press, 1981), 457. Arthur Dudden, "The City Embraces 'Normalcy,' 1919–1929," in Weigley, *Philadelphia*, 575–76.

5. Letter from John Price Jackson, executive director, sesquicentennial committee on religion, to Bishop Thomas Garland of the Protestant Episcopal Church, dated Oct. 4, 1923, City of Philadelphia Archives, record group 232.6, box A-1470, Sesqui-Centennial Exposition Association, Files of Officials, Executive Committee, and Board of Directors, Philadelphia, Pa.

6. Letter from John Price Jackson to Dennis Cardinal Dougherty, archbishop of the Philadelphia Diocese, dated Oct. 4, 1923. Dougherty initially declined to participate in a civic celebration likely to promote "bitterness among the various denominations." Record Group 232.6, box A-1470, Sesqui-Centennial Exposition Association, City of Philadelphia Archives. Dougherty reversed his stand on Catholic participation in the sesquicentennial in a Sept. 16, 1926, letter to diocese clergy, Archdiocese of Philadelphia, Archives and Historical Collections, Archdiocesan Scrapbook, Overbrook, Pa., vol. 25. See also *The Catholic Standard and Times* (Philadelphia, Pa.), "Catholics Needed for a Pageant," July 31, 1926, 4; "Is This Nation Protestant?" Aug. 21, 1926, 6; "Faith and Patriotism," Sept. 18, 1926, 4 and "Mass of Thanksgiving at Stadium," Sept. 25, 1926, 4.

7. *Philadelphia Tribune,* May 16, 1925, "The Spirit of Democracy," 4; May 23, 1925, "The Spirit of the Times," 4; June 6, 1925, "200,000 Potential Power," 4; July 4, 1926, "The Glorious Fourth," 4; and July 11, 1926, "The Sesquicentennial," 4.

8. For the sesquicentennial as a celebration of Philadelphia's material progress and the work of its industrial leadership, see comments by Chamber of Commerce President Philip H. Gadsden appearing in the notebook of Louis F. Whitcomb, Apr. 2, 1926, entry, collection no. 1936, Historical Society of Penn-

sylvania, Philadelphia. Whitcomb was the assistant director of the sesquicentennial and worked in its controller's office. For the sesquicentennial as a boon to the building trades and as a symbol of their labor's struggle against capital, see *Philadelphia Daily News,* Apr. 10, 1926, "Sesqui as Topic for Prize Essays," 15; Apr. 28, 1926, "Baird—Agent of Class Tyranny," 15; May 25, 1926, "Sesqui to be Triumph for City," 15; and June 1, 1926, "How Philadelphia May Lead Again," 19.

9. *Philadelphia Inquirer,* Aug. 4, 1926, 8. *Philadelphia Public Ledger,* July 10, 1926, 1; and July 13, 1926, 10. See also Mar. 31, 1926, entry in Whitcomb Sesquicentennial Notebook, collection 1936, Historical Society of Pennsylvania. Dudden, "City Embraces 'Normalcy,'" 575. For Vare as the bane of Philadelphia reformers and the lapsing of moral authority in the governance of cities in interwar America, see Lewis Mumford, *The City in History: Its Origins, Transformations, and Its Prospects* (New York: Harcourt, Brace & World, 1961), 559. Warner, introduction to *The Private City,* and 175. Jon C. Teaford, *The Twentieth-Century American City* (Baltimore: Johns Hopkins Univ. Press, 1986), 44–73.

10. For an official version of developments in staging the sesquicentennial, see E. L. Austin and Odell Hauser, *The Sesqui-Centennial: A Record Based on Official Data and Department Records* (Philadelphia: Current Publications, 1929), 23–32. Hauser, a former Philadelphia newspaperman, was publicity director for the sesquicentennial. See also *Report of W. Freeland Kendrick, Mayor of the City of Philadelphia, 1925* (Philadelphia: City of Philadelphia, 1926), 29–30. George Morgan, *The City of Firsts* (Philadelphia: Historical Publications Society, 1926), 470–78. Nicholas B. Wainwright, *History of the Philadelphia Electric Company, 1881–1961* (Philadelphia: Philadelphia Electric Company, 1961), 185–89.

For Mayor Kendrick's long association with the Shriners, see his obituary in *New York Times,* Mar. 21, 1953, 17.

11. Press packets prepared under the direction of Odell Hauser appear in Whitcomb Sesquicentennial Papers. Collection No. 1936. See also Warner, *The Private City,* 187–93, for a summary of the upgrade to Philadelphia's mass transit in anticipation of the event.

12. See "General Order" of E. L. Austin to all department heads, dated June 24, 1926, ordering Sunday openings at the sesquicentennial, Whitcomb Sesquicentennial Papers. For the sesquicentennial's mounting financial problems see memos from the office of Odell Hauser, dated June 11, 1926, through June 24, 1926, in Sesquicentennial Exhibition, Collection 587, Historical Society of Pennsylvania. For background, see Dudden, "City Embraces 'Normalcy,'" 572.

13. "Destroying the Moral Standard," *The Presbyterian,* Apr. 1, 1926, 7. "The Sesquicentennial and the Sabbath," *The Presbyterian,* June 3, 1926, 7; and June 24, 1926, 5. "The Sesquicentennial Revives the Sunday Question,"

The Lutheran, July 8, 1926, 14. "The Sabbath Opening of the Sesquicenten-nial," *The United Presbyterian,* July 22, 1926, 5.

14. *Philadelphia Record,* June 7, 1926, 1. *Philadelphia Daily News,* June 8, 1926, 17; June 14, 1926, 13; and June 15, 1926, 1. *Philadelphia Evening Bulletin,* July 3, 1926, 1, 2; July 5, 1926, 1, 2; and July 23, 1926, 8. For the respect McLean received within the newspaper business, see, Edwin Emery, *The Press in America: An Interpretative History of Journalism* (Englewood Cliffs, N.J.: Prentice-Hall, 1962), 527, 749. Edwin Emery, *History of the American Newspaper Publishers Association* (Minneapolis: Univ. of Minnesota Press, 1950), 38, 58. *Problems of Journalism,* vol. 6 (1928): 25–29, and vol. 7 (1929): 49–50.

15. For background on McLean and his paper, see "Notes and References Relating to the History of Philadelphia Newspapers," arranged in 1937 by John M. Heim for the Free Library, Philadelphia, Pa., vol. 2: 174–78. Also, *New York Times,* July 31, 1931, 17. *The Encyclopedia Americana* (New York: Americana Corporation, 1963), vol. 18: 78.

16. *Philadelphia Record,* June 26, 1926, 1; June 28, 1926, 1, 3; July 3, 1926, 6, 12: July 7, 1926, 2; and July 8, 1926, 3. For the determination of Austin and exposition board members to handle the problem of a seven-day sesquicentennial in a "bold way," see City Archives of Philadelphia, record group 232.4, June 28, 1926 proceedings of Executive Committee of Board of Direc-tors, Minutes, and Resolutions, box A-1469.

17. For background on the Wanamakers and the history of the *Record* as a "crusading, people's paper," see *Philadelphia Record,* May 14, 1945, 2. "Notes and References Relating to the History of Philadelphia Newspapers," vol. 6: 841–54. *Checklist of United States Newspapers* (Durham, N.C.: Duke Univ. Press, 1936), 765. Emery, *The Press in America,* 416, 527–29. For background on Wanamaker as businessman and advertiser, see Herbert A. Gibbons, *John Wanamaker* (New York: Harper & Bros., 1926), vol. 2: 12–21. John H. Appel, *The Business Biography of John Wanamaker, Founder and Builder* (New York: Macmillan, 1930), 187–96.

For the role of department store advertising in newspaper editorial policy in late nineteenth and early twentieth-century America, see Gerald J. Baldasty, "The Media and the National Economy," in *The Significance of the Media in American History,* ed. James D. Startt and Wm. David Sloan (Northport, Ala.: Vision Press, 1994), 165–81.

18. The fate of Philadelphia's sesquicentennial celebration dominated the front pages of much of the city's press during the summer of 1926. See particu-larly *Philadelphia Inquirer,* June 18, 1926, 1; June 19, 1926, 1; June 28, 1926, 1, 10; July 7, 1926, 1, 6; and July 10, 1926, 1. *Philadelphia Evening Bulletin,* June 24, 1926, 1; June 28, 1926, 1; July 3, 1926, 2, 12; July 6, 1926, 1; July 13, 1926, 1; July 15, 1926, 1; July 16, 1926, 2; July 19, 1926, 3; July 22,

1926, 1; July 23, 1926, 1, 8; July 24, 1926, 1, 8; July 26, 1926, 2; July 27, 1926, 1, 8; Aug. 4, 1926, 1; Aug. 5, 1926, 2; Aug. 9, 1926, 1, 8; and Aug. 12, 1926, 1, 2. *Philadelphia Public Ledger,* July 6, 1926, 10; July 10, 1926, 1; July 13, 1926, 10; July 23, 1926, 1, 10; July 24, 1926, 10; July 26, 1926, 2, 6; July 27, 1926, 1, 10; July 31, 1926, 1; Aug. 10, 1926, 1; and Aug. 14, 1926, 6. *Philadelphia Record,* June 12, 1926, 2, 15; June 18, 1926, 6; June 19, 1926, 1, 7; June 20, 1926, 2, 8; June 23, 1926, 1; June 28, 1926, 1; June 29, 1926, 1; July 1, 1926, 1; July 3, 1926, 1, 6; July 7, 1926, 2; July 9, 1926, 1, 2; July 10, 1926, 1; July 23, 1926, 1, 2, 8; July 25, 1926, 1, 3, 7; July 27, 1926, 1, 2, 6; Aug. 1, 1926, 1; Aug. 2, 1926, 1; Aug. 4, 1926, 2; Aug. 6, 1926, 1, 2; Aug. 8, 1926, 1; Aug. 12, 1926, 1, 16; Aug. 13, 1926, 1, 6; Aug. 22, 1926, 1; Aug. 23, 1926, 1; Aug. 24, 1926, 6, 11; Aug. 25, 1926, 1, 2, 11; and Sept. 2, 1926, 1. *Philadelphia Daily News,* Mar. 25, 1926, 15; Mar. 31, 1926, 27; Apr. 12, 1926, 15; Apr. 28, 1926, 15; June 7, 1926, 27; June 8, 1926, 17; June 14, 1926, 13; June 15, 1926, 1, 15; June 16, 1926, 1; June 17, 1926, 1; June 19, 1926, 1, 15; June 21, 1926, 1; June 22, 1926, 1, 15; June 23, 1926, 17; June 26, 1926, 17; June 28, 1926, 1; June 29, 1926, 1, 15, 30; June 30, 1926, 1, 14, 15; July 1, 1926, 4, 17; July 3, 1926, 14, 15; July 9, 1926, 1; July 10, 1926, 1; July 13, 1926, 1; July 14, 1926, 1, 15; July 16, 1926, 13; July 17, 1926, 1; July 24, 1926, 1; July 26, 1926, 1, 15; Aug. 5, 1926, 15; Aug. 6, 1926, 1, 30; Aug. 7, 1926, 13; Aug. 13, 1926, 15; Aug. 17, 1926, 1; Aug. 18, 1926, 1; Aug. 23, 1926, 13; Aug. 26, 1926, 15; Sept. 6, 1926, 23; and Sept. 18, 1926, 1.

19. "Notes and References Relating to the History of Philadelphia Newspapers," vol. 4: 574–87. *Philadelphia Inquirer,* Aug. 4, 1926, 8. Emery, *The Press in America,* 356, 528, 530. *New York Times,* Jan. 22, 1929, 29; and Jan. 23, 1929, 22. The *Inquirer's* opposition to sesquicentennial boycotters is also reflected in Whitcomb Sesquicentennial Papers, entries for June 11, 1926, June 12, 1926, and June 24, 1926.

20. *Philadelphia Public Ledger,* Mar. 21, 1926, 7; July 10, 1926, 1; July 13, 1926, 10; July 16, 1926, 1; July 23, 1926, 1, 10; July 24, 1926, 10; July 26, 1926, 2, 6; July 27, 1926, 1; and July 28, 1926, 10. "Notes and References Relating to the History of Philadelphia Newspapers," vol. 6: 796–839. Emery, *The Press in America,* 356, 527–29. *New York Times,* June 7, 1933, 1, 13 ; and June 8, 1933, 18. Dudden, 593. *Problems of Journalism,* vol. 1 (1923): 122, vol. 2 (1924): 38, 128–29, and vol. 6 (1928): 25–26. Walter D. Fuller, *The Life and Times of Cyrus H. K. Curtis* (New York: Newcomen Society of England, American Branch, 1948), 10–20. John Tebbel, *George Horace Lorimer and the Saturday Evening Post* (Garden City, N.Y.: Doubleday, 1948), 123–32. Joseph C. Goulden, *The Curtis Caper* (New York: Putnam, 1965), 32–33.

21. *Philadelphia Record,* June 28, 1926, 1, 3; July 3, 1926, 1; and July 8, 1926, 3.

22. *Philadelphia Record,* June 29, 1926, 1; and July 3, 1926, 2. *Catholic*

Standard and Times (Philadelphia), June 19, 1926, 3; June 26, 1926, 10; July 3, 1926, 4; July 31, 1926, 4; Aug. 7, 1926, 1, 2; Aug. 21, 1926, 6; Sept. 11, 1926, 1, 3; Sept. 18, 1926, 1, 3, 4; Sept. 25, 1926, 1, 4; Oct. 2, 1926, 1, 3, 4; and Oct. 9, 1926, 1–4. The stand of the archdiocese in supporting the sesquicentennial and staring down religious bigotry is praised by George N. Shuster, "After Many Years," in *Ave Maria,* Oct. 30, 1926, 562–65. Dennis Cardinal Dougherty's role in organizing the march to the fairgrounds in support of Catholic rights is described in several letters dated Aug. 31, 1926; Sept. 16, 1926; Sept. 20, 1926; Sept. 23, 1926; Sept. 28, 1926; and Sept. 29, 1926 in the Archdiocesan Scrapbook, Archdiocese of Philadelphia Archives, vol. 25.

23. "Notes and References Relating to the History of Philadelphia Newspapers," vol. 5: 741–43. Philadelphia Tribune, May 16, 1925, 4; May 23, 1925, 4; May 30, 1925, 1, 4; June 13, 1925, 1; July 4, 1925, 4; July 11, 1925, 4; Aug. 22, 1925, 1; Aug. 29, 1925, 1; Sept. 5, 1925, 4; Sept. 12, 1925, 1; June 19, 1926, 4; July 3, 1926, 4; July 31, 1926, 4; and Aug. 7, 1926, 4. Also, Austin and Hauser, *Sesqui-Centennial,* 469.

24. *Philadelphia Public Ledger,* Aug. 6, 1926, 15; Aug. 19, 1926, 1, 17; and Aug. 23, 1926, 1. *Philadelphia Evening Bulletin,* Aug. 19, 1926, 1, 3, 21; Aug. 20, 1926, 1, 2; Aug. 21, 1926, 1; and Aug. 23, 1926, 1, 2. *Philadelphia Inquirer,* Aug. 19, 1926, 1, 17; Aug. 20, 1926, 1, 10, 15; Aug. 21, 1926, 1, 15; Aug. 26, 1926, 15; Aug. 27, 1926, 17; Aug. 29, 1926, 18; and Aug. 30, 1926, 15. *Philadelphia Record,* Aug. 19, 1926, 1; Aug. 20, 1926, 1; and Aug. 24, 1926, 6. *Philadelphia Daily News,* Aug. 19, 1926, 1, 5; Aug. 20, 1926, 17, 20; and Aug. 23, 1926, 1, 23, 26.

25. *Philadelphia Evening Bulletin,* Aug. 20, 1926, 1; Aug. 21, 1926, 20. *Philadelphia Inquirer,* Sept. 22, 1926, 2. *Philadelphia Public Ledger,* Sept. 22, 1926, 1.

26. *Philadelphia Public Ledger,* Aug. 24, 1926. *Philadelphia Evening Bulletin,* Aug. 27, 1926, 16; Aug. 31, 1926, 18. *Philadelphia Inquirer,* Sept. 3, 1926.

27. *Philadelphia Daily News,* Aug. 27, 1926, 30; and Sept. 2, 1926, 16. *Philadelphia Record,* Aug. 24, 1926, 11; and Sept. 10, 1926, 11. *Philadelphia Public Ledger,* Sept. 4, 1926, 19; Sept. 12, 1926, 24; and Sept. 15, 1926, 15. *Philadelphia Evening Bulletin,* Aug. 26, 1926, 18, Aug. 27, 1926, 16; and Aug. 31, 1926, 18.

28. *Philadelphia Evening Bulletin,* Aug. 26, 1926, 18; Sept. 3, 1926, 20; Sept. 9, 1926, 20; and Sept. 13, 1926, 1, 20, 31. *Philadelphia Public Ledger,* Aug. 20, 1926, 13; Sept. 12, 1926, 24; Sept. 17, 1926, 30; and Sept. 20, 1926, 1. *Philadelphia Inquirer,* Sept. 2, 1926, 17; Sept. 14, 1926, 1; Sept. 17, 1926, 1, 17; and Sept. 20, 1926, 1. On Odell Hauser's publicity apparatus, see "Celebrating 150 Years of American Independence: A Visualization of the Spiritual, Scientific, Artistic and Industrial Progress of America and the World," a booklet produced by the Sesquicentennial International Exhibition Committee in Sesqui-

centennial Papers, 1926, collection no. 1547. Historical Society of Pennsylvania, Philadelphia. Also, see *Philadelphia Evening Bulletin,* July 29, 1926, 16.

29. *Philadelphia Evening Bulletin,* Aug. 19, 1926, 1; Aug. 20, 1926, 1, 16; Aug. 26, 1926, 1; Aug. 27, 1926, 16; Sept. 2, 1926, 18; Sept. 3, 1926, 20; Sept. 9, 1926, 20; Sept. 13, 1926, 1, 20, 31; Sept. 14, 1926, 22; Sept. 16, 1926, 1; Sept. 17, 1926, 1, 22; Sept. 18, 1926, 1, 16, 17; Sept. 20, 1926, 1; Sept. 21, 1926, 1, 20; Sept. 22, 1926, 22; Sept. 23, 1926, 1, 24; Sept. 24, 1926, 1, 26; and Sept. 25, 1926, 1, 15. *Philadelphia Inquirer,* Aug. 19, 1926, 1; Aug. 20, 1926, 1; Aug. 21, 1926, 1, and sec. S, 7; Aug. 24, 1926, 1, 17; Aug. 27, 1926, 17; Aug. 29, 1926, 12; Aug. 30, 1926, 1; Aug. 31, 1926, 1; Sept. 1, 1926, 1; Sept. 2, 1926, 1, 17; Sept. 3, 1926, 17; Sept. 5, 1926, sec. S, 12; Sept. 14, 1926, 1; Sept. 15, 1926, 1; Sept. 16, 1926, 1, 19; Sept. 17, 1926, 1, 17; Sept. 18, 1926, 1; Sept. 19, 1926, 1; Sept. 20, 1926, 1; Sept. 21, 1926, 1; Sept. 22, 1926, 1; Sept. 23, 1926, 1, 19; Sept. 24, 1926, 1, 24; and Sept. 25, 1926, 1. *Philadelphia Public Ledger,* Aug. 19, 1926, 1; Aug. 24, 1926, 26; Sept. 12, 1926, 24; Sept. 17, 1926, 30; Sept. 18, 1926, 30; Sept. 19, 1926, 1; Sept. 20, 1926, 1; Sept. 21, 1926, 30; Sept. 22, 1926, 1; Sept. 23, 1926, 1; Sept. 24, 1926, 1; and Sept. 26, 1926, 24.

30. "Annual Message of W. Freeland Kendrick, Mayor of Philadelphia, Containing the Various Departments of the City of Philadelphia for the Year Ending Dec. 31, 1926." The report is dated Jan. 15, 1927, and appears in record group 232.2, box A-1480, Sesquicentennial Charter and By-Laws Reports, Official Publications, City Archives of Philadelphia. See also *New York Times,* Sept. 25, 1926, 14.

31. Gene Tunney, *A Man Must Fight* (Boston: Houghton Mifflin, 1932), 222–23. Gene Tunney, *Arms for Living* (New York: Wilfred Funk, 1941), 122–23. *New York Daily News,* Sept. 24, 1926, 42, 48. *New York Times,* Sept. 24, 1926, 1.

32. Gene Tunney, "My Fights with Jack Dempsey," in *The Aspirin Age,* ed. Isabel Leighton (New York: Simon & Schuster, 1949), 162–63. Tunney, *Arms for Living,* 123–24. Ed Van Every, *The Life of Gene Tunney: The Fighting Marine* (New York: Dell Publishing, 1926), 24–26. Nat Fleischer, *Gene Tunney: The Enigma of the Ring* (New York: The Ring, 1931), 63–64.

33. Tunney, *Arms for Living,* 112–13, 120–24. Tunney, *A Man Must Fight,* 217–19.

34. Jack Dempsey and Barbara Piatelli Dempsey, *Dempsey* (New York: Harper & Row, 1977), 197–98. Jack Dempsey and Myron M. Stearns, *Round by Round: An Autobiography* (New York: Whittlesey House, 1940), 231–33. *New York Daily News,* Sept. 11, 1926, 24. *St. Louis Post-Dispatch,* Sept. 19, 1926, part 2, 1.

35. *Chicago Evening American,* July 3, 1926, 19; July 6, 1926, 15; July 12, 1926, 11; and Sept. 20, 1926, 21. *Philadelphia Record,* Sept. 22, 1926, 1. *Detroit News,* Sept. 21, 1926, 1.

36. *Philadelphia Inquirer,* Sept. 20, 1926, 18. *New York Times,* Sept. 21, 1926, 24. *Chicago Evening American,* Sept. 21, 1926, 4. *Denver Post,* Sept. 22, 1926, 20.

37. Dempsey and Stearns, *Round by Round,* 230–32. Jack Dempsey, Bob Considine, and Bill Slocum, *Dempsey: By the Man Himself* (New York: Simon & Schuster, 1960), 193–94. Jim Tully, "Jack Dempsey," *American Mercury,* Aug. 1933, 395–98.

38. Paul Gallico, *The Golden People* (Garden City, N.Y.: Doubleday, 1965), 71–73, 85–87. Paul Gallico, *Farewell to Sport* (New York: Knopf, 1940), 13–15, 103–5.

39. *Chicago Evening American,* Sept. 20, 1926, 21; Sept. 21, 1926, 19; and Sept. 22, 1926, 25.

40. *Denver Post,* Sept. 20, 1926, 16. *New York Times,* Sept. 19, 1926, sec. 11, 2. *St. Louis Post-Dispatch,* Sept. 22, 1926, 28.

41. Grantland Rice, *The Tumult and the Shouting* (New York: A. S. Barnes, 1954), 116–18, 130–32. *St. Paul Pioneer Press,* Sept. 22, 1926, 11; and Sept. 23, 1926, 10. Grantland Rice, "The Heavyweight Peerage," *Collier's,* June 21, 1930, 22. Grantland Rice, "The Golden Fleece," *Collier's,* Sept. 17, 1927, 9, 44.

42. Dempsey and Dempsey, *Dempsey,* 199–200. Mrs. "Tex" Rickard and Arch Obeler, *Everything Happened to Him: The Story of Tex Rickard* (New York: Frederick A. Stokes, 1936), 325–26. *Philadelphia Evening Bulletin,* Sept. 23, 1926, 1. *Chicago Tribune,* Sept. 23, 1926, 17.

43. *New York Daily News,* Sept. 24, 1926, 1. *New York Times,* Sept. 23, 1926, 1, 3. *Chicago Daily News,* Sept. 23, 1926, 1. *Philadelphia Public Ledger,* Sept. 23, 1926, 1, 8. *New York Times,* Sept. 19, 1926, sec. 11, 2.

44. *St. Louis Post-Dispatch,* Sept. 18, 1926, 10. *New York Times,* Sept. 21, 1926, 24; and Sept. 23, 1926, 16. *St. Paul Pioneer Press,* Sept. 22, 1926, 9.

45. *Rocky Mountain News,* Sept. 22, 1926, 12; Sept. 23, 1926, 1; and Sept. 24, 1926, 1, 9. *Denver Post,* Sept. 18, 1926, 10; Sept. 19, 1926, sec. S, 2; Sept. 22, 1926, 20; Sept. 23, 1926, 1, 20; and Sept. 24, 1926, 1, 28.

46. *The Deseret News,* Sept. 23, 1926, 1; and Sept. 24, 1926, 1, 7. The paper claimed to have received "thousands of calls." When one young couple was handed a *News* extra after the fight, the Mormon paper reported that "the air was rent with masculine shouts of glee while the girl smothered the happy boy in an osculatory embrace which continued until their street car approached."

47. *Salt Lake Tribune,* Sept. 23, 1926, 1, 9; and Sept. 24, 1926, 1. The fight was broadcast in Salt Lake City on *Tribune*-owned KSL for fans preferring a "private" hearing.

48. *Kansas City Star,* Sept. 19, 1926, 1; Sept. 20, 1926, 13; Sept. 21, 1926, 12; Sept. 22, 1926, 1, 5; Sept. 23, 1926, 1, 19; and Sept. 24, 1926, 1, 5, 22, 23, 25, 38. *Kansas City Times,* Sept. 22, 1926, 1; Sept. 23, 1926, 1, 14; and Sept. 24, 1926, 12.

49. *Baltimore Sun*, Sept. 23, 1926, 26. *New York Times*, Sept. 19, 1926, sec. 11, 2. *Philadelphia Daily News*, Sept. 22, 1926, 30. Jack Dempsey and Charles J. McGuirk, "The Golden Gates," *Saturday Evening Post*, Oct. 20, 1934, 10–11, 73. Charles W. Wilcox, "Consider the Cauliflower," *Scribner's Magazine* 87, Mar. 1930, 445–49. John R. Tunis, "The Business of American Sports," in *America as Americans See It*, ed. Fred J. Ringel (New York: The Literary Guild, 1932), 118–22. "The 'Big Business' of Prize-Fighting," *Literary Digest*, Oct. 13, 1923, 60–67. "The Commercialized Prize Ring," *Outlook* 147, Sept. 28, 1927, 105–6.

50. *St. Paul Pioneer Press*, Sept. 13, 1926, 12. For RCA's promotion of its coverage of the Dempsey-Tunney title fights and their use in publicizing the corporation's infant radio network, NBC, see press release "Tex Rickard's Boxing Bouts to Be Broadcast on NBC," in NBC Papers (1927), correspondence, box 2, folder 61, State Historical Society of Wisconsin, Madison.

51. *St. Louis Post-Dispatch*, Sept. 24, 1926, 1, 3. The paper's promotion of radio included advice to frustrated fans. Poor reception, they were told, could be fixed by new radios. "Recently refined sets worked best," the *Post-Dispatch* advised, while recommending RCA's Radiola 25 by name. The paper saw radio coverage of sports spectaculars intimately linked to the promotion of its own circulation.

52. *Detroit News*, Sept. 21, 1926, 1; Sept. 22, 1926, 1; Sept. 23, 1926, 1; and Sept. 24, 1926, 1.

53. *St. Paul Pioneer Press*, Sept. 15, 1926, 6; Sept. 18, 1926, 1; Sept. 19, 1926, sec. 5, 10; Sept. 20, 1926, 8; Sept. 21, 1926, 1, 12; and Sept. 23, 1926, 1, 6, 10.

54. *Chicago Evening American*, Sept. 22, 1926, 26, 27; and Sept. 23, 1926, 27. *Chicago Daily News*, Sept. 23, 1926, 10; and Sept. 24, 1926, 1. *Chicago Herald and Examiner*, Sept. 21, 1926, 18; and Sept. 22, 1926, 19, 21. *Chicago Tribune*, Sept. 22, 1926, 1; and Sept. 23, 1926, 18, 19; and Sept. 24, 1926, 22.

55. *New York Times*, Sept. 19, 1926, sec. 11, 3. The *Times*, America's unofficial newspaper of record, conducted more than a hundred interviews with the well known and the often quoted, predicting the outcome of the fight. The verdict was Dempsey "by a landslide."

56. *New York Times*, Sept. 19, 1926, sec. 11, 4, 5; and Sept. 23, 1926, 17. *Philadelphia Record*, Sept. 22, 1926, 14. *Philadelphia Evening Bulletin*, Sept. 22, 1926, 19. *Philadelphia Public Ledger*, Sept. 21, 1926, 30.

57. *New York Times*, Sept. 19, 1926, sec. 11, 5; and Sept. 20, 1926, 29. *Philadelphia Daily News*, Sept. 22, 1926, 30. *Philadelphia Inquirer*, Sept. 22, 1926, 26. *Philadelphia Evening Bulletin*, Sept. 22, 1926, 19.

58. *New York Daily News*, Sept. 20, 1926, 24; Sept. 21, 1926, 36; Sept. 22, 1926, 34; and Sept. 23, 1926, 42, 44. Hunt's sentiment is echoed in by Otto Floto in *Denver Post*, Sept. 23, 1926, 20; Grantland Rice in *St. Paul Pioneer Press*, Sept. 23, 1926, 10; Elmer Davis in the *New York Times*, Sept. 23,

1926, 1, 17; Westbrook Pegler in the *Chicago Tribune,* Sept. 23, 1926, 17; and Robert Edgren in the *St. Louis Post-Dispatch,* Sept. 22, 1926, 28. See also "Corbett to Tunney on 'How to Win the Mob,'" *Literary Digest,* Jan. 14, 1928, 55–60. Gallico, *Farewell to Sport,* 93–111. Rex Lardner, *The Legendary Champions* (New York: American Heritage Press, 1972), 251–72. Jonathan Yardley, *Ring: A Biography* (New York: Random House, 1977), 307–9.

59. *New York Times,* Sept. 18, 1926, 11; Sept. 22, 1926, 21; and Sept. 23, 1926, 16. *New York Daily News,* Sept. 21, 1926, 36, 37. *The Deseret News,* Sept. 23, 1926, 2. *Chicago Daily News,* Sept. 23, 1926, 1.

60. *Chicago Tribune,* Sept. 24, 1926, 1, 21. *New York Times,* Sept. 25, 1926, 14. *New York Daily News,* Sept. 25, 1926, 28. *Philadelphia Evening Bulletin,* Sept. 24, 1926, 36.

61. *New York Times,* Sept. 24, 1926, 4. *Time,* Oct. 4, 1926, 28. Fleischer, *Gene Tunney,* 64–65.

62. Tunney, *A Man Must Fight,* 231–33. Tunney, *Arms for Living,* 124–25. Dempsey, Dempsey, *Dempsey,* 200–201. Dempsey and Stearns, *Round by Round,* 234–35. Dempsey, Considine and Slocum, *Dempsey: Himself,* 193–95. Fleischer, *Gene Tunney,* 64–65.

63. "Jack Dempsey vs. Gene Tunney, Sept. 23, 1926, Philadelphia, Pa.," *Fantastic Fights of the Century,* TM Productions, vol. 1. *New York Times,* Sept. 24, 1926, 4. Tunney, *Arms for Living,* 125. Dempsey and Dempsey, *Dempsey,* 200. *Philadelphia Evening Bulletin,* Sept. 24, 1926, 22. *New York Daily News,* Sept. 25, 1926, 18.

64. *Fantastic Fights of the Century.*

65. *Fantastic Fights of the Century. New York Times,* Sept. 24, 1926, 4. *Philadelphia Public Ledger,* Sept. 24, 1926, 17. *Philadelphia Record,* Sept. 24, 1926, 10. Graham McNamee, *You're On the Air* (New York: Harper, 1926), 46–51.

66. *Denver Post,* Sept. 24, 1926, 28. *New York Daily News,* Sept. 24, 1926, 2; and Sept. 25, 1926, 28. *Chicago Tribune,* Sept. 24, 1926, 1, 2. *Chicago Herald and Examiner,* Sept. 24, 1926, 1. On Lardner's conviction that Dempsey had thrown the fight, see Ring Lardner, Jr., *The Lardners: My Family Remembered* (New York: Harper & Row, 1973), 148–49. Those pages recount Lardner's covering for Rice when the latter was unable to file his story on the fight. Rice admits to being ill and accepting Lardner's offer. See also Rice, *Tumult and Shouting,* 147–51. The story that Lardner wrote under Rice's byline appears in *New York Tribune,* Sept. 24, 1926, 1.

67. *Chicago Evening American,* Sept. 24, 1926, 23, 27; and Dempsey and Dempsey, *Dempsey,* 201.

68. *Chicago Tribune,* Sept. 24, 1926, 23. Nat Fleischer, *Jack Dempsey, The Idol of Fistiana* (New York: The Ring, 1929), 254–55. John Lardner, *White Hopes and Other Tigers* (Philadelphia: J. B. Lippincott, 1951), 181–82. *New York Times,* Sept. 24, 1926, 5. *New York Daily News,* Sept. 25, 1926, 31.

69. *New York Times,* Sept. 24, 1926, 6.
70. *Chicago Evening American,* Sept. 24, 1926, 27.
71. *New York Times,* Sept. 24, 1926, 4.

Chapter 6
The Comeback, the Chicago Fight, and Its Aftermath

1. Jack Dempsey and Barbara Piatelli Dempsey, *Dempsey* (New York: Harper & Row, 1977), 205–8. *Chicago Tribune,* Sept. 26, 1926, 12. *Chicago Evening American,* Sept. 27, 1926, 9.

2. Randy Roberts, *Jack Dempsey: The Manassa Mauler* (Baton Rouge: Louisiana State Univ. Press, 1979), 235–38. *New York Times,* Jan. 21, 1927, 11. Dempsey and Dempsey, *Dempsey,* 205.

3. *Chicago Daily News,* Sept. 19, 1927, 19. *New York World,* Sept. 19, 1927, 10. *St. Paul Pioneer Press,* Sept. 20, 1927, 8. *Minneapolis Daily Star,* Sept. 19, 1927, 10. *Denver Post,* Sept. 20, 1927, 28.

4. *Chicago Herald and Examiner,* Sept. 19, 1927, 1, 4. *Chicago Tribune,* Sept. 19, 1927, 1, 25. *New York Times,* Sept. 19, 1927, 20. *New York Daily News,* Sept. 19, 1927, 23. *Kansas City Times,* Sept. 19, 1927, 1. *Salt Lake Tribune,* Sept. 19, 1927, 12.

5. *Chicago Evening American,* Sept. 19, 1927, 1. *Chicago Daily Journal,* Sept. 19, 1927, 12. *The Deseret News* (Salt Lake City), Sept. 19, 1927, 1. *Kansas City Star,* Sept. 19, 127, 11.

6. *New York Daily News,* Sept. 20, 1927, 38. *Chicago Tribune,* Sept. 21, 1927, 23. *Chicago Daily Journal,* Sept. 19, 1927, 12.

7. *New York Daily News,* Sept. 20, 1927, 1. *Chicago Tribune,* Sept. 17, 1927, 19. *Salt Lake Tribune,* Sept. 18, 1927, 2. *Chicago Daily News,* Sept. 16, 1927, 1. *Chicago Evening Post,* Sept. 15, 1927, 10.

8. For NBC's success in exploiting the Dempsey-Tunney fights while establishing its national broadcast network, see correspondence, box 2, folder 61, NBC Papers (1927), State Historical Society of Wisconsin. Madison, Wisc. NBC's sixty-station network for the Chicago fight represented one-tenth of all radio stations on the air in the United States in the fall of 1927. See also *Chicago Tribune,* Sept. 17, 1927, 20. *New York Times,* Sept. 16, 1927, 18. *Chicago Herald and Examiner,* Sept. 21, 1927, 20.

9. *Problems of Journalism,* vol. 5 (1927): 86–91, and vol. 6 (1928): 26–28, 48, 57. *New York Times,* Sept. 16, 1927, 18. *Chicago Tribune,* Sept. 17, 1927, 20.

10. Joseph Medill Patterson to Robert R. McCormick, July 22, 1927. Papers of Col. Robert R. McCormick, box 52, folder 3. Donnelley Library, Lake Forest

College, Lake Forest, Ill. The two newspapers had combined advertising revenues of $32 million in 1927. See Price, Waterhouse Audit Report for the year in Board of Directors Minutes, *Chicago Tribune* Publishing Company. Papers of Joseph Medill Patterson, box 48, folder 1, Donnelley Library, Lake Forest College.

11. *Chicago Herald and Examiner,* Sept. 22, 1927, 12. *Chicago Tribune,* Sept. 19, 1927, 28. *Chicago Evening American,* Sept. 22, 1927, 37. *Chicago Daily News,* Sept. 16, 1927, 32. *Chicago Evening Post,* Sept. 8, 1927, 10.

12. *Problems of Journalism,* vol. 5 (1927): 103–4. *Chicago Tribune,* Sept. 20, 1927, 21. *Chicago Evening Post,* Sept. 24. 1927, 6. *Southtown* (Chicago) *Economist,* Aug. 31, 1926, 1, 10. Chicago's newspapers had a strong ally in the battle to broadcast the Dempsey-Tunney fight. The South Park board, which controlled Soldier Field, insisted on "microphone privileges" for the city's newspapers as a precondition to signing a $100,000 rental agreement with Tex Rickard for the use of the stadium. See *St. Paul Pioneer Press,* Sept. 9, 1927, 8.

13. *Chicago Daily News,* Sept. 23, 1927, 52. For the impact of the Dempsey-Tunney fights in stimulating circulation in newspapers across the United States, see *Problems of Journalism,* vol. 5 (1927): 96–119.

14. *Chicago Evening American,* Sept. 19, 1927, 2. *New York Times,* Feb. 24, 1927, 19. *Chicago Tribune,* July 4, 1927, 24. "A Million Dollar Query: Can Dempsey Come Back?" *Literary Digest,* July 9, 1927, 47–50. Charles Samuels, *The Magnificent Rube: The Life and Gaudy Times of Tex Rickard* (New York: McGraw-Hill, 1957), 288–89.

15. *New York Times,* July 17, 1927, sec. 9, 1, 5; July 19, 1927, 17; July 20, 1927, 18; July 21, 1927, 1, 15; and July 22, 1927, 1, 9, 10, 11. *New York Daily News,* July 12, 1927, 1, 26; July 14, 1927, 34; July 15, 1927, 30, 31; July 17, 1927, 1, 52, 53, 54, 55; July 19, 1927, 2, 30, 32; July 20, 1927, 1, 30; July 20, 1927, 2, 4; July 21, 1927, 1, 2, 19; and July 22, 1927, 1, 2, 3, 19. *New York Evening Journal,* July 21, 1927, 1; and July 22, 1927, 1, 2. NBC was now boasting that "broadcasting of a prize fight is a short and snappy affair when compared with most of our broadcasts. A network is so much an ordinary occurrence now that fifty-one stations means no more than three as far as the actual broadcasting is concerned." See correspondence, box 2, folder 61, NBC Papers, State Historical Society of Wisconsin.

16. *Chicago Tribune,* Sept. 8, 1927, 23. James Langland, ed., *The Daily News Almanac and Year-book* (Chicago: Chicago Daily News, 1928), 435–37. George Fulmer Getz Scrapbook. F38DA G335. Chicago Historical Society. Chicago, Ill. *Editor and Publisher,* Aug. 27, 1927, 7.

17. *Literary Digest,* July 9, 1927, 47–48. *New York Times,* July 17, 1927, sec. S, 5.

18. *New York Times,* July 22, 1927, 1, 9, 10. *Chicago Tribune,* July 22, 1927, 1, 15. *New York Daily News,* July 22, 1927, 1, 32.

19. "Jack Dempsey vs. Jack Sharkey, July 22, 1927, New York, N.Y." *Fantastic Fights of the Century,* TM Productions, vol. 2. See also *Chicago Tribune,* July 22, 1927, 15. *New York Herald-Tribune,* July 22, 1927, 1.

20. *New York Times,* July 22, 1927, 9; July 23, 1927, 1, 6; and July 24, 1927, sec. 9, 1, 6. *New York Evening World,* July 22, 1927, 1. *New York American,* July 22, 1927, 1. *New York Daily News,* July 22, 1927, 1, 32; and July 23, 1927, 1, 2. *Chicago Tribune,* July 22, 1927, 1, 15; and July 23, 1927, 6.

21. *New York Daily News,* July 23, 1927, 1, 2, 11. *Chicago Tribune,* July 23, 1927, part 2, 3; and July 29, 1927, 8. *Chicago Herald and Examiner,* July 25, 1927, 17. *Chicago Evening American,* July 30, 1927, 16.

22. *New York Evening Post,* July 23, 1927, 12. *New York World,* July 29, 1927, 16. *New York Times,* Sept. 18, 1927, sec. S, 4.

23. "The Tunney-Dempsey Fight: A World Spectacle," *Literary Digest,* Sept. 17, 1927, 41. "It Seems to Heywood Broun," *The Nation,* Sept. 28, 1927, 305.

24. Mel Heimer, *The Long Count* (New York: Atheneum, 1969), 59–64. *Chicago Tribune,* Sept. 20, 1927, 22. Paul Gallico, *The Golden People* (Garden City, N.Y.: Doubleday, 1965), 95–97. *New York Daily News,* July 27, 1927, 28.

25. *Chicago Evening American,* Sept. 20, 1927, 22. Nat Fleischer, *Gene Tunney: The Enigma of the Ring* (New York: The Ring, 1931), 56–62 and 102–5. John Lardner, *White Hopes and Other Tigers* (Philadelphia: J. B. Lippincott, 1951), 168–70. Gene Tunney, *A Man Must Fight* (Boston: Houghton Mifflin, 1932), 2–5. Gene Tunney, *Arms for Living* (New York: Wilfred Funk, 1941), 227–33.

26. *Chicago Evening American,* Sept. 21, 1927, 26. *Chicago Herald and Examiner,* July 8, 1927, 17; Sept. 20, 1927, 18; and Sept. 21, 1927, 24.

27. The frustrated reporter was George Barry of the *Minneapolis Daily Star.* His story appears in *Minneapolis Daily Star,* Sept. 13, 1927, 11. See also *New York Times,* Aug. 27, 1927, 11. *New York Daily News,* July 22, 1927, 32. *Chicago Evening Post,* Sept. 1, 1927, 9. *Hyde Park Herald,* Sept. 16, 1927, 1, 12. *Daily Calumet,* Sept. 21, 1927, 1.

28. *Chicago Tribune,* July 26, 1927, 15. *Chicago Evening American,* July 26, 1927, 1, 4. *Chicago Herald and Examiner,* July 26, 1927, 13, 16. *St. Paul Pioneer Press,* Sept. 14, 1927, 6; and Sept. 18, 1927, sec. 5, 1.

29. *Chicago Tribune,* July 29, 1927, 8; and Sept. 1, 1927, 10. *New York Daily News,* July 27, 1927, 28. *Chicago Evening Post,* Sept. 1, 1927, 9. *Chicago Eagle,* Sept. 17, 1927, 1.

30. Lloyd Wendt and Herman Kogan, *Big Bill of Chicago* (Indianapolis: Bobbs-Merrill, 1953), 274–75. John Bright, *Hizzoner Big Bill Thompson* (New York: Jonathan Cape & Harrison Smith, 1930), 177–82. Paul M. Green and Melvin G. Holli, *The Mayors: The Chicago Political Tradition* (Carbondale: Southern Illinois Univ. Press, 1987), 71–77. June Skinner Sawyers, *Chicago*

Portraits: Biographies of 250 Famous Chicagoans (Chicago: Loyola Univ. Press, 1991), 251–52. Laurence J. McCaffrey, Ellen Skerrett, Michael F. Funchion, and Chris Fanning, *The Irish in Chicago* (Urbana: Univ. of Illinois Press, 1987), 79–88.

31. The Getz scrapbook at the Chicago Historical Society shows Getz to have been a wheeler dealer in more than coal. He sailed to Africa to stock his private zoo in Holland, Mich., which was run by a staff of thirty-five, and seen, if one is to believe Getz's own publicity, by 800,000 visitors a year. See also *Christian Science Monitor,* Sept. 19, 1927, 1. *Chicago Herald and Examiner,* July 26, 1927, 13. *Chicago Evening American,* July 29, 1927, 19. *New York Times,* July 26, 1927, 12.

32. *New York Daily News,* July 28, 1927, 33. *Chicago Herald and Examiner,* Aug. 2, 1927, 1. *Chicago Tribune,* July 26, 1927, 15. Green and Holli, *The Mayors,* 76–77. Robert Cromie, *A Short History of Chicago* (San Francisco: Lexikos, 1984), 116–18.

33. *Chicago Defender,* Sept. 10, 1927, 8. *The New Republic,* Sept. 21, 1927, 109. *Literary Digest,* Sept. 17, 1927, 36, 41. *New York Evening Post,* Sept. 11, 1927, 11. *New York Herald-Tribune,* Sept. 13, 1927, 12.

34. *New York Daily News,* July 29, 1927, 36; July 30, 1927, 24, 25; and Aug. 2, 1927, 26. *New York Times,* July 27, 1927, 19; July 28, 1927, 11; July 29, 1927, 12; July 30, 1927, 9; and July 31, 1927, sec. 9, 6. *Chicago Daily News,* Sept. 16, 1927, 32. *Southtown (Chicago) Economist,* Aug. 31, 1927, 1. *Chicago Daily Journal,* Aug. 29, 1927, 11. Mrs. Tex Rickard and Arch Obeler, *Everything Happened to Him: The Story of Tex Rickard* (New York: Frederick Stokes, 1936), 328–29.

35. *St. Paul Pioneer Press,* Sept. 16, 1927, 11. *Chicago Evening American,* Sept. 22 1927, 1, 3. *Chicago Tribune,* Sept. 18, 1927, part 2, 5.

36. *Chicago Tribune,* Sept. 20, 1927, 22; and Sept. 23, 1927, 4, 6. *New York Times,* Sept. 22, 1927, 20, 21; and Sept. 23, 1927, 19, 20. *Deseret News,* Sept. 23, 1927, 4. *St. Louis Post-Dispatch,* Sept. 22, 1927, 14. *New York Herald-Tribune,* Sept. 22, 1927, 11.

37. *New York Times,* Sept. 22, 1927, 21. *Problems of Journalism,* vol. 6 (1928): 12–19; and vol. 7 (1929): 25–29, 91. See also Kent Cooper, *Kent Cooper and the Associated Press* (New York: Random House, 1959), 212–22. Victor Rosewater, *History of Cooperative News-Gathering in the United States* (New York: D. Appleton, 1930), 242–47. Oliver Grambling, *AP: The Story of News* (New York: Farrar and Rinehart, 1940), 262–73. "Editors Set 1928 Goals for Journalism," *Editor and Publisher,* Dec. 31, 1927, 7, 42. NBC's efforts to promote itself as the "fight network" are described in NBC Papers (1927), correspondence, box 2, folder 61, State Historical Society of Wisconsin.

38. *New York Times,* Sept. 22, 1927, 21. *Chicago Daily News,* Sept. 17, 1927, 1; Sept. 20, 1927, 23; Sept. 22, 1927, 27. See also William Ray Mofield,

"Broadcasting Comes of Age, 1900–1945," in *The Media in America: A History,* ed. Wm. David Sloan and James G. Stovall (Worthington, Ohio: Publishing Horizons, 1989), 313–21. Lewis J. Paper, *William S. Paley and the Making of CBS* (New York: St. Martin's Press, 1987), 117–32. J. Fred MacDonald, *Don't Touch That Dial: Radio Programming in American Life from 1920 to 1960* (Chicago: Nelson-Hall, 1979), 89–101. Erik Barnouw, *A Tower in Babel: A History of Broadcasting in the United States to 1933* (New York: Oxford Univ. Press, 1966), 125–52. Reynold Wik, "The Radio in Rural America during the 1920's," *Agricultural History* 55 (1981): 339–50. Francis Chase, Jr., *Sound and Fury* (New York: Harper, 1942), 67–83. Philip Collins, *Radio: The Golden Age* (New York: Chronicle Books, 1988), 34–45.

39. *New York Times,* Aug. 27, 1927, 11. *Chicago Evening Post,* Sept. 1, 1927, 9. *Denver Post,* Sept. 24, 1927, 29, 31. *Minneapolis Star Tribune,* Sept. 15, 1927, 10.

40. *Christian Century,* Sept. 22, 1927, 1091–92. Getz Scrapbook, Chicago Historical Society. *Chicago Eagle,* Sept. 3, 1927, 5. *New York Times,* Aug. 14, 1927, sec. S, 6; Aug. 22, 1927, 13; and Sept. 15, 1927, 27. *Chicago Tribune,* Aug. 23, 1927, 17; and Sept. 18, 1927, part 2, 4.

41. Getz Scrapbook, Chicago Historical Society. *New York Times,* July 25, 1927, 17; and Aug. 21, 1927, sec. 9, 7. *Chicago Evening Post,* Aug. 31, 1927, 11; Sept. 3, 1927, 7; and Sept. 22, 1927, 11. *Chicago Herald and Examiner,* Sept. 17, 1927, 13. *Chicago Evening American,* Sept. 16, 1927, 1, 37. *Kansas City Times,* Sept. 21, 1927, 26.

42. *New York Times,* Aug. 26, 1927, 13; and Sept. 18, 1927, 9. *Chicago Herald and Examiner,* Aug. 5, 1927, 15. *Chicago Evening Post,* Sept. 20, 1927, 20. *Chicago Daily Journal,* Sept. 22, 1927, 15.

43. *New York Times,* Sept. 22, 1927, 20. *Chicago Daily News,* Sept. 21, 1927, 1, 27. *Chicago Evening Post,* Sept. 21, 1927 1. *Hyde Park Herald,* Sept. 23, 1927, 1. *Daily Calumet,* Sept. 21, 1927, 1.

44. A. T. Andreas, *History of Chicago* (New York: Arno Press, 1975), vol. 1: 13–21. Bessie Louise Pierce, *A History of Chicago* (New York: Knopf, 1937), vol. 1: 5–13. Emmett Dedmon, *Fabulous Chicago* (New York: Atheneum, 1981), 27–31. Harold Mayer and Richard Wade, *Chicago: Growth of a Metropolis* (Chicago: Univ. of Chicago Press, 1969), 87–102. Reid Badger, *The Great American Fair: The World's Columbian Exposition and American Culture* (Chicago: Nelson-Hall, 1979), 126–30. David F. Burg, *Chicago's White City of 1893* (Lexington: Univ. of Kentucky Press, 1976), 277–91. *Chicago Herald and Examiner,* Sept. 3, 1927, 4. *Chicago Evening American,* Sept. 21, 1927, 5. *New York Times,* Sept. 18, 1927, sec. S, 5; and Sept. 22, 1927, 21. *New York Daily News,* Sept. 23, 1927, 60.

45. *New York Times,* Sept. 20, 1927, 20. *Chicago Tribune,* Sept. 21, 1927, 26. *Chicago Evening American,* Sept. 19, 1927, 5. *Minneapolis Daily Star,* Sept.

16, 1927, 20. *Salt Lake Tribune,* Sept. 19, 1927, 17. *Kansas City Times,* Sept. 23, 1927, 14. *Rocky Mountain News,* Sept. 23, 1927, 1.

46. *St. Paul Pioneer Press,* Sept. 19, 1927, sec. 2, 3. *New York Times,* Sept. 23, 1927, 1, 18. *Denver Post,* Sept. 23, 1927, 3. *Time,* Oct. 3, 1927, 29.

47. *New York Herald-Tribune,* Sept. 23, 1927, 1. *Chicago Herald and Examiner,* Sept. 23, 1927, 1, 2. Dempsey and Dempsey, *Dempsey,* 210–15. Tunney, *A Man Must Fight,* 262–63. *Chicago Evening American,* Sept. 23, 1927, 3. *Chicago Evening Post,* Sept. 23, 1927, 10. *New York Times,* Sept. 18, 1927, section S, 5. *Chicago Tribune,* Sept. 22, 1927, 1.

48. *New York Times,* Sept. 23, 1927, 20, 21. *Chicago Evening American,* Sept. 16, 1927, 39; Sept. 19, 1927, 20. *St. Paul Pioneer Press,* Sept. 23, 1927, 9. *Denver Post,* Sept. 23, 1927, 1. *Chicago Herald and Examiner,* Sept. 23, 1927, 3. *New York Daily News,* Sept. 23, 1927, 2. Nat Fleischer, *Jack Dempsey* (New Rochelle, N.Y.: Arlington House, 1972), 168–69. *Rocky Mountain News,* Sept. 23, 1927, 1, 13.

49. "Jack Dempsey vs. Gene Tunney, Sept. 22, 1927, Chicago, Ill.," *Fantastic Fights of the Century,* TM Productions, vol. 1. Fleischer, *Jack Dempsey,* 172. Tunney, *A Man Must Fight,* 268–69. *New York Journal,* Sept. 23, 1927, 1. *Chicago Daily News,* Sept. 23, 1927, 1. *New York Times,* Sept. 23, 1927, 21; and Sept. 24, 1927, 10. *Chicago Evening American,* Sept. 23, 1927, 3. *New York Daily News,* Sept. 23, 1927, 1.

50. "Dempsey vs. Tunney," *Fantastic Fights of the Century. New York Times,* Sept. 23, 1927, 21 and Sept. 24, 1927, 10. *Chicago Evening American,* Sept. 23, 1927, 17, 55. *Chicago Tribune,* Sept. 23, 1927, 1; and Sept. 24, 1927, 4. *Chicago Herald and Examiner,* Sept. 24, 1927, 1. *Chicago Daily Journal,* Sept. 23, 1927, 1.

51. "Dempsey vs. Tunney," *Fantastic Fights of the Century.* Tunney, *A Man Must Fight,* 269–73. Heimer, *The Long Count,* 247–51. Roberts, *Manassa Mauler,* 259–62. Gene Tunney, "My Fights with Jack Dempsey," in *The Aspirin Age,* ed. Isabel Leighton (New York: Simon & Schuster, 1949), 163–68.

52. "Dempsey vs. Tunney," *Fantastic Fights of the Century. New York Times,* Sept. 23, 1927, 21. Tunney, *Arms for Living,* 135–38. John Durant and Edward Rice, *Come Out Fighting* (New York: Essential Books, 1946), 105. Tim Cohane, *Bypaths of Glory: A Sportswriter Looks Back* (New York: Harper & Row, 1963), 90–92. *Chicago Tribune,* Sept. 24, 1927, 8.

53. *Chicago Herald and Examiner,* Sept. 22, 1927, 23, 24; Sept. 23, 1927, 1, 2. *New York Daily News,* Sept. 23, 1927, 2. *Chicago Evening Post,* Sept. 23, 1927. 10.

54. *Chicago Daily News,* Sept. 23, 1927, 52. *Chicago Evening Post,* Sept. 23, 1927, 8. *Chicago Tribune,* Sept. 24, 1927, 8. Cohane, *Bypaths of Glory,* 91–92. *New York Times,* Sept. 29, 1927, 20. *Chicago Evening Journal,* Sept. 23, 1927, 4. *Christian Century,* Sept. 22, 1927, 1091–92.

55. *Chicago Daily Journal,* Sept. 23, 1927, 4, 11. *Chicago Evening Post,*

Sept. 23, 1927, 3. *Chicago Daily News*, Sept. 23, 1927, 5. *Chicago Evening American*, Sept. 23, 1927, 9. *Daily Calumet*, Sept. 23, 1927, 1.

56. *Chicago Herald and Examiner*, Sept. 23, 1927, 5. *Chicago Eagle*, Sept. 24, 1927, 1. *Salt Lake Tribune*, Sept. 23, 1927, 5. *Deseret News*, Sept. 22, 1927, 3. *Chicago Tribune*, Sept. 23, 1927, 2. *Chicago Evening American*, Sept. 23, 1927, 11. That Piltdown was a fake was a fact that lay hidden from Fowler in his metaphor making.

57. *Chicago Herald and Examiner*, Sept. 23, 1927, 4, 6. *Chicago Evening American*, Sept. 23, 1927, 18. NBC Papers (1927), correspondence, box 2, folder 61, State Historical Society of Wisconsin, Madison. *Minneapolis Daily Star*, Sept. 24, 1927, 16.

58. *Chicago Herald and Examiner*, Sept. 24, 1927, 2. *Chicago Evening American*, Sept. 23, 1927, 55. *New York Daily News*, Sept. 25, 1927, 59. *New York Times*, Sept. 25, 1927, 17. *The Nation*, Sept. 28, 1927, 305. *Christian Century*, Sept. 22, 1927, 1091–92.

59. *New York Times*, Sept. 24, 1927, 9, 10. *Philadelphia Inquirer*, Aug. 23, 1928, 21. *Philadelphia Public-Ledger*, Aug. 31, 1928, 12.

60. *New York Times*, July 27, 1928, 1, 14; and July 28, 1940, 20. *New York Daily News*, July 27, 1928, 2, 32. *New York Herald-Tribune*, July 27, 1928, 16. See also Gene Tunney, preface to *Ten and Out: The Complete Story of the Prize Ring in America* by Alexander Johnston (New York: Ives Washburn, 1927). Cohane, *Bypaths of Glory*, 91–92. Tunney, *Arms for Living*, 228–43. Tunney, *A Man Must Fight*, 282–83. Benny Green, *Shaw's Champions: G. B. S. and Prizefighting from Cashel Byron to Gene Tunney* (London: Elm Tree Books, 1978), 137–46, 176–85. *The Nation*, Aug. 8, 1928, 125. Gene Tunney, "The Blow That Hurts," *Atlantic Monthly*, June 1939, 839–41.

61. *New York Times*, Jan. 3, 1929, 23; Jan. 5, 1929, 1; Jan. 6, 1929, 1, 30; and Jan. 7, 1929, 1, 24. *New York Daily News*, Jan. 5, 1929, 1; and Jan. 7, 1929, 1.

62. *New York Times*, Jan. 7, 1929, 1, 24. *New York Daily News*, Jan. 7, 1929, 1. *New York Herald-Tribune*, Jan. 7, 1929, 1. *Minneapolis Daily Star*, Jan. 7, 1929, 1, 10. *Kansas City Star*, Jan. 7, 1929, 1, 14. *St. Louis Post-Dispatch*, Jan. 7, 1929, 1, 18.

63. *New York Times*, Jan. 7, 1929, 22; Jan. 8, 1929, 36; and Jan. 9, 1929, 1. *New York Morning World*, Jan. 9, 1929, 1. *New York Daily News*, Jan. 9, 1929, 1, 2.

64. *New York Times*, Jan. 7, 1929, 28; and Jan. 9, 1929, 1, 35. Samuels, *Magnificent Rube*, 292–96. Rickard and Obeler, *Everything Happened*, 366–68. Gallico, *Golden People*, 191–95. Grantland Rice, *The Tumult and the Shouting* (New York: A. S. Barnes, 1954), 134–37. James Dawson, "Boxing," in *Sport's Golden Decade: A Close-up of the Fabulous Twenties*, ed. Allison Danzig and Peter Brandwein, (Freeport: N.Y.: Books for Libraries, 1948), 84–85.

65. Dempsey and Dempsey, *Dempsey*, 227–32. Roberts, *Manassa Mauler*,

264–65. NBC Papers (1930), correspondence, box 2, folder 61, State Historical Society of Wisconsin.

66. Roberts, *Manassa Mauler,* 265–66. Gene Fowler, *Skyline: A Reporter's Reminiscence of the 1920's* (New York: Viking Press, 1961), 310–14. Jack Kearns and Oscar Fraley, *The Million Dollar Gate* (New York: Macmillan, 1966), 329–34. Robert H. Elias, *"Entangling Alliances with None": An Essay on the Individual in the American Twenties* (New York: W. W. Norton, 1973), 163–65. Orrin E. Klapp, *Heroes, Villains, and Fools: The Changing American Character* (Englewood Cliffs, N.J.: Prentice-Hall, 1962), 35–37, 98–101. Elliot J. Gorn, *The Manly Art: Bare-Knuckle Prize Fighting in America* (Ithaca, N.Y.: Cornell Univ. Press, 1986), 248–54. See also William E. Leuchtenburg, *The Perils of Prosperity, 1914–1932* (Chicago: Univ. of Chicago Press, 1958), 158–77. Henry F. May, *The End of American Innocence: A Study of the First Years of Our Time, 1912–1917* (New York: Knopf, 1959), 363–98. Joseph F. Kett, *Rites of Passage: Adolescence in America, 1790 to the Present* (New York: Basic Books, 1978), 254–64. John G. Cawelti, *Apostles of the Self-Made Man* (Chicago: Univ. of Chicago Press, 1965), 1–6. Peter N. Stearns, *Be a Man! Males in Modern Society* (New York: Holmes and Meier, 1990), 157–64. Robert M. Crunden, *From Self to Society, 1919–1941* (Englewood Cliffs, N.J.: Prentice-Hall, 1972), 72–73.

67. *New York Times,* June 1, 1983, 1, 4. *Chicago Tribune,* June 1, 1983, 1, 20. Jerome Holtzman, *No Cheering in the Press Box* (New York: Holt, Rinehart and Winston, 1974), 243–59.

68. *New York Times,* June 2, 1983, 22, sec. 2, 11, 12; June 4, 1983, 4; and June 5, 1983, sec. S, 2, sec. 5, 3. *Chicago Tribune,* June 5, 1983, sec. 3, 15.

Bibliography

COLLECTIONS

American Society of Newspaper Editors. Archives. Newspaper Center. Reston, Va.

Archdiocese of Philadelphia. Archives and Historical Collections. Overbrook, Pa.

Balch Institute for Ethnic Studies. Ethnic Press Collection. Research Library. Philadelphia, Pa.

Chicago Historical Society. Newspaper Collection. George Fulmer Getz Scrapbook. Chicago, Ill.

Colorado Historical Society. Stephen H. Hart Library. Colorado State Museum. Newspaper & Special Collections. Denver, Colo.

Concordia Theological Seminary. Special Collections. Fort Wayne, Ind.

Creager, Marvin. Papers. State Historical Society of Wisconsin. Madison, Wisc.

DePaul Univ. Special Collections. Newspaper Collection. Chicago, Ill.

Detroit News and *Detroit Free Press* Archives. Malcolm Bingay Papers. Detroit, Mich.

Joplin Globe. Edwin H. McReynolds Files. Joplin, Mo.

Kansas City Public Library. Newspaper Collection. Kansas City, Mo.

McCormick, Robert R. Papers. Newspaper Collection. Donnelly Library. Lake Forest College. Lake Forest, Ill.

Minnesota Historical Society. Newspaper Collection. St. Paul, Minn.

NBC Papers. State Historical Society of Wisconsin. Madison, Wisc.

Newspaper Collection. Free Library of Philadelphia. Philadelphia, Pennsylvania.

Patterson, Joseph Medill. Papers. Donnelly Library. Lake Forest College. Newspaper Collection. Lake Forest, Ill.

Presbyterian Church (U.S.A.). Periodical Collection. Office of History. Philadelphia, Pa.

Salt Lake Library. Newspaper Collection. Special Collections. Salt Lake City, Utah.

Sesquicentennial Collection. Louis F. Whitcomb Collection. Historical Society of Pennsylvania. Philadelphia, Pa.

Sesquicentennial Exposition Association. Files of Officials, Executive Committee and Board of Directors. Minutes of City Council Meetings. City Archives of Philadelphia. Philadelphia, Pa.

State Historical Society of Missouri. Newspaper Collections. Columbia, Mo.

Urban Archives. Temple Univ. Philadelphia, Pa.

Yost, Caspar S. Papers. Estate of Caspar S. Yost. Webster Grove, Mo.

NEWSPAPERS

Alamosa Independent-Journal
Antonio Ledger
Atlanta Constitution
Baltimore Sun
Boston Evening Transcript
Boston Globe
Brooklyn Eagle
Catholic Standard and Times
    (Philadelphia, Pa.)
Chicago Daily Inter-Ocean
Chicago Daily Journal
Chicago Daily News
Chicago Defender
Chicago Eagle
Chicago Evening American
Chicago Evening Post
Chicago Herald and Examiner
Chicago Tribune
Christian Science Monitor
Cleveland Plain Dealer
Craig (Colo.) Courier
Creede (Colo.) Candle
Daily Calumet
Denver Morning Telegram
Denver Post
Deseret News
Detroit News
Hyde Park Journal
Indianapolis Star
Joplin Globe and News Herald
Kansas City Call
Kansas City Star
Kansas City Times
Leadville (Colo.) Carbonate Weekly
    Chronicle
Leadville (Colo.) Evening Journal
Meeker (Colo.) Herald
Miami News
Milwaukee Journal
Minneapolis Daily Star
Moffat County (Colo.) Courier
National Police Gazette

New Orleans Picayune
New York American
New York Daily News
New York Evening Journal
New York Herald-Tribune
New York Journal
New York Press
New York Times
New York Tribune
New York World
Philadelphia Daily News
Philadelphia Evening Bulletin
Philadelphia Inquirer
Philadelphia Public Ledger
Philadelphia Record
Philadelphia Tribune
Pittsburgh Ledger
Rocky Mountain News
Routt County (Colo.) Sentinel
St. Louis Globe Democrat
St. Louis Post-Dispatch
St. Paul Pioneer Press
Sacramento Bee
Salt Lake Tribune
San Francisco Chronicle
San Francisco Examiner
Seattle Post-Intelligencer
Southtown (Chicago) Economist
Steamboat Springs (Colo.) Pilot
The Times (of London)
Toledo Blade

BOOKS

Addams, Jane. *Twenty Years at Hull House*. New York: Macmillan, 1910.

Adney, Tappan. *The Klondike Stampede*. New York: Harper & Bros., 1900.

Alexander, Charles C. *John McGraw*. New York: Viking, 1988.

Andreas, A. T. *History of Chicago*. Chicago: A. T. Andreas, 1885.

Andrews, Wayne. *Battle for Chicago*. New York: Harcourt, Brace, 1946.

Applebaum, Stanley. *The Chicago World's Fair of 1893: A Photographic Record*. New York: Dover, 1980.

Asbury, Herbert. *Gem of the Prairie: An Informal History of the Chicago Underworld*. New York: Garden City Publishers, 1942.

Athearn, Robert G. *The Mythic West in Twentieth Century America*. Lawrence: Univ. Press of Kansas, 1986.

Aylesworth, Thomas G., and Virginia L. Aylesworth, *Chicago: The Glamorous Years, 1919–1941*. Greenwich, Conn.: W. H. Smith Publishers, 1986.

Badger, Reid. *The Great American Fair: The World's Columbian Exposition and American Culture*. Chicago: Nelson-Hall, 1979.

Ballowe, James, ed. *George Santayana's America: Essays on Literature and Culture*. Urbana: Univ. of Illinois Press, 1967.

Banks, Louis Albert. *The Story of the Hall of Fame, Including the Lives and Portraits of the Elect and of Those Who Barely Missed Election*. New York: Christian Herald, 1902.

Bankson, Russell R. *The Klondike Nugget*. Caldwell, Idaho: Caxton Printers, 1935.

Barclay, Morgan, and Charles N. Glaab. *Toledo: Gateway to the Great Lakes*. Tulsa, Okla.: Heritage Press, 1982.

Barnouw, Erik. *A Tower in Babel: A History of Broadcasting in the United States to 1933*. New York: Oxford Univ. Press, 1966.

Beach, Rex. *The Barrier*. New York: Harper, 1908.

Beach, Rex, *Personal Exposures*. New York: Harper & Bros., 1940.

Beach, Rex. *The Silver Horde*. New York: Harper, 1907.

Beach, Rex. *The Spoilers*. New York: Harper, 1906.

Beard, Charles A., ed. *Whither Mankind: A Panorama of Modern Civilization*. New York: Longmans, Green, 1928.

Beaver, Daniel R. *Newton D. Baker and the American War Effort, 1917–1919*. Lincoln: Univ. of Nebraska Press, 1966.

Bellows, Emma L. *The Paintings of George Bellows*. New York: Knopf, 1929.

Bennett, Bruce L., ed. *Proceedings of the Big Ten Symposium on the History of Physical Education and Sport at Ohio State University, Columbus, Ohio on Mar. 1–3, 1971*. Chicago: The Athletic Institute, 1972.

Bennion, Sherilyn C. *Equal to the Occasion: Women Editors of the 19th Century West*. Reno: Univ. of Nevada Press, 1990.

Bent, Silas. *Ballyhoo: The Voice of the Press*. New York: Boni and Liveright, 1927.

Bent, Silas. *Man Made Machine*. New York: Farrar and Rinehart, 1930.

Berger, Meyer. *The Story of the New York Times, 1851–1951*. New York: Simon & Schuster, 1951.

Berthoff, Rowland. *An Unsettled People: Social Order and Disorder in American History.* New York: Harper & Row, 1971.

Bessie, Simon M. *Jazz Journalism.* New York: E. P. Dutton, 1938.

Bledstein, Burton J. *The Culture of Professionalism: The Middle Class and the Development of Higher Education in America.* New York: W. W. Norton, 1976.

Bogen, Boris D. *Born a Jew.* New York: Macmillan, 1930.

Bond, F. Fraser. *Mr. Miller of "The Times."* New York: Charles Scribner's Sons, 1931.

Boswell, Jr., Peyton. *George Bellows.* New York: Crown Publishers, 1942.

Boyle, Robert. *Sport: Mirror of American Life.* Boston: Little, Brown & Co., 1963.

Brady, William A. *Showman* New York: E. P. Dutton, 1937.

Bright, John. *Hizzoner Big Bill Thompson.* New York: Jonathan Cape & Harrison Smith, 1930.

Britt, George. *Forty Years, Forty Millions: The Career of Frank A. Munsey.* New York: Farrar and Rinehart, 1935.

Bromberg, Lester. *Boxing's Unforgettable Fights.* New York: Ronald Press, 1962.

Broun, Heywood. *The Sun Field.* New York: G. P. Putnam's Sons, 1923.

Burg, David F. *Chicago's White City of 1893.* Lexington: Univ. of Kentucky Press, 1976.

Burgess, Ernest W., ed. *The Urban Community: Selected Papers from the Proceedings of the American Sociological Society, 1925.* Chicago: Univ. of Chicago Press, 1926.

Burlingame, Roger. *Don't Let Them Scare You: The Life of Elmer Davis.* Philadelphia: J. B. Lippincott, 1961.

Cahan, Abraham. *Bleter Fun Mein Lebe, Leaves from My Life.* New York: Forward Association, 1926.

Cahan, Abraham. *The Rise of David Levinsky.* Gloucester, Mass.: Peter Smith, 1969.

Carlson, Oliver, and Ernest Sutherland. *Hearst: Lord of San Simeon.* New York: Viking, 1936.

Carr-Sanders, A. M. *Professions: Their Organization and Place in Society.* Oxford: Clarendon Press, 1928.

Carr-Sanders, A. M. and P. A. Wilson. *The Professions.* Oxford: Clarendon Press, 1933.

Cavallo, Dominick. *Muscles and Morals: Organized Playgrounds and Urban Reform, 1880–1920.* Philadelphia: Univ. of Pennsylvania Press, 1981.

Cawelti, John G. *Apostles of the Self-Made Man.* Chicago: Univ. of Chicago Press, 1965.

Champlin, John Denison, ed. *Orations, Addresses and Speeches of Chauncey M. Depew.* New York: Depew Trust, 1910.

Chapman, John. *Tell It to Sweeney: The Informal History of the New York Daily News.* Garden City, N.Y.: Doubleday, 1961.

Chase, Jr., Francis. *Sound and Fury.* New York: Harper, 1942.

Chicago Vice Commission, *The Social Evil of Chicago.* Chicago: Chicago Vice Commission, 1911.

Cloud, Barbara. *The Business of Newspapers on the Western Frontier.* Reno: Univ. of Nevada Press, 1992.

Coffin, Tristram Potter, and Hennig Cohen, eds. *The Parade of Heroes: Legendary Figures in American Lore.* Garden City, N.Y.: Doubleday, 1978.

Cohane, Tim. *Bypaths of Glory: A Sportswriter Looks Back*. New York: Harper & Row, 1963.

Collins, Philip. *Radio: The Golden Age*. New York: Chronicle Books, 1988.

Connery, Thomas B., ed. *A Sourcebook of Literary Journalism: Representative Writers in an Emerging Genre*. New York: Greenwood Press, 1992.

Cooper, Kent. *Kent Cooper and the Associated Press: An Autobiography*. New York: Random House, 1959.

Corbett, James J. *The Roar of the Crowd: The True Tale of the Rise and Fall of a Champion*. New York: G. P. Putnam's Sons, 1925.

Counts, George S. *School and Society in Chicago*. New York: Harcourt, Brace, 1928.

Cox, James M. *Journey Through My Years*. New York: Simon & Schuster, 1946.

Crawford, Nelson A. *The Ethics of Journalism*. New York: Knopf, 1924.

Cronon, William, George Miles, and Jay Gitlin, eds. *Under an Open Sky: Rethinking America's Western Past*. New York: W. W. Norton, 1992.

Crowley, David and Paul Heyer, eds. *Communication in History: Technology, Culture, Society*. New York: Longman Publishing Group, 1991.

Crunden, Robert M. *From Self to Society, 1919–1941*. Englewood Cliffs, N.J.: Prentice-Hall, 1972.

Czitrom, Daniel J. *Media and the American Mind: From Morse to McLuhan*. Chapel Hill: Univ. of North Carolina Press, 1982.

Dance, Stanley. *The World of Earl Hines*. New York: Charles Scribner's Sons, 1977.

Daniels, Jonathan. *They Will Be Heard: America's Crusading Newspaper Editors*. New York: McGraw-Hill, 1965.

Danzig, Allison, and Peter Brandwein, eds. *Sport's Golden Decade: A Close-up of the Fabulous Twenties*. New York: Books for Libraries, 1948.

Davis, Elmer, *History of the New York Times*. New York: New York Times, 1921.

De Coubertin, Pierre. *The Olympic Idea: Discourses and Essays*. Stuttgart: Olympischer Sport-Verlag, 1967.

De Quille, Dan. *An Authentic Account of the Discovery, History and Working of the World Renowned Comstock Lode of Nevada, Including Present Conditions of Various Mines Situated Thereon, Sketches of the Most Prominent Men Interested in Them, Incidents and Adventures Connected with Mining, the Indians and the Country, Amusing Stories, Experiences, Anecdotes and a Full Exposition of the Production of Pure Silver*. New York: Knopf, 1947.

Dedmon, Emmett. *Fabulous Chicago*. New York: Random House, 1953.

Dempsey, Jack, Bob Considine, and Bill Slocum. *Dempsey: By the Man Himself*. New York: Simon & Schuster, 1960.

Dempsey, Jack, and Barbara Piatelli Dempsey. *Dempsey*. New York: Harper & Row, 1977.

Dempsey, Jack, and Myron M. Stearns. *Round by Round: An Autobiography*. New York: Whittlesey House, 1940.

Denney, Reuel. *The Astonished Muse*. Chicago: Univ. of Chicago Press, 1957.

Dennis, Charles H. *Victor Lawson, His Time and His Work*. Chicago: Univ. of Chicago Press, 1935.

Depew, Chauncey M. *My Memories of Eighty Years.* New York: Charles Scribner's Sons, 1922.

Dozema, Marianne. *George Bellows and Urban America.* New Haven: Yale Univ. Press, 1992.

Drake, St. Clair, and Horace R. Clayton, *Black Metropolis: A Study of Negro Life in a Northern City.* New York: Harcourt, Brace, 1945.

Duddert, Joe L. *A Man's Place: Masculinity in Transition.* Englewood Cliffs, N.J.: Prentice-Hall, 1979.

Dulles, Foster Rhea. *America Learns to Play: A History of Popular Recreation, 1607–1940.* Gloucester, Mass.: Peter Smith, 1963.

Durant, John. *The Heavyweight Champions.* New York: Hastings House, 1971.

Durant, John, and Edward Rice. *Come Out Fighting.* New York: Essential Books, 1946.

Durkheim, Emile. *The Elementary Forms of Religious Life.* New York: Free Press, 1965.

Durso, Joseph. *Madison Square Garden: One Hundred Years of History.* New York: Simon & Schuster, 1979.

Eastman, Max. *Journalism vs. Art.* New York: Knopf, 1916.

Edwards, Harry. *Sociology of Sport.* Homewood, Ill.: Dorsey, 1973.

Egan, Pierce. *Boxiana or Sketches of Ancient and Modern Pugilism from the Days of the Renowned James Figg and Jack Broughton to the Heroes of the Later Milling Era.* London: The Folio Society, 1976.

Elias, Robert H. *"Entangling Alliances with None": An Essay on the Individual in the American Twenties.* New York: W. W. Norton, 1973.

Epstein, Melech. *Profiles of Eleven.* Detroit: Wayne State Univ. Press, 1965.

Etulian, Richard W., ed. *Writing Western History: Essays on Major Western. Historians* Albuquerque: Univ. of New Mexico Press, 1991.

Emery, Edwin. *The Press and America: An Interpretative History of Journalism.* Englewood Cliffs, N.J.: Prentice-Hall, 1962.

Evans, Frank B. *Pennsylvania Politics, 1872–1877: A Study of Political Leadership.* Harrisburg, Pa.: Pennsylvania Historical and Museum Commission, 1966.

Farley, James A. *Behind the Ballots: The Personal History of a Politician.* New York: Harcourt, Brace, 1938.

Fetherline, Doug. *The Five Lives of Ben Hecht.* Toronto: Lester and Orpen, 1977.

Fine, Barnett. *A Giant of the Press.* New York: Editor & Publisher Library, 1933.

Fisher, Dorothy Canfield. *The Brimming Cup.* New York: Harcourt, Brace, 1921.

Fisher, Dorothy Canfield. *Hillsboro People.* New York: Grosset and Dunlap, 1915.

Fisher, Dorothy Canfield. *Raw Material.* New York: Harcourt, Brace, 1925.

Fleischer, Nat. *Fifty Years at Ringside.* New York: Fleet, 1958.

Fleischer, Nat. *Gene Tunney: The Enigma of the Ring.* New York: The Ring, 1931.

Fleischer, Nat. *The Heavyweight Championship: An Informal History of Heavyweight Boxing from 1719 to the Present Day.* New York: G. P. Putnam's Sons, 1949.

Fleischer, Nat. *Jack Dempsey.* New Rochelle, N.Y.: Arlington House, 1972.

Fleischer, Nat. *Jack Dempsey: The Idol of Fistiana.* New York: The Ring, 1929.

Flint, Leon N. *The Conscience of a Newspaper: A Case Book in the Principles and Problems of Journalism*. New York: D. Appleton, 1925.

Folkerts, Jean, and Dwight Teeter, eds. *Media Voices: An Historical Perspective*. New York: Macmillan, 1992.

Fosdick, Raymond B. *Chronicle of a Generation: An Autobiography*. New York: Harper, 1958.

Fowler, Gene. *Beau James*. New York: Viking, 1949.

Fowler, Gene. *Skyline: A Reporter's Reminiscence of the 1920's*. New York: Viking, 1961.

Friedrich, Otto. *Ring Lardner* Minneapolis: Univ. of Minnesota Press, 1965.

Friedman, Elisha M., ed. *America and the New Era: A Symposium on Social Reconstruction*. New York: E. P. Dutton, 1920.

Fuller, Walter D. *The Life and Times of Cyrus H. K. Curtis*. New York: Newcomen Society of England, American Branch, 1948.

Fullerton, Hugh S. *Two-Fisted Jeff*. Chicago: Consolidated, 1929.

Gallico, Paul. *Farewell to Sport*. New York: Knopf, 1940.

Gallico, Paul. *The Golden People*. Garden City, N.Y.: Doubleday, 1965.

Gardner, Dorsey, ed. *United States Centennial Commission: International Exhibition, 1876, Grounds and Buildings of the Centennial Exhibition, Philadelphia, 1876*. Philadelphia: J. B. Lippincott, 1878.

Garland, Hamlin. *The Son of the Middle Border*. New York: Macmillan, 1917.

Gauvreau, Emile. *Hot News*. New York: Macaulay, 1931.

Geertz, Clifford. *The Interpretation of Cultures*. New York: Basic Books, 1973.

Geismar, Maxwell, ed. *The Ring Lardner Reader*. New York: Charles Scribner's Sons, 1963.

Gies, Joseph. *The Colonel of Chicago*. New York: E. P. Dutton, 1979.

Gilmore, Al-Tony. *Bad Nigger! The National Impact of Jack Johnson*. Port Washington, N.Y.: National Univ. Publications, 1975.

Glassberg, David. *American Historical Pageantry: The Uses of Tradition in the Early Twentieth Century*. Chapel Hill: Univ. of North Carolina Press, 1990.

Goodman, Cary. *Choosing Sides: Playgrounds and Street Life on the Lower East Side*. New York: Schocken Books, 1979.

Gorn, Elliot J. *The Manly Art: Bare-Knuckle Prize Fighting in America*. Ithaca: Cornell Univ. Press, 1986.

Gosnell, Harold F. *Negro Politicians: The Rise of Negro Politics in Chicago*. Chicago: Univ. of Chicago Press, 1935.

Goulden, Joseph C. *The Curtis Caper*. New York: G. P. Putnam's Sons, 1965.

Grambling, Oliver. *AP: The Story of News*. New York: Farrar and Rinehart, 1940.

Green, Benny. *Shaw's Champions: George Bernard Shaw and Prizefighting from Cashel Byron to Gene Tunney*. London: Elm Tree Books, 1978.

Green, Paul M., and Melvin G. Holli, *The Mayors: The Chicago Political Tradition*. Carbondale: Southern Illinois Univ. Press, 1987.

Griffith, Sally Foreman. *Home Town News: William Allen White and the Emporia Gazette*. New York: Oxford Univ. Press, 1989.

Gronbeck, Bruce E., Thomas J. Farrell, and Paul A. Soukop, eds. *Media, Consciousness and Culture: Explorations of Walter Ong's Thought.* Newbury Park, Calif.: Sage, 1991.

Halaas, David Fridtjof. *Boom Town Newspapers: Journalism on the Rocky Mountain Mining Frontier, 1859–1881.* Albuquerque: Univ. of New Mexico Press, 1981.

Hapgood, Hutchins. *Spirit of the Ghetto.* New York: Funk and Wagnalls, 1965.

Harbord, James G. *The American Army in France, 1917–1919.* Boston: Little, Brown & Co., 1936.

Hardy, Stephen. *How Boston Played: Sport, Recreation, and Community, 1865–1915.* Boston: Northeastern Univ. Press, 1982.

Harris, A. S. *Alaska and the Klondike Goldfields.* Chicago: Monroe Book Company, 1897.

Harrison, Carter H. *Stormy Years.* Indianapolis: Bobbs-Merrill, 1935.

Haskell, Thomas L. *The Emergence of Professional Social Science: The American Social Science Association and the 19th Century Crisis of Authority.* Urbana: Univ. of Illinois Press, 1977.

Hauser, Odell. *The Sesqui-Centennial: A Record Based on Official Data and Department Records.* Philadelphia: Current Publications, 1929.

Healey, Paul F. *Cissy: The Biography of Eleanor M. "Cissy" Patterson.* Garden City, N.Y.: Doubleday, 1966.

Hecht, Ben. *A Child of the Century.* New York: Simon & Schuster, 1954.

Heimer, Mel. *The Long Count.* New York: Atheneum, 1969.

Heinz, W. C., ed. *The Fireside Book of Boxing.* New York: Simon & Schuster, 1961.

Hershberg, Theodore, ed. *Philadelphia: Work, Space, Family, and Group Existence in the Nineteenth Century.* New York: Oxford Univ. Press, 1981.

Higham, John, and Paul Conkin, eds. *New Directions in American Intellectual History.* Baltimore: Johns Hopkins Univ. Press, 1979.

Higinbotham, H. N. *Report of the President to the Board of Directors of the World's Columbian Exposition.* Chicago: Rand McNally, 1898.

Hillquit, Morris. *Loose Leaves from a Busy Life.* New York: Macmillan, 1934.

Hirsch, Susan E., and Robert I. Goler, eds. *A City Comes of Age: Chicago in the 1890's.* Chicago: Chicago Historical Society, 1990.

Hoge, Alice Albright. *Cissy Patterson.* New York: Random House, 1966.

Hollander, Zander, ed. *Madison Square Garden: A Century of Sport and Spectacle on the World's Most Versatile Stage.* New York: Hawthorn Publishers, 1973.

Holtzman, Jerome. *No Cheering in the Press Box.* New York: Holt, Rinehart & Winston, 1974.

Hostetter, Gordon L., and Thomas Quinn Beesley. *It's a Racket!* Chicago: Univ. of Chicago Press, 1929.

Hough, Emerson. *The Story of the Cowboy.* New York: D. Appleton, 1931.

Howe, Daniel Walker, ed. *Victorian America.* Philadelphia: Univ. of Pennsylvania Press, 1972.

Howe, Irving, and Kenneth Libo, *How We Lived: A Documentary History of Immigrant Life in America, 1880–1930.* New York: Richard Marek, 1979.

Howe, Irving. *World of Our Fathers.* New York: Harcourt Brace Jovanovich, 1976.

Hughes, Helen M. *News and the Human Interest Story.* Chicago: Univ. of Chicago Press, 1940.

Huizinga, Johan. *America: A Dutch Historian's View from Afar and Near.* New York: Harper & Row, 1972.

Hunter, John Marvin. *The Trail Drivers of Texas.* Nashville: Cokesburg Press, 1925.

Hutchinson, William T. *Cyrus Hall McCormick: Harvest, 1856–1884.* New York: D. Appleton-Century, 1935.

Huxley, Aldous. *On the Margin: Notes and Essays.* London: Chatto and Windus, 1923.

Ingersoll, Ernest. *In Richest Alaska and the Goldfields of the Klondike.* Chicago: The Dominion Company, 1897.

Inglis, William *Champions Off Guard.* New York: Vanguard Press, 1932.

Ingram, J. S. *The Centennial Exposition, Described and Illustrated, Being a Concise and Graphic Description of This Grand Enterprise Commemorative of the First Centenary of American Independence.* Philadelphia: Hubbard Bros., 1876.

Isenberg, Michael T. *John L. Sullivan and His America.* Urbana: Univ. of Illinois Press, 1988.

Jensen, Joli. *Redeeming Modernity: Contradictions in Media Criticism.* Newbury Park, Calif.: Sage, 1990.

Johnson, Gerald W. *An Honorable Titan: A Biographical Study of Adolph S. Ochs.* New York: Harper & Bros., 1946.

Johnson, Jack. *Jack Johnson in the Ring and Out.* Chicago: National Sports Publishing, 1927.

Johnston, Alexander. *Ten and Out! The Complete Story of the Prize Ring in America.* New York: Ives Washburn, 1927.

Kammen, Michael, ed. *The Past Before Us: Contemporary Historical Writing in the United States.* Ithaca, N.Y.: Cornell Univ. Press, 1980.

Kearns, Jack, and Oscar Fraley. *The Million Dollar Gate.* New York: Macmillan, 1966.

Kelly, John. *Leisure Identities and Interactions.* London: George Allen and Unwin, 1983.

Kett, Joseph F. *Rites of Passage: Adolescence in America, 1790 to the Present.* New York: Basic Books, 1978.

Kinsley, Philip. *The Chicago Tribune: Its First Hundred Years.* Vol 1. New York: Knopf, 1943.

———. *The Chicago Tribune: Its First Hundred Years.* Vol. 2. Chicago: Chicago Tribune Company, 1945.

———. *The Chicago Tribune: Its First Hundred Years.* Vol. 3. Chicago: Chicago Tribune Company, 1946.

Klapp, Orrin E. *Heroes, Villains and Fools: The Changing American Character.* Englewood Cliffs, N.J.: Prentice-Hall, 1962.

———. *Symbolic Leaders: Public Dramas and Public Men.* Chicago: Aldine, 1964.

Knight, Robert, and Lucius H. Zeuch. *The Location of the Chicago Portage Route of the Seventeenth Century.* Chicago: Univ. of Chicago Press, 1928.

Kuklick, Bruce. *To Every Thing a Season: Shibe Park and Urban Philadelphia, 1909–1976*. Princeton: Princeton Univ. Press, 1991.

LaCapra, Dominick. *Soundings in Critical Theory*. Ithaca, N.Y.: Cornell Univ. Press, 1989.

Ladue, Joseph. *Klondike Facts*. New York: American Technical Book Company, 1897.

Lakey, Thomas A. *The Morals of Newspaper Making*. Notre Dame: Univ. Press, 1924.

Landesco, John. *Organized Crime in Chicago*. Chicago: Univ. of Chicago Press, 1968.

Langland, James, ed. *The Daily News Almanac and Year-book*. Chicago: Chicago Daily News, 1928.

Lanier, Henry Wisham. *Greenwich Village Today and Yesterday*. New York: Harper, 1949.

Lardner, John. *White Hopes and Other Tigers*. Philadelphia: J. B. Lippincott, 1947.

Lardner, Rex. *The Legendary Champions*. New York: American Heritage Press, 1972.

Lardner, Ring. *First and Last*. New York: Charles Scribner's Sons, 1934.

———. *Gullible's Travels*. Indianapolis: Bobbs-Merrill, 1917.

———. *The Real Dope*. Indianapolis: Bobbs-Merrill, 1919.

———. *You Know Me Al*. New York: George H. Doran, 1916.

Lardner, Jr., Ring. *The Lardners: My Family Remembered*. New York: Harper & Row, 1973.

Learsi, Rufus. *The Jews in America: A History*. New York: World, 1954.

Lee, Alfred M. *The Daily Newspaper in America*. New York: Macmillan, 1937.

Lehman, Harvey C., and Paul A. Witty, *The Psychology of Play Activities*. New York: A. S. Barnes, 1927.

Leighton, Isabel, ed. *The Aspirin Age*. New York: Simon & Schuster, 1949.

Lerner, Max. *America as a Civilization: Life and Thought in the United States Today*. New York: Simon & Schuster, 1957.

Leuchtenburg, William E. *The Perils of Prosperity, 1914–1932*. Chicago: Univ. of Chicago Press, 1958.

Levine, Lawrence A., and Robert Middlekauff, eds., *The National Temper: Readings in American Culture and Society*. New York: Harcourt Brace Jovanovich, 1972.

Lewis, Frederick Allen. *Only Yesterday: An Informal History of the 1920's*. New York: Harper & Row, 1959.

Lewis, Lloyd, and Henry Justin Smith. *Chicago: The History of Its Reputation*. New York: Harcourt, Brace, 1929.

Liebling, A. J. *The Sweet Science*. New York: Viking, 1956.

Limerick, Patricia Nelson, Clyde A. Milner, and Charles E. Rankin, eds. *Trails Toward a New Western History*. Lawrence: Univ. Press of Kansas, 1991.

Linn, James Weber. *James Keeley, Newspaperman*. Indianapolis: Bobbs-Merrill, 1937.

Lipsyte, Robert. *Sports World: An American Dreamland*. New York: New York Times Book Company, 1975.

Lockwood, Sarah M. *New York: Not So Little and Not So Old*. Garden City, N.Y.: Doubleday, 1926.

Longstreet, Stephen. *Chicago: An Intimate Portrait of People, Pleasures and Power, 1860–1919*. New York: David McKay, 1973.

Lloyd, Alan. *The Great Prize Fight.* New York: Coward, McCann and Geohegan, 1977.

Lundberg, Ferdinand. *Imperial Hearst: A Social Biography.* New York: Equinox Cooperative Press, 1936.

Maass, John. *The Glorious Enterprise: The Centennial Exhibition of 1876 and H. J. Schwartzmann, Architect-in-Chief.* Watkins Glen, N.Y.: American Life Foundation, 1973.

MacAloon, John J. *Rite, Drama, Festival, Spectacle.* Philadelphia: Institute for the Study of Human Issues, 1984.

MacDonald, J. Fred. *Don't Touch That Dial: Radio Programming in American Life from 1920 to 1960.* Chicago: Nelson-Hall, 1979.

MacIver, Robert M. *The Pursuit of Happiness.* New York: Simon & Schuster, 1955.

MacNeil, Neil. *Without Fear or Favor.* New York: Harcourt, Brace, 1940.

Mandell, Richard D. *Sport: A Cultural History.* New York: Columbia Univ. Press, 1984.

Mangan, J. A., and James Walvin, eds. *Manliness and Morality: Middle Class Masculinity in Britain and America, 1800–1940.* Manchester: Manchester Univ. Press, 1987.

Marcuse, Maxwell F. *This Was New York! A Nostalgic Picture of Gotham in the Gaslight Era.* New York: LIM Press, 1969.

May, Henry F. *The End of American Innocence: A Study of the First Years of Our Time, 1912–1917.* New York: Knopf, 1959.

Mayer, Harold, and Richard Wade. *Chicago: Growth of a Metropolis.* Chicago: Univ. of Chicago Press, 1969.

McCaffrey, Laurence J., Ellen Skerrett, Michael F. Funchion, and Chris Fanning. *The Irish in Chicago.* Urbana: Univ. of Illinois Press, 1987.

McDarrah, Fred W. *Greenwich Village.* New York: Corinth Books, 1963.

McLuhan, Marshall. *Understanding Media: The Extensions of Man.* New York: New American Library, 1965.

McNamee, Graham. *You're On the Air.* New York: Harper, 1926.

McPhaul, John J. *Deadlines and Monkeyshines: The Fabled World of Chicago Journalism.* Westport, Conn.: Greenwood Press, 1973.

McPherson, Barry, James E. Curtis, and John Loy. *The Significance of Sport: An Introduction to the Sociology of Sport.* Champaign, Ill.: Human Kinetics, 1989.

Meany, Tom, ed. *Collier's Greatest Sports Stories.* New York: A. S. Barnes, 1955.

Merriam, Charles E. *Chicago: A More Intimate View of Urban Politics.* New York: Macmillan, 1929.

Messenger, Christian K. *Sport and the Spirit of Play in American Fiction: Hawthorne to Faulkner.* New York: Columbia Univ. Press, 1981.

Metzker, Isaac, ed. *A Bintel Brief.* New York: Ballantine, 1977.

Mizner, Wilson. *The Many Mizners.* New York: Sears Publishing, 1932.

Montgomery, Royal E. *Industrial Relations in the Chicago Building Trades.* Chicago: Univ. of Chicago Press, 1927.

Moore, Charles. *Daniel H. Burnham: Architect Planner of Cities.* New York: De Capo Press, 1968.

Moore, William T. *Dateline Chicago: A Veteran Newsman Recalls Its Heyday.* New York: Taplinger Publishing, 1973.

Morris, Joe Alex. *Deadline Every Minute: The Story of the United Press.* New York: Doubleday, 1957.

Morris, Lloyd. *Incredible New York: High Life and Low Life of the Last Hundred Years.* New York: Random House, 1951.

Mott, Frank Luther. *American Journalism: A History of Newspapers in the United States Through 250 Years, 1690–1940.* New York: Macmillan, 1947.

Mott, Frank Luther. *The News in America.* Cambridge: Harvard Univ. Press, 1952.

Mowry, George, ed. *The Twenties: Fords, Flappers and Fanatics.* Englewood Cliffs, N.J.: Prentice-Hall, 1963.

Mrozek, Donald J. *Sport and American Mentality, 1880–1910.* Knoxville: Univ. of Tennessee Press, 1983.

Muldoon, William. *Modern Gladiator: Being an Account of the Exploits and the Experiences of the World's Greatest Fighter, John L. Sullivan.* St. Louis: The Athletic Publishing Company, 1889.

Mumford, Lewis. *The City in History: Its Origins, Transformations, and Its Prospects.* New York: Harcourt, Brace & World, 1961.

Murray, Jesse G. *The Madhouse on Madison Street.* Chicago: Follett, 1965.

Nash, Gerald D. *Creating the West: Historical Interpretations, 1890–1990.* Albuquerque: Univ. of New Mexico Press, 1991.

Nash, Jay Robert. *People to See: An Anecdotal History of Chicago's Makers and Breakers.* Piscataway, N.J.: New Century Publishers, 1981.

Nash, Roderick. *The Call of the Wild: 1900–1916.* New York: George Braziller, 1970.

Nash, Roderick. *The Nervous Generation: American Thought, 1917–1930.* Chicago: Rand McNally, 1970.

Nash, Roderick. *Wilderness and the American Mind.* New Haven: Yale Univ. Press, 1967.

Noverr, Douglas A., and Lawrence E. Ziewacz. *The Games They Played: Sports in American History, 1865–1980.* Chicago: Nelson-Hall, 1983.

Ong, Walter J. *Interfaces of the Word: Studies in the Evolution of Consciousness and Culture.* Ithaca, N.Y.: Cornell Univ. Press, 1977.

Oriard, Michael. *Reading Football: How the Popular Press Created an American Spectacle.* Chapel Hill: Univ. of North Carolina Press, 1993.

Paper, Lewis J. *William S. Paley and the Making of CBS.* New York: St. Martin's Press, 1987.

Park, Robert E., Ernest W. Burgess, and Roderick D. McKenzie, eds. *The City.* Chicago: Univ. of Chicago Press, 1925.

Patterson, Joseph Medill. *A Little Brother of the Rich.* New York: Reilley and Britton, 1908.

Patterson, Joseph Medill. *The Notebook of a Neutral.* New York: Duffield, 1916.

Patrick, Walter R. *Ring Lardner.* New York: Twayne Publishers, 1963.

Paxson, Frederic Logan. *The Last American Frontier.* New York: Macmillan, 1910.

Paxton, Harry T., ed. *Sport U.S.A.: The Best of the Saturday Evening Post.* New York: Thomas Nelson, 1961.

Perkin, Robert L. *The First Hundred Years: An Informal History of Denver and the Rocky Mountain News.* New York: Doubleday, 1959.

Pershing, John J. *My Experiences in the World War.* Blue Ridge, Pa.: Tab Books, 1989.

Peterson, Virgil W. *Barbarians in Our Midst.* Boston: Little, Brown & Co., 1952.

Pierce, Bessie Louise, ed. *As Others See Chicago: Impressions of Visitors, 1673–1933.* Chicago: Univ. of Chicago Press, 1933.

———. *A History of Chicago.* Vol. 1. New York: Knopf, 1937.

Pitts, Alice Fox. *Read All About It!—Fifty Years of the American Society of Newspaper Editors.* Washington: American Society of Newspaper Editors, 1927.

Polachek, Hilda Satt. *I Came a Stranger: The Story of a Hull House Girl.* Urbana: Univ. of Illinois Press, 1989.

Poole, Ernest. *Giants Gone: Men Who Made Chicago.* New York: McGraw-Hill, 1943.

Porter, Tana Moshier. *Toledo Profile: A Sesquicentennial History.* Toledo: Toledo Sesquicentennial Commission, 1987.

Problems of Journalism. 7 vols. Washington, D.C.: American Society of Newspaper Editors, 1923–29.

Quaife, Milo M. *Checagou, From Indian Wigwam to Modern City, 1673–1835.* Chicago: Univ. of Chicago Press, 1933.

Quaife, Milo M. *The Development of Chicago.* Chicago: Univ. of Chicago Press, 1916.

Quint, Howard H. and Milton Cantor. *Men, Women, and Issues in American History.* Homewood, Ill.: Dorsey Press, 1975.

Rader, Benjamin G. *American Sports: From the Age of Folk Games to the Age of Spectators.* Englewood Cliffs, N.J.: Prentice-Hall, 1983.

Rascoe, Burton. *We Were Interrupted.* Garden City, N.Y.: Doubleday, 1947.

Report of W. Freeland Kendrick, Mayor of the City of Philadelphia, 1925. Philadelphia: City of Philadelphia, 1926.

Rice, Grantland. *The Tumult and the Shouting.* New York: A. S. Barnes, 1954.

Rickard, Mrs. Tex, and Arch Obeler. *Everything Happened to Him: The Story of Tex Rickard.* New York: Frederick A. Stokes, 1936.

Riess, Steven A. *City Games: The Evolution of American Urban Society and the Rise of Sports.* Urbana: Univ. of Illinois, 1989.

Riis, Jacob. *How the Other Half Lives.* New York: Irvington, 1972.

Ringel, Fred J., ed. *America as Americans See It.* New York: Literary Guild, 1932.

Rischin, Moses. *The Promised City: New York Jews, 1870–1914.* Cambridge: Harvard Univ., 1962.

Roberts, Randy. *Jack Dempsey: The Manassa Mauler.* Baton Rouge: Louisiana State Univ., 1979.

———. *Papa Jack: Jack Johnson and the Era of White Hopes.* New York: Free Press, 1983.

Rodgers, Daniel T. *The Work Ethic in Industrial America, 1850–1920.* Chicago: Univ. of Chicago Press, 1978.

Rojek, Chris. *Capitalism and Leisure Theory.* London: Tavistock, 1985.

Rosewater, Victor. *History of Cooperative News-Gathering in the United States.* New York: D. Appleton, 1930.

Ross, Ishbel. *Silhouette in Diamonds: The Life of Mrs. Potter Palmer.* New York: Harper & Bros., 1960.

Russell, Bertrand. *In Praise of Idleness and Other Essays.* New York: W. W. Norton, 1935.

Rydell, Robert W. *All the World's a Fair: Visions of Empire at American International Expositions, 1876–1916.* Chicago: Univ. of Chicago Press, 1984.

Sage, George H. *Power and Ideology in American Sport.* Champaign, Ill.: Human Kinetics, 1990.

Sammons, Jeffrey T. *Beyond the Ring: The Role of Boxing in American Society.* Urbana: Univ. of Illinois Press, 1988.

Samuels, Charles. *The Magnificent Rube: The Life and Gaudy Times of Tex Rickard.* New York: McGraw-Hill, 1957.

Sandburg, Carl. *Chicago Poems.* New York: Holt, Rinehart & Winston, 1916.

———. *The Complete Poems of Carl Sandburg.* New York: Harcourt Brace Jovanovich, 1970.

———. *Cornhuskers.* New York: Holt, Rinehart & Winston, 1918.

———. *Slabs of the Sunburnt West.* New York: Harcourt, Brace, 1922.

Sanders, Ronald. *The Downtown Jews: Portrait of an Immigrant Generation.* New York: Harper & Row, 1969.

———. *Shores of Refuge: A Hundred Years of Jewish Immigration.* New York: Henry Holt, 1988.

Schudson, Michael. *Discovering the News: A Social History of American Newspapers.* New York: Basic Books, 1978.

Shergold, Peter R. *Working Class Life: The 'American Standard' in Comparative Perspective, 1899–1913.* Pittsburgh: Univ. of Pittsburgh, 1982.

Sloan, William David, James G. Stovall, and James D. Startt, *The Media in America.* Worthington, Ohio: Publishing Horizons, 1989.

Slosson, Preston William. *The Great Crusade and After, 1914–1928.* New York: Macmillan, 1930.

Slovensko, Ralph, and James A. Knight., eds. *Motivations in Play, Games and Sport.* Springfield, Ill.: Charles C. Thomas, 1967.

Smith, Henry Justin. *Chicago's Great Century.* Chicago: Univ. of Chicago Press, 1933.

Smith, Henry Nash. *Virgin Land: The American West as Symbol and Myth.* New York: Vintage Books, 1957.

Spear, Allan H. *Black Chicago: The Making of a Negro Ghetto, 1890–1920.* Chicago: Univ. of Chicago Press, 1967.

Spivey, Donald, ed. *Sport in America: New Historical Perspectives.* Westport, Conn.: Greenwood Press, 1985.

Standish, Burt L. *Frank Merriwell at Yale.* Philadelphia: David McKay, 1903.

Startt, James D., and William David Sloan. *The Significance of the Media in American History.* Northpoint, Ala.: Vision Press, 1993.

Standish, Burt L. *Frank Merriwell's 'Father': An Autobiography.* Norman: Univ. of Oklahoma Press, 1964.

Stead, William T. *If Christ Came to Chicago.* Chicago: Laird and Leer, 1894.

Stearns, Harold E., ed. *Civilization in the United States: An Inquiry by Thirty Americans.* New York: Harcourt, Brace, 1932.

Stearns, Peter N. *Be a Man! Males in Modern Society.* New York: Holmes & Meier, 1990.

Steffens, Lincoln. *The Shame of the Cities.* New York: Sangamore Press, 1957.

Stevens, Wayne Edson. *The Northwest Fur Trade, 1763–1800.* Urbana: Univ. of Illinois Press, 1928.

Stewart, Kenneth, and John Tebbel, *Makers of Modern Journalism.* New York: Prentice-Hall, 1952.

Stone, Melville E. *Fifty Years a Journalist.* Garden City, N.Y.: Doubleday, 1921.

———, Melville E. *"M.E.S." His Book.* New York: Harper & Bros., 1918.

Strading, Charles T. *Ruled by the Press.* Los Angeles: George Rissman Publishing, 1917.

Strauss, Anselm L. *Images of the American City.* New Brunswick: Transaction Books, 1976.

Sullivan, Edward Dean. *Rattling the Cup on Chicago Crime.* Freeport, N.Y.: Books for Libraries Press, 1971.

Sullivan, John L. *Life and Reminiscences of a 19th Century Gladiator.* Boston: James A. Hearn, 1892.

Sullivan, Mark. *Our Times, 1900–1925.* Vol. 6, *The Twenties.* New York: Charles Scribner's Sons, 1972.

Sutton, Albert A. *Education for Journalism in the United States from Its Beginning to 1940.* Evanston, Ill.: Northwestern Univ., 1940.

Swados, Harvey, ed. *The American Writer and the Great Depression.* Indianapolis: Bobbs-Merrill, 1966.

Swanberg, W. A. *Citizen Hearst.* New York: Charles Scribner's Sons, 1961.

Swanson, Walter. *The Thin Gold Watch: A Personal History of the Newspaper Copleys.* New York: Macmillan, 1964.

Talamini, John T., and Charles H. Sage, eds. *Sport and Society: An Anthology.* Boston: Little, Brown & Co., 1973.

Taylor, Graham. *Pioneering on Social Frontiers.* Chicago: Univ. of Chicago Press, 1930.

Teaford, Jon C. *The Twentieth-Century American City.* Baltimore: Johns Hopkins Univ. Press, 1986.

Tebbel, John. *An American Dynasty: The Story of the McCormicks, Medills and Pattersons.* Garden City, N.Y.: Doubleday, 1947.

———. *George Horace Lorimer and the Saturday Evening Post.* Garden City, N.Y.: Doubleday, 1948.

———. *The Life and Times of William Randolph Hearst.* New York: E. P. Dutton, 1952.

Travis, Dempsey J. *The Autobiography of Black Chicago.* Chicago: Urban Research Institute, 1981.

Tunis, John R. *The American Way in Sport.* New York: Duell, Sloan and Pearce, 1958.

———. *Sports Heroics and Hysterics.* New York: John Day, 1928.

Tunney, Gene. *A Man Must Fight.* Boston: Houghton Mifflin, 1932.

———. *Arms for Living.* New York: Wilfred Funk, 1941.

Turner, Frederick Jackson. *The Frontier in American History*. New York: Henry Holt, 1920.

———. *Rise of the New West: 1819–1829*. New York: Harper & Bros., 1906.

Turner, Victor. *Dramas, Fields and Metaphors*. Ithaca, N.Y.: Cornell Univ. Press, 1974.

———. *Schism and Continuity*. Manchester: Manchester Univ. Press, 1957.

Van Every, Edward. *The Life of Gene Tunney: The Fighting Marine*. New York: Dell Publishing, 1927.

———. *Muldoon: The Solid Man of Sport*. New York: Frederick A. Stokes, 1929.

Veblen, Theodore. *The Theory of the Leisure Class*. New York: B. W. Huebsch, 1926.

Villard, Oswald Garrison. *The Disappearing Daily: Chapters in American Newspaper Revolution*. New York: Knopf, 1944.

———. *Prophets, True and False*. New York: Knopf, 1928.

———. *Some Newspapers and Newspaper-men*. New York: Knopf, 1926.

Wade, Louise C. *Graham Taylor: Pioneer for Social Justice, 1851–1938*. Chicago: Univ. of Chicago Press, 1964.

Wainwright, Nicholas B. *History of the Philadelphia National Bank: A Century and a Half of Philadelphia Banking, 1803–1953*. Philadelphia: Philadelphia National Bank, 1953.

Waldrop, Frank C. *McCormick of Chicago: An Unconventional Portrait of a Conventional Figure*. Englewood Cliffs, N. J.: Prentice-Hall, 1966.

Walker, Stanley. *City Editor*. New York: Frederick A. Stokes, 1934.

Ward, John William. *Red, White, and Blue: Men, Books, and Ideas in American Culture*. New York: Oxford Univ. Press, 1969.

Warner, Sam Bass. *The Private City: Philadelphia in Three Periods of Its Growth*. Philadelphia: Univ. of Pennsylvania Press, 1968.

———. *The Urban Wilderness: A History of the American City*. New York: Harper & Row, 1972.

Wecter, Dixon. *The Hero in America: A Chronicle of Hero-Worship*. New York: Charles Scribner's Sons, 1941.

Weigley, Russell F. *Philadelphia: A 300-Year History*. New York: W. W. Norton, 1982.

Weiss, John, ed. *The Origins of Modern Consciousness*. Detroit: Wayne State Univ., 1965.

Wendt, Lloyd. *Chicago Tribune: The Rise of a Great American Newspaper*. Chicago: Rand McNally, 1979.

Wendt, Lloyd and Herman Kogan. *Big Bill of Chicago*. Indianapolis: Bobbs-Merrill, 1953.

———. *Lords of the Levee: The Story of Bathhouse John and Hinky Dink*. Indianapolis: Bobbs-Merrill, 1943.

West, Elliott. *The Saloon on the Rocky Mountain Mining Frontier*. Lincoln: Univ. of Nebraska Press, 1979.

Weston, Stanley. *The Heavyweight Champions*. New York: Ace Books, 1976.

Whitlock, Brand. *Forty Years of It: An Autobiography*. New York: D. Appleton, 1920.

Whitlock, Brand. *On the Enforcement of Laws in Cities*. Indianapolis: Bobbs-Merrill, 1913.

Wignall, Trevor C. *Ringside*. London: Hutchinson, 1941.

Will, Allen S. *Education for Newspaper Life*. Newark: Essex Press, 1931.

Williams, Sarah Lockwood. *Twenty Years of Education in Journalism*. Columbia, Mo.: E. W. Stephens Publishing, 1929.

Williamson, Samuel T. *Imprint of a Publisher: The Story of Frank Gannett and His Newspapers*. New York: R. M. McBride, 1948.

Wilson, Edmund. *The Twenties: From Notebooks and Diaries of the Period*. New York: Farrar, Straus and Giroux, 1975.

Wilson, Howard. *Mary McDowell, Neighbor*. Chicago: Univ. of Chicago Press, 1928.

Woodward, Stanley. *Sports Page*. New York: Simon & Schuster, 1949.

Worster, Donald. *Under Western Skies: Nature and History in the American West*. New York: Oxford Univ. Press, 1992.

Writers Project of the Works Progress Administration in the State of Nevada. Sponsored by Jeanne Elizabeth Wier. Nevada State Historical Society, Inc., *Nevada: A Guide to the Silver State*. Portland, Oreg.: Binfords and Mort, 1940.

Yardley, Jonathan. *Ring: A Biography of Ring Lardner*. New York: Random House, 1977.

Yost, Caspar S. *The Principles of Journalism*. New York: D. Appleton, 1924.

Zingg, Paul Z., ed. *The Sporting Image: Readings in American Sport History*. Lanham: Univ. Press of America, 1988.

Zorbaugh, Harvey Warren. *The Gold Coast and the Slum: A Sociological Study of Chicago's Near North Side*. Chicago: Univ. of Chicago Press, 1976.

ARTICLES

Alexander, Jack. "Vox Populi." *New Yorker,* Aug. 6, 1938, 27–32.

———. "Vox Populi." *New Yorker,* Aug. 20, 1938, 38–41.

Allen, Frederick L. "Newspapers and the Truth." *Atlantic Monthly,* Jan. 1922, 44–54.

"American Newspapers as a Whole Are Clean, Free, Capable and Meet Responsibility Honestly: An Inspiring Interview with Adolph S. Ochs." *Editor and Publisher,* Feb. 16, 1924, 1, 4.

Benet, Stephen Vincent. "The United Press." *Fortune,* May 1933, 67–68.

"The 'Big Business' of Prize Fighting." *Literary Digest,* Oct. 13, 1923, 60–67.

"Big Names and Little Stuff." *Editor and Publisher,* Jan. 5, 1924, 36.

Boatright, Mody C. "The Myth of Frontier Individualism." *Southwestern Social Science Quarterly* 22 (1941): 14–32.

Bliven, Bruce. "Arc Lights and Blood: Ringside Notes at the Dempsey-Firpo Fight." *New Republic,* Sept. 26, 1923, 115.

Brazil, John R. "Murder Trials, Murder and Twenties America." *American Quarterly* 33 (Spring 1981): 163–69.

Breuning, Margaret. "Bellows in National Gallery." *Art Digest,* Jan. 1, 1945, 22.

Broun, Heywood. "It Seems to Heywood Broun." *The Nation,* Sept. 28, 1927, 305.

———. "Personal Journalism Is Coming Back—Broun." *Editor and Publisher,* Mar. 15, 1924, 7.

Brown, Ira V. "Pennsylvania and the Rights of the Negro." *Pennsylvania History* 28 (1961): 52–54.

Bryce, James. "America Revisited: The Changes of a Quarter Century." *Outlook,* 1905, 738–39.

Camp, Walter. "What Are Athletics Good For?" *Outing,* Dec. 1913, 259–72.

Chinello, James. "The Great Goldfield Foul." *Westways* 68 (Sept. 1976): 27–29.

Cloud, Barbara. "Establishing the Frontier Newspaper: A Study of Eight Western Territories." *Journalism Quarterly* 61 (1984): 805–11.

Coleman, Lee R. "What Is American: A Study of Alleged American Traits." *Social Forces* 19 (1941): 492–99.

Collins, Herbert. "The Sedentary Society." *The Scientific Monthly,* Nov. 1954, 288–92.

"Colonel McCormick Defines a Newspaper." *Editor and Publisher,* Nov. 8, 1924, 4.

"The Commercialized Prize Ring." *Outlook,* Sept. 28, 1927, 28–32.

"Corbett to Tunney on 'How to Win the Mob.'" *Literary Digest,* Jan. 14, 1928, 55–60.

Cornuelle, R. C. "Remembrance of the *Times*: From the Papers of Garet Garrett." *The American Scholar* 36 (1967): 433–44.

Cox, James A. "Mr. Jake vs. the Great John L." *Smithsonian,* Dec. 1984, 157–61.

Croak, Thomas M. "The Professionalization of Prizefighting: Pittsburgh at the Turn of the Century." *Western Pennsylvania Historical Magazine* 62 (1979): 333–43.

Cunningham, William. "No Wonder They Want to Fight!" *Collier's,* Sept. 13, 1924, 14, 45.

Davenport, Walter. "The Dirt Disher." *Collier's,* Mar. 24, 1928, 26, 30, 52–53.

———. "The Nickel Shocker." *Collier's,* Mar. 10, 1928, 26, 28, 40.

Dempsey, Jack, and Barbara Piatelli Dempsey. "The Destruction of a Giant: How I Beat Jess Willard." *American Heritage,* Apr. 1977, 76–81.

Dempsey, Jack, and Charles J. McGuirk. "The Golden Gates." *Saturday Evening Post,* Oct. 20, 1934, 10–11, 73.

Duffus, Robert L. "The Age of Play." *The Independent,* Dec. 20, 1924, 539.

Edgren, Robert. "The Modern Gladiator." *Outing,* Mar. 1903, 298–306.

"Editors Mean Business." *Editor and Publisher,* May 3, 1924, 26.

"Editors Set 1928 Goals for Journalism." *Editor and Publisher,* Dec. 31, 1927, 7, 42.

Goldman, Robert, and John Wilson. "The Rationalization of Leisure." *Politics and Society* 7 (1977): 185–86.

Green, Norma, Stephen Lacy, and Jean Folkerts. "Chicago Journalists at the Turn of the Century: Bohemians All?" *Journalism Quarterly* 66 (1989): 812–21.

Greuning, Ernest. "Can Journalism Be a Profession? A Study in Conflicting Tendencies." *Century,* Sept. 1924, 693–97.

Gruneau, Richard. "Freedom and Constraint: The Paradoxes of Play, Games, and Sports." *Journal of Sport History* 7 (Winter 1980): 68–86.

Gorn, Elliot J. "Gouge and Bite, Pull Hair and Scratch: The Social Significance of Fighting in the Southern Backcountry." *American Historical Review* 90 (1985): 18–43.

———. "The Manassa Mauler and the Fighting Marine: An Interpretation of the Dempsey-Tunney Fights." *Journal of American Studies* 19 (1985): 36–37.

Guttmann, Allen. "Who's On First?, or, Books on the History of American Sports." *Journal of American History* 66 (1979): 353–54.

Haller, Mark H. "Urban Crime and Criminal Justice: The Chicago Case." *Journal of American History* 57 (1970): 619–35.

Hardy, Stephen, and Alan G. Ingham. "Games, Structures, and Agency: Historians on the American Play Movement." *Journal of Social History* 17 (1983): 285–301.

Harrison, Richard Edes. "AP." *Fortune,* Feb. 1937, 89–90.

Howells, William Dean. "Letters of an Altrurian Traveller." *Cosmopolitan,* Dec. 1893, 218–32.

Humphreys, Joe. "The Rickard I Knew." *Collier's,* Nov. 9, 1929, 28, 59–60.

"In Interview Hearst Speaks Plainly of Policies of His Organization." *Editor and Publisher,* June 14, 1924, 3–4.

Irwin, Will. "United Press." *Harper's,* Apr. 25, 1914, 6–7.

Jacoby, Russell. "A New Intellectual History?" *American Historical Review* 97 (1992): 405–24.

Katz, William. "The Western Printer and His Publications, 1850–1890." *Journalism Quarterly* 44 (1967): 708–14.

Keeler, Clinton. "The White City and the Black City: The Dream of Civilization." *American Quarterly* 2 (Summer 1950): 112–17.

Kent, Christopher. "Higher Journalism and the Mid-Victorian Clerisy." *Victorian Studies* 13 (Dec. 1969): 181–98.

Klapp, Orrin E. "Hero Worship in America." *American Sociological Review* 14 (1949): 53–62.

Knapp, Richard. "The National Recreation Association, 1906–1950." *Parks and Recreation* 7 (Aug. 1972): 48–49.

Kofoed, Jack. "The Master of Ballyhoo." *North American Review,* Mar. 1929, 282–86.

Kramer, William M., and Norton B. Stern. "San Francisco's Fighting Jew." *California Historical Quarterly* 53 (1974): 333–45.

Lardner, Ring. "The Battle of the Century." *Saturday Evening Post,* Oct. 29, 1921, 12, 84–86.

"Lawson Falls at 75 from Overwork Serving His Great Press Ideal." *Editor and Publisher,* Aug. 22, 1925, 1, 4.

Lewis, Guy. "Sport, Youth Culture and Conventionality, 1920–1970." *Journal of Sport History* 4 (Summer 1977): 129–33.

———. "World War I and the Emergence of Sport for the Masses." *The Maryland Historian* 4 (Fall 1973): 109–11.

Loetscher, Lefferts. "Presbyterianism and Revivals in Philadelphia since 1875." *Pennsylvania Magazine of History and Biography* 69 (1944): 57–58.

Lowe, Benjamin, and Mark H. Payne. "To Be a Red-Blooded American Boy." *Journal of Popular Culture* 8 (1974): 383–91.

Luce, Jr., Ralph A. "From Hero to Robot: Masculinity in America—Stereotype and Reality." *Psychoanalytic Review* 54 (1967): 53–74.

May, Henry F. "Shifting Perspectives on the 1920's." *Mississippi Valley Historical Review* 43 (1956): 405–27.

McGeehan, W. O. "The Last Gladiator." *Saturday Evening Post,* Sept. 28, 1929, 37, 149–50, 153.

Messenger, Christian. "Tom Buchanan and the Demise of the Ivy League Athletic Hero." *Journal of Popular Culture* 8 (1974): 402–10.

"*Milwaukee Journal* Reflects Its Editor's Character." *Bulletin of the American Society of Newspaper Editors,* Sept. 15, 1926, 1.

Nixon, Raymond B. "Changes in Reader Attitudes Toward Daily Newspapers." *Journalism Quarterly* 31 (Fall 1954): 21–22.

Nord, David Paul. "The Public Community: The Urbanization of Journalism in Chicago." *Journal of Urban History* 11 (1985): 412–14.

Norris, Wendell W. "The Transient Frontier Weekly as a Stimulant to Homesteading." *Journalism Quarterly* 30 (1953): 44–48.

Nugent, Henry. "The Sports Section." *American Mercury* 16 (Mar. 1929): 336.

"Our Faith and Action." *Editor and Publisher,* Feb. 23, 1924, 44.

Parsons, Talcott. "The Professions and Social Structure." *Social Forces* 17 (1939): 437–67.

Paxson, Frederic Logan. "The Rise of Sport." *Mississippi Valley Historical Review* 4 (1917): 143–68.

Pew, Matthew. "Ogden Reid Says Public Is Best Served by Fewer but Better Papers." *Editor and Publisher,* Mar. 29, 1924, 1.

Rader, Benjamin G. "Compensatory Sports Heroes: Ruth, Grange and Dempsey." *Journal of Popular Culture* 16 (1983): 18–21.

———. "The Quest for Subcommunities and the Rise of Sport," *American Quarterly* 24 (1977): 368–69.

"Remarks of Dorothy Canfield Fisher." *Graduate Magazine* (Univ. of Kansas) 26, 1928, 8–9.

Rice, Grantland. "The Golden Fleece." *Collier's,* Sept. 17, 1927, 9, 44.

———. "The Heavyweight Peerage." *Collier's,* June 21, 1930, 22.

Santayana, George. "Philosophy on the Bleachers." *Harvard Monthly* 18 (July 1894): 181–90.

Schiller, Dan. "An Historical Approach to Objectivity and Professionalism in American News Reporting." *Journal of Communication* 29 (Autumn 1979): 46–57.

Schneider, Walter E. "Fabulous Rise of the *N.Y. Daily News.*" *Editor and Publisher,* June 24, 1939, 5.

"Sell the Papers! The Malady of American Journalism." *Harper's,* June 1925, 1–9.

Sloan, William David. "Historians and the American Press, 1900–1945." *American Journalism* 3 (1986): 154–66.

Smith, Garry. "The Sports Hero: An Endangered Species." *Quest* 19 (1973): 59–70.

Smith, Robert. "Heroes and Hurrahs: Sports in Brooklyn, 1890–1898." *Journal of Long Island History* 11 (1975): 7–8.

Smythe, Ted Curtis. "The Reporter, 1880–1900: Working Conditions and Their Influence on News." *Journalism History* 7 (1980): 1–10.

Sojka, Gregory S. "Evolution of the Student-Athlete in America." *Journal of Popular Culture* 16 (Spring 1983): 55–67.

Somers, Dale A. "The Leisure Revolution: Recreation in the American City, 1820–1920." *Journal of Popular Culture* 5 (Summer 1971): 125–47.

Stave, Bruce M. "A Conversation with Sam Bass Warner, Jr.: Ten Years Later." *Journal of Urban History* 11 (Nov. 1984): 109.

Stearns, Myron M. "Champion Ex-Champion." *Harper's,* Sept. 1939, 417.

Stearns, Peter N. "Modernization and Social History: Some Suggestions, and a Muted Cheer." *Journal of Social History* 14 (1980): 191–95.

Stehlin, Stewart A. "Philadelphia on the Eve of the Nation's Centennial: A Visitor's Description in 1873–1874." *Pennsylvania History* 44 (1977): 25–36.

Stolberg, Benjamin. "The Man Behind the 'Times.'" *Atlantic Monthly,* Dec. 1926, 721–30.

Stone, Gregory. "American Sports: Play and Dis-Play." *Chicago Review,* Fall 1955, 83–100.

Taylor, Graham. "Between the Lines in Chicago's Industrial Civil War." *The Commons,* Apr. 30, 1900, 1–5.

———. "Chicago as Viewed by Its Intimate Friends." *Chicago Theological Seminary,* Jan. 1930, 8–11.

———. "An Epidemic of Strikes in Chicago." *The Survey,* Aug. 2, 1919, 645–46.

———. "Revitalizing Chicago." *Journal of Education* 82 (Aug. 26, 1915): 150.

Thompson, Maurice. "Vigorous Men, a Vigorous Nation." *Independent,* Sept. 1, 1898, 609–11.

Towers, Wayne M. "World Series Coverage in New York City in the 1920's." *Journalism Monographs* 73 (1981): 3–23.

Tully, Jim. "Jack Dempsey." *American Mercury,* Aug. 1933, 398–99.

Tunis, John R. "Changing Trends in Sports." *Harper's,* Dec. 1934, 78.

Tunney, Gene. "The Blow That Hurts." *Atlantic Monthly,* June 1939, 839–41.

"The Tunney-Dempsey Fight: A World Spectacle." *Literary Digest,* Sept. 17, 1927, 41.

"The Value of College Athletics." *Outlook,* Jan. 27, 1906, 151–52.

Walden, Daniel. "Urbanism, Technology and the Ghetto in Novels by Abraham Cahan, Henry Roth and Saul Bellow." *American Jewish History* 23 (1984): 296–300.

Watson, Elmo Scott. "A History of Newspaper Syndicates in the United States, 1865–1935." Supplement to *Publisher's Auxiliary,* Nov. 16, 1935, 5–21.

Weigle, Clifford F. "The Young Scripps Editor: Keystone of E. W.'s System." *Journalism Quarterly* 41 (1964): 360–66.

Weinberg, S. Kirson, and Henry Arond. "The Occupational Culture of the Boxer." *American Journal of Sociology* 57 (1952): 460–69.

"What Is the Lure of the Tabloid Press?" *Editor and Publisher,* July 26, 1924, 7, 34.

Wik, Reynold. "The Radio in Rural America during the 1920's." *Agricultural History* 55 (1981): 339–50.

Wilcox, Charles W. "Consider the Cauliflower." *Scribner's Magazine,* Mar. 1930, 445–49.

Wilson, Dale. "Marvin Creager and the Kansas City Crowd." *Historical Messenger* (of the Milwaukee County Historical Society), Sept. 1961, 2–4.
Woods, Alan. "James J. Corbett: Theatrical Star." *Journal of Sports History* 3 (1976) 174–75.
Zeisel, Joseph S. "The Workweek in American Industry, 1850–1956." *Monthly Labor Review* 81, Jan. 1958, 23–29.

ENCYCLOPEDIA REFERENCES

Andrews, Tom S. and C. R. Diegle. *Ring Battles of Centuries.* New York: Tom Andrews Record Book, 1924.
Burrill, Bob. *Who's Who in Boxing.* New Rochelle, N.Y.: Arlington House, 1974.
"James Middleton Cox," *Encyclopedia Americana.* Vol. 13. New York: Americana Corporation, 1963, 139–40.
Marquis, Albert Nelson. *The Book of Chicagoans: A Biographical Dictionary of Leading Living Men of the City of Chicago.* Chicago: A. N. Marquis, 1911.
Pictured Encyclopedia of the World's Greatest Newspaper. Chicago: Chicago Tribune Publishing, 1928.
"William McLean," *Encyclopedia Americana.* Vol. 18. New York: Americana Corporation, 1963, 78.
Sawyers, June Skinner. *Chicago Portraits: Biographies of 250 Famous Chicagoans.* Chicago: Loyola Univ. Press, 1991.
The World's Greatest Newspaper: A Handbook of Newspaper Administration, Editorials, Advertising, Production, and Circulation, Minutely Depicting the Word and Picture of How It's Done by the World's Greatest Newspaper. Chicago: Chicago Tribune Publishing, 1922.

UNPUBLISHED WORKS

Bevans, George Esdras. "How Workingmen Spend Their Spare Time." Ph.D. diss., Columbia Univ., 1913.
Cebula, Larry. "For Want of Actual Necessaries of Life: Survival Strategies of Frontier Journalists in the Trans-Mississippi West." Paper presented at a meeting of the American Journalism Historians Association, Salt Lake City, Utah, Oct. 7, 1993.
Furst, Terry. "Boxing Stereotypes versus the Culture of the Professional Boxer: A Sociological Decision." Master's thesis, Staten Island Community College, 1971.
Heim, John M. "Notes and References Relating to the History of Philadelphia Newspapers," 1937. Free Library. Philadelphia.
Lloyd, Franklin Robert. "Big Men and Regular Fellows: Popular Heroes of the 1920's." Ph.D. diss., Univ. of Iowa, 1975.
Sesquicentennial International Exhibition Committee. "Celebrating 150 Years of American Independence: A Visualization of the Spiritual, Scientific, Artistic

and Industrial Progress of America and the World," 1926. Sesquicentennial Papers. Historical Society of Pennsylvania. Philadelphia.

FILM AND TELEVISION

"Jack Dempsey vs. Jess Willard, July 4, 1919, Toledo, Ohio." *Boxing's Great Bouts*. NBC Television.

"Jack Dempsey vs. Gene Tunney, Sept. 23, 1926, Philadelphia, Pa." *Fantastic Fights of the Century*. Vol. 1. Collectors Series. TM Productions.

"Jack Dempsey vs. Jack Sharkey, July 21, 1927, New York, N.Y." *Fantastic Fights of the Century*. Vol. 2. Collectors Series. TM Productions.

"Jack Dempsey vs. Gene Tunney, Sept. 22, 1927, Chicago, Ill." *Fantastic Fights of the Century*. Vol. 1. Collectors Series. TM Productions.

Index